THE DIARIES OF KENNETH TYNAN

D1324713

THE DIARIES OF
KENNETH TYNAN

EDITED BY JOHN LAHR

BLOOMSBURY

First published 2001
This paperback edition published 2002

Copyright © 2001 by Tracy Tynan
Introduction copyright © 2001 by John Lahr

The moral right of the authors has been asserted

Bloomsbury Publishing Plc, 38 Soho Square, London W1D 3HB

A CIP catalogue record for this book
is available from the British Library

Every reasonable effort has been made to ascertain and acknowledge
the ownership of copyrighted photographs, illustrations and
quoted material included in this volume. Any errors
that have inadvertently occurred will be corrected in
subsequent editions provided notification is sent to the publisher.

ISBN 0 7475 5841 8

10 9 8 7 6 5 4 3 2

Typeset by Hewer Text Ltd, Edinburgh
Printed in Great Britain by Clays Ltd, St Ives Plc

CONTENTS

Illustrations	*vii*
Editor's Note	*1*
Introduction	*5*
1971	*17*
1972	*81*
1973	*115*
1974	*167*
1975	*213*
1976	*295*
THE HOLLYWOOD YEARS	*345*
1977	*361*
1978	*399*
1979	*413*
1980	*417*
INDEX	*421*

ILLUSTRATIONS

Section 1

1. *Isis*, 1947
   Tynan at twenty-first birthday party on Thames, April 1948
2. The Bright Young Thing
3. Acting in e e cummings' *Him*, 1950
4. The young director, 1952 (Roger Wood)
5. Tynan and Cecil Beaton (Paul Tanqueray)
6. Tynan and Elaine Dundy, *c.* 1953
7. Tynan with daughter Tracy
8. The young critic ('Menswear')

Section 2

1. The young Turk, 1953 (Louise Dahl-Wolf/*Harper's Bazaar*)
2. Tynan with Claire Bloom (Maurice Ambler/Hulton Archive)
3. Tynan in Spain, *c.* 1954 (Duncan Melvin)
4. Tynan fourth row on the aisle, *c.* 1957
5. Tynan at *The New Yorker*, 1961 (Condé Nast)
   Tynan with S. J. Perelman and Groucho Marx (Jane Bown)
6. Tynan with Vivien Leigh, *c.* 1963
7. Tynan and Laurence Olivier (The Estate of Mark Boxer)
8. Tynan with Truman Capote, 1966 (Thames Television)

Section 3

1. Tynan, 1964 (Mary Evans/Roger Maine)
2–3. Wedding Day with Marlene Dietrich in tow, 30 June 1967
4. Tynan with son Matthew, 1972 (Tynan Family Archives)
   Tynan and Kathleen, Valencia, 1968 (Tynan Family Archive)

5. At memorial service for Dominic Elwes, November 1975 (Press Association Photos)
6. With Roman Polanski (Baron Wolman)
7. With Kathleen, 1969 (The Estate of Sir Alfred Ayer)
8. Tynan as 'Louise Brooks' and Kathleen, 1976 (Tim Jenkins)

Section 4

1. Tynan and Kathleen, Hollywood, 1979 (Roddy McDowall)
2. The celebrity circuit (*l. to. r.*): Roxana, Kathleen, Tony Richardson, Gore Vidal, Jack Nicholson, Matthew Tynan, Princess Margaret (Roddy McDowall)
3. At home in Brentwood, 1979 (Roddy McDowall)
4. Tynan in the sun (Roddy McDowall)
5. Tynan and Kathleen, 1979 (Roddy McDowall)
6–7. Tynan's burial, 1980
8. The last portrait, 1979 (Roddy McDowall)

One day in the last year of his life, Kenneth Tynan called his eldest daughter, Tracy, from the hospital and told her that he had something important he wanted to talk about. Over the last years, Tracy had been a frequent visitor to her father's bedside, as Tynan struggled, in the polluted Los Angeles air, with an hereditary form of emphysema, exacerbated by his two-pack-a-day smoking habit. On her previous visit, emboldened by a few swigs of Tynan's favorite cheap champagne, Chandon Blanc Des Noirs, which she'd smuggled into the hospital and which they surreptitiously drank from paper cups, Tracy suddenly said, 'You know, Daddy, I never told you this, but I . . . I . . . love you.' Her words came in a rush. 'He reached out and held my hand briefly,' Tracy recalled. 'I felt relieved.' Tynan drained the bottle of champagne and said, 'Now let's talk about something else. This is beginning to sound like a bad hospital movie.' Tracy was, she says, 'crushed'. She quickly invented a business appointment and soon found herself in the brightness of the Santa Monica day, sitting in her grey VW Rabbit in tears.

For a month or so, she'd stayed away from her father leaving the bedside watch to Tynan's dutiful wife Kathleen; now, an hour after his call, she was back at the familiar battle station. Kathleen, Tynan told her, was away on a business trip. Then Tynan announced 'that he had decided to bequeath his diaries to me', Tracy said. 'I was surprised. He said that they contained, amongst other things, an explicit account of the sado-masochistic affair he had been carrying on for the last ten years. He was concerned that Kathleen might try and destroy it. In fact, there was evidence that she had already made an attempt.' She added, 'I knew that Kathleen would be furious when she found out what my father had done: she would consider it an insult and a betrayal. And in a way it was.'

A fortnight later, when Tracy next visited her father, Tynan asked her if she'd signed the codicil to his will. She hadn't. 'Well, you had better hurry up,' Tynan said. 'Kathleen's back. She found out that I am giving you the diaries, and she's furious.'

'How did she find out?' Tracy asked. Tynan poured himself a slug of champagne. 'I told her,' he said. Tracy went home, signed the codicil. 'I never discussed it again with my father or Kathleen,' she said. Not, at least, until Tynan's memorial service, in London in September of 1980, when Tracy and Kathleen found themselves alone in the beige bedroom of Kathleen's basement Kensington flat getting ready to go to the post-memorial party. As Tracy recalled the exchange, Kathleen turned to her and said, 'Have you told anyone about the diaries?' ' "No," I lied.' ' "They belong to me," Kathleen said. "How could you do this?" ' 'I think he was afraid that something might happen to them,' Tracy said.

'I was angry. I tore out some pages but then I put them back,' Kathleen said. 'And besides, I need them for the biography I am writing on your father.' This was news – bizarre news – to Tracy.

After a prolonged legal investigation, Tracy learned that she could not claim her inheritance because the codicil had been typed and was therefore required by law to have four witnessing signatures. Tracy was one signature short. She did not have the money or the will to challenge Kathleen further in the English courts; angry and hurt, she gave in. 'The rift between us never healed,' she said. Tracy did receive a conciliatory note from Kathleen offering to split the proceeds of the journals when and if they were sold; otherwise, Tracy's inheritance from her father was a gold watch and a pen.

Kathleen died in 1995. Tynan's two younger children, Roxana and Matthew, who had inherited the rights to their father's work, returned the diaries to Tracy because, she says, 'they felt it was the right thing to do'. The hand-over took place a few months later in LA, when Roxana gave Tracy a small canvas bag containing twelve slim volumes of her father's diaries from 1970–80. 'It was the first time I had actually seen them in the flesh,' Tracy said. 'They were so small. Barely four inches by six inches, loose-leaf leather binders. Not very elegant or practical but they were unmistakably his: filled with pages of his elegant, barely legible handwriting.'

Almost all of those little black books are now decoded and between hard covers. Although a few passages were excised for fear of libel claims, very little has been cut: a Zen mantra, an account of a trip to Sri Lanka, Test Match cricket descriptions, and passages that trail off because a subsequent page has 'gone missing'. For reasons of narrative impact and focus, the diaries have been judiciously topped and tailed, with the cut information folded into the book primarily via the footnotes, which have been compiled with the help of my *New Yorker* cohort Dan Kaufman. I have not footnoted those people whose fame, by my lights, translates across the Atlantic or who are sufficiently identified in context. But, since Tynan's diaries are being published both here and in America, cross-cultural references are vexing, especially to a name-dropper like Tynan. Morecambe and Wise, Max Wall, and Bobby Moore, for instance, are household names in England, but draw a blank in America. Here, I hope, the footnotes are not – as Edmund Wilson called them – 'scholarly barbed wire', but a way of increasing the reader's pleasure in Tynan's social landscape, his gossip, and his high style.

John Lahr
The New Yorker
20 March 2001

INTRODUCTION

At Oxford, where he became a post-war legend, Kenneth Tynan cut a lanky, gaunt, romantic figure. He liked to characterise himself to the Bright Young Things as a kind of meteor who would burn brightly on the English scene only to be extinguished before his thirtieth year. 'By then,' he said, 'I will have said everything I have to say.' In fact, Tynan's skyrocketing crash-and-burn scenario took nearly twice as long to come to pass. With his reputation for brilliance more or less intact, he died too young, from emphysema, at the age of fifty-three in July, 1980. At his memorial service, the playwright Tom Stoppard turned to Tynan's three young children, Tracy, Roxana, and Matthew. 'For those of us who were working in the English-speaking theatre during those years,' he said, of the period between 1950 and 1963 when Tynan's drama criticism was as much a public event as the plays he reviewed, 'for those of us who shared his time, your father was part of the luck we had.'

Critics do not make theatre; they are made by it. Tynan's luck was to be the right age at the right place with the right credentials, the right vocabulary, and the right impudent temperament to savour the new British theatrical resurgence – certainly the greatest flowering of dramatic talent in England since Elizabeth I. With his hard-won intellectual precocity and his rebellious instincts ('Rouse tempers, goad and lacerate, raise whirlwinds' was the quotation – his own, as it happens – pinned above his writing desk), Tynan was the old and the new Brit rolled into one well-tailored package. Of the many qualities that made him an outstanding critic – qualities of wit, language, knowledge, style, and fun – perhaps the most important and the most surprising was his profound awareness of death, which fed both his voracity for pleasure – for food, for drink, for sex, for talk ('Talking to gifted and/or funny people,' he wrote, 'is evidence both of intense curiosity and of jaded palate') – and his desire to memorialise it. 'When working or satisfying his appetites,' Tynan wrote, in an analysis of himself at forty in the preface for *Tynan Right and Left* (1967), 'he knows precisely who he is; but with the cessation of these pursuits, his identity tends to blur and disappear. Can seldom banish from his mind the fact of approaching mortality.' As a critic, Tynan's sense of being present, a kind of fervid alertness to the event before him, was fuelled by this profound fear of absence. 'I remember about thirty times a day between waking and sleeping and always while I'm asleep that I am going to die,' he said. 'And the more scared I am, the more pleasure and enlightenment I want to squeeze from every moment.'

For Tynan, writing was a hedge against loss, a way of keeping the consoling dramatic pleasures alive inside himself by making them live for others. 'I mummify transience,' he wrote, at the age of twenty-three, in the epilogue to his first book, *He That Plays the King* (1950), an almost delusional rant intended as an exercise in what he called 'the athletics of personality' – the pronoun 'I' is used thirty-two times in two pages – with which he launched himself from Oxford into the waiting world. Tynan went on: 'I am an echo, a mould which recasts things, set-pieces, atmospheres, manners, gestures into something more weatherproof. My business is to accustom every sight, or sound, or smell to the companionship of good words.'

Tynan, who as a youngster had gobbled up American movies, writers, and music, also had a very American sense of individualism. He incarnated Whitman's 'destiny of me', in which egotism imposes itself on life as a form of gallantry. As a boy and an inveterate fan, he had collected the autographs of such contemporary heroes as Winston Churchill, Neville Chamberlain, and Joseph Kennedy, but he soon became his own star. Orson Welles's 'incomparable bravura personality' was Tynan's model. 'Have a new pose: arrogance, bass voice, hanging lower lip. Which reads O–R–S–O–N,' he wrote, in a letter to a friend, in 1944, just three years before buttonholing the bemused Welles himself to write the preface to his first book. ('Dear Mr Tynan then – by the way, what are you?' Welles's introduction begins.)

Tynan fancied himself *sui generis*. He was his own greatest invention, and he loved his Maker. When he told his life story, he downplayed his humdrum provincial Midlands origins. He called his birthplace, Birmingham, 'the ugliest city in the world, that cemetery without walls'. 'In any real sense of the word, I was born at Oxford,' he said. 'I have no more connection with my early life and with Birmingham than I have with Timbuctoo.' Even as a youth, he was a dandy whose swagger was pitched against the oppressive and 'sterile emptiness' of his home town. He wanted glamour, which was not easy to excavate in the threadbare blandness of post-war England. 'No cafés. No good restaurants. Clothes were still "austerity" from the war, dismal and ugly. Everyone was indoors by ten, and the streets were empty . . . Rationing was still on,' Doris Lessing wrote, and that was of raffish London not baggy Birmingham.

That deadliness leached into Tynan's childhood, where the unsolid ground of his family life had a habit of shifting. His older sister had died at birth. His father, the taciturn, successful Sir Peter Peacock, who was fifty-five when Tynan was born, spent weekdays up the road in Warrington, where he was the Mayor for six terms and a self-made businessman, and where, unbeknownst to his son, he kept another family. (He had never married Tynan's mother, and Tynan flaunted his father's name only as his own middle name; at seventeen, when his father died and his illegitimacy became official knowledge, Tynan dropped the name Peacock but kept the posture.) Tynan's mother, Rose, who ended her life in a mental institution, was a kindly, depressed, modestly educated former laundress with aspirations for respectability, from whose tastes and personality Tynan felt increasingly estranged. In 1958, unkempt and confused, Rose was picked up by Yorkshire police carrying a suitcase on which was written: 'I DON'T KNOW WHERE I'M GOING BUT I'M GOING TO THOSE WHO LOVE ME.' It certainly wasn't Tynan who, until the end of his days, felt shame and self-loathing about how he'd abandoned his mother. 'I could have postponed her death at the expense of my own absorption in self-advancement. I chose not to,' he said. As a teenager, he turned the family's déclassé oil paintings of cows in pasture to the wall, but his sense of parental detachment was born out of issues deeper than taste. 'A Caesarean, a bastard and a contemptible object,' is how Tynan characterised himself in infancy, in notes during his psychoanalysis in 1962. 'A bedwetter. I soiled my mother and she punished me by refusing to feed me.'

In the end, like all narcissists, Tynan fed himself. His passion for intellectual distraction was part of the agitation he liked to generate, his way of fending off what he called 'my meddlesome bug-bear, solitude'. Insofar as Tynan ever had a mission, it was a war against stagnation in art and in himself. He had grown up with a lie at the centre of his family; even before he knew what it was, he felt unmoored by the family silences. ('Electrically charged but not properly earthed' is how his second wife, Kathleen, described him, in her excellent 1987 biography *The Life of Kenneth Tynan*.) Tynan didn't know what to make of his parents, and his astonishing intelligence made him equally bewildering to them. They indulged their son's eclectic enthusiasms. His mother introduced him to music-hall and the 'high-definition performance', which he began to chronicle, even as a young man, because, he said later, 'It seemed unfair to me that an art so potent should also be so transient, and I was deeply seduced by the challenge of perpetuating it in print.' Together, Tynan and his mother travelled to London to see Ivor Novello, the Crazy Gang, Gilbert and Sullivan operettas, Donald Wolfitt's hectoring Shakespearian performances. For his ninth Christmas, Tynan asked for and received one hundred books from his parents, who on one occasion even splurged on a monocle for their little show-off, whose large vocabulary was marred by a permanent stutter.

If it was hard for Tynan to be understood at home, he was compelled to make the world at large pay proper attention. From an early age, he became something of a mythomane. 'As long as I'm not ignored you know quite well I'm perfectly happy,' the teenage Tynan wrote to a friend. At King Edward's School, which he attended on a scholarship, he won twelve major prizes, ran the debating and literary societies, and edited the school magazine. At eleven, Tynan appointed a school chum to be his Boswell; at fifteen he addressed the literary society on 'Art and I' ('a History of the Influences that have Gone into the Making of K.P.T.'); at sixteen he played Hamlet; at twenty-three, he published his first book of criticism; and by twenty-seven, he was the famous drama critic of the *Observer*. Tynan's life was proof of one of his most famous aphorisms: 'A man who strives after an effect not infrequently achieves it.'

Tynan's performance of personality – the flamboyant dress (dove-grey suits and velvet collars, pastel shirts), mannerisms (cigarette held between the third and fourth finger), and word-horde – embraced the notion of the extraordinary that he'd studied on stage and screen. 'This sad age needs to be dazzled, shaped and spurred by the spectacle of heroism,' he wrote, and certainly he needed it. (He began the preface to his first book by declaring 'a passionate preoccupation with large and towering personalities: a sort of hero worship of which I am not the least ashamed and which I think the theatre ought to encourage'.) Tynan aspired to a hero's daring and dimension: big magic as an antidote to big hurt. 'I was illegitimate and I was made to know it by my father and my family,' he wrote later to his first wife, the American writer Elaine Dundy. 'I was the boy . . . at whom everyone smiled knowingly and despisingly, and I have pretended ever since to be somebody – anybody – else.' His first published piece of prose in the *King Edward's School Chronicle* spelled out the credo by which he would more or less live for the rest of his life: 'In every community there exists a certain element of the insignificant,' he wrote at the age of fourteen. 'The undistinguished person: the person who never argues, never shouts, and whose presence is not immediately noticed . . . As I watch the useless lives of these people, so foolish, so wasted and so ordinary, I become afraid and try desperately to forget them.'

Tynan arrived at Magdalen College, Oxford, in 1945, and immediately plunged into a whirlwind of public display that included directing, acting, writing and debating, and only intensified what he called his 'superiority complex'. 'Nothing can ever top the sense of privileged exhilaration I felt then,' he said. By his own calculation, his experience at Oxford amounted to 72 weeks, 300 parties, and one 6,000-word essay a week, or the equivalent of five full-length books. Tynan's tutor was C.S. Lewis, the Renaissance scholar, more famous for his enduring moral writings, who taught Tynan how to deploy paradox properly and how to make his verbal firepower more accurate. 'Keep a strict eye on eulogistic and dyslogistic adjectives – they should diagnose (not merely blame) and distinguish (not merely praise),' Lewis wrote on a Tynan essay about early English drama. Tynan learned his lessons well; he quickly acquired an impertinent authority.

By the end of his three years, Tynan was already attacking members of the British critical fraternity and their impoverished sensibilities, setting them up like so many ten pins only to knock them down name by name. 'A sham necklace of bitter brevities or false, hollow eulogy will not do for criticism,' he brayed, in the first chapter of *He That Plays the King* (1950). 'The fixed quizzical grin, the bar-fly impressionism, the epicene tartness, which most critics affect, is no substitute for awe, hate, or rapture.' He went on: 'What I am saying is that attack, not apology, passion, not sympathy, should be behind the decorous columns of our drama critics . . . Criticism has taken a wrong turning into imperturbability and casualness; it has ceased to worry about communicating excitement or scorn; it is away and somewhere else; not vitally interested . . . It calls for great flexibility of reaction and above all, great flair and cocksureness.' In other words, in calling for a new cultivated response and a new amperage of passion, what Tynan was really proposing as the Rx for the parlous state of English dramatic criticism was himself. A stripling aesthete, he prophesied: 'My collected works will bulk small but precious.' (His subsequent dashing and incomparable *oeuvre* of dramatic criticism is currently out of print on both sides of the Atlantic.)

After a year of directing theatre in the provinces (he was the youngest professional director in Britain) and subsequently being ignominiously fired by the star of a London production of Cocteau's *Les Parents Terribles*, in 1950, Tynan followed the line of least resistance – into journalism, where he was his own star turn. 'I liked the realistic way he understood and accepted that in his ferocious pursuit of notoriety, he was making himself a target which was going to get hit,' wrote Elaine Dundy, who became the first Mrs Tynan on 25 January 1951, but who was not, by a long chalk, the first woman to whom Tynan had proposed. He was twenty-three when they met and twenty-four when they married. 'They often marry young, Destiny's tots,' Dundy wrote, of their tempestuous marriage, which ended in 1964. 'The truth is they need company for their journey. They need someone at their side to watch all the wonderful things that are happening; someone to watch them coming into being.'

As a critic, Tynan emerged on the English scene virtually fully formed. He was poised; he was knowledgeable; he was fun. He was also – and always – spoiling for a fight. He inherited a moribund theatrical scene, where, as he wrote, 'Two out of three London theatres were inhabited by detective stories, Pineroesque melodramas, quarter-witted farces, débutante comedies, overweight musicals and unreviewable revues . . . The accepted new playwrights then were Fry, Eliot, and Anouilh.' He wrote as a man of the theatre not as a man of the reading room, and his style blasted prolix Victorian waffle from critical discourse. Here, for instance, writing on Shakespeare's *Henry IV* in 1946, is James Agate, the leading theatre critic of his day, whose style Tynan mocked for its 'breathless punch-drunk downrightness':

'England,' announces the programme. And who is to set the first half of this great play in its country and period, not one thinks, the wan and shaken King, nor yet his priggish, pragmatical son; and surely the Percys and the Mortimers, Douglases and Glendowers have long been piffle before the wind.

Instead of the highfalutin, Tynan developed an artful, pungent, sly tone, which might be called 'lowfalutin'. His pomp had a knockdown wink in it. Of Rodgers' and Hammerstein's excursion into contemporary Chinese culture in *Flower Drum Song*, Tynan wrote: 'Perhaps as a riposte to Joshua Logan's *The World of Suzy Wong*, Rodgers and Hammerstein have given us what, if I had any self-control at all, I would refrain from describing as a world of woozy song.'

In print, Tynan's limpid style presented him to the world as a specimen of perfect individualism without wound or worry. 'I know nothing of ardour and am not dogged: to write, for me, is not necessary as gunpowder needs to explode . . . I do this because I can, not because I have to,' he said in *He That Plays the King*. Tynan protested too much. He did have a need, and that need was to align himself, in a kind of symbiotic way, with the extraordinary souls whose work onstage he matched with his own literary performance. Fame, and the celebrated company he kept, legitimised him. 'I am a stringed instrument, a base Aeolian harp with one motif astray in every mood: this motif is a wish to perfect and complete the thing seen,' he wrote. He continued. 'I dramatise all that passes into me or plays upon me, for the act of dramatisation is the act of making unreal and perfect images of what is real and imperfect.' The word 'fame' has its etymological root in the Latin word for rumour; Tynan had the power both to spread the word and to make it memorable.

While he wrote well about plays, Tynan was wonderful on actors. 'The study of actors should be a full-time task, and worthy of the same passionate scholarship which lepidopterists devote to butterflies,' he wrote. He had a language beyond the usual lit-crit stammer, and it conveyed the subtlety of a craft that was undergoing profound sociological changes. The 1945 Education Act had enabled many talented young people to get scholarships to universities and to acting schools that before the Second World War had been the privilege of the rich. This created a dynamic new pool of working-class talent – actors like Rita Tushingham, Joan Plowright, Peter O'Toole, Kenneth Haigh, Tom Courtenay, Albert Finney, and Richard Burton, who came to the stage with different energies, different behaviours, different connections to British experience, and who in a short time would require a different kind of play. Tynan was on their wavelength. Of Burton's Henry IV, for instance, he wrote, in 1951: 'Fluent and sparing of gesture, compact and spruce of build, Burton smiles where other Hals have guffawed; relaxes where they have strained; and Falstaff . . . must work hard to divert him. In battle, Burton's voice cuts urgent and keen – always likeable, always inaccessible.' Tynan was also not shy about shivering the timbers of the English acting establishment. On Vivien Leigh's Cleopatra: 'Taking a deep breath and resolutely focusing her periwinkle charm, she launches another of her careful readings; ably and passionately she picks her way among its great challenges, presenting a glibly mown lawn where her author had imagined a jungle.' Still, as in the case of Margaret Rutherford's man-eating Lady Wishfort in Congreve's *Way of the World*, Tynan's power of analogy could kiss as unforgettably as it could kill. 'Miss Rutherford is filled with a monstrous vitality,' he wrote. 'The soul of Cleopatra has somehow got trapped in the corporate shape of an entire lacrosse team.'

Because Tynan understood glamour and the discipline of planting and keeping the idea of self in the public mind, stars found themselves deconstructed by him with unusual finesse. 'To be famous young and to make fame last – the secret of combining the two is glandular: it depends on energy,' Tynan wrote with particular prescience, in a review of the debut of Noël Coward's famous nightclub act at the Café Royal. He went on: 'Someone once asked Demosthenes what was the most important quality in an orator. "Action," he said. And the second. "Action." And the third? "Action." So with talent.' Tynan, who aspired to be a spellbinder, was never more compelling than when he was under the spell of others: Marlene Dietrich 'shows herself to the audience and delivers the sacred goods'; Katherine Hepburn is 'wide open yet without breaches in her armour. It is the paradox which makes stars'; Judy Garland at the Palace '. . . embodies the persistence of youth so completely that we forbid her to develop, and permit her no maturity. Even in young middle age, she must continue to sing about adolescence and all the pain and nostalgia that go with it. When the voice pours out, as rich and pleading as ever, we know where, and how moved we are – in the presence of a star, and embarrassed by tears.'

Tynan never succumbed to what he called 'the critic's scourge: atrophy of love'. He was passionate, nowhere more so than in his review of John Osborne's Look Back in Anger (1956). 'I doubt if I could love anyone who did not wish to see Look Back in Anger. It is the best young play of its decade,' he wrote famously. But Tynan's review, which proved to be a rallying cry for the theatre's New Wave and which praised the play for catching the contemporary mood of the young – 'the drift towards anarchy, the instinctive leftishness, the automatic rejection of "official" attitudes, the casual promiscuity, the sense of lacking a crusade worth fighting for' – represented an instructive volte-face. Tynan had begun his critical career on a High Tory note, insisting that theatre 'is a tale of unique men and women, whom one can imagine in palaces or hovels, but never somehow in semi-detached villas'. By 1954, he was singing a new socialist tune: 'We need plays about cabmen and demi-gods, plays about warriors, politicians, and grocers . . . I counsel aggression because, as a critic, I had rather be a war correspondent than a necrologist.'

But theatre is a recalcitrant beast; even with Tynan's brilliant prodding it didn't move quickly in his direction. At the end of the fifties he concluded that English theatre was 'desperately enfeebled' and that 'the strongest and most unmistakable influence on our drama in the last ten years has been transatlantic'. Having discovered Brecht and tried in vain to transplant his enthusiasm for political drama into the English landscape, Tynan took himself off for an infusion of American energy, in 1958, and was the senior drama critic of The New Yorker for two years. As the sixties wore on, however, he found himself with less to say about Britain's writers (Pinter, Orton, Bond), and more to say about the establishment of a National Theatre, where the sprouts of their theatrical renaissance could be properly nurtured.

In 1962, having just attacked the newly appointed head of the National Theatre, Sir Laurence Olivier, for his season of plays at the Chichester Festival Theatre, Tynan wrote to Olivier asking to be made the National Theatre's first dramaturg. 'How shall we slaughter the little bastard?' Olivier fumed to his wife, the actress Joan Plowright, who nonetheless liked the idea because 'young audiences would be thrilled with the mixture of you and Ken'. In a letter inviting Tynan to work as an in-house critic and to help plan the seasons, as well as take charge of all published material, a position Tynan held from 1963 to 1973, Olivier added a postscript: 'God – anything to get you off that *Observer.*'

The job added both to Tynan's public prestige and to his private frustration. Once again, he was a middle man; his light hidden under a theatrical bureaucracy. Of the seventy-two plays mounted on his watch, according to Kathleen Tynan, 'thirty-two of these were Ken's ideas; twenty were chosen with his collaboration'. This kind of defensive scorekeeping is typical of the dramaturg's dilemma; the success or failures of the theatre may be of his choosing but not of his accomplishing. Neither odium nor glory fall finally to him: both inside and outside the theatre, the critic's role, Tynan knew to his cost, was one without risk. In 1970, comparing his relationship with Olivier to 'a tugboat nudging an ocean greyhound into harbour', Tynan put a bright face on a strained, often punishing relationship:

> L.O. calls me into his office to discuss the 1971 repertoire. He goes through my familiar list of plays, making remarks he has made a hundred times before about each of them . . . The odd thing is that he should have such a low opinion of me to think I would be mollified by a few kind words from the Godhead. I conclude he is a man of no imagination or sense of contemporary theatre, sluggish of mind and insensitive to current definitions of talent, interested only in hanging on to power.

When he looked back on his life, Tynan often regretted opting to be an onlooker rather than director. 'I took the safer course and became a full-time critic,' he wrote in his journal. 'That is why today I am everybody's adviser – Roman Polanski's, Larry Olivier's, Michael White's – and nobody's boss, not even my own.' As some kind of bona fide literary figure, he assumed a star's front-row seat, but in the workplace he was forced to take a back seat. 'Such is servility,' he wrote in 1972, when Olivier had gone behind his back to ask the director Peter Hall his opinion of a play that Tynan had suggested. And when Olivier appointed Hall as his successor, rather than choosing one of his colleagues at the National, Tynan wrote, 'He has passed a vote of no confidence in us all. He has hired us, stolen our kudos, and shows no compunction about discarding us.' The National kept Tynan busy but did not allow him to accomplish his mission. In its tenth anniversary year, Tynan noted in his journal that the theatre 'will have discovered one new playwright (Tom Stoppard) and no new directors'. He added: 'It's a sad reflection on the way in which I've occupied my time for the past decade.'

Over the next nine years – the time covered by his journal – Tynan's sense of regret and self-loathing grew. He heard himself described as the greatest English theatre critic since George Bernard Shaw, but, unlike Shaw, he had no other forum in which to express himself. Renown requires deeds, and where were Tynan's? He tried and failed to float the idea of himself as a stage and film director. He could manage the sprint of a newspaper column but not the long-distance run of a sustained piece of work. None of the books for which he took advances got written. (He got halfway through a study of Wilhelm Reich but dropped it.) The routine of reviewing had palled, and the anomie it had once kept at bay now filtered deeper into his life. 'The sensation of vanishing. Nothing registers on me: I register nothing,' he wrote. He seemed unable to claim new meaningful territory for himself. He sought distractions outside himself, in sex, society, and celebrity. There were always causes to debate and to keep him in the middle of things: Vietnam, sexual liberation, censorship (he was the first person to break the BBC sound barrier by saying 'fuck'). He produced two West End shows that failed and two sex revues, including Oh! Calcutta!, which is listed in the Guinness Book of Records as the longest-running revue. In the late sixties, he had characterised his inner life as a battle between a 'Super-Ego of tremendous power' and 'an equally powerful Id'. 'Caught between these mighty adversaries,' he wrote of himself, 'his Ego is ground to dust, like a neutral principality in a polarised world.' Tynan's self-lacerating spirit was increasingly channelled into his sado-masochistic obsessions (he had an appetite for spanking and caning), which are recounted in his diaries. More and more, he smiled at the world with cold teeth. 'Still a non-smoker, but alas, a non-worker,' he wrote to Louise Brooks, of whom he had written a marvellous profile for The New Yorker, while living in Los Angeles, where he took up permanent residence in the late seventies.

At the beginning of Tynan's career, when he was still inventing himself in *He That Plays the King*, he turned his emptiness into a kind of heroic self-advertisement, depicting himself variously as a 'soft blotting-pad', a 'shell', a 'spying-glass', a 'chameleon', an 'echo'. As a critic, he hitched that emptiness to stars and to productions whose energy he absorbed and reflected back. Over time, though, the increasing momentum of his fame led to a sort of disintegration. His emphysema compounded a lassitude that he could neither control nor quite understand. 'I used to take Dexamyl to give me enough confidence to start work,' he wrote in 1971. 'Now I take it to give me enough confidence not to.' The frequent high spirits in Tynan's sad tale make his diaries all the more poignant. 'Was Elaine a trial?' the critic Cyril Connolly asks him about his first wife. 'No, more of a jury,' Tynan answers.

On his death-bed, he whispered the words 'a small talent for brilliance'. If he was speaking of himself, his judgement is too harsh. The diaries he left behind bear witness to his own advice: 'Be light, stinging, insolent, and melancholy.' They demonstrate both his brilliance and his struggle to find a place in the world for his intelligence to shine. Unwittingly, in their accounts of Tynan's restless and wayward sexual exploits, they also track a larger human theme, which *Oh! Calcutta!* tried and failed to dramatise – what one of Tynan's famous friends, Tennessee Williams, once called the 'mad pilgrimage of the flesh'.

– John Lahr

1971

11 January

Affinity towards string quartets, small jazz groups, dinner parties of no more than six people – distaste for symphonies, big bands, large parties – in this state I find myself: a committed chamber musician, unhappy in all crowds. Hence a parlour politician, never an activist. All the applause I need is supplied in my private life. Those lacking such applause (or approval) seek it in public, becoming politicians.

Soubriquets
Miss Botty Bumhole
Miss Randy Spankable
Miss Clarissa Cabbage
(who grimbles)

15 January

Talent apart, what enables one to exercise talent is the ability to impose oneself (*s'imposer*). Roman,[1] Larry,[2] Welles[3] Brando, Pinter can *s'imposer*. Definition of an imposer: one about whom one worries whether his response to one's next remark will be a smile or a snarl. With imposers there is always danger, even if one isn't employed by them (e.g. Hemingway).

---

1. Roman Polanski (1933–).
2. Sir Laurence Olivier (1907–89).
3. Orson Welles (1915–85). One of Tynan's early idols whom, at the age of twenty-two, he tracked down in Paris to write an Introductory Letter to his first book *He That Plays the King*. 'If you don't write the preface, I can't get it published,' Tynan told Welles. Afterwards, Tynan recalled: 'The fog and the stammer helped.' In his Introductory Letter, Welles wrote: 'You know how to cheer, you are not afraid to hiss, you are audible (to put it mildly) and transparently in love. Even crotchety old fuss-budgets like me find that irresistible. You even go so far as to interest yourself passionately in acting for acting's own sweet sake. One is grateful for so rare and unfashionable a preoccupation, but one is nevertheless suspicious . . . Are you the new Garrick, Mr Tynan? Never mind, stay where your fellow actors really need you: on the other side of the footlights. The necessary side.'

16 January

When one burst of work was finished (in 1921), Wittgenstein gave up philosophy for eight years, until another major idea came along. So with me and journalism. I hated to submit doodles to a *Daily Telegraph* feature. I today sent off two examples . . . one, when inverted, showed a kneeling girl clutching a caned bottom, while the other was a pattern made up of a longhand scrawl that read: 'Self-conscious doodle'.

It is my theory that most 'work' in the arts (and criticism) is either the projection – in a concealed form – of the artist's emotional (including sexual) preferences and impulses, or a species of game. If one feels no need to express one's impulses in disguise, or if one has ceased to enjoy the 'game' aspect of art, why concern oneself with artistic 'work' at all?

Idea: A history of World War II based on movies about it. E.g. Start with map of the world and place pins as if indicating principal wartime activities. John Mills reaches beach at Dunkirk just as John Mills goes down with submarine in *We Dive at Dawn*. Kirk Douglas is blowing up heavy-water installation in Norway as Burt Lancaster prevents Impressionist paintings from leaving occupied France. Burt Lancaster fucks Deborah Kerr on eve of Pearl Harbor in *From Here to Eternity*. John Wayne is also nearby in *In Harm's Way*. Attenborough[1] snivels in *In Which We Serve* while crashing to his death in *The Way to the Stars* – etc. etc. (getting the films right, which I haven't). You would find, I suspect, that in one war picture or another, John Mills played every rank, commissioned and non-commissioned, in all the fighting services. It would be nice to intercut sequences so that Captain Mills, after accepting a salute from Corporal Mills, went off to report to Colonel Mills . . .

17 January

(Dream) – footnote in a biography of Maurice Richardson,[2] author and journalist: 'finger to crown of hat'. Richardson always claimed special privileges for the intelligentsia, of which he indicated his membership by

1. Sir Richard Attenborough (1923–). Actor, film producer and director.
2. Maurice Richardson (1907–78). Richardson was a Fleet Street character and habitué of the Colony Rooms and the rough-and-tumble Soho of the forties and fifties.

tapping the crown of his pork pie hat significantly with his index finger. I have seen him go confidently to the head of a queue in a betting shop, tapping the crown of his hat as he did so. (Nothing gainsaid him). When introduced by a friend to a stranger, he would screw up his face interrogatively, look at the friend and tap his hat, a piece of mime that meant: 'Is he all right up there?' The friend would respond with a shrug, a balancing motion of the hand or an enthusiastic nod; but after the meeting was over, Richardson would usually remark with ill-concealed disgust: 'Not exactly Lord Heawood of Luton, is he?' (referring to a once celebrated but now forgotten Edwardian mathematician).

20 January

The Garcia[1] situation reaching a climax: L.O. disturbed by momentary nudity of Anthony Hopkins at dress rehearsal. Garcia – five feet high, frizzed black hair, plaintive ochre face – has coped with L.O. with a nonchalant effrontery that fills us all with admiration. When he arrived for rehearsals in December, L.O. spent a night going over the Arrabal text, marking 200 passages that disturbed or offended him. On meeting Garcia he said: '*Cher maître* – there are just a few things I'd like to ask you about the play . . .' Garcia stepped forward and took the script from Larry's hand, between thumb and forefinger as if it were contaminated. With frigid distaste he dropped it into the wastepaper basket. 'Sir Laurence,' he said, smiling wanly, 'I detest literature. I abominate the theatre. I have a horror of culture. I am only interested in magic!' Collapse of L.O. who later recovers to ask nervously: 'There's a scene towards the end where the Architect *eats* the Emperor. How do you intend to stage that?' 'Sir Laurence,' said Garcia, sweetly as to a child, 'I *could* tell you; but it would scare the shit out of you; so I will *not* tell you.' After the first dress rehearsal, L.O. tentatively complained that the

---

1. Victor Garcia (1935–82). Diminutive Argentine director whom Tynan had invited to do Arrabal's *The Architect and the Emperor of Assyria* at the National Theatre. In Tynan's undated diary entry for November, 1970, he writes: 'L.O.: "Has Arrabal approved your designs for this play?" "I am equally as important as Arrabal, Sir Laurence. *Je ne suis pas un employé.*" 10 December 1970: 'Victor Garcia complains about the humiliating, amateurish treatment he has been getting from the NT – no co-operation from the technical people, money doled out in £5 envelopes per day ("*Comme une putain*"), a flat with only one bed for himself and his designer – he has now refused to sign his contract and threatens to leave for Paris unless L.O. is willing to help. "It is like working in an under-developed country. Please explain that because I am foreign I am not insane *or* a revolutionary." '

sound effects were ruining one of the longest speeches in the play. 'I quite agree,' said Garcia. 'We must have twice as much noise.' So – incredibly – a new sound system is being installed, at a cost of £2,000. When challenged in one area, he attacks in another. Hearing that L.O. was worried about Hopkins' nudity, he casually remarked that he needed a choir of *thirty counter-tenors*. All day yesterday the organisation was scouring the country for counter-tenors: the nudity was forgotten.

22 January

Lord Eccles[1] (Minister for the Arts) says in a speech in the City that he and the Arts Council are working on a plan to prevent subsidised theatres from staging 'blasphemous' or 'pornographic' plays. Thus, in a typical Tory move, censorship – abolished under the Labour Government – is to be restored, *but not for the commercial theatre*.

This government hardens all the time. How bitterly one reflects that no matter what their differences, all right-wingers unite in one positive cause – to hang on to what they've got. Whereas the Left splits and splinters, divided by uncertainties over how to get what they've never had (i.e. *control* of property).

The Industrial Relations Bill has already provoked parliamentary socialists to disorder in the House – and they *support* many of its provisions. I hope the workers react with outright fury. As Brecht[2] said, we have seen enough of their divine patience. By Don Siegel:[3] Anti-human forces (source unspecified) plant foetus-bearing pods in a Californian town: they bear fully grown human bodies identical with the inhabitants, whom they replace. The difference is that the alien creatures are dehumanised conformists with no individual emotions. A young doctor and his girlfriend are the last human survivors in a town taken over by the pods. What is fascinating is the ambivalence of the message. To Siegel, one suspects, the doctor-hero represents the last radical non-conformist in a world of Eisenhower, post-McCarthyite

---

1. Viscount Eccles (1904–99). Minister in cabinets of Winston Churchill, Anthony Eden, Harold Macmillan and Edward Heath. As the Arts Minister in the Heath government, sought to introduce the highly unpopular policy of charging the public fees to enter museums.
2. Bertolt Brecht (1898–56). German playwright, poet, theatrical innovator. Tynan was Brecht's English champion.
3. Don Siegel (1912–91). American film director and producer; his films include *Invasion of the Body Snatchers* (1956), *Dirty Harry* (1971).

capitalism. To the producers, however, he must have represented the last Eisenhower, post-McCarthyite capitalist in a world about to be conquered by creeping Communism. In this way, the mass media reconcile Marx and Mammon. (I don't suggest, by the way, that Siegel is a Marxist or even a liberal. It may be that he deliberately made the film ambiguous in order to appeal to conservatives and dissenters alike.)

24 January

First big row over 'prudence and property' (Blake's phrase). Should I pay £19,000 for a fifty-five-year lease on our house – or leave the money to accumulate and give up the house after the present twelve-year lease is over? Kathleen[1] says pay up and have security; I say save and retain mobility. I rashly quote Samuel Butler's[2] line: 'A brigand demands your money or your life; a woman demands both.' K. insists that she is my equal partner. I riposte that she is kept and thence cannot claim partnership. This shocks her to tears; she says she has never before realised that she was 'kept' in the Victorian sense. I cannot believe that, as a supporter (like me) of Women's Lib, she is so naive. In any case she cannot both be kept and decide the disposition of the husband's earnings. I cannot see an easy compromise. She wants roots and solid property; I want mobility and liquid money.

I eventually took her advice and paid for the extension of the lease. Financially it was a wise decision: with a fifty-five-year lease the house is probably worth more than £100,000.

Morality and its intrusion into professional life in Britain: when Bobby Moore,[3] the English football captain, drinks a beer in a night-club at 1.30 a.m. before a game, he is not just fined (as he might be in American football), he is reviled for immorality. (Partly, of course, because he is not upper class and because his fame makes him 'an example to youth'.) But the headmastery tones of the editorials on this subject would be

---

1. Kathleen Halton Tynan (1937–95). Married Ken Tynan 30 June 1967, the second marriage for both; mother of Roxana and Matthew Tynan; the author of *The Life of Kenneth Tynan* (1987), editor of *Kenneth Tynan Letters* (1994).
2. Samuel Butler (1835–1902). Novelist and critic, author of *Erewhon* (1872), *The Way of All Flesh* (1903).
3. Bobby Moore (1941–93). One of the great defenders in the history of English football, who led the team to World Cup victory in 1966.

impossible anywhere else on earth – 'Moore on the carpet' – 'Moore gets the stick' – one-line school phrases are inevitable and sadly revealing. Few Englishmen *ever* leave school: they spend their lives in thrall not to their *own* approval but to the headmaster's. And if they fail it is not just a pity or bad luck, it is an awful warning to the rest of the school . . . (cf. Byron and Stephen Ward.[1])

The Post Office strikers cannot win, to judge by the press: Either (a) they are causing chaos and inconvenience, thereby turning public opinion against them which means that they have failed, *or* (b) they have *not* caused chaos or inconvenience, which *also* means that they have failed.

Sometimes one finds both prongs of this attack in the same newspaper.

The most difficult financial gulf to negotiate is that between being top of the little league and bottom of the big league. I, a top English journalist, have recently become a small theatrical tycoon. To be the poorest of the rich causes more anxiety than to be the richest of the poor.

Supper with Roman, Kathleen, Iain Quarrier (co-producer of the Godard-Mick Jagger film *One Plus One*): Quarrier attacks Godard, admits to being Tory, and I am forced on to the defensive. Oddly, Kathleen finds herself intuitively compelled to support those (i.e. Quarrier) who look and sound trendy and suave. I snarl briefly at her and the talk returns to normal. At home, later, our row continues; we sleep on separate floors. Things look bad. Only last night we continued the quarrel over the house – my offer being to buy the lease but in my own name, with guarantee that I wouldn't sell in less than fifteen years, and that when I did I would share the proceeds with K. This seems fair enough to me, but not to her: she demands partnership now. Last night we supped together in South Ken, and her rage was such that she walked out of the restaurant and drove home without me.

Roman tells of a Persian friend who gets rigidly stoned every evening. They went out to dinner with a party of friends, the Persian having

---

1. Dr Stephen Ward (1913–63). A society osteopath involved in the 1963 Profumo scandal; Ward, who introduced Christine Keeler to John Profumo, killed himself after he was found guilty of living off immoral earnings.

announced: 'I am estoned.' (Persians are like Spanish, they put an 'e' before 's'.) The group ordered *blanquette de veau* and when they had waited for some time the Persian, who had been sitting in total silence with bowed head, suddenly said quite distinctly: 'I want to change my wheel.' The others assumed that he was hallucinating and asked whether he would like his oil changed as well and whether he would like a phone in the back seat. Dourly he insisted: 'I want to change my wheel,' until somebody remembered that they had ordered veal and realised that all he wanted was to eat something else.

So we beat on, canes against the buttocks, borne back ceaselessly into the past.[1]

Disapproval shades into envy and then into admiration – and it is at that point that one spiritually sets out (of Fitzgerald's admiration for Gatsby and Monroe Stahr[2]).

3 February

Arrabal opening, after two dress rehearsals, which reduced its length from $3\frac{3}{4}$ hours to $2\frac{1}{2}$. Garcia's ignorance of the English language, does, I fear, show: dialogue is performed with little variety of pace and emphasis, when it seems to call out for light and shade. But the visuals are extraordinary – the forklift truck, the parachute which becomes an angelic robe with central halo, the burning carbon arc lamps which at one point turn the actors into stark and shrivelled survivors of a nuclear war. All this gives a strange sense that, in Beckett's phrase, *'quelque chose suit son cours'*: the twin protagonists are not masters of life and death, but midgets caught up in some ghastly mechanical process which goes on independently of them. In short, there really *is* a God in the machine.

But I wish the translation and the delivery were more *nuanced*. (Press is mixed, but generally bad. The English specialise in the barely concealed yawn when faced with something surprising. Philip Hope-Wallace[3] of the

---

1. Tynan's parody of the last lines of F. Scott Fitzgerald's *The Great Gatsby*: 'So we beat on, boats against the current, borne back ceaselessly into the past.'

2. Monroe Stahr, the Irving Thalberg-inspired hero of F. Scott Fitzgerald's *The Last Tycoon* (1941).

3. Philip Hope-Wallace (1911–79). Journalist and critic for *The Times*, 1935–39 and the *Guardian*, 1946–76; compared Tynan's Oxford production of *Hamlet* to those of Tyrone Guthrie and Vsevolod Meyerhold.

Guardian is famous for always reacting to novelty with: 'This took me back to Vienna in the early twenties.' I wondered what Garcia and Arrabal would take him back to: the answer was: 'This will scarcely be new to anyone familiar with recent ballet . . .' Thus he remains one-up, yawn duly half-stifled.)

Joke conceived in the loo yesterday: what would the *Variety* headline be if Rex Harrison slugged an autograph collector? Answer: SHIT HITS FAN.

5 February

Triple stye in eye induces gloomy introspection. Around 1952 – when Clunes[1] fired me from the Arts production – I had a choice between hanging back as an onlooker and plunging in as a participant – i.e. continuing as a director. I took the safer course and became a full-time critic. That is why, today, I am everyone's adviser – Roman's, Larry's, Michael White's,[2] – and nobody's boss, not even my own.

From a bleak day in the country, two *vignettes*: (1) Customer of *chic* country restaurant to the *patron*: 'Most of the waiters are Greek or Cypriot – they don't understand this country. Some of 'em haven't been here much more than fifteen or twenty years.' (2) *Patron* of another restaurant as he serves duck to Kathleen: 'It's a dirty bird, isn't it, a filthy bird? Ducks are *horrible* birds.' The same eccentric had said when we arrived and booked a room: 'What on earth made you choose *this* place?'

10 February

After hearing the adagio of a Schubert chamber work: there is nothing more beautiful than the happy moments of unhappy men. This might serve as a definition of art.

1. Alec Clunes (1912–70). Hired Tynan, just down from Oxford, to direct Jean Cocteau's *Les Parents Terribles* at the Arts Theatre Club. The show's star, Fay Compton, had no confidence in Tynan as a director and demanded Clunes fire him.
2. Michael White (1936–). British theatre and film producer, including Tynan's *Oh! Calcutta!* (1970) as well as such films as *Monty Python and the Holy Grail* (1974); *My Dinner with André* (1984).

11 February

Roman directing the murder of Lady Macduff's little daughters. He explains that they must pretend to be dead – it's a *game* – while he puts funny paint (i.e. blood) on their faces. He arranges the smaller girl sprawled in a cradle. As he sprinkles the blood, he says, 'And what's your name?' 'Sharon,'[1] she says.

12–15 February

A lost weekend in Hamburg with Kathleen and George and Joan Axelrod[2]. At the Salambo Erotic Theatre I see fucking on the stage for the first time and to my surprise am enchanted. So are we all. A group of well-built, clean and mutually affectionate young people constitute the show, which is imaginatively lit with evocatively orgasmic sound effects. Cocks are sweetly and diligently sucked, and the leading pair (the girl is a Scot) fuck for eighteen minutes – four times a night – in a variety of postures, the man's penis never leaving the girl's cunt. The full rectal presentation, with the dear Scot's bum outstretched to bursting, as the pink piston of prick slides up and down, is something I shall never forget.

Also: the bizarre use of candles, here and elsewhere in Hamburg. A girl lies down naked, feet to the audience, and then raises her splayed legs over her head. She then inserts two lighted candles into her cunt and bumhole. Bagpipe music is then heard and a kilted Scot enters with a cigar which he proceeds to light at the vaginal candle. He then exits and the bagpipes fade. *Why is he Scots?* No answer is provided. It is worth noting that the theatre, which seats about 200, is plushly decorated and attracts audiences of families and young lovers, not the traditional mackintosh men. There are upwards of a dozen such places in Hamburg, where fucking – single or multiple – is an accepted part of the entertainment. Warren Beatty, who is filming in Hamburg, tells me that he met the Scots girl at the Salambo. She told him that her partner never came on stage (surely a stupendous triumph of self-control) and

---

1. The actress Sharon Tate (1943–69). Polanski's wife; murdered along with four others at her Los Angeles home on 9 August 1969 by Charles Manson and his followers.
2. George Axelrod (1922–). Screenwriter, playwright, producer, director. Famous for his Broadway comedy *The Seven Year Itch* (1953) which two years later became a star vehicle for Marilyn Monroe in the Billy Wilder film version.

denied that she herself achieved orgasm. She seemed to imply that it would somehow be unprofessional to lose control: as she put it, 'The day I come, I quit.'

At another joint a boisterous plump blonde in her thirties romps on the stage, nude except for black boots and a belt, from which four huge false phalluses hang like trophies. In each hand she carries a couple of whips. These, however, she soon discards. With merry cries she squirts water from the rubber cocks over the audience and then distributes them to front-row spectators, whom she invites – by bending over, rear projected, at the edge of the stage – to insert them into cunt or bumhole, as their whim dictates. When a dildo has been pushed in up to the mock scrotum, she bends over even further and – no hands! – expels it with a loud pop on a count of three. Later she invites a male spectator on to the stage, unzips his fly, licks his limp penis into shape, and squats on his lap bouncing up and down. Such is her good humour that one is not shocked. This is another instance of the super-vulgarity that lies on the other side of sophistication – and is in fact more sophisticated than sophistication. I return from the city sexually refreshed and laden with some well-chosen pornography.

16 February

Roman shoots the nude sleepwalking scene. Francesca[1] does it very sportingly and with no fuss about her nudity – though of course the set is closed, great curtains are drawn around the acting area whenever a take is imminent, and the wardrobe mistress, rushes to cover Francesca with a dressing gown the instant Roman says, 'Cut.' After Hamburg those furtive precautions seem ludicrous. At lunch I opine that Francesca has *'fesses tristes'*. Roman agrees, adding that he much prefers bottoms to breasts. We discuss which stars have the sexiest bottoms. I say Natalie Wood; he says Jane Fonda. I reply that hers is boyish. 'Why not?' says Roman. 'As a matter of fact *I* have the sexiest bottom in the film industry.' (And he gets up to model it.) I then put in a word for Marilyn

1. Francesca Annis (1945–). British actress who played Lady Macbeth in Roman Polanski's *Macbeth* (1971), for which Tynan co-wrote the screenplay.

Monroe. Roman says, 'Oh, if we're going to talk about *dead* people, Sharon's bottom wasn't bad.' It does not seem to occur to him that his tribute could have been less callously phrased.

Roman (with bemused pleasure): I fucked a Chinese lawyer!

Note R.'s use of phials of amyl nitrate to produce emotion in actors.

'He was fucking one of those girls you find everywhere – somewhere between a starlet and a secretary.'

R. never apologises, no matter how he offends.

R. pouring blood over the little girls' corpses in Lady Macduff scene: he is totally armoured against sentiment. His motto is the Captain's in *The Dance of Death*: 'Cancel – and pass on!'

My present passion for chamber music is not evidence of maturing taste. What it indicates is in fact growing personal insecurity. Nowadays I feel guiltily idle when listening to jazz or pop; but when listening to a Bach prelude or a Schubert quartet I feel – though equally idle – that I am at least improving myself at the same time.

25 *February*

After dinner to Peter Sellers' Chelsea flat, where I talk to George Harrison of the Beatles (hair at least 2′ 6″ long) about the forthcoming NT musical about William Blake's 'Tyger'. I hope to get some suggestions from him about composers. It painfully emerges, after a long conversation, that he was 'never very much into English literature' and that he has never, in fact, *heard* of William Blake. Which is surprising and sad. It's a pity that he should think himself a poet without having had the chance to compare himself with a poet like Blake.

'Whatever the public blames you for, cultivate it: it is yourself.' (Cocteau)

'Watch out: that man is no revolutionary. He's just a diehard anarchist of the old guard.' (Cocteau)

From a letter written by Cocteau in 1916: 'Let us not forget that we are in a phase of Mars – in which the moon grows full, *art is transformed, and the prospect is for thirty years of wars*.' (My italics)

Satie on Ravel: 'Ravel refuses the Legion of Honour, but all his music accepts it.'

All weakness corrupts, and absolute weakness corrupts absolutely.

'After *Le Coq et l'Arlequin*, we ran the risk of being taken seriously, which is the beginning of death.' (Cocteau in 1921 – so he took over a bar in the Rue Duphot.)

Cocteau on seeing Proust's corpse, with the MS of *À La Recherche* piled on the mantelpiece: 'That pile of paper on his left was still alive, like watches ticking on the wrists of dead soldiers.'

Cocteau: 'Fashion must be beautiful first, and ugly afterwards. Art must be ugly first, thus beautiful afterwards.'

Being busy is the best excuse for not working.

4 March

We consider and finally abandon the idea of buying a 1955 Cadillac hearse, recently offered for sale in the King's Road. The owner, a young American, asks only £500 for it, since superstition deters many potential buyers, and I'm attracted by the brass buckles and knobs on it, which light up at night, and by the thought of swishing through reverently uncovered crowds of peasants in French and Italian villages. Taken for a trial spin in the sepulchral flivver, we are pleased by the eagerness with which other traffic gives way for us, but disturbed by a tendency on the part of hospitals to flag us in as we drive past. But in spite of the conversational possibilities ('His and Hearse', etc.) we drop the project, Kathleen claiming that the thing is too big for her to manoeuvre.

I am convinced that my old Oxford chum Alan Beesley[1] is a CIA agent, probably a medium-ranking courier. Evidence; he goes down from Oxford in 1948 and disappears to Helsinki – near a most sensitive cold war frontier – for several years, ostensibly translating pop songs into Finnish. Then, with no radio experience, he is sent to Nigeria – newly independent – by the Ford Foundation to set up a radio network there. Thus he has his own transmitter and Ford Foundation protection! He then reappears in my life after a long absence, making no secret of his right-wing views (rather as Guy Burgess made no secret of his Leftist sympathies – and Burgess, like Alan, was scruffy and a heavy drinker, whom nobody suspected precisely because it seemed nobody would employ such a garrulous and disorganised person as a spy). *Soon* he is the only right-winger present when I take him to Clive Goodwin's[2] party for Danny Cohn-Bendit[3] during the Paris riots. Last year he goes to Ireland, just after the Belfast upheavals erupt, ostensibly to work on a travel book but probably to investigate IRA activists and gun-runners. He asks me for a list of people he could contact to find out what is really going on in Ireland. I give him letters to people like Claud Cockburn[4] and Conor Cruise O'Brien[5], who later writes to me wondering why he has not contacted them. Obvious answer: there is no book, and what he was hoping for was a list of Irish revolutionaries.

His present alleged job – an American publishing firm – is the ideal cover, since it explains his constant mobility and gives him an excuse for going anywhere. In London, he stays with us probably as a bolt hole where rival intelligence services cannot track him down. (Who would think of looking for a *CIA agent* in the spare bedroom of a prominent left-wing journalist?) Significant that he has never shown us any of the books he claims to have written for the US publisher. They include

1. Alan Beesley (1924–74). Close friend of Tynan's since Oxford. In *Isis* (1947), Tynan wrote: 'Alan Beesley thrust and bored into Oxford in October 1945, and it was like a kick in the midriff. Amongst other things he founded the Author-Critic Club and made about five hundred friends . . . Alan wears things out quickly, including himself. He lights his candle at both ends: tremulous, hypnotic flames which he snuffs regretfully, always just before both ends meet. While it burns, and you are with the subjective, not the objective, Alan, you are mesmerised by that relentless personality – so shaming and humiliating that it might be tangible.'
2. Clive Goodwin (1936–77). British actor, editor, Leftist journalist and literary agent.
3. Daniel Cohn-Bendit (1945–). French political activist; a leader in the 1968 Paris student revolt. Elected to the European Parliament as Green Party candidate in 1994.
4. Claud Cockburn (1904–81). British journalist and novelist; veteran of the Spanish Civil War and a Marxist, he wrote many suspense novels including *Beat the Devil* (1952).
5. Conor Cruise O'Brien (1917–). Irish critic and historian.

phrase-books – a wildly unlikely story when I come to think of it, because Alan is hopelessly bad at languages. Q: What should my attitude be to him now? E.M. Forster said that if he had to choose between betraying his country and his friend, he hoped he would have the courage to betray his country. But my dilemma is different. I have to choose between my loyalty to my friend and my loyalty to the international ideals that the CIA is mobilised to destroy. If Alan is part of this organisation, then there is a direct link between his activities and those of Lt. Calley[1] in My Lai. Often, during our post-war years at Oxford, gentlemen in quiet tweed suits would descend from London to give discreet glasses of sherry to undergraduates who might be political recruits for intelligence work. Alan and I knew of these interviews and mocked them. The mocking may have been hollower than I imagined.

8 March

No Communist country has ever dropped a bomb on a civilian. Repeat and remember that. *No Communist country has ever dropped a bomb on a civilian.* (Yesterday 1,000 planes bombed Laos. 1,000.)

Morecambe and Wise[2] gag, courtesy of George Melly:

Wise: What would you do if you found a man in bed with your wife?
Morecambe: Strangle his dog and break his white stick.

French au pair girl on phone to me: 'Mrs Morton leave there is fur minutes.' (i.e. Mrs M. left ten minutes ago.)

'When will the world know that peace and propagation are the two most delightful things in it.' (Horace Walpole, 1778)

---

1. Lt. William Calley, Jr. (1943–). US Army commander of a platoon that in 1968 massacred more
   than 100 civilians in the village of My Lai, Vietnam.
2. Eric Morecambe (1926–84) and Ernie Wise (1925–99). Beloved British comedy team. 'The
   characters they present in their act are both fixed at a mental and emotional age of approximately
   fifteen,' Tynan writes in *The Sound of Two Hands Clapping* (1975). 'They ape the manners and
   vocabulary of adults, but are always falling back on the idioms, habits, and local references of a
   North-country childhood. Hence they cannot deal with adult sex, except indirectly, through
   innuendo, as in their famous TV encounter with Frank ('Casanova') Finlay:
   Finlay (furtively): I have a *long felt want*.
   Morecambe (after subliminal pause): There's no answer to that.'

On closed circuit TV at 5 a.m. K. and I see the defeat of Mohammed Ali. Belated epitaph of the sixties: flair, audacity, imagination, outrageous aplomb, cut down by stubborn, obdurate, 'hard-hat' persistence. We may come to look back on the sixties as the Indian summer of the Western imagination, of the last aristocrats of Western taste. Beginning with Kennedy, the era ends with Nixon and Joe Frazier, his hatchet-man. In Clay's towering vulnerability, his apparent unconcern about exposing himself to punishment, there is breathtaking hubris, as well as the death wish remarked on by more than one commentator. He reminds one of a beautiful butch queer savouring the ecstasy of being beaten up and rolled by a bit of rough trade from the docks. Cavaliers had better beware. The Roundheads are back in force.

Idea for a short comedy: a TV producer buys a new and advanced laughter machine which can provide laughter of greater subtlety and variety than his old one. His problem: to find writers who can provide lines to fit the laughs.

'In films,' says Larry, 'there is no performance. You just shoot a lot of rehearsals and pick the best.'

11 March

Coincidentally, following my recent entry about Alan Beesley, the man himself telephones and says he would like to come and stay with us on Saturday night. I phone Clive G. and discuss my suspicions. After I do so, Kathleen says that if Alan *is* an agent, he will certainly not be one for long since Clive's phone is probably tapped. I have in fact blown Alan's cover: he is now a burnt-out agent.

13 March

Alan arrives. He is clearly in a depressed state, though hiding it buoyantly. When we are alone he confides that his American employer – the publisher – invited him to dinner last night and told him he was fired; part of an economy drive, consequence of US recession, new projects having to be scrapped, etc. – but I am of course stunned. K.'s prediction has come true. Alan *is* burnt-out. I confess my suspicions. He laughs merrily throughout, and when I have finished, says: 'Wouldn't it be a fantastic

Kafka situation if they were using me as an agent *and I didn't know it?*' He really does seem quietly desperate about getting another job in publishing soon. My suspicions fade, but do not entirely vanish.

Friendless virtually at forty-three: I have alienated my traditionalist friends by my left-wing politics, and my left-wing friends by my love of pleasure.

Headline: 'LOYAL ROLLS WORKER FINED'. The story is of a motor worker fined by his union for strike breaking. Thus loyalty, in newspaper language, means loyalty to one's employer, not to one's fellow-workers.

What is the vilest thing I have known one person do to another? High on the list would be what John Osborne and Jill Bennett did to Penelope G.[1] last year. Penelope was then living with Mike Nichols, who has suffered since birth from the disability of being totally hairless. (He even wears false eyebrows.) Nolan, Penelope and John's little daughter, had been staying with her father in London, and when she returned to New York her luggage contained a parcel addressed to Penelope 'With love from John and Jill'. It contained one of Nolan's dolls, which at first Penelope did not recognise, so curiously had it been maltreated. *Every hair had been pulled out of its head.*
  Penelope still cannot recall that moment without bursting into tears.

19 March

Deadlock at rehearsals of the NT *Coriolanus*, which started on Monday, with Christopher Plummer in the lead and Joachim Tenschert and Manfred Wekworth of the Berliner Ensemble directing. Plummer broke off rehearsals on Thursday to insist that twenty substantial cuts in his part should be restored and that new costumes should be designed for him. He also indicated disapproval of the interpretation – though it was he who chose them from a list of possible directors we submitted to him. Tenschert and Wekworth patiently agreed to the textual restorations (most of which were justified) but pointed out that they could

---

1. Penelope Gilliatt (1932–93). British film critic for *The New Yorker* magazine, 1968–79, also wrote the screenplay *Sunday, Bloody Sunday* (1971).

hardly jettison their interpretation of the play, since they had worked on it for years with Brecht and embodied it in one of the Ensemble's most brilliant productions.

Today Plummer arrives at rehearsal and as soon as his entrance arrives, refuses to take direction, insists on doing it his way, and makes jokes about T. and W. in front of the company. Whereupon T. and W. call off the rehearsal and retire to their hotel until such time as Christopher will apologise to them. All this, of course, is a re-enactment of *Coriolanus* – Plummer versus the two people's tribunes, too proud to bow the head and atone for his insults. He is crassly in the wrong, of course, but I fear in this case it will be the tribunes, and not Coriolanus, who are banished.

20 March

My *Coriolanus* prediction is happily wrong. After a night of telephoning from John Dexter[1], Michael Blakemore[2], and myself, Larry sees the point that we must not bend to the whim of visiting stars. His first impulse was to take the actor's side, fire the Germans and ask Michael Blakemore to take over the production – appealing to the latter's loyalty. I pointed out to Michael that the captain who scuttles the ship has no right to invite loyalty when asking one to bail out the bilgewater. Faced with a choice between the values of two ex-leaders of the Berliner Ensemble and the values of the star of *The Sound of Music*, which do we choose. After forty-eight hours of worry, much of it sleepless, on all our parts, Larry calls a company meeting to hear how the actors feel. To a man, they express loyalty to the Germans – a gratifying and (for me) unexpected result. Larry then breaks the news to a dumbfounded Plummer that he has been voted out of the consulship. Anthony Hopkins will take over the part. The whole episode a splendid vindication of the new collective leadership at the NT.

---

1. John Dexter (1925–90). Theatre and opera director; joined the National Theatre at Olivier's invitation in 1963.
2. Michael Blakemore (1928–). Australian-born actor and director; an associate artistic director at the National Theatre in 1971 and directed several notable successes there including *Long Day's Journey into Night* (1971), *The Front Page* (1972) and *The Cherry Orchard* (1973).

22 March

Gala dinner at the Dorchester in aid of the United Nations Association. Bumper assembly of posh fascists. On my right Lady Rotherwick who says she can't read *The Times* since it became 'Communistic'. 'When was that?' I ask. 'When the Astors sold it.' She says things are getting worse all over the world. 'We're Union Castle, you know. Ten years ago we had 150 ships. Now – how many d'you think?' I shake my head. '*Barely fifty*' – as if to say, '*Meat only once a week.*' Her opening sentence was uniquely calculated, in all its aspects, to start my adrenalin running. 'We've just been on a business trip to South Africa with the Rothermeres – it's a real paradise, isn't it?' She adds, 'That's the place to buy land – it's marvellous for spec' (i.e. speculative building). She confides that she and her husband own 'a lot of Rhodesia'. He is called Bunny and looks like a polished pink snooker ball. They have estates in Oxfordshire, Scotland, the Mediterranean and (of course) Rhodesia. She asks what I do. I say work at the National Theatre. 'Oh, where is that?' 'At the Old Vic,' I say. Hearing that I work for L.O., she observes, 'Vivien Leigh – oh yes, she died of cancer.' I quietly contradict her. '*I think you'll find she did,*' pipes this cheery, assured, empty-headed, infinitely tedious battener on thousands of lives. She looks about thirty-five but: 'Bunny and I have been married twenty years,' she says. The rich have the gift of elastic youth, which *can* be bought.

Laughingly, she tells me how a picture of her husband and herself at a night-club in Cape Town appeared with the caption: Lord and Lady *Rotherstein* – 'As if we were *Jewish*, my dear!'

26 March

We arrive late at night at Emma Cockburn's cottage in Wiltshire, which we have taken for two weeks. Next morning is halcyon. The cottage, thatched but furbished with all the books and minor luxuries of the left-wing rich, overlooks a lovely loop of the Avon, to which the grass gently slopes down. The first book I pick up – *The Mozart Companion* – falls open at an essay by Hans Keller in which I read that Mozart's String Quintets in C (K.515), G.Min (K.516) and D (K. 592) are: 'The greatest and most original . . . in existence, and the greatest and most original symphonic structures of Mozart, chamber-musical or otherwise.' An auspicious coincidence since the dozen or so records I have brought down from London include these very quintets. I stand on the terrace surveying all the green, pigeon-cooing, river-lapping *douceur*. Inside the cottage a Bartok Quartet on the gramophone speaks distantly of conflict and unease.

27 March

Alan Bennett said of Christopher Plummer: 'He's his own worst enemy – but only just.'

1 April

'Live each day as if it were your last' – the old stoic maxim, so far from giving me strength to endure, has been my undoing: for who, given a wife and child like mine, could spend his last hours doing anything but looking at them and smiling with foolish gratitude? Thus I spend each day.

4 April

Living a mile from Stonehenge, near the heart of Old Albion and the places of Arthur, I again come across the books of C.S. Lewis[1] – on sale in Salisbury Cathedral. I read *That Hideous Strength* and once more the old tug reasserts itself – a tug of genuine war with my recent self. How thrilling he makes goodness seem – how tangible and radiant! But what problems he raises! It is good to work, so I am bad in that I am not working. But whose work am I doing? I'm writing a magazine piece on Roman Polanski – at best a morally neutral act. But the film Andy Braunsberg[2] wants me to write and – greatest, most consummate of temptations – to *direct* has an erotic and anally sadistic theme. To do this work may well be a wicked act. Am I being tempted with sin, or tested with the chance of committing myself to responsible work? While solving the problem, I remain idle.

---

1. C.S. Lewis (1898–63). Author and scholar, best known for *The Screwtape Letters* (1942) and other volumes of Christian apologetics. Tynan's tutor at Magdalen College, Oxford.
2. Andrew Braunsberg (1942–). Film producer of among others Polanski's *Fearless Vampire Killers* (1967).

I must record here a story Marlene Dietrich[1] told me several years ago. She was a friend, in the thirties, of Joseph P. Kennedy, and her daughter swam with his boys on the Riviera before the war. In the autumn of 1962 she was appearing in cabaret in Washington. Bobby and Teddy came to see her, but of course the President does not attend night-clubs; and she was sad about this until she received a summons to have drinks at the White House the following Saturday at 6 p.m. She accepted, although at 7 p.m. she had to be at the Statler Hotel, where the Jewish War Veterans were holding a dinner to honour her for her wartime work to aid Jewish refugees.

So at 6 she arrived at the White House and was shown by a Press attaché into the President's sanctum. A bottle of German wine was cooling in an ice bucket. 'The President remembered that when he last dined with you in New York you said this was your favourite wine.' The attaché poured her a glass and withdrew. The clock reached 6.15 before J.F.K. loped in, kissed her, poured himself some wine, took her out on the balcony and talked about Lincoln. 'I hope you aren't in a hurry,' he said. Marlene explained that, alas, 2,000 Jews were waiting to give her a plaque at 7 p.m., and it was now 6.30 . . . 'That – doesn't give us much time, does it?' said J.F.K., looking straight into her eyes. Marlene confesses that she likes powerful men and enjoys hanging their scalps on her belt. So she looked straight back and said: 'No, Jack, I guess it doesn't.'

With that, he took her glass and led the way out into a corridor and then round a corner into – the presidential bedroom. And then, in M.D.'s words:

> I remembered about his bad back – that wartime injury. I looked at him and he was already undressing. He was unwinding rolls of bandage from around his middle – he looked like Laocoön and that snake, you know? Now I'm an old lady, and I said to myself: I'd like to sleep with the President, sure, but I'll be goddammed if I'm going to be on top!

But it seems everything was OK; J.F.K. took the superior position; and it was all over sweetly and very soon.

1. Marlene Dietrich (1901–92). Tynan's good friend from 1954 when he first caught her attention with a sentence: 'She has sex but no gender.' Said Dietrich: 'There were all these people trying to guess me out and he understood the whole thing.'

And then he went to sleep. I looked at my watch and it was
6.50. I got dressed and shook him – because I didn't know my
way around the place, and I couldn't just call for a cab. I said:
'Jack – wake up! 2,000 Jews are waiting! For Christ's sake get
me out of here!' So he grabbed a towel and wrapped it round
his waist and took me along this corridor to an elevator. He
told the elevator man to get me a car to the Statler immediately – standing right there in his towel, without any
embarrassment, as if it was an everyday event – which in his
life it probably was. Just as I was getting into the elevator, he
said: 'There's just one thing I'd like to know.' 'What is it,
Jack?' I said. 'Did you ever make it with my father?' he said.
'No, Jack,' I answered truthfully, 'I never did.' 'Well,' he
replied, 'that's one place I'm in first.' Then the lift door closed
and I never saw him again.

5 April

Lunch with Cecil Beaton at Broadchalk, after which he shows us his
new hothouse, wearing a brown puma-skin overcoat and a deep
chestnut pleated-velvet cap. He has aged beautifully and (as Kathleen
points out) is prepared for the loneliness of old age since life as a solitary
queer has prepared him for it better than married life prepares husbands
or wives. As we leave he urges us to work: 'Tap, tap, tap, like
woodpeckers.'

From Leonardo's *Trattato della Pittura*: 'For if you are alone you are
completely yourself, but if you are accompanied by a single companion
you are only half yourself.'

12 April

I draft (but don't send) a letter to *The Times*:

Dear Sir,
    I am in possession of a thin circular disc of what seems to
be shellac, bearing faint concentric striations and a label

reading: 'Down Mexico Way with Dame Clara Butt'.[1] Is this
a record?

I am, etc . . .

The most unexpected thing I ever heard said: after a dinner party in the
mid-fifties. The host desultorily asked the guests to name the three things
they loved most in the world. The answers ranged from the predictably
serious ('Schubert Quartets') to the predictably skittish ('onyx cufflinks')
until Kitty Freud[2] shook her dark hair and said with trembling candour:
'Travel, good food, and being spanked on my bottom with a hairbrush.'

16 April

In Paris.

Drinks with exiled princeling – Alexander of Yugoslavia – who says,
apropos of the West Indies, 'You can educate these blackies, but you
cannot civilise them.' Then dinner at the Tour d'Argent with Tom
Curtiss,[3] Noel Annan[4] and wife, and Paulette Goddard. The ex-Madame
Remarque is bronzed, beminked, and bewrinkled – a loud face, lively
eyes and a need to keep sparkling, even when she has nothing to say. She
is going to go on a tour of the Loire Châteaux with Anita Loos for
Holiday magazine. She tells of her dislike for Kate Hepburn, which began
when they were both appearing on stage in Detroit not so long ago.
'Come and let me show you the *real* America,' said Kate: and took P.
Goddard on a guided tour of the Ford factory *on Sunday*. It was then that
P. Goddard decided that Kate had no sense of humour – and too much
dedication. P.G. has not since appeared on the stage.

I draft a press announcement stating, with as little pomp as my French will
allow, that I cannot be held responsible for the Paris version of *Oh!
Calcutta!* due to open on 10 May. Less than half the material comes from
the English-language versions; the gaps are filled in by sketches written by

---

1. Dame Clara Butt (1872–1936). Opera singer.
2. Kitty Freud (1926–). First wife of the artist Lucian Freud; the model for some of his most arresting work.
3. Thomas Quinn Curtiss (1915–2000). A film and drama critic for the *International Herald Tribune*.
4. Noel Annan (1916–2000). British academic and liberal social critic; a regular contributor of essays to the *New York Review of Books*. Annan led the successful fight against the introduction of museum fees proposed by Viscount Eccles.

Parisian authors. All hints of heterosexual deviations are ruthlessly cut; and it seems that even the most liberal French audience would walk out if it heard on a stage the vernacular words for prick and cunt. Instead we have pseudo-poetic sketches about men in love with goats and trees and women in love with *haute cuisine*. For the hundredth time one laments that the French have never had a theatrical tradition that reflected the faces of everyday French life. Reality must be *transcended*, they insist, never shown. Hence their disdain for most of the good work done in the English-speaking theatre since the war.

At the Olympia: Jerry Lewis opens to a tout-Paris audience including Aznavour, Bardot, etc. His finesse, his daintiness, his delicate mimetic skill are riveting: cleverly adapting his act so that it avoids language (he speaks no French) and focuses on mime, song, gesture, dance and miming to music, he shows a command of vaudeville techniques such as I may never see again and such as this audience has probably never seen before. Miming to a thirties big-band record, he transforms its snarling riffs and growling trumpets into a bar-room brawl – *brilliant*!

A nostalgic pilgrimage to the Hotel de Lutèce, in the rue Jules Chaplain, a hundred yards from the Dôme and the Coupole in Montparnasse. In this quiet, cheap little hotel – 35 francs for a double bed and bath even as late as last December – I have stayed on every trip to Paris in the past twenty years. Many of the clients were retired circus performers and vaudevillians (I met the late Jimmy Savo[1] there in the fifties); many were one-night lovers. Every room had a double *and* a single bed (in case one partner wanted to sleep in cool sheets) and mirrors built into the walls alongside the beds. Opposite the Lutèce was (and is) a genuine whores' hotel, with rooms available by the hour. But the Lutèce was my Paris base – first shared with Elaine[2] in our early and

---

1. Jimmy Savo (1896–1960). Broadway comedian.
2. Elaine Dundy (1921–). Tynan's first wife, mother of Tracy Tynan. Married 1951. Author of among other books *The Dud Avocado* (1958) in which Tynan appears as the flamboyant Max Ramage. 'Although the spotlight seemed his natural element and he preened himself in it, it scared him too,' Dundy wrote in a 1994 article about her marriage to Tynan. 'And at those times his stammer would rise in his throat as if to choke him. I liked the realistic way he understood and accepted that in his ferocious pursuit of notoriety, he was making himself a target that was going to get hit. His pose was very decadent, *fin-de-siècle*, Yellow Book, Oxford flamboyant, etc. In other words, the things that drove other people crazy about him, I thought marvellous. I adored him.' She added: 'We drank a lot. We drank alcoholically; thought alcoholically; and fought alcoholically . . .' They divorced in 1964.

good years, then with Addie Herder,[1] then with Evans[2] (whom I saw tonight at the Tour d'Argent with her husband John Frankenheimer) – and latterly with my last and best love, Kathleen. I phoned last week for my usual reservation, and a strange voice told me the hotel was '*définitivement fermé*': it has been bought by a nameless 'association'. So perishes the heart of my Paris. Living in a friend's apartment near the Gare des Invalides, I feel as if I were in Siberia.

The biggest cultural event of my early life was *Citizen Kane*. Believing all I read (and Welles said) about it, I thought it was a one-man show, conceived, produced, written, directed and predominantly played by Orson. This notion of a work of art as a solo performance affected all my attitudes towards theatre, cinema and my own career for many years. I didn't come to face this idea of art as collaboration for a very long while. Now Pauline Kael's pieces on *Citizen Kane* in *The New Yorker* prove beyond dispute that Welles did not work a line of *Kane*: that the concept and its execution (right up to the shooting script stage) were the unaided work of Herman J. Mankiewicz.[3] I'm delighted, of course, by this confirmation of my belief that film is as much (if not more) a writer's medium as a director's: but it is deeply undermining to find that so much of my earliest definition of art was based on a lie.

Elizabeth Hardwick[4], wife of Robert Lowell, has lost her husband to Caroline Citkovitz. Beata Rosmer, wife of Rosmer, loses her husband to Rebecca West in Ibsen's play. Rebecca's victory is hollow, and she and Rosmer finish by drowning themselves as Beata did. In the *New York Review of Books* Elizabeth writes an enormously long revaluation of *Rosmersholm*, concluding that its moral is: 'In the end, nothing will turn out to have been worth the destruction of others and of oneself.' I have seldom seen an autobiography so cleverly disguised as criticism.

1. Addie Herder (1920–). American painter; Tynan began an affair with her in 1959 while travelling in Europe.
2. Evans Evans (1936–). Actress, wife of movie director John Frankenheimer; appeared as Velma in *Bonnie and Clyde* (1967).
3. Herman J. Mankiewicz (1897–1953). Famous American wit, screenwriter and first drama critic of *The New Yorker*.
4. Elizabeth Hardwick (1916–). Novelist and critic, co-founder with her husband, the poet Robert Lowell, of the *New York Review of Books* in 1963.

19 April

A huge supper at Max Rayne's[1] to celebrate the twenty-first anniversary of the Festival Ballet. We arrive late with Pam and David Harlech[2] to find most of the guests (300 of them) already seated in this modern Hampstead palace. Princess Margaret, the guest of honour, has not yet taken her place; we kiss, chat and she suggests we go in to dine. As we do so, everyone rises. The joy is that among the guests, reverently on their feet, are dozens of people who would like to see me in prison – Tory industrialists, Catholic MPs, peers and snobs in general. As I pass among them to the top table I incline my head to them with what I hope looks like radiant contempt.

In 1584, Reginald Scot[3] mentioned, in a list of supernatural creatures used to frighten children: 'The spoom, the man in the oke, the fire-drake, the puckle, Tom Thombe, Tom Tumbler boneless, and such other bugs.' I might call my autobiography *Tumbler Boneless*.

20 April

Rally for George Jackson[4] and the Soledad Brothers – blacks imprisoned for racist reasons in a Californian jail – at the Central Hall. The star speaker is James Baldwin, who says: 'If their children and my children have no future, nobody in this hall has any future.' He takes a straight socialist line, equating the suffering of the Soledad blacks with that of oppressed people everywhere. I recall arguing with him twelve years ago, when he was battling for integration and equal opportunity: I begged him to find the answers in Marxism rather than racism. More argument followed in stage 2 (the black separatist phase) of the black revolution. At this period I met Martin Luther King at Harry Bela-

---

1. Sir Max Rayne (1918–). Former chairman of London Merchant Securities and patron of the arts.
2. Lord David Harlech (1918–85). British Ambassador to the United States during the Kennedy Administration and a friend of J.F.K. Pamela (1934–) was his second wife.
3. Reginald Scot (1538–99). Author whose *Discoverie of Witchcraft* (1584) debunked many of the superstitions surrounding witches and witchcraft. Shakespeare was said to have read and admired Scot's book.
4. George Jackson (1941–71). One of the Soledad Brothers; murdered a white prison guard in 1970. He was the author of *Soledad Brother: The Prison Letters of George Jackson* (1970). He was killed in an escape attempt.

fonte's house in New York and asked why he did not make the point that it was economic exploitation that kept the Negro down. 'If I said that,' he replied, 'they would call me a Communist. Christianity is safer.' Phase 3 of the black revolt is the realisation that it is a part of the worldwide revolt against private ownership and profit. Jimmy B. has just arrived at this analysis. One can only say, 'Welcome to the club.'

28 April

Farewell party at the Axelrods' – Harlechs, Lenny Bernstein, David Hockney, Tony Curtis, Jules Stein, Josh Logan[1]. Talking to the latter (about Vietnam), David rolls a joint and passes it around. The first time Josh passes it on; the second time he takes a puff. Immediately his bashful face falls and he turns to me. 'My God – that's the first time I've smoked pot since I met Benny Goodman in 1938!' He has bought a house in Chelsea and intends to live half of the year here. He opposes the Vietnam War.

30 April

From *The Big Store* (1940): late Marx Brothers minor rating, but plenty of instant movie nostalgia – Virginia O'Brien, Douglas Dumbville (angry rumours), Margaret Dumont, the overrated Harpo, the overspecialised Chico (a Jewish wop!) and a slightly overtired Groucho. We prize these films because of the world they *send us out into* – the world of our teens. I set down some forgotten lines from Tony Martin's *Tenement Symphony*:

> The Cohens, the Kelleys,
> The Campbells and Vermicellis –
> They all have a part
> In my Tenement Symphony . . .
> O Maria, O Maria –
> You'll be late
> For your date
> With Izzy . . .

---

1. Joshua Logan (1908–88). Theatre and film director; among his many distinguished productions, *Annie Get Your Gun* (1946), *Mister Roberts* (1948) and *South Pacific* (1949).

The songs of the ghetto
Inspire the allegretto –
You'll find it
In my Tenement Symphony . . .
Hully Gee! –
Hully Gee! –
Gotta stop!
Hey, Jakie! . . .
And from this confusion
I dreamed up a grand illusion
My Tenement Symphony
In four flats.

The phony, warm-hearted Depression togetherness of it all – just before the war brought the boom and cancelled the need for that kind of interracial cheer-up music. Also worth noting: another credit from the past – the vocal team called Six Hits and a Miss.

3 May

Adrian Mitchell's[1] marvellous bawdy celebration of William Blake, *Tyger*, is scheduled to open in July. Larry expressed early on his horrified qualms about four-letter words, scatology and randy references in the text; but he has postponed issuing an ultimatum on the subject until now, when the production has been announced and advertised. He is counting on the directors (John Dexter and Michael Blakemore) and the author being willing to compromise rather, than have a public row. Further, he says he must get Lord Chandos' approval of the text. This incites me to explosion. First he has no need to obtain anyone's approval; I spent two years on an Arts Council inquiry which unanimously asserted the right of the Artistic Director – *not* the Board – to have the final say on choice of plays in subsidised theatres.

The Arts Council endorsed this recommendation and it's now official policy. So Larry cannot hide behind Chandos' skirts in

---

1. Adrian Mitchell (1932–). British poet, novelist, playwright; his *Tyger: A Celebration of the Life and Work of William Blake* was staged by the National Theatre in 1971.

censoring this play. Nor will I let him intimidate and unnerve dear good-natured Adrian with some such ploy as: 'Dear boy, it's just a question of the odd line and song here and there – of course you're entitled to withdraw the play and make a fuss about being censored – but if we leave the dirty bits in then I'm in awful trouble with my Board – and what with Lord Eccles cracking down on obscenity in subsidised theatres, we might even get our grant cut . . .' Etc. etc. I must tell Adrian to be absolutely firm. Of course *all* the disputed lines are not *necessary*: but 'Reason not the *need*' – they are Adrian's, they are part of his play, and they must be included. The supreme irony is that the play deals precisely with the way in which England and the Establishment try to gag and castrate their revolutionary poets. Adrian must not fall victim to the very practices against which his play protests.

Two kinds of schoolboys often turn out to be artistically gifted. There are those who do impersonations: those are the talented. And there are the ones they are impersonating: these are the geniuses.

Excerpt from any jazzman's autobiography:

One night after our last set a little guy stepped out of the smoky haze of the Biltmore Ballroom. He was a little beat-up guy and he had a beat-up little case with a beat-up little horn in it. He asked Doc whether he could sit in and jam with us and Doc said OK. That's the way it was along the West 50s in that never-to-be-forgotten, hell-for-leather heyday of gutbucket and jive. So the beat-up little guy pulled out his beat-up horn and for two hours he blew miraculous labyrinths of harmony that would have made the angels weep. Then he put his beat-up horn back into its beat-up case and walked out into the blue Chicago dawn. His name was Bertolt Brecht.

Glassy-eyed debby girl at party, smiling wildly to conceal the fact that she is pissed out of her mind. I say chattily: 'Nice and cool today.' Deb: 'Yes. There's a bresh, frisk wind.'

6 May

To Elstree, where I tape the *Dick Cavett Show* with Jack Hawkins[1] and George Brown[2]. Hawkins and I (and a large studio audience) are kept waiting for two hours while Brown is found, poured into a cab and transported protesting to the studio. I talk about sex and *Macbeth*, repeating myself with hypnotised efficiency. Brown lurches and rambles and expostulates, speaking moistly of how he 'shared the agony' of L.B.J. over Vietnam. It was apparently an agony in a garden – the garden of the White House: 'L.B. and I walked up and down and he unburdened his heart to me. I felt I knew that great man like a brother.' I interrupt to say that if he knew L.B.J. well enough to call him 'L.B.' maybe next time he could just call him 'L.'. Then Brown is off about how the pledge made to Vietnam must be kept: 'I can't weep over the men whose lives are being lost,' he says, with the barbarous complacency of the self-righteous untouched. Afterwards, behaving with the rhetorical expansiveness with which he has doubt-less learned, over the years, to conceal the fact that he is pissed as a newt, he begs me to lunch with him so that he can explain his point of view. (He is the kind of man who paws you as he talks.) 'We burned and tortured and maimed in Malaya,' he intones, waving a gin. 'And *we were right*' (this with fat jowls thrust forward, Churchill turned into Billy Bunter[3]). 'Where war is concerned, in for a penny, in for a pound! Never look back! Never go back on your word!' i.e. never admit you were wrong. Brown is led slowly to his car by his wife Sophie, saying, 'It's getting late, George,' for what must be the 500 millionth time. To think that this wet-brained clown was once our Foreign Secretary!

11 May

First musical read-through of *Tyger*: the whole cast stunned and exhilarated. Tonight Larry calls Adrian to find out if he will agree

---

1. Jack Hawkins (1910–73). Actor.
2. George Brown, Baron (1914–85). Vice-chairman and Deputy Leader of the Labour Party, 1960–70, Labour Foreign Secretary, 1966–68.
3. Billy Bunter. Anti-hero of Frank Richards' stories, originally published in the boys' weekly paper *Magnet*.

to the cuts: I almost hope Larry withdraws the play so that I can do it with Michael White and astound London and New York. I weep shamelessly at Mike Westbrook's setting of Adrian's lovely song 'The Children of William Blake' (I must have this recorded for K.'s parturition next month)[1]. And the Vic rehearsal room rocks to the hymn-like rhythms of the first act finale, 'Everything that lives is holy', a simple descending phrase repeated by the whole cast hundreds of times while Gerald James (as Blake) cries prophecies of victory over squalor and repression at the audience. It is overwhelming and the show must be a triumph. Partly mine, since I commissioned it.

Supper at the Savoy Grill (best food in London). At the next table, on one of his brief visits to England, is Noël Coward with his curious court – Graham Payn[2], Gladys Calthrop[3], and Joyce Carey[4]. How sad that Noël should cherish this drab circle – nice enough people, but so second rate. He greets us as he rises to go, explaining that he's *en route* from winter in Jamaica to summer in Switzerland. 'You've chosen a good time to come,' says Kathleen, thinking of the splendid summery weather. 'Do you *swear* it?' says Noël with a grave twinkle, unconsciously quoting from his early one-actor *Shadow Play*. He turns to go, and we see with a shock that he can hardly hobble and has to be helped by Graham and Joyce Carey. The rubicund face and confident lips have fooled us. This is an old man on the last of his legs. Probably I shall not see him again.

13 May

While I think of it: the story of Britt Ekland's knickers. About a year ago, arriving at my office at the National Theatre, I pulled a book out of

---

1. The director John Dexter would not allow the song to be recorded. 'I promised her this song as a welcoming present for the child – she has not yet heard the score,' Tynan wrote to Dexter in June 1971. 'It was to have been recorded outside rehearsal hours with a simple piano accompaniment. It would have been heard by nobody except Kathleen and myself (and the baby). The recording would have taken, at the most, five minutes. (You will be aware that the poem is all of nine lines long.). I now hear that you have forbidden the taping to take place. Forgive me if I am speechless.'
2. Graham Payn (1918–). British actor, Coward's life-long companion after World War II, made his debut in Coward's revue *Words and Music* (1932).
3. Gladys Calthrop (1897–1980). Costume and set designer, close companion of Noël Coward, many of whose shows she worked on.
4. Joyce Carey (1898–1993). British actress; befriended Coward in 1924, appeared in many of his plays including *Present Laughter* (1942) and *This Happy Breed* (1942).

my coat pocket and there came out with it a pair of Kathleen's knickers. They fell on the floor under the eyes of Rozina [Tynan's secretary at the National Theatre]. Out of mischief and a desire to test the speed and durability of gossip, I decided to invent a story about how the knickers came to be there. (The truth was that to enliven a dull taxi ride I had asked K. to remove them to pay a forfeit. I'd then forgotten they were in my pocket.) So I told Rozina – which was true – that the previous night I'd been at a party to celebrate the wedding anniversary of Princess Margaret and Tony, given by the Rupert Nevilles. The Queen, Prince Philip and the Queen Mum were also there. Showbiz was represented by Britt Ekland, John Dankworth, Cleo Laine and me.

Then began the lie. I said I'd noticed the Queen Mother drink half-pints of a clear liquid from a tankard. 'Gin of course,' I remarked to Britt. 'Surely not,' she replied. 'It must be water.' 'I'll bet you,' I said, 'your knickers to a pair of first-night seats for *Oh! Calcutta!* that it's gin.' 'You're on,' she said. So I called over a liveried waiter, tipped him 10 shillings and asked the question. 'Gordon's gin, sir,' he said. Whereon Britt retired to the loo and returned to hand me her knickers. Three days later I was accosted by a gossip columnist at a club. 'Is it true about you and Britt Ekland's panties?' he asked. 'You'd better ask her,' I said. Next day the whole story appeared under his name in the *Daily Mirror.* And when, later in the year, Britt sold her own life story to the *People*, she devoted almost a whole issue to perpetrating my myth.

The Common Market, into which we are being remorselessly shoved, is (a) the greatest historical vulgarity since Hitler's 1,000-year Reich – a capitalist bloc of Germany, Italy, France, Spain, England and the Low Countries, directed against socialism. (b) the deathknell of socialism in Western Europe – which is why right-wing Labour as well as the Tory centre supports it.

Victor Hugo held audiences in his later years, attended by hundreds of worshippers. A throne would wait empty on a dais until he appeared. One morning he entered, took his seat, and, after pondering for a long minute, uttered: '*Quant à moi, je crois à Dieu.*' An elderly lady in the audience turned to her friend and whispered: '*Quel merveille! Un Dieu qui croit à Dieu!*'

25 May

Note on Fecund Critic:

Mrs Brendan Gill[1]
Never takes the pill
Though when all's said and done,
Her husband is one.

26 May

Overheard in lobby of Hotel de la Paix, Geneva: American woman, obviously rich and obviously regarded as the intellectual of her group, says: 'Naturally I don't believe in fostering mediocrity with handouts because, of course, it completely destroys initiative' – she who has lived on handouts every mediocre minute of her married life.

17–26 May

These days spent in an attic room at the Château de Meyrargues, a lofty ironbound medieval fortress (converted into a hotel with twelve rooms and a first-rate restaurant) ten miles north of Aix-en-Provence. Here I write the first 1/2-hour of my film script, at present called, *Our Life with Alex and Florence*. I intended to stay longer but was driven home by loneliness: when work ended in the afternoon I was faced with six hours empty of society and converse; and even *haute cuisine* could not fill the gap. I visited leafy Aix, which was more bijou and prettier than I looked for; Avignon, a tourist-packed nuisance, with the Palais des Papes a resonantly useless and hollow monument, best seen from across the river, dominating the city like the two cathedrals dominate Salamanca. Chill and desolate to explore: no paintings and muddy, mediocre frescos.

A memorable dinner nearby at the Auberge de Noves, which lost its third Michelin star a year or two ago and clearly deserves to have it back. 1st course: *Le Triomphe du Golfe* (lobster soufflé with truffles) –

---

1. Brendan Gill (1914–98). *New Yorker* writer from 1936 until his death; the magazine's senior drama critic 1968–87.

followed by *Caneton en Papillote*, the whole bird cooked in a paper bag and served with a separate green sauce of rosemary, thyme and tarragon. Evidence of seriousness: I had chosen a ½ bottle of Claret at 60F to go with the duck, but the patron insisted that I take a Rhône wine at 12F!

Books read at the Château included Arnold Bennett's Journals (superb) and – most memorably – *The Joint* by James Blake: letters written from a variety of American prisons by a forty-ish recidivist, chronically queer, masochist and intellectual. For wry, stylish wit I've read nothing to touch this in American literature for a decade. Blake cannot cope with the mad competitive life of 'freedom': he finds his only fulfilment in the relative peace and order of prison life where he can read, play piano, and get his kicks by sucking off psychopaths. This is Genet without the martyr complex and the pretensions. A startling book.

Triple coincidence: during my stay at Meyrargues, I invented an imaginary château called Peyrargues in which my film takes place. After flying from Nice to Geneva, I went to dinner at the Parc des Eaux Vives, and on the way bought a paperback to re-read – Waugh's *Brideshead Revisited*. On page 26 I came across a passage in which Sebastian Flyte invites the narrator, Charles Ryder, to come for a drive, eat strawberries and drink a wine called *Peyrargues* – 'And don't pretend you've ever heard of it, because you haven't'. Hardly had I noted this coincidence when the waiter offered me the wine list. I asked if he had any special recommendation. 'This,' he said, 'is really excellent,' pointing to *Château Fleuris Peyrargues*, at 50F! of which, needless to say, I had never heard in my life.

9 June

At 3:30 p.m., a son – 7lb. 3 ½ oz. – to be called Matthew (after K.'s father) Blake (after William Blake and James Blake, the American convict author) Tynan. I had thought I could sire only girls and rather wanted a third. She would have been exquisitely named Angelica Tiffany Tynan and when the nurse told me the child was a boy, I spoke aloud a short farewell to Angelica Tiffany, who had emerged briefly from the shadows and now receded into them. What I feared was a husky thug of a boy: I do not like male competition – in fact I am not all that crazy about men *per se* – so I was much relieved to find that Matthew is sensitive, almost *girlish* – looking – resembles Roxana when she was born. So long as he develops my feminine streak he will be very welcome. I shall shortly buy him a few pretty frocks and enter him for Sadler's Wells Ballet School. K. is positively glowing with earth-motherliness. She has always wanted a boy and now she *has* one. I begin to feel almost superfluous. The problem about this second child will not be that *Roxana* may feel overshadowed, but that *I* may – a situation of which Freud had omitted to warn me.

Chronically idle since my return from France two weeks ago. I used to take Dexamyl to give me enough confidence to start work. Now I take it to give me enough confidence not to.

As the Common Market debate gets hotter, here are my feelings. If we want a Europe permanently divided along East-West lines; a mutual protection society for Western capitalism; the death of all hopes for socialism (as opposed to Willy Brandt's Social Democracy) in Europe; if, in short, we want to resurrect Hitler's 1,000-year Reich – a Western European bloc dominated by Germany, implacably opposed to the socialist world, and even including countries like Spain, which Hitler failed to incorporate – then we must make haste into the Common Market. If on the other hand we want *true* internationalism (instead of the parochial variety), we must stay out. I understand why right-wing Labour Party members want us in. There are two reasons – (1) the general politicians' fantasy of governing a still larger territory and population, and (2) the knowledge that, once in the Common Market, they need no longer fear the Labour Left, which will be rendered impotent.

The Tory attitude: the EEC is a challenge for British industry. There will be unemployment and higher prices and small businesses will go to the wall: but all this is presented as if it were somehow an inevitable and character-building ordeal, like the prospect of execution which concentrated the mind of the Major in Pepys so wonderfully. The English people really think there is some miraculous panacea in the Common Market which Heath has not seen fit to reveal to them. They cannot believe what is in fact the truth: that he genuinely believes that suffering is the way to bring the workers to heel. Tory politicians seldom appeal in vain to the British public's appetite for suffering.

Phrase from BBC 2 documentary on wartime bombing policy: in an RAF instructional film we hear that 'many a promising young fire has been extinguished before it has destroyed a house'.

Why do women have babies? In order to be loved by babies.

But don't you hate yourself for being so idle?
Oh yes.
Why don't you do something about it?
Because I dislike hating myself slightly less than I dislike effort.

I.O. on Peter Glenville's[1] story on how he became queer: his mother, the famous pantomime principal boy Dorothy Ward,[2] decided against breast-feeding him when he was born, since Christmas was approaching and she had to bind her breasts flat in order to be an acceptable male. But in April when the pantomime was over she had a sudden access of maternal feeling and, removing the bottle, offered her nipples to Peter G. 'I adored my bottle,' he said. 'And suddenly there was this great dangling strawberry thrust into my mouth. I remember it distinctly; and I've hated women ever since.'

6 July

Disturbed by sudden, widespread praise (in the narrative arts) of the smooth *vis-à-vis* the hairy. Discretion, tact, restraint, kid gloves, the snaffle and the bit with no sign of the bloody horse – these are the virtues presently being acclaimed. Examples: Pinter's *Old Times* (how thin, how trivial, how – yes – *bourgeois* compared to the profoundly eccentric and many-sided characters in *The Caretaker*!) – *Sunday, Bloody Sunday* (with its careful understatement, its so-British acceptance of the *mystique* of making the best of a bad blow-job) – *Le Genou de Claire* (in which pseudo-literary dialogue – which would be insufferable on the

---

1. Peter Glenville (1913–96). Theatre and film director, most notably of Jean Anouilh's *Becket* (1960) with Laurence Olivier and Anthony Quinn.
2. Dorothy Ward (1890–1987). Actress and singer.

stage or in a novel – is rendered bearable by summer-holiday photography of the Lake of Annecy) – and, though I haven't yet seen it, the Pinter-Losey version of *The Go-Between*. I begin to fear that *Tyger*, in this new world of bloodless ambiguities, will seem embarrassing and even 'primitive' in its passion and directness.

Afterthought: all these films have a puritanism that is not merely aesthetic – Rohmer the Catholic, for whom the touching of a girl's flesh (Claire's knee) exists not as a pleasurable act but as the illustration of a moral decision – the self-destructive sex in *The Go-Between* – the dwelling on bygone moments of erotic obsession which traps the husband and the wife's best friend in *Old Times* – and the gloomy ruefulness with which, in *Bloody Sunday*, the hero and heroine squander their affection and regard on a cool and uncaring erotic object – the boy.

Both *post* and *ante* (and usually *during*) coitus, everything must be resolutely *triste*.

In an age when everyone talks of 'lifestyle', nobody talks of life content.

13 July

First public preview of *Tyger* – not well received: the direction hasn't released the spontaneous, audience-embracing warmth that is in the show. And of course there were technical gaffes of all kinds which can be put right. I see Larry looking fogged and harassed and uncomprehending. Several times the audience longed to applaud but were not allowed to, no pause being granted them. This is a gross error: bottled applause turns sour. (Tynan's 2nd Law of Theatre.) Next day Larry and I meet Dexter and Blakemore to exchange notes. L. says he asked Binkie Beaumont[1] (member of the Board) to see the performance last night and quotes Binkie as saying that the show is subversive and seditious and that public money should not be spent on such things. L. begs for deletion of line: 'God damn the Queen.' I am deputed to ask Adrian to consent to cuts.

---

1. Hugh 'Binkie' Beaumont (1908–73). West End impresario who ran the H.M. Tennant empire for many years.

16 July

Fourth preview of *Tyger*: already a tenfold improvement: solidarity between actors, musicians and audience is tangible in the theatre. But before the show an astounding scene in Donald Albery's[1] office with Larry, John Dexter, Michael Blakemore and myself. L.O. insists that 'God damn the Queen' be deleted. Adrian has refused. John and Michael make passionate speeches: 'We're both over twenty-one,' says Michael, and M. just stops short of threatening resignation. I explain that Adrian really has republican sympathies, as do I: 'Why don't you go and live in a republic then?' says L.O. He also cannot understand the supermarket scene, in which Blake confronts and repudiates the idea of Private Property; and he thinks the scene parodying a 'British Cultural Committee' is libellous to Lord Goodman[2]. How one longs to reveal that if *Tyger* succeeds it will be in the teeth of panic-stricken opposition from this obtuse lick-spittal, L.O., who would rather insult and outrage a poet than cause a moment's dismay to Her Majesty. How ironic that the show, which deals with the efforts of snobbish and conservative officialdom to censor a revolutionary poet, should have a backstage plot that precisely echoes the one on stage! Later in the meeting I propose a production of *Lysistrata*, to be adapted by Germaine Greer. Instantly L.O.'s sad old brain sniffs danger: 'Won't she fill it up with cocks and cunts?' And his entourage – Michael Halifax and Tony Easterbrook – dutifully bleats agreement.

19 July

The last night before the opening and a tremendously loving night, with most of the audience staying on to dance with the Mike Westbrook band. Afterwards, an astonishing scene: Joan Plowright has been sent by Larry to tell John Dexter, Michael Blakemore and myself that the Queen-bothering line must be cut or the show will not go on. An hour of debate (with John claiming that without her support the National Theatre would never have put on any intelligent new plays) results in deadlock: Michael B. offers three alternatives – (1) L.O. forgets about the whole

---

1. Donald Albery (1914–88). West End theatre producer.
2. Lord Goodman (1913–95). The portly and powerful British lawyer who held many important public positions including the chairmanship of the Arts Council from 1965–72.

thing, in which case we will forget it as well – (2) L.O. announces to the press that the show has been performed without his approval – (3) L.O. calls together the company and personally instructs Gerald James (who plays Blake) to delete the offending word. We shall see which choice he will make. Whichever it is, it will outrage the central character and his author by treating them as children.

25 July

Worst fears realised – *Tyger* receives – from the middle-aged critics – the most venomous reviews I can remember. After a first night weakly played in the later stages, the press split down the middle on generation-gap lines: the pity, from our point of view, being that the overwhelming majority of the critics are over forty. This is unhealthy for the theatre, because it means that standards are being set by men who have mostly settled in their own careers for second-best, for compromise, for values acceptable to their editors and their readers. Nobody among the newspaper critics has a radical vision of life and theatre – and I don't mean just *politically* radical: I use the word in a far more general sense, meaning a free, open, unconstrained, unblinkered, exuberant, back-to-grass-roots view of human possibilities. Michael Billington in *The Times* is enthusiastic about the show, and he is a young man employed as Irving Wardle's second string. (Wardle is in his forties.) Hobson of the *Sunday Times* is sixty-seven. B.A. Young of the *Financial Times* is c. fifty-eight; Shulman of the *Evening Standard* is fifty-nine. Our only supporters (Billington apart) are *O2*, *Ink*, *New Society*, *Time Out*, Charles Marowitz on radio – who calls the show 'a true theatre poem' and says it's the only indication in sight that the London theatre is alive and kicking. For myself, I am alarmed. As I predicted in a gloomy moment some weeks ago, *Tyger* has outraged the new conformism of understatement, tact and compromise. The fury, however, has been far greater and more vindictive than I could ever have imagined.[1]

---

1. Tynan to Penelope Gilliatt, 5 August 1971: 'The National is in a bit of a slough, since Adrian Mitchell's outrageous insurgent musical about William Blake *Tyger* was trampled on by most of the middle-aged critics (and most of them *are* middle-aged now; average age, I discovered is over fifty; whereas I was twenty-six when I took over the *Observer*, and adored by the underground press. I thought it 70 per cent marvellous and agreed with Charlie Marowitz when he called it on radio 'a theatre poem'; but I see that it's too passionate and extreme for modish taste, which is mostly formed these days by critics who prefer the sigh and shrug and the stoically tightened up lip . . . Ah well, or wellish.'

3 August

Disgraceful production of *Danton's Death* at the New Theatre (for the NT) by Jonathan Miller. Mumbled and inaudible; the mob scenes inexcusably excised; Danton – guillotined in his mid-thirties – played by Christopher Plummer as a mannered eccentric in late middle age, rather like Benjamin Franklin; Robespierre (Charles Kay) the traditional thin-lipped villain of Hollywood epics; nineteenth-century songs wantonly added; the central and crucial scene in prison with Tom Paine omitted altogether; the set consisting of headless waxworks in boxes, underlining the fairly obvious point that the play has to do with decapitations. I cannot exaggerate my rage at this mixture of arid intellectualising and naive oversimplification. There had been talk earlier in the day of asking Jonathan M. to direct *The Bacchae* for the NT. It would be like giving a bomb to a member of the Bomb Disposal Squad.

Harold Pinter *has* a theme, I reflect, after reading reviews of the film version he has written of L.P. Hartley's *The Go-Between*. It is: The betrayal and spoliation of innocence and purity. *Vide*: the abduction of the hero in *The Birthday Party*, the electric shocks applied to Aston in *The Caretaker*, the erosion performed by time upon the pure romantic memories of the wife in *Landscape* and the husband in *Old Times*.

'Four flops in a row,' Larry murmurs to me during the rehearsal of *Danton's Death*. 'Now they'll *have* to ask me to go.' He is only half kidding. Larry's torpid fatalism is exactly like Danton's: he ruminates and reminisces as the hatchet-men gather in the shadows. And always, at the back of his mind, is the unspoken thought which Danton actually utters: 'They'll never *dare* . . .'

4 August

The reviews – with only a couple of exceptions – are uniformly good. High praise to Jonathan for his brilliantly analytical production, to the actors for their exquisite control. Larry calls me up in bewilderment. 'I don't know what to think any longer,' he says. For different reasons both of us now feel that theatre as defined by the working critics of today is something alien to us, dedicated to purposes we find restricted and antipathetic. This does not mean that we are *behind* the times. (I am still younger than the average critical age). It means that we are *apart* from them. Perhaps we should both resign.

Afterthought: perhaps the real reason for the critical approval is simpler than I thought. *Tyger* is openly revolutionary; *Danton's Death* says that revolution breeds terror. Who need wonder that the latter message is more acceptable to anti-revolutionary critics?

8 August

Ken Russell's film of *The Devils* (based on Huxley's book about the berserk nun of Loudun) causes us to walk out – sickened by the vulgar brutality of it all. It's like Orwell's image of Nazism – a jackboot perpetually stamping on a human face. There are illiteracies in the script (e.g. 'in remembrance of he who was your archbishop') to parallel the gross visual overstatements that abound. Vanessa (as the Abbess) licking dried blood from the wounds of an imaginary Christ; plague victims with rotting faces being treated with live hornets; and the spectacle of Oliver Reed *à la presse* and then charcoal-broiled for which one didn't wait. It is as if Francis Bacon's subconscious had somehow mated with that of Cecil B. De Mille. A fanatical film about fanaticism. Vanessa gets a curious and gargantuan enema – vaginal, to judge from her position, which is flat on her back on the altar. Rumour says that – rectal or vaginal – she insisted on having the enema in the interest of realism, with the result that she lost her baby. I find this hard to believe; but I have no doubt that – as rumour also insists – Russell shot the actual penetration of the instrument though fully aware that the sequence would have to be omitted from the finished film.

13 August

With Larry and Joan to a preview of John Osborne's new play, *West of Suez*. J.O. has lately taken to abusing L.O. and me in print whenever he has the chance, berating the National Theatre for rejecting his last two plays and revealing that he and Tony Richardson[1] once discussed hiring

---

1. Tony Richardson (1928–91). Theatre and film director, directed John Osborne's *Look Back in Anger* (1956). His marriage to Vanessa Redgrave produced the actresses Natasha Richardson and Joely Richardson.

a thug to beat us up. He has become a friendless and mean-spirited man who feeds on hostility and only feels fully alive when he is hating or hated. His new hero (lovely owlish-blimpish performance by Ralph Richardson) is a writer with four daughters (one more sister than in Chekhov, with whom J.O. clearly hopes now to be compared). He is visiting a West Indian island, recently granted independence, and loses no opportunity to record his opinion of the natives as a mixture of 'lethargy and hysteria, brutality and sentimentalism' – not a bad description of J.O. himself. Finally two black guerrillas shoot the old man in cold blood, just after he has been mindlessly abused by an American hippie. This peevishly melodramatic ending is the only action in one of the most *wasteful* plays I can remember.

There are nineteen characters doing the dramatic work that could be done by half a dozen; people are lengthily and drearily established, only to disappear without trace; and although the occasional barbed line stands out and scratches at the memory, most of the conversation is like a child with a good ear reproducing the *noise* made by intelligent and/or sophisticated people, but getting the *words* subtly wrong. J.O.'s plays are more and more like extracts from an interior monologue of increasing bad temper and incoherence. Jill Bennett plays the principal daughter: she is anguished and in pain and at odds with her husband. Why? No answer. Running through the play is a snobbism of pain. People who suffer mental pain are held up for our reverence like secular martyrs, although no attempt is made to define the nature of this pain or to explain it. Characters are always qualifying their lines with: '. . . if that means anything, which I doubt' – tell-tale defensive sign of loose writing.

A very sad evening – illiberal, self-absorbed, self-indulgent – which will doubtless be hailed by the critics as mature, autumnal and (yes) Chekhovian. The opening dialogue between Jill Bennett and her (stage) husband is oddly Pinterish. Osborne too has moved into the fashionable artistic territory where the minor gripes and peccadilloes of the British middle class are interminably pondered and analysed. Also his hero is a writer (there are two other writers in the play) – cf. the screenwriter hero of *The Hotel in Amsterdam* and the movie director hero of *Old Times*. These authors should move in a wider social circle. *West of Suez* is about as universal and Chekhovian as N.C. Hunter's *A Day by the Sea*, a Haymarket hit of the fifties which it much resembles.

Ironically, it was from N.C. Hunter and his school that J.O. was alleged to have saved the English theatre.

Over supper at Mimmo's we lament J.O.'s general decline and specific *nastiness*. Joan says that Jill is fond of explaining in public that John can't make her come and has trouble getting an erection. When she is working on a TV play or a film, John takes to his bed and drinks champagne all day long. Larry derides J.O.'s repeated assertions to the press of unswerving loyalty to the Royal Court, his artistic cradle, spiritual home, etc: it's pure balls – he's only doing the new play there because every West End management turned it down. Anthony Page[1], the director, dislikes the play and has only staged it out of loyalty.

By the end of supper Larry is fairly tight and reveals grave doubts about the influence he has had on English actors: 'I once saw the National Youth Theatre give a performance of Shakespeare when all the actors – every bloody one of them – were imitating my Henry V scream. I was absolutely horrified and I looked at them and said to myself: "Jesus Christ, is this what I have spawned?"'

17 *August*

Dinner with Roman and Sandy Whitelaw[2]. Sandy says he has made a list of the countries in the world where it is possible to live a free and liberal life. There are five of them: Sweden, Norway, Denmark, Holland and Britain. And what (he asks) have they in common? Answer: They are all monarchies. This worries him, since he is a convinced republican.

Reading Hemingway's *Across the River and Into the Trees* for the first time: I conclude that he forged a style perfectly designed to express the ideas of the underprivileged and later found himself drifting into a frame of mind that compelled him to use the same style to express the ideas of the authoritarian and sophisticated. And it did not fit.

When I knew Hemingway he drank steadily and strongly, but I had not realised what his standards were until I analysed the alcoholic intake of Colonel Cantwell and his teenaged beloved, Renata, during their

---

1. Anthony Page (1935–). Stage, film and television director; Artistic Director of the Royal Court Theatre 1964–65.
2. Alexander 'Sandy' Whitelaw (1930–). American film director and former studio executive.

first evening together in *Across the River*. Before meeting Renata, the
Colonel drinks three double dry martinis with the head waiter and has a
double gin and Campari in his bedroom. In Harry's Bar he and his girl
share eight double 'Montgomerys' (dry martinis at a ratio of 15 to 1, this
being the ratio of superiority at which, according to Hemingway, Field
Marshal Montgomery preferred to do battle). Over dinner at the Gritti
the couple drink one bottle of Capri Bianco, one of Valpolicella and
two of Roederer Brut '42. Later in a gondola they down a bottle of
Perrier-Jouet. Total: Seven double martinis and one double gin for the
Colonel, four double martinis for the girl, plus five shared bottles of
wine. Finally, the Colonel retires to his room and empties another
bottle of Valpolicella.

Sentence that wins, outright the Unsupported Hemingway General-
isation Prize: '. . . you do not say that you buy sausages for a dog in
Italy.'

19 August

Château St Martin in Vence. I read in the *Herald Tribune* that the Café
Chauveron in New York has closed, one of the last *grande luxe* French
restaurants in the city. It was here, in the last years of the fuddled fifties,
that I was a founder-member – with Cecil Hardwicke and Richard
Watts[1] – of a luncheon club meeting every Friday at what came to be
known as the 'Square Table'. The level of wit was not perhaps as high as
at the Algonquin thirty years earlier, because the Algonquin was a dry
hotel, while the voices shouting for the limelight at the Chauveron
were usually thickened by liquor well beyond the point of intellig-
ibility. Other attendees at the Square Table included Alan DeLynn (a
pimp for all seasons), Leonard Lyons[2], George Stevens[3] and his son, John
Crosby[4] (who will almost certainly not remember), and visiting fa-
mouses like Frank Norman[5] and a small publicity man from the Coast

1. Richard Watts (1898–1981). Journalist and drama critic for the *New York Post*, 1946–76.
2. Leonard Lyons (1906–76). Gossip columnist for the *New York Post* from 1934–74.
3. George Stevens (1904–75). Film director; among his films *A Place in the Sun* (1951) and *Giant* (1956).
4. John Crosby (1912–91). Television critic for the *New York Herald Tribune*, 1946–65.
5. Frank Norman (1930–80). Playwright and novelist, best known for his comedy of Cockney life *Fings Ain't Wot They Used T'Be* (1959) which won the *London Evening Standard* Drama Award.

named 'Scooper' Conlon, who wore a green celluloid eyeshade and had once, in journalistic days long past, chalked up one minor scoop. Many other boring people, attracted by the volume and intensity of the boredom at our table, would sit down and order; and it would usually be assumed by our founder-member that one of the others (or he himself in an amnesiac alcoholic moment) had invited him: so that many total strangers got free lunches due to the generosity and general stupidity of the Squares. I was about forty years younger than most of them and Christ knows what I was doing amid that lovable, bawdy throng of deaf, drunken, droning monologuists.

20 August

K., surveying herself in a bikini and suspecting that she is putting on weight, says to me plaintively: 'If you saw me across a swimming-pool, would you think I was Miss Happen?' It emerges that she has been pronouncing 'misshapen' like this all her life.

23 August

Germaine Greer visits us in Sardinia to discuss the adaptation of *Lysistrata* that I have commissioned her to make for the NT. She talks about the eagerness with which magazines now print everything she writes: 'If I peed on the paper, they'd print the stain.'

27 August

We move in for a few days with Peter Saunders and wife on the Costa Smeralda. P.S., a hearty fighting-fit businessman of German origins, says of the people who own the villa next door: 'Basically they're just a typical pair of pushy Northern textile Jews.'

At dinner last night I sat next to a woman who thought that female nudity on the beach was 'bestial' and a prime cause of homosexuality in men, and said that if her daughter married a black, she would kill herself. The five days we are spending on this inbred country-club land for the rich is like a sojourn in an occupied country. I lurk in my room as late each morning as I dare, fearful that when I emerge I shall be arrested, condemned at a damned court-martial and shot.

Sentence heard in a dream: due to local calendar variations and the regional chronology employed in French agriculture, it is never 6 p.m. in Dijon.

2 September

In Cordoba (a fetid yawn of a city) K. returns to the subject of my conversation with Liz Wallace about stripping on beaches. 'You sounded,' she says, 'so *uncool* – like a Savonarola, a propagandist for stripping.' Of course I deny this but she boringly persists and reiterates. Finally I remind her that if she wishes to retain the ears of intelligent men (or women) in conversation, she must continue to take care of her looks. '*Drive carefully*,' I say, wagging a finger. This infuriates her.

The mad menu translator strikes again in Cordoba: at the Restaurante Siena we find the following: 'Crema de Ave' (Crème de Volaille) rendered as 'Bird Cream', and 'Savage Asparagus on Stewed-in Pan'. Ordering white wine of the region at lunch, we are brought a bottle of sherry. That is Cordoba for us: savage asparagus washed down with a decent bottle of sherry.

Much as I hate remarks of the kind parodied by J.B. Morton[1] when he said: 'Wagner is the Puccini of music', I can't help observing that Cordoba is the Avignon of Spain. Look at the similarities: two ancient cities, each on the northern bank of a great river spanned by a famous bridge, each notable for a vast religious edifice (the Palais des Papes, the Mezquita) which has had no perceptible religious importance for many centuries. (True, there are still services in the Christian cathedral within the mosque, but its Moslem significance vanished 700 years ago.) In both cases a tremendous structure was built to house something or someone that did not belong there – the Anti-Pope and the Caliph. And both cities, of course, as a reward for having backed the wrong religious house, are stifled by tourism.

Since Jules Feiffer[2] acquired a middle-aged spread, he and his wife are known as Paunch and Judy.

1. J.B. Morton (1893–1979). Journalist and satirist, wrote the 'Beachcomber' column for the *Daily Express*, 1924–75.
2. Jules Feiffer (1929–). Satirical cartoonist, playwright, author.

Superbly cryptic, all-purpose conversation-stopping aphorism coined by Fernand Léger apropos of abstract art: 'You don't make a nail with a nail, but with iron.' I am still not clear whether Léger approved or disapproved of abstract art.

5 September

Spending a weekend at La Consula, I recall the many periods of residence that Cyril Connolly[1] passed here in the fifties. He was a dominating guest who not only decided who else was to be invited but supervised all *placements* and menus and drew strict distinctions between people who could be asked for lunch and people who could only be asked for a swim *before* lunch. Himself a hater of bullfights he evolved many ploys for disconcerting *aficionados* like myself. 'Did you read about the bull in Barcelona yesterday?' he would enquire, raising his head from a newspaper as we returned from the *corrida*. 'Didn't want to die. *Wouldn't take his medicine.* They had to give him black *banderillas*. What a disgrace. Never live that down, will he?' If we bored him by discussing technicalities, about *derechazos* and *naturales*, he would riposte by murmuring: 'Of course the difference between Big Jim Sims of Middlesex and Little Ticer Freeman of Hampshire was that Jim gave his googly more air. He'd toss it well up, and it would whip across from the off stump and take the leg bail . . .' He would keep this up until we stopped.

Cyril had a fantasy about owning a *ganadería* where he would train bulls to murder matadors. Lifesize models of *toreros* would be dotted around the ranch with the vital organs clearly marked. Bulls attacking these areas would receive extra food, thus setting up a conditioned reflex. 'And in the unlikely event of any matador surviving long enough to go in for the kill,' Cyril mused, 'each of my bulls would have a cyanide capsule under its tongue, to cheat the executioner.'

During one visit to La Consula, he spent his free moments (which

---

1. Cyril Connolly (1903–74). Tynan became friendly with Connolly after writing him an apology letter for a missed luncheon date. He laid the blame on Ava Gardner. 'Miss Gardner, whom I hardly know, is a convivial girl and not easily discouraged when she gets the smell of riot in her nostrils, and I allowed myself to be swept in an open car twice across London with her engaging entourage, which was joined at odd times by a policeman and a rich swimmer named Esther Williams . . . on whose presence Miss Gardner insisted, saying that a party wasn't a party without a drunken bitch in tears.'

were many) improvising a pornographic novel about the other guests. One was a premature hippie named Hetty McGee, who figured in the novel as 'Lady Hetty'. I remember the opening sentence: '"Call that a prick?" said Lady Hetty, screwing her monocle more firmly into her eye.' We once made a trip to some recently excavated Roman baths in the neighbourhood, and as we entered I heard Cyril saying: ' "What a wonderful place for the Fucking Bee," enthused Lady Hetty.'

8 September

Tomas Osborne, member of the brandy and sherry family who are entertaining us in Puerto de Santa Maria, says: 'I have one hundred and thirty-five first cousins.'

Maids lurking about and giggling and slapping each other in the corridors of Spanish hotels. Where else would these girls be safely employed were it not for the hotel *bonne*? Hotels are the convents of tourism. (And it's clear that the girls or their parents are aware of the potential dangers to their virginity. Nowadays when you ring for the chambermaid, *two* girls usually come, like policemen patrolling *louche* districts in pairs. Or am I generalising rashly? This hotel after all adjoins an American naval base.)

To ensure immediate arrival of breakfast in hotels: lock the door, remove all your clothes and go to the lavatory.

9–11 September

In Ronda, Puerto de Santa Maria and Jerez with the explosively funny Dominic Elwes[1] and his girlfriend Helen Jay. Apropos of journalists, the once-notorious Dominic (alleged bounder, cad and fortune-hunter) says, 'I thought I was a hermit and found I was a pariah.' Driving back from a bullfight in Jerez, Dominic makes me laugh until I fear for the safety of my emphysematic lungs as he retells what he had heard from Tomas Osborne about a friend of his – a *rejoneador* – who was killed in the ring: 'He was kill in the ring and then he was getting dead in the house and then he was completely dead. I had a meeting with him in a

---

1. Dominic Elwes (1931–75). British painter and socialite.

restaurant, but he did not come to the restaurant because he was getting dead in the house, and then he was completely dead . . .' All this in a perfect thick, Andaluz accent.

Tomas is blond and looks like the younger son of a Hamburg shipbuilding family. He claims to sleep only three hours a night, is bombed most of the time (according to Dominic) on brandy, and suffers from brain damage due to constant exposure to tomatoes, the meat of pigs, and the craft of public relations, in which branch of the Osborne industry he works. Dominic observes that rich Spaniards are of two kinds: the tall fair-haired ones who look like Englishmen and talk in impenetrable bullfight accents; and little, black ones who look like gypsies and say: 'I'm most *frightfully* sorry but these ghastly Spanish clowns simply don't know their arse from their elbow.'

The reason for the transience of the wit of people like Dominic is not due to any alleged 'magic'. It resides simply in the fact that much of their humour consists of recreating – in their own image – events in which you have just participated with them. E.g. you have to have been at lunch with Dominic to laugh at his account of the party. He's a past master of the *post mortem*.

13 September

An extraordinary occasion. Rafael Osborne, the withered sixty-ish queer of the family, married to a Texan woman who appears to have left him, turns up at a table at a fish restaurant in Puerto de Santa Maria, pays our bill without consulting us, and invites us to have a nightcap at his 'little house' nearby in the country, where he lives with his spinster daughter. He has the skull face of late Cocteau and has clearly suffered the fate of the sensitive queer amid the *machismo* of Spanish society, which alone in Europe has not yet accepted the homosexual. (At lunch in a pavilion at the Jerez *feria*, a very sophisticated sherry heiress told us that she had had a brilliant cook who happened to be queer; she then had a baby son, so 'of course I had to fire the cook in case he molested the child'.)

So we drive out to a miniature Versailles, a strange gutted palace approached by a floodlit column of cypresses. The palace, built in 1620, collapsed, and Rafael is rebuilding it at his own deliberate speed. Open sky overhangs the great foyer, with its sweeping staircase that lacks banisters. Vast dining-rooms, big enough to seat fifty people – people whom this fastidious pederast would never wish to invite – yearn unfinished, the windows unglazed rectangles.

The garden, seen suddenly through one of the latter, is a magic postcard – rows of plane trees surrounding a swimming-pool lit from within and a brilliantly designed decorative fountain. This formal pattern, glimpsed through and framed by the ruins, is one of the most startling vistas I have ever seen. Rafael lives with his daughter and twelve-year-old Siamese cat in a wing of the house, decorated à la française with panels and chandeliers, the whole place reeking of tuberoses. It is as if the house were a symbol of dusty, empty, feudal Spain, out of which Rafael has carved a delicate corner in which to indulge his despised and exquisite fancies. What hell it must be to be born such a monster in a society as inbred, parochial, hypocritical and anti-intellectual as that of rich Andalucía. Driving the other day through a little village near Cordoba, we saw a house with a word scratched in chalk on the front door, 'Maricón' (queer). I don't think this could happen anywhere else in Europe.

There is a street in Jerez de La Frontera named Calle Taxdirt. I cannot think why.

16 September

'A quiet dinner for about eight people,' said George Weidenfeld's[1] secretary. When we sat down, we were, I suppose, about fifty: Cecil Beaton, Cyril Connolly, Mary McCarthy in places of honour. A tiring rout, made doubly so by the additional hordes who poured in after dinner, making it necessary to talk standing up, a thing I hate to do after about ten-thirty. Seeing Cyril prompted me to rephrase his most famous aphorism: inside every Weidenfeld soirée a dinner party for eight people is wildly signalling to be let out.

1. George Weidenfeld (1919–). Book publisher.

20 September

An outsider – a user of many masks. A secret superior being. A dope addict. A master of esoteric skills. An upholder of no class and seemingly a member of none. A despiser of officialdom and established authority. A lover of music. In whom do all these attributes reside? In a composite portrait of the nineteenth-century artist? No: you have guessed it: in Sherlock Holmes.

No one has ever achieved anything in the arts if he (or she) felt compelled to debate the desirability of the project with his (or her) spouse before embarking on it. The decision to *do* must be singly taken. Which is strong counsel against matrimony.

The Trouble Shooters – a popular BBC serial about the fight for power at the top of an oil company – is the most naked propaganda for capitalism available on British TV. The question at issue is which of a selection of more or less power-crazy chaps will become Managing Director. Those in favour of entry into 'Europe' are painted as fighting liberals, the rest as old-fashioned but possibly teachable conservatives. 'Will he become boss?' is the question raised by this kind of series. 'Will he go on the dole?' is a question raised by no TV programme known to me.

A pustulant = a nun with acne.

25 September

The anti-porn campaigners took Trafalgar Square for a 'Festival of Light' this afternoon. The same faces one saw at Billy Graham's crusades at Harringay Arena fifteen years ago – mostly plain or downright ugly people whom life (due to the insanely high valuation put by capitalism on physical attractiveness) had never invited to its party, but who found themselves bidden by the Rev. Billy to an eternal party in heaven. Looking at them, and hearing their veneration for Lord Longford and his like, I coin a slogan for them: 'Tug your forelock, not your foreskin.'

26 September

With Clive and Michael at Don Luigi's to discuss the poet C. Logue[1] with a former girlfriend of his, who says that on one occasion, finding himself alone (with her) for the evening, he wept, saying that the world would never be changed as he wanted it to be. Me: 'I'm not surprised. When you're over forty there is nothing to do after 11 p.m. except cry or fuck.'

28 September

T.E. Lawrence's RAF record, auctioned yesterday, has the following entry: 'Identification marks: scars both buttocks.' This confirms the story of one of Lawrence's service friends that he regularly beat him. Odd how upper-class British life between the wars was full of steely, dapper men with blazing eyes who took tea in ducal conservatories and then retired to furnished rooms to take down their trousers and be whipped. I met some of them in Oxford after the war, mostly minor gentry, many of them slightly sinister, planning to buy and operate private schools for boys (an easy thing to do then, because inspection of such schools was cursory and infrequent) of which the main function would be to act as laboratories for experiments with the cane.

Larry (of an actor suggested for a comedy part): 'He's about as funny as a baby's open grave.'

1 October

Losey's film of *The Go-Between* isn't half as moving as the book and doesn't solve the problem that has bedevilled all the people who have previously tried to carve a script out of it – e.g. how to put across a book told entirely in first-person narrative (by an adult looking back on his childhood) without resorting to voice-over narration. Pinter's flash-forward device to the narrator as an old man is merely distracting and adds little. He says the book made him weep; how many will weep at

---

1. Christopher Logue (1926–). British poet and political radical, author of *Songs* (1959) and *War Music* (1981).

the film? Also Losey misses the easy, stupendously effortless authority and nonchalant power of the Edwardian (and in some respects the contemporary) upper classes, the steely impregnability beneath the *douceur de vivre*. Accents, gestures, the whole physical bearing of the people − all are subtly wrong. The boy − not an aristocrat but an outsider − is excellent. (So is Edward Fox as the heroine's respectable lover.) But the film doesn't deserve its accolades. It's another of the over-praised species we've noticed before − study of emotionally deprived or crippled English folk leading lives of quiet desperation in well-to-do circumstances and settling for second-best because that's how life is. What attracts Pinter here is his old recurrent theme: the destruction of (the boy's) innocence. Threatened innocence always attracts Harold: the child in him is not far beneath the smooth bespectacled mask.

5 October

Dinner at Brighton with Larry, Joan, Sidney Bernstein[1] and Jennie Lee.[2] Jennie L. says that the purpose of this Tory government is to push through the Industrial Relations Bill, to get into the Common Market and to lose the next election. They will then take up their City directorships, cash in handsomely, and leave the baby of rising prices and unemployment in the lap of Labour.

10 October

On Channel 5, New York, David Susskind[3] talks to seven lesbians. One is an ordained black minister who told her mother she was a lesbian at nine, married and had four children, left her husband and founded 'a church for gay people' in Boston. The audience cheers its approval. How sanely − but how incredibly − things have changed in a decade.

---

1. Sidney Bernstein (1899–1993). Film and media tycoon; Bernstein owned Granada Television among many other holdings. He was also a lifelong socialist and Labour Party backer.
2. Jennie Lee (1904–88). Labour politician, Minister of Arts under Harold Wilson's government, 1964–70. She worked closely with Lord Goodman and was also instrumental in creating the Open University.
3. David Susskind (1920–87). American television producer and talk-show host.

In Chicago as guest of *Playboy* magazine, who are holding a 'Writers' Convocation' at their hotel, the Playboy Towers. Those present include George Axelrod, Kenneth Galbraith, Arthur Schlesinger (sedulously denying that he is supporting Teddy Kennedy for the presidency in '72, though it's perfectly clear that he's thinking of nothing else), Art Buchwald[1] (addressing Hugh Hefner as 'Your Holiness'), Jules Feiffer, Murray Kempton[2], Moravia[3], V.S. Pritchett, Alan Watts[4] and sad-eyed, gentle, transparently ailing Augie Spectorsky, the magazine's Editorial Director, whose idea the whole junket was, and whom (though nobody put the thought into words) I fear we may not see again.

There are panel discussions on sex, politics, journalism and urban life – the emphasis is relentlessly on 'personalised interpretations of phenomena', so that objective journalism is regarded with scorn alongside journalism that records the emotional climate reigning (or raging) within the journalist; politics is never discussed in terms of capitalism or socialism but in terms of the individual psychology of the candidates ('politics is about people'); the panel on the problems of American cities is headed: 'Paranoia: the New Urban Lifestyle'; only when sex is the subject does this sub Freudian approach seem appropriate.

Many of the panellists cease, on achieving panel membership, to speak English. Instead they speak panelese. Otherwise intelligent men, with delicately nurtured minds and impeccable intellectual credentials, are transformed by the proximity of a microphone into pundits, saying things like: 'Hopefully we shall be making some insightful and non-judgemental contributions in the area of relating to the paranoia of urban lifestyles and the banalisation of caringness.'

My favourite guest is the English-born philosopher Alan Watts, who has gone native for the past two decades in California, where he writes about Zen and the hippie life. Wearing a purple smock and sporting an out-thrust grey beard, Watts wanders through the conference inexplicably laughing to himself – whether because LSD and other drugs have conferred on him euphoria or brain damage it is hard to say.

1. Art Buchwald (1925–). American political humorist and journalist.
2. Murray Kempton (1917–97). Journalist and New York newspaper institution; wrote in a high style and championed the underdog.
3. Alberto Moravia (1907–90). Journalist, novelist and major figure in Italian literature whose many works include *The Conformist* (1951).
4. Alan Watts (1915–73). Author and scholar of Eastern religions, especially Zen Buddhism.

Turning a corner in the hotel, one sees him walking alone down an empty corridor, shaking with laughter. During the banquets at night, he grows restless and after the soup rises to his feet and passes among the other guests, pausing here and there to rest a kindly hand on people's shoulders and, bending down, to bestow on them some of his vast store of excess chuckle, which seems to come from inside him, like distant Sydney Greenstreet. He seldom speaks.

11 October

Dichotomy = operation performed on lesbians to make them normal. Schlepper colony = department store.

13 October

Contrary to horrific rumour, everyone now in New York seems kindly, warm-hearted, eager to please. I am recognised by waiters, box-office staff and cab-drivers far more often than in London. In a record store a middle-aged assistant welcomes me back to the city and sells me a new recording of a Mozart serenade – 'It's really a dazzler. The last person I sold it to was Mr W.H. Auden.' How many salesmen in English stores would ever have heard of – let alone be able to recognise – W.H. Auden? But of course my impression of a radiantly life-loving city is illusory, as I am reminded by Anthony West[1], whom we encounter at a party. An English friend of his recently spent six months in New York and formed exactly the same impression as I have done – until the day before he was to leave, when he went for a stroll by daylight in Central Park. He was beaten up and robbed by a gang of teenagers. Then five minutes later as he was staggering homewards, a second gang accosted him, and, when they found he had no money, beat him up again and broke both his arms. West, who is middle-aged, has an American wife and has lived most of his working life in New York, is returning to England in the New Year: he says he will not bring up his children in conditions of such danger.

1. Anthony West (1914–88). The illegitimate son of Rebecca West and H. G. Wells. A frequent *New Yorker* contributor.

17 October

Having last night seen Ariane Mnouchkine's[1] breathtaking company in *1789* at the Round House, I attend a discussion of the production with Mnouchkine, Arnold Wesker and Jonathan Miller. Wesker views the show darkly, saying that collective authorship can lead to 'group hysteria' and in any case must always lack the 'focus' that a single writer can bring to bear on events. I rise to say that it is precisely that single focus that has led to the state of drama today – too many private plays about private middle-class people. When such authors attempt historical subjects, they always see them through the eyes of *individuals* (usually prominent or powerful figures). Collective authorship, on the other hand, dispenses with individual psychology and is thus uniquely fitted to present the movements of masses, classes and social groups. Mnouchkine's company, for instance, uses five or six different *actors* to play Louis XVI in various different guises and situations; so that it's impossible for us to identify with him. Arnold, I fear, is still enslaved to the idea of a play as the private property of the author – a strange bourgeois hangover. Mnouchkine points out that she was not allowed to register the play with the Société des Auteurs as the joint work of Le Théâtre du Soleil: it *had* to be attributed to one named person. Thus does the law carry out its appointed duty to keep property private.

18 October

We meet Muhammad Ali at a dinner party at Tsai Chin's.[2] A great thrill: apart from Mao and Chou En-lai, he is one of the few celebrities I still long to know. (Explanation for his presence at Tsai's: she is having an affair with a black actor named Calvin Lockhart who is pally with Ali.) Someone at the party says: 'Whatever happened to Danny Cohn-Bendit?' At once I am back in Clive Goodwin's flat, packed with every literary Leftist in London for the party he gave in the spring of '68 to celebrate Cohn-Bendit's flying visit to London. The barricades were up

---

1. Ariane Mnouchkine (1934–). French theatre director who formed the theatre collective Théâtre du Soleil in 1964. *1789* premièred in 1970.
2. Tsai Chin (1937–). Chinese actress who appeared in *The World of Suzie Wong* (1960) and Wayne Wang's *The Joy Luck Club* (1993). Known as 'Dear Brat' to Tynan who had an affair with her in the early sixties.

in Paris; everybody was talking about 'instant revolution'; and when Cohn-Bendit held a question-and-answer session with the guests, I made myself immediately unpopular by asking: 'What's your strategy? What is the next step the students will take?' C.B. said impatiently: 'The whole point of our revolution is that we do not follow plans. It is a spontaneous permanent revolution. We improvise. It is like jazz.' Everyone applauded and reproved my carping. I went on to ask: 'Nobody ever had a successful revolution without the support of the army – are you trying to form any links with the military?' C.B. again brushed the question aside as an irrelevance: 'The army is no problem. Many young officers agree with us.' At the very moment, as we discovered later, de Gaulle was quietly testing the army's loyalty; assured that he had it, he knew that he was sitting pretty and that the revolution, for all its tumult and euphoria, was a paper tiger.

19 October

American talent does not survive sophistication. It needs to preserve a certain *naïveté*, a hayseed element, even a touch of the child, and the primitive, if it is to retain its juice and energy. This is true of *Huckleberry Finn*, of Scott Fitzgerald (always an outsider in Paris and the Côte d'Azur), of Hemingway (with the boyish braggarty of his virility cult), of the *out-of-towners* who founded and wrote for *The New Yorker*, of Ring Lardner's ingrained and obsessive provincialisms, of Whitman, Sherwood Anderson, Runyon, John Ford . . . When urban sophistication lays its hand on the American artist, it is like frost on a bud – witness the aridity of Edward Albee's recent work and the nonexistence of Truman Capote's. Tennessee Williams and Arthur Miller, so different in almost every respect, have more in common with each other than either has with – say – Nabokov. When US talent goes elegant, New York really becomes what Spectorsky calls it – 'a road-company Europe'. Exception: Cole Porter is about the only one I can think of.

21 October

Dinner with Mike Bessie, my publisher, whom I owe a book two years late in delivery. Is it only laziness that makes me work-shy? Not *only*. I disbelieve in art because I no longer believe that there is a secret something inside me which, when properly expressed, will take on a higher reality and deserve the name of 'art'. What I do believe is simply that a good painting makes you see what I (the painter) saw; and a good book makes you experience what I (the author) experienced. The best books are works of personal testimony – letters, reportage, intimate biography, autobiography. But they are merely reflections of events, they do not express an 'inner reality'. B.F. Skinner, the behaviourist, is right to attack the idea that human behaviour is caused by 'indwelling agents' – the postulate so brilliantly demolished by Gilbert Ryle in *The Concept of Mind* and by such latter-day proponents of oriental philosophy as Alan Watts, who says, 'I do not *have* a body. I am a body.' The prime cause of confusion in the artistic and/or intellectual world today lies in the failure to accept the erosion of the ancient duality of mind and matter, soul and body, ego and carcass, inner life and outer life. Until we realise that there is only *one* life, we shall have little peace and even less joy; and most of what we write will be infected by the germs of an archaic etymology.

22 October

A late evening with the British journalistic intelligentsia, Anthony Sampson[1], Karl Miller[2], John Gross[3], David Caute[4], etc.) in their blue suits with their defensive, hedging, qualifying manner, as if all were in fear of being blackballed from some nameless club of which all aspired to be members. God, the lack of selfhood and certainty! I can talk about *not* writing with more passion than they talk about writing. They look about as vivacious as a group portrait of the Bulgarian chess team.

24 October

B.F. Skinner is providing me with an apt vocabulary in which to analyse my own condition. I have received incommensurate good fortune

---

1. Anthony Sampson (1926–). Journalist and author of among other books *Mandela: The Authorised Biography* (1999).
2. Karl Miller (1931–). Editor and academic. Edited the *London Review of Books*, 1979–92.
3. John Gross (1935–). Editor of the *Times Literary Supplement*, 1974–81. Since 1989 the theatre critic for the *Sunday Telegraph*.
4. David Caute (1936–). Left-wing British journalist and playwright.

(from *Oh! Calcutta!*[1]) which has produced indolence. But I have also received incommensurate *blame* (in the press, etc.) which I resent since it deprives me of due credit. So: why should I work to gain the approval of those who do not approve of my work?

30 October

X is a man I have consistently defended against his detractors. The other day at dinner he was snobbish and bullying. I have often wondered what other people failed to see in him, and now I know.

8 November

A public opinion poll shows that a majority of people think that entry into the Common Market will be good for Britain. Equally, a majority think it will be *bad* for themselves. Here is the paradox of this country in a nutshell – why cannot the people see that if entry is bad for a majority of them, it is by definition bad for England, since they *are* England. Instead they cling to the belief that there is a separate abstract entity called 'the good of the country', in the name of which they are willing to abnegate themselves. So brilliantly are they hoodwinked that they fail to realise that, in this case as in so many others, 'the good of the country' equals 'the good of big business'.

11 November

Loss of an old friend: the always faintly preposterous but likeable Vera Russell.[2] She arrives for lunch and over preliminary drinks she says she is going to visit Auden. I make a casual remark about regretting that he has chosen to erase his own past history – i.e. in the political poems. Without any warning she says with icy contempt: 'A person like you is in no position to criticise *anybody*. You have destroyed yourself – you have sold yourself for sensationalism. I went to your *thing* (*Oh! Calcutta!*) the other night and it's the most blatant piece of money-making I have

---

1. *Oh! Calcutta!*. Revue devised by Tynan which ran 3,918 performances in London and 5,852 on Broadway.
2. Vera Russell (1911–92). Stage name Vera Lindsay, actress, broadcaster and journalist and with her second husband Gerald Barry was very involved in the planning of the Festival of Britain.

ever seen.' Naturally I cannot lunch with her after this, so go out, leaving her rather cravenly to Kathleen. Later I write her an appropriately corrosive letter.

15 November

Roman's advice: never attempt anything in a situation when you cannot get done what you want done, because this leads to black rages and frustration – therefore never go into politics. Only second-rate people become politicians (he says); first-rate people go into the arts and sciences. This is very tempting to me, and conceivably true. Politics for me increasingly means nocturnal debates from which, even if I win them, nothing tangible can come, except sacrifice of irreplaceable brain cells.

One basic difference between socialist and Tory is that the former is concerned mainly with *who is governing* (what class?) the latter with *how to govern* (the technique of imposing, of managing people, of pragmatic administration). The Tory is not concerned with the democratic base of government; he believes that *all* government is essentially unequal since it is always carried out by a small ruling group. Therefore what does it matter if, at any given time, the members of that group are drawn from the same class? If pressed, he will maintain that the ruling class is better equipped in the technique of ruling. In this context he will use the same argument as those who claim that US blacks are less intelligent than whites because of heredity: the intelligent Africans did not allow themselves to be captured and transported as slaves. Hence (the analogical argument runs) the really bright cavemen did not become serfs.

20 November

The man who fears failure will choose the arts rather than the sciences. The scientist must be tough enough to face being proved wrong; for him the verdict is yes or no. The artist can never be proved wrong; for him there is always the loophole of 'perhaps'. This is why so many artists are neurotic: they need the nourishment of perhaps to protect them against the death-blow of no.

4 December

Herewith a letter sent by me to *The Times* and then withdrawn, since I felt it might cause adverse comment on the NT, which has *also* just applied for an increased grant:

> Dear Sir,
>
> It was very satirical of the Select Committee to announce the Monarch's dramatic pay increase at a time when nearly a million of her subjects are earning nothing and Christmas is just three weeks away. A case, you might say, of having her cake and letting them eat it.
>
> That will certainly show them, and such is the mood of these decorous days that they are more likely to emit a royal cheer than to rush out and burn down a castle or two, as their ancestors a few centuries ago were wont to do when royal depredations on this scale were mooted.
>
> £980,000 to Her Majesty; 970,000 jobless. It cannot be an accident that the numbers are so close. Surely it must represent a deliberate plan to keep the Queen's remuneration pegged to the unemployment figures. If so, I trust we can count on the government to pull its finger out and make it £2,000,000 by next Christmas.
>
> Yours sincerely.

12 December

A new magazine has appeared called *Mentor*, entirely made up of letters from fetishistic readers, rather like the pre-war *London Life*. *Mentor* is a unique example of a democratically run magazine with full reader-power. It is controlled by its readers, most of whom are crying out to be oppressed (i.e. by fetter, gag, chain, corset or cane).

17 December

While it is in my mind, a brief account of one of the oddest evenings of my life (recalled because somebody at the NT yesterday was playing a game involving unlikely dinner parties). This was the occasion in 1967 when our guests were Peter Cook[1], Harold Pinter and his wife Vivien Merchant[2], and the Snowdons. We had rigged up a double film screen made of a sheet and planned, after dinner, to show some American experimental films simultaneously with outtakes from British nudipix (cf. scenes when the model accidentally dropped towel, bra or knickers) and Jean Genet's erotic film *Chant d'Amour*.

The evening started less than charmingly when Mrs Pinter, in belligerent mood, merely extended a vague hand on being introduced to Princess M., not bothering either to get up or to interrupt what she was saying to Peter Cook. At dinner I put her next to Tony, who had just photographed her as Lady Macbeth at Stratford, which she was playing (very boringly) to Paul Scofield's Macbeth. I overheard her saying: 'Of course, the only reason we *artistes* let you take our pictures is because of *her* –' The last was accompanied by a stabbing finger toward H.R.H. Hereabouts Harold began to drink steadily. Indeed, everyone did. Princess M. was awkwardly unruffled, but every word had registered on that watchful little psyche.

After dinner we settled down to the films, which at first went well. I had warned Tony that there would be some pretty blue material, and he said, 'It would be good for M.' – and so, for a while, it seemed. The English bits were amateurish and charming, with odd flashes of nipple and pubic bush; and the American stuff with fish-eye lens and zoom was so technically self-conscious that the occasional bits of explicit sex passed almost unnoticed – e.g. a fast zoom along an erect prick looked like a flash zoom up a factory chimney. But when the Genet started the atmosphere began to freeze.

Genet's film is about convicts in love with one another and themselves, and it contains many quite unmistakable shots of cocks – cocks limp and stiff, cocks being waved, brandished, massaged or just waggled – intercut with lyrical fantasy sequences as the convicts imagine themselves frolicking in vernal undergrowth. Silence became gelid in the room: no one was laughing now. Suddenly the inspired Peter Cook came to the rescue. *Chant d'Amour* is a silent film, and he supplied a commentary, treating the movie as if it were a long

---

1. Peter Cook (1937–95). Legendary British comedian; with Dudley Moore, Jonathan Miller and Alan Bennett starred in *Beyond the Fringe* (1963).
2. Vivien Merchant (1929–82). Actress, first wife of Harold Pinter. She appeared memorably in Pinter's *The Homecoming* (1967).

commercial for Cadbury's Milk Flake Chocolate and brilliantly seizing on the similarity between Genet's woodland fantasies and the sylvan capering that inevitably accompanies, on TV, the sale of anything from cigarettes to Rolls-Royces.

Within five minutes we were all helplessly rocking with laughter, Princess M. included. It was a performance of genius that saved a situation which – in those 'pre-permissive' days – could have been distinctly tricky; and it didn't matter, afterwards, that Harold was so drunk that, having solemnly taken his leave, he fell all the way downstairs. I hugged Peter for one of the funniest improvisations I have ever heard in my life.

1972

6 January

After a few drinks, Laurence Harvey took Elaine, Mamie Van Doren and myself to downtown Los Angeles to show us the wonderful low life on view in the bars there. 'It's *fiendishly* exciting,' he said. 'But we really ought to have had a little more to drink.' 'You're right, Laurence,' I said. 'One swallow doesn't make a slummer.' (Date: *circa* 1956)

7 January

Reading the proofs of John Berger's[1] new novel (*G*), I conclude that he is too good and exemplary a man to be a good novelist – quite apart from the fact that he lacks the sense of humour I look for in any writer I am going to love. Not only is everything he says too important, too weighty; it is also too *fair*. Few if any of the great novelists are people one would like to know as friends. Hemingway the bully; Proust the snob; Waugh the snobbish bully; Fitzgerald the drunk; Dickens the exhibitionist – they are all great novelists because they like to exploit and manipulate people, to mock and devastate people, to torment and trample on people – and we are talking, remember, of people they have themselves created. This takes a calculating kind of near-sadism to which John Berger – great critic though he is – is a stranger. (Playwrights are different and often nicer – their characters exist publicly, in the improvisations of actors, to be appreciated publicly, in the presence of audiences. The person-to-person torture-chamber privacy of the novel cannot exist in the theatre.)

15 January

What is the best theatrical impromptu I've ever heard? Probably John Gielgud's during the dress rehearsal of Peter Brook's production of

---

1. John Berger (1926–). Marxist art critic, playwright and novelist.

Seneca's *Oedipus* at the Vic. Irene Worth as Jocasta had to pretend to impale herself vaginally on a large wooden sword fixed point upwards on the stage. To do this she went through a lot of protracted squatting motions, with appropriately agonised expressions. At the dress rehearsal she stopped in mid-squat and, shading her eyes, peered out into the auditorium. 'Peter,' she said, plaintively. 'The last time I did this it was much larger and it was on a plinth.' 'Plinth Charles?' said John G. 'Or Plinth Philip?'

18 January

Seeing a uxorious writer friend at a party, I rather please myself by saying: 'He's put his talent into his work and his genius into his wife.'

19 January

A Freudian spoonerism, uttered by me to Kathleen yesterday: 'Did you remember to close the deadroom bore?'

13 February

The *Guardian* table of temperatures reveals that Luxor is the warmest place within striking distance of Europe. So thither we go to escape cloud and sleet and find sun to work. The trip is a revelation. Not only no rain but no cloud; the muddy Nile oozing past the old Winter Palace Hotel; tourists plentiful, but not so numerous as before the Six-Day War; begging ubiquitous, thieving common, prices high; *but*: this is where European (i.e. world) civilisation started and for the poor nothing has changed. A mud hut, a couple of wives, an oil lamp for the long nights, a donkey, the hope of a boat or a smallholding, meat once a week, fish once a week, the rest rice and bananas and tea, plus a puff of hash for the men – and that is all. And yet if I had to choose between this Nile-side life and that of – say – a Lancashire factory worker, compensated as he is by more money, entertainment and mobility for the appalling weather, I am not sure how I would decide. The Upper Nile can never be industrialised and hence never rich in any sense of the word. In the 5,000 years since the Old Kingdom was founded, have we changed the life of the Egyptians – and can we? And *should* we? (Beyond the obvious improvements in welfare and sanitation). These are disturbing thoughts for a socialist.

We have been befriended by a boatman called Mukhta Ali, half-Nubian, in his early twenties and recently married to his second wife, a fifteen-year-old Alexandrian girl. Today he took us in his exquisite felucca (not *his*: he mans it for someone else) to his village, a mile upstream, and gave us a lunch of fish, rice, bread and herbs in his mud hut: the wife kept strictly outside, along with in-laws, chickens, and donkey. On the way back to Luxor I ask him: 'When you see a rich man, with a big house and two cars, are you angry?' He grins and says: 'Angry, yes. Very angry.' He is not so fatalistic after all: the socialist is reassured. I refrain from pointing out to him that *I* have a big house and two cars.

14 February

The Valley of the Kings, the temples of Luxor and Karnak, the tombs of the nobles: one feels like the Frenchman Denon who came here with Napoleon's army in 1798, a terrible lack of theatres, arenas, *pleasure-domes*. It is a humourless, monolithically ceremonial civilisation. But of an ordered beauty, a hierarchical span linking peasant with sun-god, that casts a very deep spell. Luxor will be the next sacrifice on this altar of tourism. Already the first high-rise hotel has gone up. When the war-scare dies down, others will follow.

21 March

We are invited to a party at Grosvenor House to celebrate the tenth birthday of the *Sunday Times* colour magazine. The invitation card speaks of a decade of creative achievement and a chance to meet some of the people who made it great. All very pretentious; but we go expecting to meet some good writers and interesting people. Instead we are confronted by about 2,000 advertising executives in blue suits. Fewer than twenty women are there (I had to plead quite hard to get my invitation extended to cover Kathleen) because revelling over the spoils – which is soon revealed as the purpose of this junket – is traditionally the male prerogative. At each table of twelve advertising men sits one token celebrity – Alan Whicker[1], Huw Wheldon[2], Tony Snowdon, Jonathan Miller, Peter Cook, Alan Bennett, myself, etc.

Lord Thomson[3] makes a speech in which he refers to the phenomenal surge of advertising revenue the magazine has achieved. He does not mention the editor or any of the people who have written for the magazine. The vice-president, J. Walter Thompson, replies to the toast. He, too, has glowing praise for the opportunities the magazine has offered to the advertising industry, and fails to name a single person who has contributed to its pages. This insulting occasion outrages me more than it should have. I am perfectly aware that the function of a journalist is to draw the readers' attention to the ads, and that when writing for *The New Yorker* (for instance) my primary duty is to sell vodka. But what horrifies one is the new Tory *blatancy* about these things, the assumption that there is no longer any need to pretend that writers are anything more than adjuncts to the advertising industry. I suppose I should be glad that the old hypocrisies are no longer operative.

As the guests are dispersing, Peter Cook mounts the speakers' podium (where the microphone has been switched off) and begins a drunken harangue, attacking the Thomson organisation for their 'fucking stupidity and rudeness' in refusing to allow the guests to bring their wives or mistresses. He makes little impact: this is in any case a side-issue. Sad to see Peter so incoherent: one had heard rumours that he had become a lush.

22 March

Fascinating tit-bit from Hugh Millais[4] about the poet Logue. Some years ago (according to Millais) the University of Houston awarded $7,000 a year for life to Robert Graves, John Betjeman and Christopher in return for a promise that the poets would donate their mss. to the university library. This Logue is not the hermit ascetic he claims to be,

---

1. Alan Whicker (1925–). Broadcaster and writer, he created numerous documentaries and was the host of the BBC's *Whicker's World* for many years.
2. Huw Wheldon (1916–86). Broadcaster. When Tynan appeared on a late-night programme, *BBC 3*, and uttered, for the first time on British television, the word 'fuck' in a discussion about censorship, Wheldon was the only member of the BBC's top brass to defend completely Tynan's use of the word.
3. Lord Thomson of Fleet (Kenneth R. Thomson) (1923–). Canadian-born publishing executive.
4. Hugh Millais (1929–). Actor; appeared in, among other films, Robert Altman's *McCabe and Mrs Miller* (1971).

living on crusts and dependent on the charity of his friends for his very existence. Unlike most other writers, he has a guaranteed income for life – and from a southern university, too, a citadel of all that Logue the Leftist professes to despise. When next he knocks me for contributing to *Playboy*, I shall have my answer pat.

24 March

George Axelrod and his wife have bought and redecorated a house near Eaton Square. I am shown over it and particularly envy the huge oak-beamed second-floor room – the largest in the building – which is designated by Joan Axelrod (a professional interior decorator) as 'George's work-room'. My own 'work-room' – wrested from my secretary after long hassles with my wife, who wanted it for herself – is a small dank closet on the ground floor with one small window and an irreparable heating problem. 'At least,' I say, to Joan Axelrod, 'if George has a work problem, he can always take a walk around the writer's block.'

30 March

Spinoza said that a man's duty, when he surveyed the world, was 'neither to laugh nor to weep, but to understand'. This is also the ultimate duty of the theatre.

5 April

We are discussing how I use Kathleen (and all men use their wives) as housekeeper-drudges when word comes of yet another crack in the roof. 'Oh, those bloody plumbers!' cries Kathleen. 'They're so incompetent.' 'It's a bad tool,' I point out, 'that blames its own workmen.'

10 April

Dining at the Cheval Rouge in Montoire with the Pierre Salingers,[1] I am called from London by Rozina. She says that yesterday's *Observer*

---

1. Pierre Salinger (1925–). Journalist and politician; Press Secretary during the Kennedy Administration, later became a correspondent and editor for ABC News, 1979–93.

and today's *Guardian* contain hard announcements that Peter Hall has been signed to replace Larry at the National. I call Larry, whose story is that two weeks ago he was summoned by Sir Max Rayne, the property tycoon who has been chairman of the NT since last summer, and told that the Board had decided on Peter Hall. He told Larry to keep his mouth shut, and that was that. L.O. swears that this was the first he knew about the approach to P.H. and that he was given no chance to suggest alternatives. Clearly he should not have agreed to the vow of silence: he ought to have insisted on discussing the appointment with his colleagues – me, John Dexter and Michael Blakemore – the latter especially, since he is the logical successor to L.O., not the burnt-out conservative P.H.

11 April

K. drives me back to Paris, cutting short our holiday, and I return to London. From John Mortimer[1] (a Board member) I learn that he was under the impression that the artistic executive had been consulted. I call Michael Blakemore in Biarritz (it's a sad coincidence that both he and John Dexter are abroad at this crucial point); he is outraged at the lack of consultation and feels betrayed by L.O. In the afternoon L.O. calls a company meeting and explains that P.H.'s appointment is not fixed and that nobody's job will be imperilled when the company moves into the new theatre, in January 1974. (But what kind of demoralised twilight regime will prevail until then?) To a question from me, he replies that he will stay as Artistic Director until the company is established in the new theatre. I leak this story promptly and accurately to the *Evening Standard*. This provokes a statement from the Board that Peter Hall's appointment is not fixed and that L.O. will stay on into 1974. At least a bombing pause has been gained.

12 April

I talk to John Dexter (who's leaving in 1974 anyway but believes in *group* leadership) and Frank Dunlop[2] (who is cynically disgusted by

---

1. Sir John Mortimer (1923–). British novelist, playwright and progressive barrister.
2. Frank Dunlop (1927–). Theatre director; associate director of the National Theatre, 1967–71, Director of the Edinburgh International Festival, 1983–91.

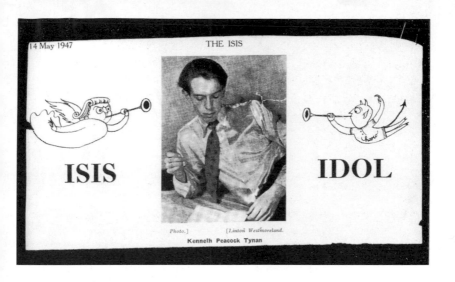

THE ISIS

14 May 1947

ISIS IDOL

Photo.] [Linton Westmoreland.

Kenneth Peacock Tynan

L.O.'s willingness to sell us all to P. Hall without any consultation). I speak to P. Hall, who has just flown back from the US to a Board meeting today: he insists that he had no idea there had been any lack of consultation about his appointment, and asks me to tell Dexter, Dunlop and Blakemore that he was not trying to go over their heads. He adds that the amount of power wielded by the NT Board worries him; it is far greater than that which is executed by the RSC Board.

Joan Plowright tells me that she quarrelled with L.O. over his decision not to tell J. Dexter, M. Blakemore and me about the Board's choice of P.H. which he heard on 11 March. When I went to Brighton over two weeks ago (on 24 March) and had to drink with them, she was about to break L.O.'s word and tell me when Tracy and her boyfriend joined us for drinks. Throughout the following week we were discussing future plans for the new theatre which he knew were purely academic, yet he never chose to tell us what he knew.

At three-thirty I go to Max Rayne's office to present our (i.e. M.B.'s, J.D.'s, F.D.'s, Patrick Donnell's and mine) point of view. He begins by saying that when he was appointed Chairman less than a year ago, Larry came to him and said: 'I expect you want my resignation.' He was amazed and said why? Larry said he thought a new broom would want to sweep clean. Max said he expected L.O. to stay on at least until the new theatre opened. This was agreed. When Max asked who Larry would nominate as his successor he said: 'Would the Board consider a Lady Directress?' Spotting what he meant, Max said he doubted whether the Board would accept the suggestion. L.O. then proposed – *Richard Attenborough*! Max claims that he thought Larry's ideas had our support. I explained that most of the important decisions of the last few years had been taken by a group of us, myself being a dominant factor, and that many of the *bad* ones had been taken on occasions when we had allowed Larry a free rein. I presented Max with the proposal that the Board should meet M.B., J.D., F.D., P.D. and myself on equal terms to hear our ideas about the succession. Max's first response was: Why couldn't we present our ideas to *him* for transmission to the Board? I demurred. So why couldn't we submit our opinion *in writing*? Again I demurred. He finally said he would put my proposal to the Board today and let me know the result.

Footnote: Max said that when he put the case for P. Hall to Larry two weeks ago, he told him that negotiations would only be continued if Larry approved. Larry gave his wholehearted approval. In fact – as I have learned from a friend of my secretary, who is secretary to Laurie Evans (Larry's agent *and* Peter Hall's) – a contract between P.H. and the N.T. was already in an advanced stage of drafting four weeks ago. In other words, it was already virtually irreversible by the time L.O. was informed.

I hate the most important decision in the administrative history of the English theatre being taken by a property tycoon (Rayne) and a lawyer (Goodman), without any word from the people who planned, created and evolved the National Theatre. When I mentioned Michael Blakemore's name to Max, he said blandly: 'Alas, I've never met Mr Blakemore.' He also regretted that I had not consulted him about the succession six months ago. I pointed out that he was the titular boss, and if he had wanted to know my opinion he had only to pick up the telephone.

What emerges from all this is that Larry has behaved appallingly. He has sold us all down the river without a single pang – by refusing to nominate a possible successor from his own colleagues, he has passed a vote of no confidence in us all. He never wanted to work with anyone who might replace him, either as actor or director. He has hired us, stolen our kudos, and now shows no compunction about discarding us. I cannot recall his ever saying a word in public that gave any credit to anyone connected with the NT except himself.

11 p.m. L.O. calls in confusion – confirms most of what Max Rayne says – states that Max called him this evening asking why he wasn't at the crucial Board meeting to which Larry replied that he couldn't recall having been invited. He still isn't sure whether he was or not. 'I'm afraid I don't remember things very well nowadays,' he says to me, seeking sympathy. He says he did suggest Dicky Attenborough and David William[1] (!) but not Joan, except as a member of what he calls a 'college of cardinals', to include Jonathan Miller, Paul Scofield, myself and a dozen others, to advise on policy and the succession. I say that the Board would never have accepted this, since it would have looked like a Counter-Board. He apologises for the present situation and for causing Michael and me (especially) to feel betrayed; but says he could not in conscience recommend Michael for the job of Director *now*.

---

1. David William (1926–). Director and actor, the Director of the Stratford Festival in Canada from 1989–93.

Later he adds: 'Maybe in five years' time . . .' I say categorically: 'If you had taken us into your confidence a year or so ago, we could have reached a joint conclusion and put it to the Board.' But L.O. is not a man for joint conclusions. He does not trust anybody. He does not understand participation.

13 April

L.O. furious that I have told *The Times* that I went to see Max Rayne to arrange a meeting with the Board. Reading Reich, I find an explanation of his deep anxiety and fear in such situations. He would like to dominate the chairman (father) but is terrified of offending him and causing him to react with anger. In other words, the Oedipal impulse is frustrated by castration anxiety. (N.B. How Larry adopts a *passive-feminine* persona when in the presence of authority – such as the chairman, i.e. *he anticipates* the castration by taking on the manner of a woman – mother.) I recall what Gadge Kazan[1] once said to me: 'Above everything else, Larry is a *coquette!*'

16 April

Lord Goodman, who leaked the news of Peter Hall's appointment to the *Observer* last week in accordance with a proviso that he, as chairman of the *Observer* trustees, would let the paper have the story first, today says in the *Sunday Times* that some 'disturbed person' at the NT (clearly a reference to me) had leaked the story because he wanted 'a final convulsion'. We are dealing with liars on a fairly grand scale in this business.

From a book review in the *Sunday Times* by Michael Howard, the right-wing military historian: 'Hitler was in fact the archetypical man in the pub: affable, generous, sentimental, arrogant, bigoted, ignorant and (when the drink begins to bring out his real prejudices) rather nasty. No wonder millions of common men could identify with him . . .' Consider that sentence and what it tells us about the ruling class's real opinion of democracy.

---

1. Elia 'Gadge' Kazan (1909–). The doyen of American stage and film directors, directed *A Streetcar Named Desire* (1945), *Death of a Salesman* (1949) on Broadway; in film *On the Waterfront* (1954); co-founded the Actors' Studio.

Sidelight on the NT affair: L.O. and Peter Hall have the same agent, Laury Evans. Last month Evans's office were drawing up Peter Hall's contract with the NT, trying desperately to conceal the negotiations from L.O. whose own contract with the NT was clearly being violated by Hall's.

17 April

Michael Blakemore tells me that when he was appointed associate, Larry asked him whether he'd like John Dexter or Jonathan Miller as his colleague. On grounds of NT experience he chose Dexter, but on the understanding that they should get the same salary. Shortly afterwards he brought this to Larry's attention, reminded him of his understanding and protested: 'Really, you can't do this!' Larry frosted over those grey eyes, swivelled his head away and said: 'I can do whatever I like.'

18 April

Rozina: In all this NT affair, Larry has been the nigger in the woodpile. *Me*: No – the Uncle Tom.

20 April

Michael B. reveals a nugget he has uncovered from Gaia Mostyn-Owen. Peter Hall told him that Goodman offered him the National Theatre job *before* he left Covent Garden. No wonder Lord Drogheda[1] hates him. Michael also tells me that Larry has strongly opposed our joint suggestion (with John Dexter and Frank Dunlop) that we should henceforth be allowed to attend Board meetings. What a traitor he has turned out to be.[2]

---

1. Lord Drogheda (1910–89). Chairman of the Board, Royal Opera House, Covent Garden, 1958–74.
2. Tynan to Peter Hall, 20 April 1972: 'I trust you suffered no lasting wounds from being caught in the flurry of crossfire between the Board and the executive. I told the Board on Tuesday (and you last week), none of us had anything against you personally. What we deplored about the whole exercise was the total lack of consultations. My own feeling was that within a year or two Michael Blakemore might have emerged as a candidate, and it shook me to learn that Max Rayne had never even met him; but if the appointment was to be made now, then it obviously had to be you . . . So: congratulations – and I needn't warn as wary a bird as you to keep a sharp eye on the Board and its doings.'

21 April

When it actually seems as if real democracy might be about to exert some genuine influence on the nation's life, the ruling class produces an antibody to counter it. The antibody in our time is Lord Goodman. A man who has never held elective office, he has wielded more power than anyone in the country, except the Prime Minister during the past decade – and during Harold Wilson's stewardship. I am not sure Goodman didn't rule him. Can John Dexter's story be true, that the youthful Goodman looked at his image in the mirror, already obese and hirsute and porcine (and probably speckled with acne as well), and murmured to himself: 'Arnold, you're going to have to be very clever.'

It's a great error to suppose that fanaticism is only to be found in extremists. Goodman, for instance, is a fanatical *compromiser*, ruthless in his passion for what he thinks of as the middle way. (Remember that he who drives in the middle of the road runs over the most people.)

5 May

Constantine (in *The Madras House* by Granville-Barker[1]: '. . . the aristocratic method of government [is] the only ultimate method . . . all others are interim plans for sifting out aristocracies.'

Constantine: Rebellion against nature brings no happiness, Phil.
Philip (his son): What else is civilisation?
Constantine: And what better condemnation of about half of it?
Philip: Thoughts curdling into words . . . and into more thought and more words. Yes . . . it leaves one lifeless.

10 May

Poem for Tracy's twentieth birthday:

---

1. Harley Granville-Barker (1877–1946). Playwright, producer, actor and theatre scholar; a progressive dramatic force at the beginning of the twentieth century.

Twenty
Is plenty
For most girls, who then
Cease to be people
And live through their men.
You, on the other hand,
Take the long view –
Mankind your brother and
Womankind too.
Ever a chooser
And never a beggar
(Quoting Marcuse
And even Heidegger),
Herewith I wish you
Health, love and gaiety –
Down with the preachers
And up with the laity!
Down with the tyrants,
The prudes and the owners!
Arriba the rebels,
The clowns and the loners!
Be an empiricist
In socialism and sex!
Read Wilhelm Reich
And remember the Czechs!
Weep for the world
Yet seldom look sad –
And never kick sand on
Your much-loving dad.

12 May

Final unforgivable social servility by Kathleen to wealth and prejudice
and vindictiveness. Winston Churchill forces us to spend three years in
suspense, followed by £6,000 damages and £14,000 of crooked
expenses. He is a total enemy to whom I owe justified hatred.
We go to a party given by Lord Melchett[1] (under protest on my

1. Lord Melchett (1925–73). Merchant banker and first head of British Steel, 1967–73.

part, since I loathe such soirées, but she weeps and I succumb) and I am grabbed by Michael Foot's wife, Jill,[1] with whom I sit for supper. Meanwhile Winston Junior arrives. Kathleen sees him, greets him (coolly, she later alleges), but omits to tell me that he is there. She knows that, although he is a competent skier, I would probably have hit him quite hard. But she dares not risk causing a scene at Lord Melchett's. This is like not telling a Jew that Martin Bormann[2] has entered the room. It is why England is a country whose citizens would rather be pissed on by the ruling class than cause embarrassment by making trouble.

[Entry of Kathleen Tynan's:
I was the one who wanted to fight Churchill in the courts. You wouldn't do it – too scared of losing money. That's where you should have shown *courage*, not in somebody's drawing-room. Irrelevant to me whether you met, or even knocked down Winston Churchill. In the courts you would really have *defeated* him.]

When one takes a sexual or political line as intransigent as Reich's, one is going to end up without much succour and without many friends. The attack from outside will be fairly unremitting. The only comfort and fulfilment to be derived from the situation is the knowledge that such situations cannot bring comfort or fulfilment.

21 May

Line overheard in a dream, spoken by an actress: 'Whenever I wear a mild hat, all I can hear is distant islands.' I laugh till I cry at the delicate truth of this.

22 May

Idly contemplating suicide (very idly), I remember the occasion around

---

1. Michael Foot (1913–). Labour politician and writer; leader of the House of Commons, 1976–79 and leader of the Labour Party, 1980–83. Jill Foot (1914–99). Documentary filmmaker and socialist.
2. Martin Bormann (1900–1945?). Nazi leader and close aide to Adolf Hitler, signed the series of edicts ordering the deportation of Jews to concentration camps in the east.

1952 – when I called Derek Lindsay[1] to invite him to a party the following Saturday. He consulted his diary and then said: 'Alas, Peacock, I'd love to come, but I'm committing suicide on Friday.' A typical Deaconism, I thought: but when Saturday came and the party started and Deacon failed to show up, I couldn't help telephoning him to see what, if anything, had happened. A woman's voice, sounding strained and anxious, answered – Deacon's aunt, as I later discovered, with whom he lodged. 'Derek's not very well,' she said. I pressed her to tell me what was the matter, but got nowhere until suddenly Deacon's voice broke in: he had obviously been listening in on the extension. He sounded faint and exhausted. 'My dear Peacock,' he said. 'Not only can our physicians not cure us, they cannot even kill us. By subtle and judicious questioning I obtained from several medical friends their estimates of what constituted a fatal dose of Seconal. Last night I took it – plus ten. Picture my chagrin, dear Peacock, when an hour ago my eyes opened on yet another grey London afternoon.'

25 May

Supper at the Savoy with Harold and Evelyn Stern and Marlene, who called up during the afternoon to complain about her press reception. (She is in London to do a two-week *tour de chant* at the Queen's Theatre.) Her impresario, she said, was a rich pop-concert promoter who said not a word during the reception but stood by the door, 'Wearing a raincoat!' Marlene has clearly undergone some facial renovation: cheeks and neck are smooth and unwrinkled, and although she claims to be suffering from arteriosclerosis, she walks with sprightly bounciness (so unlike her buddy Noël, whom she blames for bad diet, reliance on the advice of parasites, etc.). At supper she reveals her current favourite writer: Rex Stout, whose Nero Wolfe novels she wants Orson to enact on TV. Her last literary pet was Paustovsky: no one can say her tastes aren't catholic.

27 May

Flying to New York to research my Wilhelm Reich piece for *The New Yorker* I buy and read Cecil Beaton's latest book of diaries. How lucky –

---

1. Derek (Deacon) Lindsay (1926–). Oxford friend of Tynan's. Writer; under the name A.E. Ellis wrote the widely acclaimed and classic novel about life in a TB sanatorium, *The Rack* (1958).

in this one sense – he is to be queer and unmarried, and thus constrained to use a diary as the receptacle for his outer life and inner thoughts. In marriage the partners share the outer life, which thus goes unrecorded, and leak away their inner thoughts to each other and probable oblivion. Yet (writing this halfway across the Atlantic) I would not swap Kathleen for the authorship of a masterpiece.

28 May

To New York, staying with Adolph and Phyllis Green.[1] We have supper at Sardi's and are joined by Groucho Marx and his sexy but undoubtedly daunting young secretary-manager-girlfriend, who makes no secret of her hope of making a fortune out of his memoirs. She is so unabashed that her ambition seems almost innocent. I ask him how he felt about the BBC interview that Frank Muir filmed with him last week. (Muir had taped me singing the great Kalmer-Ruby song, 'Show Me a Rose', and played the tape to Groucho to jog his memory.) Groucho swivelled his eyes at me suspiciously and said: 'Isn't he rather *tall* to be an interviewer? And he's right. Muir is over six feet and all interviewers (vide Cavett, Carson, Frost) should be under five feet eight inches. Later Groucho is introduced to Frederic Morton.[2] 'He wrote *The Rothschilds*,' says the introducer. 'Did you get an answer?' says Groucho, without a second's pause.

30 June

Two great beauties on two successive nights: yesterday, Louise Brooks[3] in Pabst's *Pandora's Box* on TV. Eton-cropped, with a fringe swirled forward at earlobe height and a face open to any sexual suggestion, candid and mischievous, full of delight and magnetism; the prototype of

1. Adolph Green (1915–). Lyricist and librettist; his collaboration with Betty Comden (1915–) is the longest-lived partnership in the history of the Broadway musical; their shows include *On the Town* (1944), *Wonderful Town* (1953), *Bells Are Ringing* (1953), also such classic film musicals as *Singin' in the Rain* (1952). Phyllis Newman (1935–). Actress and singer, wife of Adolph Green.
2. Frederic Morton (1924–). Austrian-born author and journalist, best known for *The Rothschilds* (1962).
3. Louise Brooks (1906–85). American film actress with extraordinary sexual charisma; German director G.W. Pabst (1885–1967) starred her in *Pandora's Box* (1929) and *Diary of a Lost Girl* (1929). She returned to America, where her career went into steady decline. She retired in 1938; the subject of one of Tynan's best profiles in *The New Yorker*, 11 June 1979.

Sally Bowles. Is her broad-necked bisexuality part of the attraction? At all events: Louise B. is *unarmoured*, in the Reichian sense of the word. (A sense which, since reading Reich, I find indispensable in everyday conversation.) The second beauty: Natalia Makarova, the defector from the Kirov Ballet, tonight seen with the Royal Ballet for the first time in *Swan Lake*. If all ballet were like this performance, I would find this vulgar Victorian after-dinner entertainment defensible. As Odette (Electra forbidden to fuck her father), she really is a bird, quivering and volatile; in the Second Act she glows, infinitely vulnerable because capable of surrender. As Odile in Act III she glitters: the bird becomes a snake; sinuous within its flexible armour. From the waist upwards, she is the greatest female dancer I have ever seen; the wave-like motions of her arms, the arc of her neck, are not forgettable. Whenever she leaves the stage, and the *corps de ballet* appears, you unfairly think: Who are these elephants? She has high cheekbones and predatory teeth and will doubtless keep this threadbare and spendthrift pseudo-art – eked out by the nostalgia of poor artists and the *arrivisme* of snobs – alive for a few years longer than it deserves.

5 July

In my office at the NT the house phone rings and it's Peter Hall popping in for a friendly but fairly definitive chat. He pays extravagant but (I think) sincere tribute to my part in creating the NT and adds (not '*but*' adds – he is too much the diplomat even to *imply* 'but') that he hopes I don't envisage that I'm to be thrown out. Nevertheless, he's not entirely sure (and wants my views on) whether we shall get on, both being so good at politicking, both with such strong ideas. I disabuse him of the thought that I ever intended (even under Michael Blakemore) to stay on after the move to the new building, when I would like to be phased out. I sense he is privately relieved, though not surprised.

He outlines some of his ideas for the new operation. My policy of having no policy was, of course, partly tailored to the limitations (and strengths) of Larry's temperament – pragmatic, empirical, wary of grand designs or distant goals. Peter is far more the Man with a Plan. He says he wants to do far fewer major productions and rehearse them longer, so that each when it appears is a model of 'the pursuit of excellence'. (He mentions the early days of the Brecht theatre as an analogy.) At the same time he wants far more experimental productions, mobile productions – a proliferation of new work put on at white heat, with no worry if perfection isn't achieved. We both agree that a team of new young directors must be recruited for this. I tell Peter that in my view the failure to recruit or encourage young directors has been the greatest weakness of Larry's administration. I hope he will bring Roland Joffe on, among others; good politician that he is, he has already had his ear to the ground and realises that Roland (and of course Michael) has the company's affection and respect.

I feel, of course, a slight pang now that all has been said and the end of the chapter settled. It *would* be exciting to plan a new NT with a new policy . . . But enough of this vicarious living. I must go back to taking responsibility for what I do, which is *write*.

8 July

The Front Page a gigantic hit – following my earlier choices, *Long Day's Journey* and *Jumpers*, to make a Tynan grand slam. Larry sees me backstage after the curtain and proffers personal thanks. I take the next day off to celebrate.

Sandra Weidenfeld, to David Somerset, on visiting the latter's ancestral home for the first time: 'It's *divine* – how long did it take you to find it?' (Somerset nearly said: 'About 500 years.')

12 July

A Gestalt prayer:

I do my thing and you do your thing.
I am not in this world to live up to your expectations.
And you are not in this world to live up to mine.
You are you and I am I.
And if by chance we find each other, it's beautiful.
If not, it can't be helped.
Shalom.

16 July

My comment on the Wimbledon men's singles final: Smith only wins when he is playing above his best, Nastase only loses when he is playing below his best.

20 July

I am certain that the full potential of the cinema will not be achieved until it concentrates on the development of *full-length cartoons*. (I've suspected this since I saw the brilliant and highly erotic Japanese cartoon, *1001 Nights*, two years ago.) I do not, by this, mean stylised drawings of talking animals; nor would anyone imagine anything so absurd were it not for the fact that Walt Disney's accidental domination of the cartoon scene has made it impossible for us to think of it except in terms of clothed, speaking animals and birds going through motions designed to entertain the nursery. It's significant that the first X-rated or 'adult' cartoon, *Fritz the Cat*, has pigs, crows and cats in its cast but no people. It is as if the first oil painter had painted only trees, and the art of painting had subsequently been defined as the art of painting trees.

What the cinema ought to be doing (and to have done) is to present coloured *images* of reality (or fantasy) designed by *artists*. At present – by using the camera merely to photograph *reality* – it is confining itself to a function that is part newsreel and part photographed theatre. In pure cinema there would be no real actors and no real backgrounds; there would be drawn (or painted) people in drawn (or painted) settings. Only thus will cinema achieve its historic mission of rising above and eventually replacing the novel.

I note that several critics refer to sexual situations in *Fritz the Cat* [1] that would never be tolerated by the censor in 'real-life' cinema. Exactly: art laughs at censorious locksmiths. And the erotic possibilities of pure cinema are infinitely greater than those of 'filmed reality'.

Why have the movies never exploited this obvious line of devel-

1. *Fritz the Cat* (1971). Animated, sexually explicit film based on the cartoons of Robert Crumb.

opment? Partly because of Disney's power (already mentioned) but partly, too, because of his weakness. Because he failed, in *Snow White*, to draw a credibly human hero and heroine, it was assumed that no one else could succeed.

I must do something with this insight before a thousand others beat me to it. How?

Male voices on British TV and radio come in only two tones: respectful and cheeky. *All* disc jockeys talk like cheeky sons-in-law chatting up mums-in-law. No BBC voice addresses the viewer or listener as an equal.

10 August

In Turkey, having just seen the carnage left by a car crash with four corpses. Bad – i.e. fast and reckless – driving tends to exist in inverse ratio to democratic institutions. In an authoritarian state, the only place where the little man achieves equality with the big is in heavy traffic. Only there can he actually *overtake*. Hence the cut corner, the risks taken, the savage abuse exchanged.

15 August

A dream: I am interviewing Orphan Ramyx, a blue-eyed blonde whom I introduce as 'TV's tittering bumhole girl!'. She explains that she acquired this description by appearances on a talk show where all she did was flash her anus and titter. Her bumhole is now nationally famous. 'It is inlaid with semi-precious stones,' she whispers, 'and its fumes are reputed to be good for arthritis.'

20 August

At Cuarton. Dominic Elwes spends five minutes in the company of a raffish, middle-aged widow and immediately afterwards describes her as follows: '. . . her brain rotted by a lifetime of warm vodka-tonics before lunch, varicose veins exploding beneath her support stockings and her face eaten away by white lead make-up repeatedly condemned under the Pure Food and Drugs Act . . .'

5 September

If one proves by rational, scientific procedures that ghosts exist, then one has demonstrated that the world is not governed by rational scientific laws. Therefore the procedures one has used are inapplicable. Therefore ghosts do not exist.

1 October

I see Andy Braunsberg and, because of K.'s real horror of the gossip that will surround my proposed film, give him two phony reasons for postponing it indefinitely – (a) that two publishers are insisting that I fulfil a long-overdue contract for a book by next spring or repay £5,000 and (b) that the new British film censor rigorously cuts all spanking scenes. Thus I erase my hope of becoming a film director. In the evening I tell K. what I have done. Her immediate reaction: 'And what forfeit do you expect me to pay?' The lack of understanding is – chilling, so much so that I almost reconsider. Have I done right to deny myself a career to spare her feelings, since she seems so impervious to mine? This sacrifice represents eighteen months' intermittent work, and the shelving of a lifetime ambition; and she does not even thank me.[1]

---

1. Kathleen Tynan writes in *The Life of Kenneth Tynan*: 'Ken was intent on exposing and demonstrating his sexual life, about which he felt a mixture of the deepest guilt and the deepest reverence; while his wife, who had refused this exploration – or so he believed – waited in hopeless hope for her old world to be made whole.' Tracy Tynan: 'He was very open with Kathleen about it and it hurt her deeply. Partly in response and as a result of the widening gap between them, she also started having affairs but very discreetly.'

9 October

One major difference between the London theatre today and twenty years ago is: the relative paucity of queers. In the heyday of Noël C. and John G., a high proportion of the best young actors, directors and playwrights was queer. Nowadays: it's hard to think of more than a handful – Ian McKellen, Robin Phillips, Alec McCowan, the late Joe Orton. If true, what does this indicate? That permissiveness, bringing wider sexual opportunities to adolescents, has allowed many 'don't-knows' to opt for heterosexuality instead of homosexuality. That social change has swelled the upper ranks of West End actors with alumni of state schools, where queers are relatively uncommon, instead of boys from public schools, where homosexuality flourishes? I'm not sure and would like to know.

Psychoanalysis, so far from dissolving the guilt attached to sexual fetishes, has in fact intensified it. To the Victorian an interest in spanking was an eccentricity; to the Freudian it is evidence of a pre-genital fixation, it is an offence against the sacrosanct ideal of the Exclusively Genital Orgasm. Freud hypothesised an ideal sexual act, from which all deviations were heresies to be purified by confession and rooted out in the annealing fires of analysis. To the Victorian only sodomitical deviations (in men or women), incest and bestiality were considered unnatural: to the Freudian it is not merely eccentric, it is *against nature* for the prick to stiffen at the sight of a corset or the smell of a pair of knickers. In other words, the new orthodoxy finds many more things anathema than the old.

Which twentieth-century artists are beyond criticism – i.e. accepted by *everyone* as masters to question whose status would be blasphemous? Not Joyce (it's OK to dislike Finnegan); not Stravinsky (OK to find the latter works arid); not Picasso (John Berger's book); not Eisenstein (OK to hold his work distorted by Stalinism); not Chaplin (OK to prefer Keaton); not Brecht (OK to hold his work corrupted by dogmatic Marxism); not Shaw (OK to find him shallow); not Hemingway (infantile aggressions); etc. etc. The only exceptions I can think of are: Chekhov and Proust – and it's stretching a point to call Chekhov a twentieth-century figure. (Footnote: to this list Mary McCarthy – on 10 December – suggests an addition: Kafka.)

11 October

Most vivid memory of this summer's trip to Turkey: the fearful night of torment in Antalya. We had driven 300 miles on fairly lunar roads before arriving at this overgrown coastal resort (in Southern Turkey) in a heatwave of 107 degrees. Instead of the air-conditioned room with bath that we had booked, the hotel could offer only a glorified linen cupboard on the top floor (no lift) without even a shower. Just outside the window of this hotel (recommended in the guidebooks for its tranquillity) there was a large open-air night-club. The floor show began shortly after dusk, with deafening amplification, and consisted of an interminable Turkish variety bill, including everything from pop groups to stand-up comics. At 10 p.m., I called the concierge to ask when the festivities would cease. At 11 p.m., he said.

At twelve midnight, they were still in full swing and I boiled over. I consulted my little Turkish dictionary. As I expected, the word for 'shit' was not listed. On the next page (it was an eccentric little book) my eye caught the word 'sweepings', the Turkish for which was: '*süpruntu*'. I then looked up horrible ('*iğrene*') and when the next performer on the bill finished her act – she was a folk singer – I leaned out of the window and bellowed: '*Iğrene süpruntu!*' Whether because of the surprising nature of the insult ('Horrible sweepings!' cannot be a common form of abuse, even in Turkey) or because it is virtually impossible to *shout* the 'u' sound (which is pronounced like the French '*u*'), nobody paid any attention. Returning to my dictionary, I turned to 'manure' ('*gubre*'') and, combining it with 'nasty' ('*pis*'), let the next act – a crooner – have it with both barrels of '*Pis gubre!*' a far more gratifying and resonant cat-call. Again, there was no reaction that I could see or hear, although I was certainly audible and there is nothing equivocal about being called 'Nasty manure'. I could only conclude that my voice was lost amid a general clamour of other dissidents in the audience who were *already* shouting, '*Pis gubre.*'

At 1 a.m. the cabaret ended and I had just fallen asleep when a tremendous clattering announced the arrival beneath my window of a full-scale construction gang. It was now about 2.30 a.m. In Southern Turkey during heat waves it is too hot to do intensive manual work by day, and hence a good deal of construction work is done at night. I peered out of the window and saw dozens of men in steel helmets, a dozen glaring arc-lights, welding torches, trip hammers and pneumatic drills going full blast. It was an infernal spectacle. Shouting was useless; I even removed some stones from the windowbox and flung them feebly at the throng. Repeated calls of protest to the concierge finally took effect. A complaint was lodged with the police and at 4.30 a.m. a squad car drove up and ordered the team to make less noise. It was a triumph of sorts, though by then I was too hoarse and exhausted to savour it.

18 October

Larry at his most characteristic: I give him a new script to read, a fascinating comic-strip treatment of the *General Strike* by David Caute called *The Great National Holiday*. He reports that he hated it and says in the same breath that we ought to consider a dreadful piece of thirties drivel called *By Candlelight*. (He also reveals that, without telling any of us, he has already sent the *Strike* play to Peter Hall in New York for an opinion – although Peter does not take over as director for twenty months. Such is servility.)

19 October

Thoughts *re* L.O. for my book: he and John Clements[1] demonstrating strokes in front of Kay Hammond,[2] his remark about Helene Weigel's[3] lined face ('I suppose that's what comes of being peed on for thirty years'); his love of *African Genesis* and *Territorial Imperative*, his outburst against John Gelgud's *Oedipus* ('*Oedipus* is about *blood* and *guts* and *shit*'); his lack of interest in anything outside acting and gossip.

24 October

Reflections after a party for Betty Bacall: it is a mark of male chauvinism to praise actresses like her for their intelligence. *Any* actress *with a deep voice* is always hailed by male critics for her wit, shrewdness, intellec-

---

1. Sir John Clements (1910–88). Actor, director and manager; succeeded Olivier as Director of the Chichester Festival Theatre, 1966–73.
2. Kay Hammond (1909–80). Actress; wife of John Clements.
3. Helene Weigel (1900–71). Austrian actress; married Brecht in 1928 and gave definitive performances in many of his plays, especially as the mother in *Mother Courage* (1949); with Brecht co-founded the Berliner Ensemble in 1949 in East Berlin and ran it from 1956 to her death.

tuality – simply because she *sounds like a man*. Example, Bacall, Kate Hepburn, Marlene – all of them are nice women but by no stretch of the imagination mental giants.

25 October

> There are a thousand little silly softnesses which are pretty and endearing between acknowledged lovers, with which no woman would like to dispense, to which even men who are in love submit sometimes with delight; but which in other circumstances would be vulgar – and to the woman distasteful. There are closenesses and sweet approaches, smiles and nods and pleasant winkings, whispers, innuendoes and hints, little mutual admirations and assurances that there are things known to those two happy ones of which the world beyond is altogether ignorant. Much of this comes of nature, but something of it sometimes comes by art.

> (Trollope – *The Way We Live Now*.)

1 November

Odd dream symbolising (I think) the triumph of art over reality. I dream that I meet Minnie Barnum, the owner of a collection of yellowed ivory figurines of the great courtesans in various erotic postures and groupings (including spankings). The figurines, which are tiny, are set out as on a cribbage board, in the holes of which they rattle like loose teeth. Minnie Barnum (who resembles a thin Jewish Nellie Wallace[1]) tells me of her greatest achievement. At the exact instant when the suffragette threw herself under the hoofs of the King's horse on that famous Derby Day, she hired Melba to sing E above high C – thus topping the cries of the crowd, who stopped their own screaming and turned, silenced by art, to listen.

---

1. Nellie Wallace (1882–1948). British actress, singer and music-hall comedienne.

2 November

Another dream. I dictate the following letter to Jo Grimond[1] (whom I don't know):

> Dear Sir,
>   I believe that you should have a horse. I am therefore setting up the 'A Horse for Jo Grimond' fund, the aim of which will be to raise enough money, by public subscription, to ensure that an adequate and substantial animal can be secured.
>   Warmest wishes, and here's looking forward to your horse.
>   Yours sincerely –

Dinner with Gore (Vidal) at the Mirabelle. He tells me that Truman Capote's sole remaining income is two more annual instalments of the $30,000 advance from Random House on an undelivered novel: after that, the poorhouse. Gore's big revelation: Tom Driberg[2] is writing an auto-biography in which he will reveal how, in younger days, he performed a blow-job on Aneurin Bevan.[3] (This prompts me to invent a second version of *My Blue Heaven* entitled *I Blew Bevan*. The first, of course, was invented when Patrick Lichfield[4] invited us to spend a weekend at his house with David Bailey[5], and his (Bailey's) girlfriend Penelope Tree.[6] Suspecting that Patrick hoped for a general orgy which he could then film, I mused:

> Just Patrick and me
> While Bailey makes Tree –
> We're happy in our
> Blue Movie.

Later at home I play a newly issued LP of early Chevalier songs and remember a memorable remark of the ever-lamented Harry Kurnitz[7]. I was describing a lunch at Chevalier's house in Marne-la-Coquette:

1. Joseph 'Jo' Grimond (Baron) (1913–93). Scottish politician, leader of the Liberal Party 1956–67.
2. Tom Driberg (1905–76). Labour MP, 1945–55; 1959–74; flamboyant homosexual.
3. Aneurin Bevan (Rt. Hon.) (1897–1960). Influential Labour politician; Minister of Health 1945–51.
4. Patrick Lichfield (1939–). Photographer; took the famous 'Royal Wedding' photograph of Charles and Diana in 1981.
5. David Bailey (1938–). Fashion photographer; the embodiment of sixties Swinging London; the model for Antonioni's *Blow-Up* (1966).
6. Penelope Tree (1950–). A fashion model and Bailey subject.
7. Harry Kurnitz (1909–68). Screenwriter, playwright and novelist; among his many films, *Witness for the Prosecution* (1957).

K.T.: Everything in the place is a reflection of Chevalier. The dining-room table looks like a straw hat. The ashtrays are little straw hats. Even the *loo* is built like a straw hat.

Harry: And is the bidet shaped like a protruding lower lip?

16 November

In Tunisia: idly listening to the lapping Mediterranean beneath my hotel balcony, I reflect that the sound has echoes that are not wholly gentle. It *hisses* – as it would if the sea were boiling and the sand ice-cold (cf. the noise of boiling water as one tilts it towards the edge of the saucepan).

17 November

Note the baroque (or 'bavoque') lisp common to many baroque queers, whereby they pronounce 'r' not as 'w' but as 'v'. Viz: 'How does that guh-*vab* you?' or: 'He's a perfect puh-*vick*.'

Byron has given me the perfect title for an autobiography if I ever write one: *The Summer of a Dormouse*. It's from a letter:

> When one subtracts from life infancy (which is vegetation) – sleep, eating and swilling – buttoning and unbuttoning – how much remains of downright existence? The summer of a dormouse . . .

Byron, Wilde and Shakespeare would be the three English writers I'd most like to invite to dinner. Odd how nineteenth-century literature is sealed off at both ends by an anal scandal – Wilde up Bosie's[1] bum, Byron up Annabella's.[2]

---

1. Lord Alfred Douglas (1870–1945). Author and poet, chiefly remembered as 'Bosie', whose tempestuous affair with Oscar Wilde led to Wilde being labelled a 'somdomite' by Douglas's scandalised and poor-spelling father, the Marquis of Queensberry, and to the series of trials that sent Wilde first to prison and then into exile. Wilde's *De Profundis* is addressed to Douglas.
2. Anne Isabella 'Annabella' Milbanke (1792–1860). Wife of Lord Byron; married in 1815, the bland and unimaginative Annabella left Byron a year later over his ongoing affair with his half-sister Augusta Leigh. London society supported Lady Byron against Byron.

18 November

Characters – in plays and films – are intimate friends whose sufferings
we can enjoy with moral impunity. (At any rate we can do nothing to
alleviate them, which puts us in a state of guilt-free impotence.)

24 November

Memorabilia from Frank Sullivan[1] on Bostonian parochialism: 'It is
related that on occasion when Saltonstall Boylston learned that his
friend L. Cabot Lowell was leaving for a trip around the world, he
enquired of Lowell: 'Which route shall you take, L.C.?' 'Oh, I shall go
by way of Dedham, of course,' replied Mr Lowell.

Sullivan also tells of a Back Bay aristocrat asking Oliver Wendell
Romney if his ancestors came over on the *Mayflower*. 'No, they
arrived on the next boat. They sent the servants over on the
Mayflower.'

Sullivan's selection of what he calls 'wolf sentences':

Look – the lake comes right up to the shore!
There are lots of nice people in Hollywood – but not many.
This is the best salad I ever put in my whole *mouth*.
A whole bunch of men came in surrounded by a little fellow in
the middle.
He tells a thing one morning and not the others.
She had more money than she could afford.

Finally Sullivan's friend, the erratic roofmender called the Thick
Quinker, because once he had upbraided a group at the other end
of a bar with the words, 'I know what youse guys are doin' up there.
You're talkin' about me. But you ain't foolin' me any. I'm a thick
quinker.' Same guy also described himself, after a bad experience, as
'The Last Rose of The Mohicans'.

---

1. Frank Sullivan (1892–1976). Humorist and Algonquin Round Table pundit; long-time staff writer
for *The New Yorker*.

25 November

A day that should be commemorated, while I happen to think of it, is that odd Sunday of 1951. A strange American man-about-the-arts (also a painter and sculptor) named Hjalnar Bayesen invited Elaine and me to go and watch polo at Cowdray Park as the guests of his friend the Maharajah of Cooch Behar, then a much-publicised young playboy figure. 'There'll be a couple of other people coming too,' said Hjalnar. We accepted, and on Sunday morning at eleven two Rolls-Royces drew up outside our flat. In one of them sat Hjalnar, the Maharajah, and the latter's girlfriend, a starlet named Susan Shaw. In the other car was Tennessee Williams, and a White Russian actress called Maria Britneva,[1] attractive in a wild sharp-tooth way, like a very dashing stoat. We were introduced and joined Tennessee on the motorcade, which now rolled on to a little house in Chester Square.

Hjalnar rang the doorbell and, returning to the cars, said we were all asked in for drinks. We entered a small living-room, dark and shuttered despite the hot sun, full of bottles, glasses and party debris. Practical jokes were scattered everywhere, such as ashtrays in the shape of human hands and simulacra of lighted cigarettes lying on satin cushions. Laurence Harvey then staggered downstairs, in a dressing gown, obviously hungover, to be introduced to us all and to pour drinks. He was followed by Hermione Baddeley[2], wearing an egg-splattered kimono. Hjalnar talked continuously; nobody else spoke except Tennessee, who muttered to me: 'Do you know any of these people?' I shook my head. So did he. Hjalnar suggested we should leave; Miss Baddeley and Mr Harvey got dressed; and as we were stumbling through the gloom to the door, Miss Baddeley (who was at that time living with Mr Harvey) said dramatically: 'Larry – the beards!' 'My God, yes,' said Harvey, and plunged back upstairs.

He soon returned with an armful of long false beards made of crêpe hair and dyed extraordinary colours – green, yellow, purple, orange, puce. Solemnly he distributed them among the party: just as solemnly

1. Maria Britneva (Lady Maria St Just) (1921–84). Actress; of whom it was said she was 'neither a lady, nor a saint, nor just'; controversial friend of the rich and famous. Tennessee Williams called her his 'five o'clock angel', subsequently made her the quixotic executor of his Estate; her humour, ferocity, and pragmatism were Williams's inspiration for Maggie in *Cat on a Hot Tin Roof* (1955).
2. Hermione Baddeley (1906–86). Character actress.

we hooked them over our ears. This was done without any suggestion of a prank but as if it were raining and he was handing out mack-intoshes. 'We turn up everywhere in our beards,' said Miss Baddeley categorically. Flamboyantly hirsute, we piled back into the cars, and silently sped through the suburbs. As we stopped at traffic lights, people would stare curiously at the bizarre convoy, beards steadily wagging, myself in magenta quietly rabbiting with Tennessee in sky-blue.

At Cowdray Park we disembarked and the chauffeurs produced hock and cold pheasant from the boot. Some of us remained bearded, others did not. Tennessee, sipping his wine, found himself standing alongside his host, and, noting him to be a man of colour, politely observed: 'I – er – I expect you know the Aga Khan?' Cooch Behar smiled and said yes, they had met. Those were the only words he and Tennessee exchanged all day. All at once there was a scream: 'Jesus Christ!' Mr Harvey had been stung on the lip by a wasp. He danced around in a panic. 'Christ, fuck it, I'm *filming* tomorrow and what happens to the fucking close-ups if my lip's swollen up like a fucking balloon?' Miss Baddeley soothed him, procured a bottle of brandy from a chauffeur and retired with him into one of the cars, closing doors and windows and pulling blinds behind them. Outside the car, conversation re-mained becalmed in the heat. Occasionally men on horses thundered by and were lost to sight in the distance. A one-armed man rode up and was introduced as the Maharajah of Jaipur. Tennessee became silently drunk. No one had any idea why they were there. My wife and I joined Baddeley and Harvey in the car for some brandy. Harvey was moaning, Baddeley philosophically drinking. Emptying the bottle, she peered through the window and said memorably: 'I think I'll pop out for a mouthful of fresh wasp.'

Harvey followed her, so noisily in need of medical attention that the kindly Cooch Behar decided we had all better return to London. Harvey's lip had, in fact, as he predicted, begun to swell up exactly like a little pink balloon. We climbed back into the cars. My wife and I travelled with Tennessee, Miss Baddeley and Miss Shaw; our host went ahead with Hjalnar, Mr Harvey and Miss Britneva who had already shown, in a number of flashing œillades, that she had very little time for Mr Harvey's tantrums.

As we were purring (I think that's the word) past the Albert Hall the leading Rolls drew up at the kerb and Miss Britneva flew out. She ran back to our car, weeping hysterically. Opening the door, she said: 'Get me out of here, Tennessee. That shit Harvey has just spat in my face.' It turned out that she had interrupted a monologue by Harvey on the subject of his film career to deliver herself of an incisive opinion on the effect of narcissism and megalomania on talent (if any). Whereupon Mr H., who was facing her on a jump seat, had leant forward and let fly.

We decided to take the opportunity to peel off as well, and so, thanking our host sincerely, we climbed out and flagged a taxi. One lesson I learned from that day was that one should recall, when planning a party whose ingredients sound like an exciting mixture, that there are such things as Molotov cocktails.

30 November

The great obstacle of marriage: one wants to make love to a willing, co-operating *approving* female body. In fact one is expected to make love to a partner in accountancy, a fellow businessman, a joint consultant in child-rearing, a fellow voter – and in one of many of these capacities, the wife may very strongly disapprove of the husband. Yet she expects adequate love to be made nonetheless. Here is the vicious circle of true-companionship marriage: the more husband and wife share all the responsibilities of life, the more they are engaged in disputes over non-sexual matters, the less they are – what lovers must basically be – simple cock and cunt. The more 'modern' the marriage, the more extensive the sharing, the less likely is sexual union. One is not irresistibly inclined to fuck one's lawyer, bank manager and friendly neighbourhood philosopher – especially if in all three of these *personae* the wife disapproves of one's activities.

3 December

Lazy is the passive tense of selfish.

6 December

With the Snowdons to see *The Front Page* at the NT. Afterwards, at dinner, Princess M. says: 'It's a funny thing about dogs. They never like Negroes, you know. Dogs are terrible snobs.'

7 December

Dinner with John Berger, who last week outraged the polite literary world by accepting the £5,000 Booker McConnell prize for the best novel of the year (G) and announcing that he would use half of it to finance his new book about the migrant workers of Europe and give the other half to the Black Panther movement, because of the exploitation of black labour by Booker McConnell in Guyana. After his presentation speech, at a dinner at the Café Royal, Cyril Connolly's wife said to him: 'You are a very rude man. And you didn't even thank the cooks for the lovely dinner they provided.' John had stood for the loyal toast, and when he sat down his neighbour, Tom Maschler[1] of Jonathan Cape, said: 'Why did you stand to drink the Queen's health?' John replied that Tom had also stood. 'Yes,' said Tom triumphantly, *'but I didn't drink anything.'*

8 December

An annual Christmas trip[2] to Paris ruined by a bronchial attack. What is emphysema like when a bug strikes? The lungs burn and scald when coughing starts; breathing is like painfully clenching and unclenching two vast stiff fists – the lungs. Or you might say that it's as if glue were pasting the inside of the lungs together, so that the air that is forced in must prise them open. Tonight – dining at the Tour d'Argent – I am close to fainting and collapse into bed at the hotel, unable to move. I feel really fatal, though Kathleen cheers me by recalling what Dominic Elwes said when a nasty colonic ailment menaced him last year: 'It isn't time yet to say hello to Father Greensward.' Dominic's reaction to serious illness was outrage at its effrontery: 'It's absurd! Jesus Christ, I'm Peter Pan!'

1. Thomas Maschler (1933–). Publisher, Chairman of Jonathan Cape, 1970–91.
2. In *The Life of Kenneth Tynan* Kathleen Tynan writes: 'We went to Paris on our annual Christmas weekend . . . which was lavishly planned and executed. But we were not extraordinarily pleased with each other.'

1973

1 January

Remark made by Virginia Blond during weekend with Harlechs: 'Do you know that if you spray your gateposts with soda-water, moss will grow on them?' (A) How was this piece of information acquired? (i.e. who was spraying his estate with soda-water, and why? (B) Why should one *want* moss on one's gateposts?

I never return from an English country weekend without some such peerless nugget of trivia.

3 January

Wisdom of Brecht: He said that what proved the *Inferno* to be a classic was: 'You can read it out of doors.' Again: 'Communism is not radical. It is capitalism that is radical.'

5 January

If our (the NT's) planned production of *The Bacchae*, adapted by Wole Soyinka[1] and directed by Roland Joffe[2] is postponed – as it may be, due to various internal stresses in the organisation – the NT will by next October have been in existence for ten years during which it will have discovered one new playwright (Tom Stoppard) and no new directors. I mention this statistic to Larry, who is visibly shaken: he tries to counter with names like John Lennon (a one-act play adapted from two books) and Maureen Duffy[3] (another one-acter, given for six performances), but finally admits that I'm right. It's a sad reflection on the way in which I've occupied my time for the past decade.

1. Wole Soyinka (1934–). Nigerian playwright, novelist, critic and poet; received the Nobel Prize for Literature in 1986; adapted National Theatre's production of Euripides' *The Bacchae* (1973).
2. Roland Joffe (1945–). Theatre and film director; directed the National's *The Bacchae*; his films include *The Killing Fields* (1984) and *The Mission* (1986).
3. Maureen Duffy (1933–). British novelist, poet, playwright.

8 January

L.O. the good and canny arbitrator, the wise beak, solves a problem that has divided John Dexter, P. Donnell and myself by a formula of one sentence and then says: 'Right – shall we have a pillow fight or make fudge?'

9 January

Story by Michael Blakemore about Albert Finney, who told it to him. When Albert made his million on *Tom Jones* and went on his sabbatical trip around the world, he stopped at Acapulco. One evening he was drinking Dom Perignon on a balcony with the most beautiful girl in Mexico. He took her into the bedroom and put his cock into her. With every thrust he said, out loud: '*That's* for Dad, and *that's* for Mum, and *that's* for Uncle Ted, and *that's* for Cousin Jim, and *that's* for Auntie Marron . . .': A whole working-class family shared that fuck.

Dinner at Drones with (among others) Germaine.[1] She brings a nice little Australian girlfriend named Margaret. I congratulate Germaine on the nude picture of her in *Suck* which depicts her sitting facing the camera with legs apart and drawn up round her head like a wreath. I tell her (truthfully) that it turned me on far more than full frontals usually do. Germaine is prettily pleased, and bridles like an Edwardian miss whose portrait by Sargent is being praised. 'Did you like my cunt?' she says. 'I certainly did,' I say. 'And what about my arsehole?' 'I didn't notice it, darling.' 'Oh – it's there – rather large, I'm afraid – you can't miss it.' 'Oh, I thought that was your cunt.' During this exchange, which is conducted with great sincerity and warmth, I catch sight of Germaine's friend out of the corner of my eye. Her mouth is rigidly agape with astonishment.

1. Germaine Greer (1939–). Australian-born feminist icon; became widely known after *The Female Eunuch* (1970). At the opening of Tynan's second erotic revue *Carte Blanche* (30 September 1976), Greer told the London *Evening News*: 'It simply didn't come off. They couldn't sing well enough and they couldn't dance well enough.' Tynan wrote to her the next day: 'You are, of course, entitled to your opinion, and you are entitled, if you wish, to share it with a million newspaper readers. Whether you are then entitled to attend a party in celebration of the show you have just knocked, and to seek a heartfelt reconciliation with the person who devised it, I am not certain. But there is one thing to which I know you will never be entitled, and that is my friendship.'

11 January

Larry invites John Dexter, Paddy Donnell and myself to dinner with Joan and himself at Roebuck House, to announce that he has decided to resign as director of the NT in October. Amazement. We had all planned on his retiring, as *privately* agreed, in the spring of '74. He now assures us that, although he has not discussed the situation with P. Hall, he is bored to death with the administrative chores, feels no artistic excitement in the job, and would like to get out as soon as possible. We point out that we have organised our lives around leaving as soon as the NT moves into its new home (1975) or as soon as he had previously agreed to resign (spring 1974) and that he must not retire prematurely for fear of alienating the company and (by implication) us. Much good drink is consumed (Margaux '57 and Dom Perignon) and many good anecdotes are told – among them one by Paddy D. about Ralph Richardson storming on in the last act of *Macbeth* and booming at Macduff: 'Let fall thy sword on *venerable crusts* . . .' Larry's decision is left for a few days' consideration and for discussion with P. Hall.

13 January

Roxana at breakfast: 'The Lord God says you mustn't go to the loo.'

13 February

General enthusiasm at NT for Trevor Griffiths'[1] new play *The Party*. Peter Hall likes it; John Dexter wants to direct it; and Larry not only likes it but wants to play the part of the old Trotskyite, Tagg. John has given him various basic revolutionary texts to read as background. Larry confesses to me that Trevor's play has for the first time explained to him what Marxism is about. But I have doubts about him in the play. It needs – *all* its characters need – a core of burning revolutionary zeal: a passionate and caring political intensity. And Larry, for all his rage and virtuosity, is a cold actor: he can with an effort simulate passion (e.g. Othello), but it is not communicated, and often leaves an audience wondering rather shamefacedly why they haven't been more moved.

1. Trevor Griffiths (1935–). British playwright; among his best-known plays, *Comedians* (1975).

He's at his best with the contortions and turbulence of the cold heart, the extinct volcano – e.g. *Richard III, Dance of Death, Long Day's Journey*. If Tagg is played thus, he will come across as a hard and demonic monster – not as a man of feeling – and this would be disastrous.

Distaste, disdain, revulsion – the nouns of withdrawal, of contact rejected, or scorned – these evoke the characteristic behaviour of only one country. They are the nouns of England.

14 February

Story from Betty Comden about Cary Grant interviewing Kurt Frinys (queer spelling?) who wanted badly to be his agent. After questioning him about the proposed financial arrangements, Grant said: 'There is one other thing. Are you Jewish? Frinys paused for a moment, then said: 'Not *necessarily*.'

18 February

Youngish man approached me in the street in Soho and said: 'Mr Tynan – I just wanted to tell you how much I approve of everything you're doing.' I thanked him. There was a pause, after which he said: 'Er – what – er – what *are* you doing?' Good question.

20 February

Can it be that so many US musicals celebrate Outsize Women (*Annie Get Your Gun, Call Me Madam, Hello, Dolly, Gypsy, Sweet Charity,* etc.) because so many US musicals are written by Jewish mother fuckers?

We have a Young Vic for the young playgoer: how nice it would be to have a genuine Old Vic for authentic oldsters, where plays for eighty-year-olds are performed with trained nurses in attendance to look after cardiac arrests. There would be a crutch room in the lobby; and tea-trays would be served, but no tea – because of the audience's tendency to dribble its food and lose control of its bladder. In the basement an experimental theatre would stage plays by Terence Rattigan.

Once at a dull party I met the pop singer Sandie Shaw[1], who was wearing a very décolleté dress. I had been drinking ('to make other people interesting' – George Jean Nathan)[2] and began to flirt with her. Finally I decided to go home before the floor began to heave, and asked her for her telephone number, which she gave me. With great deliberation I produced a ballpoint pen and wrote it down – on her left shoulder. One more friendship that never flowered.

Thought on thirties movies: with the passage of time, the eternal things about them peel away, and only the basic trivialities remain to enchant us.

Since last November I have been seeing (and spanking) a fellow spanking addict, a girl called Nicole. Her fantasy – dormant until I met her – is precisely to be bent over with knickers taken down to be spanked, caned or otherwise punished, preferably with the buttocks parted to disclose the anus. She also enjoys exposing and spanking me. Meeting only for intensive and exhausting sexual purposes, we have delighted each other for months. Our fantasies exactly match: whereas I am conscious that Kathleen has had to *will* herself to fit into my fantasy. But for all these months my sex life with K. has languished, to her increasing distress. Two days ago, forced by real anguish on her part (blaming herself for my lack of physical interest) I told her about N. – explaining, a trifle disingenuously, that there was no competition between the two of them; that represented the curry side of my life, whereas K. represented French cooking; that I needed both, perhaps even at the same time (threesome situations are especially attractive to sado-masochists, who like an audience since they like humiliation); that it was only the guilt of concealment that had kept me from fucking her.

Remark by Nicole: 'Lovers are scenes and friends are for ever.'

Recent experiences prove once again that physical pain is not a source of pleasure even to the masochist. The apprehension, the preparation,

---

1. Sandie Shaw (1947–). Pop singer famous for her mid-sixties version of Bacharach/David's '(There's) Always Something There to Remind Me.'
2. George Jean Nathan (1882–1958). American drama critic and editor; with H.L. Mencken co-founded and edited *American Mercury*.

the threat, the exposure, the humiliation – *these* are thrilling, and so is the warmth afterwards, and the sight of the marks; but the impact of cane on bottom is no fun at all. (There used to be an ointment on sale that deadened the skin: it was a boon to masochists.) Thus Reich is right when he declares that masochism is not – as Freud claimed – a form of deathwish in that it seeks not pleasure but pain. The pain is no part of the pleasure of masochism: it is the unpleasant price that must be paid for the pleasure that precedes and follows it.

Writing about 'the subject' makes me reflect again how infinitely more varied in its excitements is sado-mas than straight sex. The sado-mas couple have all the pleasures of straight fucking *plus* the myriad variations that sado-masochism brings with it – the marks that stay for days on the bottom, giving one a reminiscent thrill with each twinge; the anticipation of punishment, which can go on for a week or more and provoke masturbation a dozen times before the whipping actually happens; the multitudinous roles one can play – priest and novice, teacher and prefect, maid and master, doctor and patient (enema department) etc. etc. – each enabling one to savour different nuances of domination or submission. (One fact worth investigation: no sadist that I know is interested in breasts. Bottoms replace them completely as sexual fetishes.) And the games one can play! Really, there is no sport to touch it: it is not just a nocturnal relaxation, it is a way of life.

23 February

Drinks at the Mostyn-Owens with Mary McCarthy, Stephen Spender, Robert Lowell, *et al.* Spender and Lowell discuss what poetry means in the twentieth century – Stephen naming Joyce and Virginia Woolf as 'poets'. I accuse him of annexing prose writers out of territorial ambition, and suggest that the existence of the word 'poetry' is no reason to postulate the existence of poets. I propose that instead of saying that writers are (or are not) poets, we should simply say that they use *metaphor*. This would include playwrights and film-makers as well as novelists and poets. Stephen agrees.

Of Eliot, Lowell says that he was probably a paranoiac when he wrote his best poems, up to and including the *Quartets*. His marriage removed the paranoia, the need to write, and the ability to write poetry. Do we prefer (the unstated question runs) the miserable creator or the contented non-creator? I have no doubt which I would vote for.

Spender and Lowell discuss Auden, who has just come to England and settled at Christ Church, Oxford. It seems he is immensely rich (from real-estate investments in Greenwich Village) and similarly mean. He accepts the charity of the college and refuses to eat out of Hall, although his megalomaniac conversation ('He talks like a driver shooting red lights,' says Natasha Spender, 'and happily tells the same story a dozen times in one evening') has led several dons to suggest that he might choose to spare them the bounty of his nightly presence. He also shows a disturbing propensity to be taken in by strange young men who turn up at his rooms claiming to be needy relations. She says she would not be at all surprised if he were to be felled (perhaps fatally) by one of those rough-trade interlopers.

6 March

With Trevor Griffiths I listen for the thousandth time to Groucho singing 'Show Me a Rose'. Definition: Groucho as singer is Al Jolson with vinegar. We watch a film on Edith Evans[1] by the unctuous Bryan Forbes.[2] She is not the great actress he and everyone else declare her to be. Her limits are too narrow: classic high comedy and genteel modern boulevard plays and that's about all. Within the limits, I don't deny her excellence. But her strongest suit by far is the curiously restricted, intensely English one of: *disdain*. Warm disdain, icy disdain, mischievous disdain, murderous disdain: but always disdain. Her voice patronises all who hear it.

7 March

At last on an *Evening Standard* placard: finally itself, the announcement nothing can follow, the ultimate bulletin of catastrophe: 'ABSOLUTE CHAOS TONIGHT – OFFICIAL.' (The reference is to a railway strike.)

---

1. Edith Evans (Dame) (1888–1976). Considered by many the definitive Lady Bracknell in Oscar Wilde's *The Importance of Being Earnest*, which she first played in 1939.
2. Bryan Forbes (1926–). British director and screenwriter.

8 March

Watching a Sunday TV show I reflect that the really soporific thing about Christianity is the sort of human being it attracts. People are the opium of religion.

9 March

Season of W.C. Fields films at the NFT. Fields in *The Old-Fashioned Way* (1934), reacting to the entrance of a flirtatious widow in a monstrous hat and flamboyantly beribboned dress: 'Looks like a well-kept grave.' And Fields in *You're Telling Me* (1934): a real find, hitherto unknown to me, including a long golfing routine at the end, photographed with a static camera, that is one of the funniest vaudeville bits I've ever seen: 'What a terrible world. Sometimes I wonder if I'll get out of it alive.'

10 March

The deep pleasure of listening to 'serious' music: it dignifies our self-pity.

12 March

Q.: What is the headline when an ancient Vietnamese city collapses on a well-dressed practical joker?
A.: Hué down upon the Soigné Ribber.

13 March

I write a few hours before a press conference at which Larry will announce that from 1 April, he and Peter Hall will be co-directors of the NT and that in October Peter will take over as sole boss. A few months ago Larry put this idea to John Dexter, Paddy Donnell and myself: we all protested that it was a breach of his promise to us that he would stay until next spring. He agreed, and we thought the matter settled. Now, a few days ago, he has gone back on his word again and unilaterally decided to quit – leaving me awkwardly placed, since Peter wants me out of the way by the autumn. Luckily I have an exchange of letters in which Peter guarantees that I stay until the move into the new theatre (now postponed to spring '75); and I think I can use this to ensure that I don't depart until April '74.

Peter and I discussed this yesterday. He began by saying how much he appreciated all I'd done for the NT and 'as far as I'm concerned, you won't leave a minute earlier than you want to. No bullshitting. I've no reason to bullshit you'. He goes on to say that it was not he but Larry who insisted that he should take over the directorship earlier: 'I quite understand – Larry wouldn't want to be kept hanging around waiting for the theatre to open.' And all this time I am squirming with embarrassment, wanting to say: 'But we are up to *here* in bullshit, Peter, and it isn't Larry who would have been kept waiting around, it's *you*. Why do you bother to put on this act?' But he continues, this quiet and genial predator who wants me out of his tank. I have a drink with him and Larry afterwards and depart with an image of them as two armoured ships ruthlessly bound for their own career harbours, no matter how many collision courses they may have to take in the process. Peter – uniquely in the theatre – has no enemies and no friends. I don't know which is the more eloquent criticism. He does not seem to be made of flesh and blood but of some resilient gelatinous substance like a jelly fish. Behind that strange round face, boyishly puckered, ruefully grinning, is a more voluptuous love of power than any I have known except possibly that of Lord Goodman. No wonder the two of them get on so well together. (Note on gamesmanship as I entered his office. P. Hall said jocularly: 'Good afternoon, *sir*.' The mode of address indicated (a) *mock*-servility, plus (b) suggestion of deference due to *age*. You have to hand it to him; and, of course, people do, on a plate.)

14 March

Going through my 1971 diary for income tax reasons, I come across the following conversation with Polanski in Saint Tropez:

R.P.: *Que penses-tu des oiseaux?*

K.T.: *Les oiseaux sont tous cons. Tous.*

R.P.: *Est-ce qu'il y a des exceptions?*

K.T.: *Non. Sont tous cons.*

R.P.: *Il n'y a pas un oiseau moins con que les autres?*

K.T.: *Non.*
R.P.: *Plus con?*
K.T.: *Ah, ca, oui*!

(It was, I recall, excellent grass.)

15 *March*

I dreamt a Shakespearian pun last night: 'Man hath no solace, Madonna, for man is *solus.*'

16 *March*

Remark by K.T. at the N.T. press conference to a journalist who didn't use it: 'When Laurence Olivier asked me to work for him, the National Theatre was merely an idea. Now it is an institution. Not bad in ten years. Our welcome to Peter Hall is heartfelt, but we would be more than human if it were not tinged with a distinct overtone of "Follow *that.*" '

20 *March*

N.B. Where most men of his age, referring to slightly unpleasant people whom they regard as inferiors, would use words like 'chap', 'fellow', 'blighter' or (in extreme cases) 'bastard', L.O. habitually calls them 'fuck-pigs'. (e.g. journalists.)

Visit from Peter Shaffer[1], the third or fourth of its kind, to work out improvements to his play *Equus*. The hero, an adolescent boy in love with horses, ends up blinding six horses with a spike. In Peter's original script, the boy is trying to fuck a girl in the stable: he forcibly undresses her, she taunts him with impotence, he is roused to fury and attacks the horses. At my suggestion he has modified this, so that the girl voluntarily strips, he fails sexually, she tries to arouse him, at which point he sees one of his worshipped horses watching them. He feels as if

---

1. Peter Shaffer (1926–). British dramatist whose *The Royal Hunt of the Sun* (1964) was the National Theatre's first success with a new play; in 1973, he had another international hit, *Equus*, which also began at the National with John Dexter directing.

he were committing adultery in his wife's bedroom or, on another level, as if he were blaspheming in church. He has violated his true religion, and this is why he madly seizes a weapon to blot out the image of his crime from the horses' eyes. Now Peter comes with the very practical problem that a young boy *could not* blind six panicky horses without being trampled. I suggest that he should approach the first horse quickly, almost reverently, and suddenly attack its eyes. Its reactions communicate themselves to the other horses: he then seizes a pitchfork and stabs them to death in their stalls. Thus at the beginning of the play the boy's psychiatrist, Dyshart, would know merely that six horses were killed – not as at present, that six were *blinded*. He would later discover, as a crucial clue, that *one* of the slain horses had had its eyes put out.

Peter (talking about Harold Hobson)[1]: He may not be clinically insane, but at the very least he's what the Victorians called 'cuckoo'.

21 March

Walking along a lane in Chichester, I saw three chalked graffiti, in different hands, on a wall, at roughly twenty-yard intervals. They read: 'Betty is silly,' 'Lucy is mad,' and 'I love E. Horne.' On the way home I compose the following Betjemanesque lyric:

> Betty is silly and Lucy is mad;
> It's the horridest day that they've both ever had.
> But God's in his heaven,
> The lark's on the thorn,
> And I'm feeling blissful,
> 'Cos I love E. Horne.

> Are you Edna or Edgar or Ethet or Ed?
> But what does it matter, together in bed,

1. Harold Hobson (1904–92). Theatre critic for the *Sunday Times*, 1947–76; met Tynan at Oxford – 'favourably resembling Jack Buchanan' – and introduced the aspiring drama critic to the publisher of his first book. When he heard he was ill in LA, Hobson wrote to Tynan. Tynan replied to Hobson, May, 1980: '. . . I certainly miss our duelling days – the trouble with our successors is that nothing seems *at stake* for them.'

Or rolling around on the elm-shaded lawn,
With my thumb up your knickers,
My darling E. Horne.

Yesterday was a superb day for ego massage. I wrote a very decent 1,000 words; dispensed advice to P. Shaffer; and was then taken out to a superb dinner at the Etoile (La Tache 1962!) to have my brains flatteringly picked by Nick Tomalin[1] for his book on the National.

22 March

At the party for Claire Bloom after the opening of *A Doll's House*, Sir Bernard Delfont[2] (as he soon will be) walked over to me. He looked astonished: 'Bloody marvellous, isn't it?' He said. 'Live acting, I mean. Bloody amazing. I thought it was *really interesting* tonight. That's the only word for it – *bloody interesting*. Just a few people standing up there in lounge suits and it's absolutely fascinating – no singing and dancing, no orchestra, just people chatting like you and me. Of course I don't get to the theatre much these days, what with all the paperwork and that – but I can tell you I wouldn't mind going again if it's as interesting as this.' What makes *this* interesting is that it comes from a man who owns or controls about six West End theatres.

At the same party, John Gielgud, renowned for dropping conversational bricks, got one on the foot from Kathleen, as follows:

K. Have you seen the ghastly performance Maggie Smith is giving in *Private Lives*?
J. (*his smile fading to a wince*): Er – I directed it.

25 March

A new stupidity has broken out in the Sunday papers: the idealisation of the impresario. Last week Harold Hobson, discussing the NT, wrote about the 'creative' contribution made by Lord Chandos[3] to the

---

1. Nicholas Tomalin (1931–73). British author and journalist; co-wrote with John Elsom *The History of the National Theatre* (1978).
2. Sir Bernard Delfont (1909–1994). Producer and theatrical impresario.
3. Lord Chandos (1893–1972). Chairman, National Theatre Board, 1962–71.

company's achievement. I had to write explaining that Chandos took no part at all in the making of artistic decisions (though he twice, through the Board, had a hand in *un*making decisions we had made). This week Hobson raves about the creative energies of Binkie Beaumont, who died on Thursday, virtually holding him responsible for the 'grace and intellectual thrust' of shows like *My Fair Lady*, or *Irma la Douce*. This is like holding Christie's artistically responsible for the pictures they sell. *My Fair Lady* was created in America, Lowe, Lerner and Moss Hart working on Shaw's original: all Binkie did was to buy the British rights, and pay the British salaries. Similarly *Irma la Douce* was a Parisian hit that Binkie shipped to London: his creative contribution was to pay the fares. (Hobson says that Binkie's taste was for Wilde's kind of theatre, in which connection he repeats about three times that Shaw was the only critic of his day who praised *The Importance of Being Earnest*, the others all disliking it because it lacked social content. Thus Binkie's taste is equated with Shaw's. It seems cruel to point out that Shaw was in fact the only contemporary critic who *didn't* like *The Importance*, which he thought feeble, mechanical and dated.) Now the *Observer*, in a profile of Peter Daubeny[1], compares this globe-trotting entrepreneur with *Diaghilev*. I wish they would hurry up and knight Daubeny so that we would not have to read any more of these inflated encomia.

26 March

A very tiresome evening with Kathleen, Tracy, Clive Goodwin and Rosie Boycott[2], editor of a Woman's Lib magazine. The tiresomeness emanates from Tracy and Miss Boycott. Regarding me as the classic trendy-Lefty of the previous generation, they make it a point of honour not to let anything I say go by without instant and clamorous contradiction. If I suggest that animal liberation, i.e. refraining from killing other species, is to be treated on the same level as racial or sexual liberation, they berate me for being a pacifist and an anti-abortionist. If I dispute their notion that laughter should accompany fucking, they

---

1. Peter Daubeny (1921–75). British theatrical impresario; brought the Berliner Ensemble, Moscow Art Theatre and the Comédie Française to England; also established the World Theatre Seasons.
2. Rosie Boycott (1951–). Editor and writer; in 1998 became the Editor of the *Independent*, the first woman in British history to edit a daily.

maintain that I have never enjoyed fucking. After three hours of this strident nit-picking I slink off to bed. Their need to attack me is, of course, identical with the tribal assault traditionally launched by the sons on the chief: the king must die. What is sad is that new women should turn out to be no more than old Adams writ large. (But perhaps if I were not so prominent a figure, they would be gentler with me.)

30 March

A recollection: when my first wife wrote to me that she had discovered a *cache* of pornography in my study, I cabled from New York:

> Dear Mrs T.
>   You tied with me
>   the knot that never loosens.
>   How sad that I
>   turned out to be.
>   Yours truly, Eugene Goosens.

(Footnote: Goosens was the celebrated musician who had recently been fined for trying to smuggle pornography into Australia.)

As we are packing to go to the country, Roxana creeps into an empty suitcase and says: 'Relax in a warm hot bath with Dracula.' And creepily closes the lid.

2 April

My birthday. Noël is dead and Muhammad Ali has broken his jaw and I am forty-six. God and bugger and fuck.

A: I can't work.
B: But you'll feel so happy if you work.
A: I don't deserve to be happy.
B: Why not?
A: Because of the pain I'm causing you.
B: You mean if I weren't in pain you could work?
A: Yes.

B: In other words, the whole thing is my fault.

A: Not exactly, but –

B: If I'm to blame, why don't you deserve to be happy?

A: Because I can't work.

(Imaginary dialogue, of course).

5 April

Dinner with Peter Hall at the Etoile. An affable occasion, remarkable for the way in which many of his views on the NT's future coincide with mine. E.g. he says permanent companies have no future (because of TV and film encroachments and the lure of Broadway); and he intends to run the new theatre as follows: (1) big classical productions, with open-ended rehearsal periods, in the Olivier Theatre (2) a separate company doing other plays in the Lyttelton Theatre (I suggest, and he agrees, that these productions should be put on for limited runs, not in repertoire) (3) a continuous firework display of experimental work in the studio theatre. The big company would feed on recruits transplanted from Lyttelton productions. We discuss the chances of persuading Larry to play Lear at the end of 1974: I explain that at one time Larry had asked me to co-direct the play with him, but add that I have no longer any territorial claims in the project. Peter says to my amazement that he sees the play in terms of Ivan the Terrible – to my amazement, because this had been my idea, too. I even ran Part II of Eisenstein's film for Larry to show him what I meant. P.H. swears he hasn't discussed production ideas with L. and I believe him: what's interesting once again is how oddly our ideas overlap. I finish by stating one claim for myself: I'd like to direct Firbank's[1] *The Princess Zoubaroff*, of which P.H. has never heard and which I give him to read. (Oh – and he also said he intended to put foreign companies into the Lyttelton for about four months of the year). We also agreed that there were only about 200 plays in the world repertoire and that we were both running out of old plays we really wanted to see.

1. Ronald Firbank (1886–1926). British comic novelist on line of high-camp wit which leads from Wilde to Coward to Orton, who was greatly influenced by him. *The Princess Zoubaroff: A Comedy* (1920), his only play, never produced in his lifetime.

9 April

Unrecorded incident: on 30 June 1967, I married Kathleen after years of legal problems, a double divorce and a last-minute obstacle nobody had foreseen. We had planned to marry in New York to avoid pictures and publicity since K. was six months pregnant; but it turned out that guilty parties in divorce cases cannot remarry in New York State until x years have elapsed. So off – on a rainy morning in a rented Cadillac with Steve Vinaver[1] (now dead, damn it), Penelope Gilliatt and Marlene as witnesses – to Englewood, New Jersey, on Columbus Day, where a suave youngish Jewish JP was rather petulantly waiting for us. (He had postponed leaving for the weekend in order to marry us.) In a little office full of golf trophies he greeted us – after our years of acrimonious legal struggle to get to this long-desired goal – with: 'You sure you want to go through with this? It's a lot of baloney anyway.' We said we did. He asked for my address. 'In New York or London?' I said. 'Whichever is quicker,' he snapped. As he filled in the form, he muttered: 'I had another marriage an hour ago and there's another after lunch, so there's my weekend down the drain.' He was elaborately unimpressed by Marlene's presence and feigned ignorance of how to spell her name. 'Right,' he said. 'Let's go and stand by the fireplace, it's more dignified over there.' So we arranged ourselves before a mantel-piece agleam with more golf trophies, and he recited the service in a resonant monotone. As he did so Marlene, to cut out the noise of typewriters from the next room, edged backwards towards a sliding door and tried to close it behind her. The judge interrupted himself with no pause or change of tone: 'And do you, Kenneth, take Kathleen for your lawful-wedded – I wouldn't stand with your ass to an open door in *this* office, lady – wife, to have and to hold . . .'

Afterwards Penelope took pictures and we went back to New York for lunch at the Forum of the 12 Caesars, where Bob Silvers[2] joined us. After a snooze at the Algonquin we went to Mike Nichols' apartment, which Mike had lent us (he was on the Coast) for a wedding party. Guests included Mary McCarthy and Norman Mailer, who have been attacking each other in print lately: but no blows were exchanged.

1. Steve Vinaver (1937–68). Songwriter.
2. Robert Silvers (1929–). Co-founder and editor of the *New York Review of Books*.

Afterwards Norman, who had drunk a whole bottle of bourbon, took us to dinner at a little place off Times Square called Frankie and Johnnie's – steak and frankfurters and red wine. Norman and I became very drunk and affectionate and I recall laying my hand on his shoulder and declaring, with tears in my eyes, that he was a pacifist at heart who would not harm a fly, to which Norman, deeply moved, assented. We both forget for the moment that a few years before he had settled a dispute with his first wife ('the painter Adele Morales', as he called her) by stabbing her in the chest with a penknife. K. felt a little excluded as Norman and I went through our blood-brotherhood act, but all ended well: it was a thrillingly happy day.

10 April

Another Larry reminiscence; of the weekend Elaine and I spent with him and Vivien at Nottley Abbey in c. 1955. I had written some pretty devastating things about Vivien, which Larry had deeply resented (indeed, at one point he unfairly told me they had given her a nervous breakdown): Vivien herself, oddly, seemed almost excited by them, and it was always she who took the initiative when we met. Anyway, we arrived at Nottley before lunch on a Saturday. Larry was away in Spain, where his brother had just died of cancer, and would not be back until dinner. Vivien was vivacious, metallic and in a high manic state, talking endlessly with eyes unnaturally bright. There was a lot to drink at lunch after which Elaine and I retired for a siesta. Our room had separate beds. No sooner had I stripped to my Y-fronts and fallen asleep than I felt the sheet slowly turned back and a hand placed on my genitals. It was Vivien, naked under a *peignoir*. I began to respond and then suddenly thought how impossible it would be to cuckold a man I venerated under his own roof – a really cock-crinkling thought. I muttered it to Vivien, who pouted a bit, but eventually rose to her feet – and tiptoed across to Elaine's bed. I hastily dressed: as I left the room, Vivien and Elaine were sleepily embracing.

Larry returned during dinner: the other guests were Vivien's mother and father, a petty bourgeois former colonial administrator, I believe. Vivien's manner with L. is haughty and derisive: how can he bear it? But he does, bearlike staying the course. After dinner V.'s mother knits, father pulls on his pipe and reads *The Times*. V. is drinking hard. 'Come with me,' she says to me, and to my consternation starts to lead me upstairs.

'What for?' I say. 'I'm going to put on Sybil's chain-mail from *St Joan* and you're going to help me,' she says. I look at Larry. 'Do as she says, Kennie,' he says wearily. So up we go to a dressing-room where hangs Sybil Thorndike's battle dress. V. points mischievously at a writing desk. 'There's a secret drawer where Larry keeps letters from all his ladies. He doesn't think I know about it. Shall we peek?' I decline the offer.

Vivien now strips down to petticoat, bra and knickers and I lower the heavy costume over her head. Thus encased, we return to the living-room, where V. proceeds to render some of the longer speeches from *St Joan*, including 'Light your fires.' On an impulse she then sheds the chain-mail. Mum is appalled: 'Now, miss,' she says, addressing the forty-eight-year-old like an errant schoolgirl. 'That's quite enough of that. You mind your manners!' 'What are you going to do, Mummy?' says V. provocatively. 'Spank me with a hairbrush?' Mum seems on the point of doing just that (what a scene *that* would have been!) when V.'s attention wanders back to me. 'Let's see how Ken looks in armour!' she cries. Larry, drinking brandy in great gulps, looks up to meet my eye, nods heavily, and goes on drinking. I retire behind a screen, remove trousers and shirt and slip on the bloody corselet. Conversation continues as before, nobody referring to the fact that I am dressed as the Maid of Orleans. A saddening but surrealist night.

Another memory of the fifties: one Sunday in 1958, Joshua Logan and his wife invited Elaine and myself for a weekend at their place in Connecticut. There were about fifty guests for lunch on Sunday, and afterwards many of them gathered to watch Ed Murrow's TV show *Small World* (on which I later appeared, strangely accompanied by Vivien and Sam Goldwyn). Murrow's guests included Archibald MacLeish[1] and the veteran Polish poet Slonimski,[2] talking direct from Warsaw. As he spoke, Josh turned to me and said. 'Look at the terror in those eyes! That is the face of a slave.' This seemed to me a bit excessive. The Poles had lately had a cultural thaw and were turning out some exceptional films, notably the Wajda[3] trilogy. I said as much to Josh. He

1. Archibald MacLeish (1892–1982). Poet; won two Pulitzer Prizes for *Conquistador* (1932), *Collected Poems* (1953).
2. Antoni Slonimski (1895–1976). Popular Polish poet and critic often at odds with the Communist regime.
3. Andrzej Wajda (1926–). Poland's greatest filmmaker; established himself after the war with a searing trilogy, *A Generation* (1954), *Kanal* (1957) and *Ashes and Diamonds* (1958).

stared at me for a moment, his mouth sagging open, and then went on watching the show. When it was over the guests returned to the living-room. Josh went straight across to his wife and said: 'Nedda, we have a Commie in the house.' He said it quite loudly, and other people stopped speaking. He repeated it: 'I tell you we have a Commie in the house. Ken Tynan is a Commie!'

One could have made a scene: but Josh had a history of nervous instability and the result might have been a vast tantrum. It seemed wiser to collect our luggage and quietly leave, which we did, Josh making no attempt to stop us. A few days later a letter of grovelling apology arrived, but an abyss had opened up: at the bottom of which we saw the real panic that McCarthyism had left in its wake.

11 April

Memory of Beverly Hills in 1955: after a few drinks, Laurence Harvey said he would take Elaine, Mamie Van Doren and myself around some of the more colourful prostitutes' bars in downtown Los Angeles.

Me: Remember, Larry, one swallow doesn't make a slummer.

13 April

A grotesque not untypical day:
10–12:30: Worked on Reich book.
12:30–1: Talk to Peter Hall about policy for the new theatres; he invites me to plan a season of artificial comedy for the Lyttelton Theatre (including *Zoubaroff*); we discuss the rumoured merger between NT and RSC (a horrid piece of businessman's thinking, based on the assumption that conglomerates are good for art because they are good for industry, also that nothing desired by Lord Goodman should be denied him).
1–4: Lunch with Nicole, who receives a one-point enema, a wiped bottom in the loo and a good smacking.
4:30–5:30: At NT for discussions about *Cherry Orchard* programme with Michael Blakemore.
6:15: Train to Oxford with K.
8:30–9:30: Interview Morecambe and Wise in their dressing-room at New Theatre.

9:30–11: See Morecambe and Wise show.
11:1: Supper at Randolph with Eric Morecambe and wife.

18 April

Q: What is the final proof that the death penalty is not a deterrent?
A: The fact (announced yesterday) that cigarette consumption is now
   higher than it was before the connection with lung cancer was first
   suggested.

Michael Blakemore tells me of an occasion when (in a dispute over
Michael's artistic authority in the TV version of his stage production of
Long Day's Journey) Larry casually betrayed him in front of a roomful of
people – in fact, he simply told him to stay out of the rehearsals. M.B.
bottled this up until he and Larry were going down in the lift from the
ATV office. He then exploded quite savagely, to Larry's alarm. I said I
thought people like Larry and P. Hall kept mental files on the tolerance
threshold of their colleagues – i.e. 'Blakemore, M. – liable to fly off handle
in lifts.' 'Tynan, K. – liable to fly off handle *in print.*' Also resignation
potential would be carefully gauged and listed. M.B. adds that he and
Jonathan Miller (who had been wildly talking of resigning over the issue
of not being consulted about the suggested outrageous merger of the NT
and RSC lately leaked to the press) were entertained last night by P. Hall
in his 33rd-floor flat in the Barbican, P.H. succeeded in mollifying them,
persuaded them that his territorial ambitions were satisfied and that the
most he would grant Trevor Nunn (of the financially desperate RSC)
would be participation in an annual season of provincial productions at
the new NT. M.B. said P.H.'s view over London is dizzying and
megalomania-inducing. You can imagine (he said) Satan taking Christ
up there and saying, 'All this can be yours – *and* Italian furniture, too.'

21 April

From *The Wisdom of Father Brown*: 'What we all dread most is a maze
that has no centre. That's why atheism is only a nightmare.' (Why
'only'? Why not 'such'?)

23 April

Terrible production of *Richard III* by the Comédie Française at the Aldwych, directed by Terry Hands in the current Stratford style – black-and-white costumes, heraldic emblems and totems ('visual metaphor') and obsessive use of synthetic materials for sets and costumes. During the more bombastic patches, I improvised a little speech for an actor involved in an RSC evocation of merry England:

Bearing th'embossed blazon of a trout,
Of polystyrene and of vinyl made,
Caparisoned in lurex, *cap à pic,*
Swathed in a rug of simulated seal,
I gird my direful sword, six feet by two,
And hie me to defend the English crown
Behind portcullises of fibre-glass.

6 May

Advice to anyone who would like to win the Grand National: buy and train carefully at Newmarket one of the wild horses that would not drag me to read Doris Lessing's new novel.

20 May

Tracy's twenty-first birthday party at The Young Vic. Wild mixture of people; it's a pleasant sign of one's heterogeneity that one is able to bring together such unlikely couples as Freddie Ayer[1] and Frankie Howerd.[2] Other guests include: Eric Morecambe, George Weidenfeld, Edna O'Brien, Peter Sellers, Stephen Sondheim, Adrian Mitchell, Lauren Bacall, Eric Hobsbawm[3], David and Pam Harlech, Liza Minnelli, Peter Cook, Joan Littlewood[4], Lulu de la Falaise[5], Jule Styne[6], Burt

1. Sir A.J. 'Freddie' Ayer (1910–89). British philosopher who espoused logical positivism.
2. Frankie Howerd (1922–92). Leering, camp British comedian.
3. Eric Hobsbawm (1917–). Historian and professor.
4. Joan Littlewood (1914–). Theatre director; founded London's experimental Theatre Workshop; her *Oh, What a Lovely War!* (1963) was its most famous production.
5. Lulu de la Falaise (1947–). Doyenne of fashion and creative associate of Yves St Laurent.
6. Jule Styne (1905–94). Broadway and Hollywood composer; his theatrical output includes *High Button Shoes* (1947), *Gentlemen Prefer Blondes* (1949), *Gypsy* (1959).

Shevelove, Robin Blackburn[1], Henry and Drue Heinz.[2] Plus a hundred chums of Tracy's. Indian food, cabaret by John Wells[3], Dudley Moore and (disastrously) Max Wall[4], and a fifties-type rock group called Shakin' Stevens at the Sunset. Very little change out of £1,000, but memorable.

22 May

The more K. is convinced that I love her, the more she suffers when I see N. But I do love her and cannot help acting lovingly.

30 May

Dee Wells[5] and Freddie Ayer's party at Hampstead Town Hall. I sit while others dance and find myself the surprised repository of information about unsatisfactory sex lives. Barbara Kelly[6], now in her fifties, married for thirty-odd years to Bernard Braden[7], calmly says she longs for the guts to break away for a Gauguin sojourn in the Pacific. Peter Quennell's[8] wife, slightly drunk, tells me that Peter has gone home in a rage and that she will be whipped when she joins him; she is therefore determined to enjoy herself thoroughly before being punished. Then Miriam Gross[9], (the beautiful wife of John Gross) who has always been named as a model of monogamy by Kathleen and many other supporters of the cult, sits beside me and reveals that she has been

1. Robin Blackburn (1940–) A Leftist historian, Blackburn wrote *The Making of New World Slavery* (1997).
2. Henry John Heinz II (1908–87). American businessman, chairman of the H.J. Heinz Co.; active in political causes and patron of the arts.
3. John Wells (1936–98). British satirist, actor; for *Private Eye* concocted the highly successful cod-confidential political columns, 'Mrs Wilson's Diary' and the 'Dear Bill Letters', the purported correspondence of Dennis Thatcher, husband of Prime Minister Margaret Thatcher.
4. Max Wall (1908–90). Hatchet-faced, feisty British comedian of note.
5. Dee Wells (1925–). American journalist and second wife of philosopher A.J. 'Freddie' Ayer.
6. Barbara Kelly (1924–). Canadian-born actress and broadcaster; appeared with husband Bernard Braden on many BBC radio and TV programmes.
7. Bernard Braden (1916–93). Canadian actor and broadcaster; well-known BBC personality, including *Leave Your Name and Number* which featured himself and Kelly as two Canadians living in London.
8. Peter Quennell (1905–93). Editor, critic and literary historian.
9. Miriam Gross (1939–). Formerly married to John Gross. Arts Editor, *Daily Telegraph*, 1986–91; since 1991 Literary Editor, *Sunday Telegraph*.

unfaithful to John three times in the last two years. The last bastions of monogamy are collapsing; even Kathleen is astonished; soon, I pray there will be a clear distinction between what makes a pair of companions and what makes a pair of lovers.

2 June

In Stratford alone for two weeks – to work and to give Kathleen and myself a period of consideration. I see John Barton's[1] production of *Richard II* at the RSC (highly praised to me by P. Hall). It is bloodless, with the curiously pedantic flamboyance for which this company is nowadays praised. The RSC (a directors' theatre) has not discovered one star actor in the twelve years since it was founded. When you lack actors, you need 'interpretation' – to supply the bloodstream that is missing. So Barton insists that Richard and Bolingbroke are mirror-images of one another (the two actors involved alternate the parts on successive nights): each is a human being who takes on the artificial 'role' of kingship. Everything is done to dehumanise the performances: actors enter on iron stilts, Richard rides in on a property horse which is a unicorn; a snowman actually appears in the scene after the line about Richard being a 'mocking king of snow' – and the whole set is a steep funicular up and down which a balcony slides, bearing Richard on it. Lines from *Henry IV* are introduced to remind us that crowned heads lie uneasy. Oh God, the effort that goes into making these ancient family squabbles take on a resonance they not only cannot but *should* not have for intelligent, modern audiences! If the play is done *straight*, then we are promulgating false ideas about the holiness of monarchy – we are in fact appealing to the sycophantic emotions that still throb in many hearts on reading of the engagement of Princess Anne. But if we try to make the play intellectually tolerable to sensible people, we must violate it. I conclude that we should stop doing it. (At Stratford dozens of bright young talents are occupied in work that could never for a moment embarrass the Establishment. No wonder the Queen is their patron.) Ian Richardson plays Richard II as a rhapsodic spinster, not unlike Franklin Pangborn. Richard Pasco tips the scale by humanising

1. John Barton (1928–). Theatre director and playwright. Co-founder with Peter Hall of the Royal Shakespeare Company; associate director, 1964–91, devised the highly successful *Wars of the Roses* (1963) and the retelling of the Trojan War, *Tantalus* (2000).

Bolingbroke, for which I'm sure his director nightly scolds him. An evening of consummately polished ennui.

3 June

Afterthought: why is it that so many RSC directors – e.g. P. Hall, Trevor Nunn, John Barton – have nervous breakdowns? Is it connected with the resolute anti-emotionalism of their production style? Emotions tightly confined on stage in steel and leather must erupt somewhere: so the private man suffers?

4 June

Inflation rides high, and I believe intentionally. A super-rich class is being built on top of the existing structure – an international-conglomerate-business rich, drawing on the US and the Common Market – with the aim of keeping the insurgent and overweening middle classes in their place, and of decisively depressing the proletariat (and restricting their aims to merely increasing their wages to keep pace with inflation). Only members of the super-rich – the new feudal class – will be able to keep their heads above the decline in the real value of money, because they are paid in perks, property, possessions and tax-exempt benefits. This is what will separate them from the rest of us, whose efforts will perforce be dedicated *not* to changing society but to keeping ourselves from drowning. Thus cunningly manipulated, inflation can *create* (as well as destroy) a ruling class.

5 June

Desired things:

Class A:
>   The sun.
>   The company of people by whom I am loved.
>   The company of people I love.
>   Good food and wine.
>   The propinquity of a female bottom I can
>   *quite freely* whip.

Class B: Admiration of my work.
          The company of intelligent people by whom I am admired.
          The company of people I admire.
          Fast quiet cars.
          A sunlit villa.
Class C: Money to afford classes A and B.

6 June

First public preview of the RSC production (by Buzz Goodbody[1] – a CP member, I learn from Trevor Griffiths) of *As You Like It*. Or *As You Lump It*, to judge from the scant desire to please that this wan staging displays. Three and a half hours and not a moment of that special flavour – like a ripe fruit spurting juice – for which this comedy has been cherished for three and a half centuries. The set is a straight crib of the Koltai[2] set for Clifford Williams'[3] NT production a few years ago (as Clifford rattily points out to me in the first interval). Maureen Lipman – another borrowing from the NT – is a lovely unaffected Celia. But Eileen Atkins' Rosalind! This is brutal miscasting: not only is Eileen too old, she mooches around the forest like a disconsolate Doris Lessing heroine who has been through it *all*, *baby*, giving the fisheye to everyone she meets and regarding Orlando with all the tremulous passion of a cod approaching a baited hook. Still, she has a week to learn how to play the part.

10 June

I read Gore's *Two Sisters*. What superb and seamless armour he wears, as befits one to whom life is a permanent battle for (social and intellectual) supremacy. It is of course a battle that cannot be won by anyone who is incapable of surrender. And Gore could never surrender (i.e. expose) himself freely to anyone. All the same, the necessity to stay on top keeps him writing. As for me my sword rusts in my scabbard.

1. Mary Ann 'Buzz' Goodbody (1947–75). British director; RSC's first woman director, committed suicide in 1975, a month before the opening of her production of *Hamlet*.
2. Ralph Koltai (1924–). Hungarian-German designer; associate designer at the Royal Shakespeare Company, 1963–66.
3. Clifford Williams (1926–). Theatre director; collaborated with Tynan on both erotic revues, *Oh! Calcutta!* and *Carte Blanche*.

20 June

Nicole is really a tremendous reaction to twenty-five years of feeling ashamed of my sexual preferences – being taunted and threatened and blackmailed with them by Elaine, who (except in moments of drunken reconciliation) spent fifteen years intimidating me by promising to tell my friends and employer all about my filthy desires unless I clove to her, and who actually *did* tell my daughter, then aged four, about them, in the small hours of one phantasmagoric night. It is appalling that K. whom I love should be suffering for Elaine's crime[1]. But I cannot allow myself to hate myself *again* – for whatever reason, even for causing K. pain.

25 June

Part of our problem is that we have hardly any life outside our own relationship. Neither of us has any family in England; Kathleen has no job to give her a link with the outside world, and my own bridgehead, the National, disappears when I move out of my office in August. At home we live among children and servants: and we are both at home most of every day. Hence our one-to-one relationship, instead of being simply the most important in our lives, is virtually the *only* one. And whenever anything goes wrong with it, it is as if the whole of life was incurably poisoned. We must remember that Nicole only occupies about 1.8 per cent of my week. The rest is Kathleen's.

Drinks with the Mark Littmans[2] and Tennessee Williams, the latter more assured and healthy-looking than I have seen him for a decade. 'Violence is useful for a writer,' he says. 'He gets rid of it in his work.' Then to the Connaught for dinner with Gore Vidal and Burt Sheve-

---

1. Elaine Dundy: 'No need to mince words: it is necessary to correct the false impression which Ken spread that his sexual sadism only involved playful spankings, for while they could serve as an aperitif, to arouse him, the headmaster's cane was his instrument of choice. To cane a woman on her bare buttocks was what gave him his greatest satisfaction . . . Although I deeply hated it, deeply hated it in theory and in practice, I submitted to his flagello-mania on five different occasions, one lasting a week, and broke four canes. Each time I did it, it was for the craven reason to keep him for myself.' 29 October 1994, the *Independent Magazine*.
2. Mark Littman (1920–). QC, company director; Marguerite Littman (1934–). American-born socialite and dialect coach for British-based productions about the American South.

love. Gore is not a bit surprised that Governor George Wallace was on Nixon's list of political 'enemies', indeed, he says he is convinced that Nixon engineered the attempted assassination of Wallace during the 1972 election campaign.

Last night, just after midnight, I was physically attacked by a man for the first time since Kathleen's first husband brought me down with a flying tackle in the driveway of her mother's house ten years ago. We were driving home from a restaurant near Covent Garden (Tennessee and Gore were among the other guests) when a lorry stopped in front of us, blocking the road, and two more behind me. The drivers calmly got out and disappeared into late-night cafés. Annoyed as I always am by the way in which market personnel assume that the whole area around the garden belongs to them after 11 p.m. I honked my horn, hoping either (a) to lure the drivers out of their cafés or (b) to attract a copper and lodge a complaint. A cop certainly arrived, but when I explained why I was honking he said he was going to prosecute me for unnecessary use of the horn. The lorry ahead now moved on and the PC asked me to pull over into a loading bay near the market. As I did so, a porter sitting with some friends on a pile of crates threw a piece of metal at the car, hitting the radiator and scratching it. I got out and told him crisply to fuck off. To my alarm, he rushed at me from a distance of about ten yards, bashed me in the chest, kneed me in the stomach and grappled me with all the strength of his twenty-odd years. The cop watched without interfering until the porter's chums had pulled him off me, and then finished taking down the number of my car etc. Three days later my ribs are still bruised and I can neither breathe fully nor cough without considerable pain. It is not quite comfort enough to hear (from Mark Littman) that this incident fits in with a general pattern of mounting class-conscious violence throughout the country in recent months.

26 June

To the first night of *Magnificence* at the Royal Court, a play by Howard Brenton about the possibility of revolution in England, which, like many similar plays, spends 90 per cent of its time explaining how neurotic, paranoiac and ineffective revolutionaries are, and only 10 per cent demonstrating why revolution is necessary. The percentages should, of course, be reversed; but it seems that no English playwright can face the derision that the critics would pour on any writer who made that his priority.

Before the curtain we met in the bar Milton Shulman[1], who told me that I owed my job on the *Evening Standard* in 1952 to the fact that he had read a brilliant article on the London Critics that I had written under a pseudonym for an undergraduate magazine; he had shown it to the Editor of the *Evening Standard*, Charles Curran. Curran, much impressed, had passed it to his drama critic, Beverly Baxter, who was fiercely attacked in the article; and this was why Baxter attacked my performance in the Alec Guinness *Hamlet*. All very plausible: except that the article in question, devastating piece of work, was written not by me but by Gavin Lambert.[2] So I owe my launching as a newspaper critic to a complete misapprehension.

30 June

Dinner at Ava Gardner's: guests include Patrick Garland[3] (whose production of *Twelfth Night* in Worcester Gardens, which I saw two weeks ago, was the most joyful and moving Shakespearian occasion I've attended for years: real Cavalier stuff after the Roundhead aridities of Stratford, totally unafraid of such unmodish qualities as emotional impact and – worst of all – charm: a heartbreakingly passionate Viola, a lovely and not over-guyed Sir Andrew and quite the best Malvolio I've ever seen, an extremely careful and bombastic speaker with no aspirates and all vowels very slightly 'off' in the Edward Heath manner. Modern dress and lyrical rock music, but for convenience's sake only: no modern parallels intruded, thank God. The finals, with the lovers rowing away across the lake while fireworks zoom up from the farther shore, almost rivalled Nevill Coghill's[4] Reinhardtian miracle in the same setting just after the war, when he ended *The Tempest* by having Ariel run out towards

1. Milton Shulman (1918–). Canadian-born film and theatre critic; mainly for the London *Evening Standard*, 1948–96.
2. Gavin Lambert (1924–). British critic, novelist, and screenwriter.
3. Patrick Garland (1935–). British writer, director and producer; Artistic Director of Chichester Festival Theatre, 1980–84, 1991–94.
4. Nevill Coghill (1899–1980). Merton Professor of English, Oxford, 1952–66; influential Shakespeare director, Oxford University Dramatic Society, 1934–66.

Prospero's departing ship apparently *across the water* but actually on a wooden jetty two inches below the surface; after which, retracing his steps, he spirited up a vast ramp to the top of a distant tree, where he vanished in a sudden magnesium flare, seeming literally to have been swallowed up by his native element, the air) and the Gregory Pecks.

Jack Benny looked in after dinner and, as usual, flattered me by remembering every detail of our first meetings, when I was just beginning on the *Evening Standard* twenty-two years ago. Just as I am marvelling at his total recall, he jolts me by telling a story about Noël Coward which he included in his memorial tribute to Noël. It is actually a story – and a very feeble one – about Henry Sherek,[1] as I know because I was present when Sherek delivered the pay-off line to Jack in the Caprice. (Story concerns Jack B. complaining that the British say *Ee*-velyn Laye[2] while the Americans say *Evv*-elyn. *Sherek*: 'But you must remember, Jack – *we were here first.*' Only Benny would find this funny in the first place, let alone worth retelling after twenty years, and attributing to Noël Coward.)

1 July

Loss of interest in sex lately due to guilt induced by K. We try to make love this morning and make no headway at all. Even deeper sense of guilt afterwards. *The self-disgust I feel at being unable to fuck K. makes me feel more self-disgusted than ever.* Can this be what is known as a vicious circle? (Compare and contrast: vicious circle and double bind.)

5 July

Much of what we call love is in fact mutually indulged laziness. We find each other's eyes, as objects of contemplation, far more rewarding than blank sheets of paper furled around typewriter cylinders.

9 July

Have been reading *Temporary Kings*, the latest in Anthony Powell's mystifyingly revered sequence of novels. Perhaps significantly, the

---

1. Henry Sherek (1900–67). Theatre producer.
2. Evelyn Laye (1900–96). Actress and singer, whose career spanned more than fifty years.

longest quote on the dustjacket comes from something published by the University of Manitoba Press: Powell is a natural for thesis-seekers. Whenever I read him, especially in the late books, I'm amazed that a writer so grammatically insecure, so prolific in blurred, circuitous sentences, should be held up for admiration as a stylist. The impression left by the series is of a man recording, with bland satisfaction, the depredations made by time and sexual and social climbing on his closest friends. This latest book, virtually without action of any kind, is boring gossip raised to the level of – gossip. He is the Jennifer of Quality Lit.

16 July

Nicole: I'm not an afraid person. (I think this is true.)

17 July

Trevor Griffiths asks me what I mean by a humanist. I say: A humanist is someone who remembers the faces of the people he spanks.

19 July

Every theatre is limited by the social and moral background of its actors. After years of prompting from me, the NT is at last doing *The Bacchae*: and having seen a run-through (and discussed it with the director, Roland Joffe) I now wonder if it was wise to attempt it. This great play is about the need to *accept* the element of outrage, violence and sexuality in our natures. Pentheus, who seeks to deny it, is destroyed by Dionysus in consequence. The Bacchantes, female followers of Dionysus, should be naked. But none of the girls will strip: if *they* cannot come to terms with their own nakedness, how can the play communicate the full hot blast of its message? Likewise Roland wants Cadmus to wear a false phallus when he dances to Dionysus: the actor, a pious Catholic, said he would rather give up the part. (And actors in repertory companies can exert such pressure far more effectively than in the commercial theatre: they cannot be fired from the company, since they are needed for other plays in the repertoire.) Roland interestingly points out that working in a predominantly classical repertory has undesirable side-effects on the actors: it makes them unduly conscious of their dignity, gives them a sense of 'respectability'. The other plays in the rep rub off on them and may unfit them for genuinely experimental work.

21 July

Preview of *Equus*. It works better than I had ever thought: and to my surprise I find it deeply moving. The truth is that I identify with the hippophile boy whose strange 'perverted' desires P. Shaffer is at such pains to extol and preserve. In all the people who are shocked by his peculiar ways I see those who have despised my love of spanking.

'The vibration acts directly upon the spinal nerve-system . . . the spanker transfers his wrath to the great will-centres in the child, and these will-centres react intensely, are vivified and educated.' (D.H. Lawrence on spanking.)

30 July

Note how a humbly democratic attitude towards oneself can lead to megalomania – *via* the argument: I refuse to believe that I am unique; therefore what I feel and think must be felt and thought by millions of others; therefore I can safely generalise and legislate from my own example.

6 August

'What we're getting, Dave, over Watergate, is the backlash of the groundswell of the backwash of the grassroots, wouldn't you say?' (Imaginary overheard)

7 August

Song of the Soccer groupie:

Cocks –
I've had a few –
From Nobby Stiles[1]

---

1. Nobby Stiles (1942–). Former Manchester United and England midfielder; one of the heroes of the 1966 English World Cup victory.

To Peter Osgood.[1]
Leeds – Don Revie[2] too –
That Eddie Gray[3] –
He really was good.
Best, and Bobby Moore –
And even Alf[4]
(Though in a shy way) –
But more,
Much more than this,
I fucked Steve Heighway.[5]

8 August

Title for my autobiography: *Sans Taste*.

9 August

From a dream:

Robert Graves[6]: What are you like as an actor?
K.T.: Irredeemably competent.

10 August

I am slowly developing the habit of indifference. I am learning how not to feel very strongly about anything. With this withdrawal of emotion goes a withdrawal of energy: only the basic needs – food and sex – now really rouse me from torpor. I shall die writhing in apathy.

12 August

Title for autobiography: *Independently Blue* – from 'Love Me Or Leave Me', the old Ruth Etting[7] song.

1. Peter Osgood (1947–). Former football star for Chelsea and Southampton.
2. Don Revie (1927–89). Managed the England team in the seventies.
3. Eddie Gray (1948–). Former Leeds United left-wing.
4. Sir Alf Ramsey (1920–99). Manager of England in its only World Cup victory in 1966.
5. Steve Heighway (1947–). Football coach and former star of the Ireland team.
6. Robert Graves (1895–1985). Author, poet, novelist, and classical scholar.
7. Ruth Etting (1907–78). American torch singer and Ziegfeld girl; enjoyed a brief comeback in the late forties.

14 August

I have just come across some notes I kept of Michael Blakemore's excellent opening address to the cast when he began rehearsals for his production of *The Cherry Orchard* at the N.T. earlier this year. He said the play was, as Chekhov had described it, a comedy, and not, as English actors so often performed it, 'an appeal for distressed gentlefolk'. He defined Chekhov's version of the comic spirit as 'common sense carried to a positively seditious degree'. He advised the cast to approach their parts as one approaches one's best friends – 'with affection, some delight in their existence, and absolutely *merciless* judgement'.

> The least sentence costs me an effort; talking, moreover, is almost as painful as writing. And I must admit too that I was becoming difficult: at the least suspicion of a thought, some cantankerous critic, always hiding deep in my mind, would rise up to ask: 'Are you sure that it's worth the trouble to . . .?' And, since the trouble was enormous, the thought immediately withdrew.
>
> (Gide's Journal, November 1904.)

17 August

Contentment is always bought at the price of one's liberty: that is what distinguishes it from happiness. And (in fairness one must add) from misery as well.

> A great drowsiness benumbs me from my awakening until evening; games occasionally shake it off, but I am gradually losing the habit of effort . . . sensual pleasure permeates everything; my finest virtues are dissipated and even the expression of my despair is blunted.
>
> (Gide, September 1905.)

And I was blaming it all on amphetamines! I expect in fact that what Gide and I have in common is simply the torpor that comes from having a little money.

The past ten days I spent with Kathleen and the children in a cottage in Wales near Harlech. There were gales and lashing rain for nine days, during which work was impossible because of depression, followed – familiar pattern! – by one day so idyllic that work was impossible because of happiness. We drove to Llanberis and picnicked in the ruins of the castle, where I improvised for Roxana the sad tale of the Fair Lady of Llanberis who, while her husband was away at the Crusades, rode off with the Black Baron of Barmouth. At this point a handsome, solitary young man in a black leather jerkin and black boots, with long Byronic hair and a bandit-style beard and moustache, walked into sight: feigning not to see him, I was able to persuade Roxana that she had seen the ghost of the Black Baron. She was delighted. We drove on to Naut Falls – one of the lovely little domesticated waterfalls in which Wales abounds: hundreds of gushing currents all in the space of a reasonably sized back garden – and then a few miles further on, we climbed through a hole in a barbed-wire fence to survey what our guidebook called 'the Mysterious Lake with the Mysterious Island' – mirror-smooth, deserted except for the odd sheep dotting the banks, and reflecting a hump-backed island in the middle, purple with heather, basking there like a great whale. Finally back to the cottage via a hillside single-track road behind Beddgellert, where we stopped for tea at a large country house hotel, attracted by a hand-written sign that said, categorically: 'SLOWLY, PLEASE – PEACOCKS.'

I am really very good at fantastic tales for children. During our week of storms, I have been amusing Roxana with a series of stories about Roy Jenkins[1] (who was to have spent last weekend with the Harlechs but cried off). My Roy Jenkins is a society-crazed super-snob who will go to any lengths and adopt any subterfuge to get into parties to which he hasn't been invited – and from which, easily unmasked, he is promptly ejected. Her favourite is the tale of how Roy Jenkins dressed up as the Duchess of Sutherland (whose invitation he had stolen) to gain admittance to the Royal Garden Party, and how he entered for the Queen's Obstacle Race, caught his wig and zipper on a nail while crawling through a pipe, and emerged in his underpants, to be instantly and ignominiously thrown out of the Palace grounds.

1. Roy Jenkins (1920–). Welsh political leader; co-founded the Social Democratic Party (1981), and MP from 1948–87.

K.H. suggests that we should collaborate on a children's book. I should like to include some of the animal poems I made up in Ceylon, e.g.:

As the moon wanes, the mighty Moose
Commits the act of self-abuse.

Look, here comes the jaunty Coypu!
Can it be a girl or boy-pu?

Behold, behold the plangent Yak.
He bears the world upon his back.
He mourns each loss, he wails each lack.
He goes away, and then comes back.

The rifle barked, the native guide fell dead.
'Have I done well?' Sir Eric Blossom said.
'No, you buffoon,' observed his wife Anita.
'I said shoot [the] Bee-Eater, not [the] beater.'

If you adopt an orphaned Rhino,
He may bring mud in on the lino.

It cannot be claimed that the specious Herring
Excels in deeds of do or derring.

Who sits at the wheel of that luxury car?
The mad, fun-loving Budgerigar.

'If I weren't such a fake,'
Moaned the False Palm Civet,
'I'd be as right
As a bloody trivet.'

In Dublin Bay there swam a Prawn
Who cursed the day that he was born.
'Jim Joyce has gone, and Brendan's dead.
Begorah, I'll be next,' he said.

The Caribou,
To name but a few,
Puts fluff and Tampax
Down the loo.

The Quail subsists on eggs and bacon
Until to heaven he is taken.

On the way home, I saw a Cobra.
Of both of us, he was the soberer.

George with his sword two mighty Saurians cleft
In twain, so that four separate bits were left.
The wrong bits mended, leaving on the Nile
A crocodator and an Alligile.

18 August

I lie awake at night craving comfort, reassurance, succour, forgiveness from K. Is this what I am really saying to her – 'Please forgive me for hurting you. Then I can go away and hurt you some more?'

19 August

A new play, *Cromwell* by David Storey,[1] has opened at the Royal Court: the reviews say it is a bleak, wintery panorama of war seen from the underside, a sort of Son of *Mother Courage* with decor by (who else?) Jocelyn Herbert.[2] It is compared to Edward Bond[3] (of the same theatre) and those who like it say that it commands respect, assuming of course that one likes being commanded. I know I shall never see it. It is the biggest disaster in the current English theatrical scene that one of the two leading national companies (the RSC) and the leading avant-garde theatre (the Royal Court) should both be run by aesthetic puritans –

---

1. David Storey (1933–). British dramatist and novelist, among his best-known work *In Celebration* (1969), *Home* (1970), *This Sporting Life* (1960), a novel turned into a film by Lindsay Anderson.
2. Jocelyn Herbert (1917–). British stage designer.
3. Edward Bond (1934–). Controversial British playwright, author of, among others, *Saved* (1985), *Lear* (1972), *The Fool* (1973).

with the NT itself conceivably going puritan under P. Hall. If only there were a dash of verve, colour, panache at the Court: it is nowhere to go for anything but a twisted smile, instantly to be wiped off the face. But I expect that to people like Lindsay A.,[1] showmanship is deeply suspect and colours like magenta are downright sinful. This sort of grimness was inherent in the Royal Court from the start, though in those days it was tempered by the occasional flamboyance of people like Tony Richardson and (verbally at least) the early Osborne. But I recalled the prophetic words of Orson Welles to the cast of a dour, downbeat musical called *The Lilywhite Boys*: 'There are many things it is permissible and desirable to do to an audience. You can provoke them, you can alarm them, you can put rockets under them and turn flamethrowers on them. But what you cannot do, in any circumstances, is to unzip your flies and pee on them.'

23 August

Freud says one must forego sensual pleasure in favour of cultural achievement. Reich says cultural achievement is valueless unless one has sensual pleasure. Following Reich, I refuse to work on my book about Reich for more than four to five hours a day, and devote the rest to pleasure. This inevitably cuts down my achievement. Thus: in order to write a Reichian book about Reich, I must delay writing a book about Reich.

24 August

Gide on returning from Turkey:

What a relaxation it is to have enlarged on the map the space one no longer wants to go and see! For too long I believed (out of love of exoticism, out of fear of chauvinistic self-satisfaction, and perhaps out of modesty), I thought that there was more than one civilisation, more than one culture that could rightfully claim our love and deserve our enthusiasm . . . Now I know that our Occidental (I was about to say French) civilisation is not only the most beautiful; I believe, I know that it is the *only* one . . .

1. Lindsay Anderson (1923–94). British theatre and film director; including many of David Storey's plays and a seminal production of Joe Orton's *What the Butler Saw* at the Royal Court Theatre.

I think so too, and wish the matter were more openly debated. For instance: can we imagine a Chinese writing that about his civilisation? (I know the Chinese think *they* are superior, as a *people*, but as a civilisation . . .?) Is Europocentrism merely conditioning? Or has it some objective validity? After all, one civilisation has to be better than the others, and how many competitors are there? (Egypt suggests itself: certainly it lasted as long and longer).

K. discovers that today is the tenth anniversary of the first time we fucked. It was at the Edinburgh Festival, 1963; and we stayed at the George Hotel. Great sense of thanksgiving.

25 August

There is one important way in which I need not be sorry for K. Never in her life has she experienced what for most people is the most powerful, savage, heart-rending and unforgettable experience in their lives – and one which is constantly and agonisingly repeated – I mean the experience of rejection – bear in mind that what she is going through for the first (and probably last) time is what 90 per cent of the human race expect to go through whenever they make a pass at a member of the opposite sex. She is like a member of an exclusive club who has lost – for some inexplicable reason – her right to park anywhere for any length of time and to use any other car parked within a mile's radius. 90 per cent of the rest of us are pedestrians, and have been so since our teens.

1 September

Embarked on gastronomic tour of Southern France with K. Lyon is now the eating capital of Europe with six three-star restaurants within its reach, including the reigning maestro Paul Bocuse, at Collages. On the way to Lyon we had a superlative lunch at the Hotel de la Poste, Avallon, which inexplicably lost its third star some years ago and which I have always found one of the half-dozen best restaurants in Europe. Last night inflation hit us at Drouant, a Paris restaurant, where dinner for three with one bottle of wine cost £50. (Ten years ago it would have been £20.) I urge K. to write a piece about Lyon into which she would incorporate all our conclusions about French *cuisine* – e.g. that the following are always terrible: *quenelles de brochet* (towel soufflé), cream sauces (especially with mushrooms), *foie gras* (liver ice-cream), *bouillabaisse* (as opposed to delicious *soupe de poissons*) and LOBSTER in all its (coarse, rubbery, tasteless) forms.

2 September

A sentence Michael Frayn[1] might have written:

> With ruthless clarity and unsparing candour, he worshipped his own virtues. So did his assistant, Peggy. With this shared assumption, they were able to work together on a footing of complete equality.

6 September

I was naked in public today for the first time in my life. After our eating tour of France we are spending a few days in St Tropez. Most of the beaches here have been topless for several years; now there is a whole stretch of rocky coast near L'Escalet beach where nudity is permitted. How long will it be before the rest of the Mediterranean coast catches up with sanity? (I recall how, only three years ago, Kathleen declined to join me in looking for an alleged nude beach in Sardinia, supposedly because a woman she didn't like very much might be there.)

The eating trip was immense. Highlights: Chez la Mère Charles at Mionnay, near Lyon, newly graced with its third Michelin star and amply living up to it. (I had *salade de pieds de mouton* with a sharp, clean mayonnaise I can still taste; *pâté d'anguilles en croûte*; cold *aiguillette de boeuf en gelée*, braised in champagne; and some staggering pastry.

Also memorable: the ever-magnificent Hotel de la Poste at Avallon (*poulet en civet*, with the superb blood sauce); and the Auberge de Noves, grandest of overnight halts, a luxe mansion outside Avignon where I had *caneton en papillote aux herbes de Provence* and a *soufflé grand Marnier*

---

1. Michael Frayn (1933–). British journalist, novelist, playwright, best known for his backstage farce *Noises Off* (1982).

that was more alcoholic than anything else I can recall *eating*. The patron here told me that in his opinion and that of most of the profession the best restaurant in France was Troisgros at Roanne (where I overate once, and left with a rather warped impression of the place). 'Whenever I go there,' he said, 'there is always one dish – often very simple, perhaps just a kidney cooked in a pan – that I know I could never make.' Of the Hotel de la Poste, he said that the patron, M. Hure, had made the error of not training anyone to succeed him: 'He has no children. When the night comes he just wants to turn off the lights. There is no glow any more.' He confirmed that, although it has caused him to suffer greatly (by chopping off his third star some years ago), the Michelin was still far and away the best gastronomic guide in existence. His own list of the best restaurants:

Troisgros (Roanne)
Lasserre (Paris)
Bocuse (Collages)
Auberge de l'Ill (Illhausern)
Moulin de Mougins (Mougins)

(The last two I haven't tried.) My own list:

Le Tour d'Argent (Paris)
La Marée (Paris)
Auberge de Noves
Chez la Mère Charles
Hotel de la Poste (Avallon)

9 September

For lunch and dinner to Tony Richardson's private village in the hills behind St Tropez. It consists of eight or nine cottages he bought seven years ago and knocked together into a rambling living unit that trickles down the side of a valley to a swimming-pool. Exquisite place and nice people, including Annie Ross[1] and Sean Lynch, and John Gielgud. I see

---

1. Annie Ross (1930–). British singer famously part of the popular vocal trio Lambert, Hendricks and Ross, 1958–62.

that John is about to read *The Joint* by James Blake: he asks me what it's about:

K.T.: It's about a masochistic convict who keeps getting himself imprisoned because he likes being sucked off by sadistic Negro murderers.

J.G.: Well, you can't quarrel with that.

J.G. does not swim and explains that like all his family he has had a lifelong horror of water. 'I even used to hate washing,' he remarks. 'I was a very dirty little boy.' Inconsequently he goes on to reveal that as a child he used to eat rubber – 'the elastic out of my suspenders, rubber bands, anything I could get my hands on'. A deeply eccentric man. At the end of dinner (taken al fresco by a mixture of moonlight and fairy-lights), he suddenly starts and cries: 'Good God! What on earth's happened to Grizelda?' Grizelda (Tony's current girlfriend) was sitting – as she had been all evening – on his left. He had temporarily omitted to notice her existence. Also at Tony's (for lunch): a splendid middle-aged Frenchwoman named Anne-Marie Savile, prominent in the Resistance, whose Anglophilia is so strong that she calls her three dogs Simpson, Fortnum and Mason, and changed her name from Schumann to Savile (after Savile Row).

10 September

A literally diabolical dream, nauseating and mephitic, with a real whiff of the pit: I awoke dry-mouthed with terror. I meet a masochistic girl, in her mid-thirties, perhaps American, not beautiful but vivacious. Together we visit several Soho bookshops, where she buys some spanking magazines. I notice the proprietor of one of the magazines taking an interest in her. He is a real person I have met: a grey-faced ageless young man with close-cropped hair and a permanent two-day growth, who looks like the Artful Dodger a week dead. Some time later I return to the shop, with a (male) friend. We discover the girl in the cellar. She is naked, covered with dust and shit-stains. Her hair has been shaved off and *dozens of drawing-pins have been driven into her head.* We learn that the shopkeeper has kept her down here for days. He has made her lick up and eat his excrement. He has forced her to make love to corpses. She can now barely speak and resembles something between Falconetti in *La Passion de Jeanne d'Arc* and an inmate of Auschwitz. And all this is my fault. What is to be done? You must get her out of it, says my friend. But the shopkeeper is in with the heavy mob, and if I rescue the girl, they will either kill or castrate me. And after all – and most sickening of all – *perhaps she likes it.* At this point I wake up filled with horror. And, at once, dogs in the hotel grounds began to bark pointlessly, as they are said to do when the King of Evil, invisible to men, passes by. I really felt as if my mind had been the temporary harbour of an evil spirit, sent to deliver an obscure and obscene warning. The sense of evil I felt was tangible enough to be an objective reality.

11 September

There are writers who have written themselves out at forty; and there are writers who have written themselves *in*. There is no third kind.

11 October

Memory of a lifelong socialist who, pointing to his cringing ten-year-old son, said to Philip Toynbee: 'If there's one thing I hate, it's racialism. And I've told that lad there that if I ever hear him calling a Negro gentleman a nigger, I'll give him a leathering he'll remember till the day he dies.' 'It's things like that,' Philip brooded, 'that shake one's faith in the proletariat.'

16 October

Life is a bountiful murderer. It comes to us bearing an armful of gifts, of which the last is a knife to the heart. It is like a Christmas morning on which one of the presents is a letter bomb. That is if one is lucky.

18 October

Story, told to me by James Thurber,[1] to illustrate the gulf that often yawns between the European man of letters and the American. Once in New York Thurber was introduced to Cyril Connolly. The two men sat for a long time in awkward silence. Then the following exchange took place:

J.T.: Tell me, are you related to One-Eyed Connolly, the Kansas City bootlegger?
C.C.: (*guardedly*): I don't believe so.
End of conversation.

19 October

To his friends' dismay, Lord Harlech's breath is seldom free from garlic.

31 October

A vogue-word I really detest is 'relevant'. The de Filippo[2] play that opened at the National last night will probably be accused by the critics of lacking 'relevance', since it deals with a middle-class Neapolitan family in 1959. But what depths of egocentricity and parochialism the use of the word betrays! To demand that a work of art should be 'relevant' to southern English late-capitalist society in 1973 is to reveal an appallingly blinkered sensibility – and a dismaying lack of curiosity. The function of a work of art is to enable us to see through the eyes of *others* – and it is vulgar narcissism to insist that those eyes should be directed at ourselves. The de Filippo play is about Naples in the fifties; and to enjoy it we must assume that Naples in the fifties is as interesting as London in

---

1. James Thurber (1894–1961). Cartoonist and humorist. Tynan on Thurber, *Profiles*: 'James Thurber is four-fifths blind, a misfortune which may have helped to make him one of the funniest writers in the world . . . Like Milton and Mister Magoo, he lives in a true world of comedy, a world dimly discerned, private and remote, peopled with exaggerations: furtive, apprehensive men, women prophetic and horrific, and animals beyond the strangest imaginings of Edward Lear. The Common Thome, Hackett's Gorm, the White Sepulchre, and the Tantamount are some of the animals: he draws them either peering aghast over their shoulders or asleep. These two conditions – acute fright or deep coma – are the most prevalent in Thurber's universe.'
2. Eduardo de Filippo (1900–84). Italian actor and playwright.

the seventies or Moscow in the 1890s. We go to plays to learn about others; if we learn about ourselves in the process, that is a bonus; but it is not part of the prescription. Later: my fears were groundless. The play had ecstatic reviews in many daily and weekly papers. It was in fact the greatest critical success the NT has ever had. Not even a qualifying clause of doubt. Larry called me up at dawn the day the reviews appeared, to say: 'Congratulations. I couldn't believe my eyes.'

2 November

I hear that Barry Humphries[1] has composed a love song to be sung by his comic-strip hero Barry McKenzie[2]. It is called: 'How Can I Say I Love You, When I Can Hardly Breathe Down Here'.

5 November

K.: You're nothing but a little slut.
N.: Yes. But I'm a *friendly* little slut.

6 November

First reading of Trevor Griffiths' *The Party* at the NT. Larry in tremendous form as John Tagg, the Glasgow Trotskyite: his long speech at the end of the first act will be the most inspiring call to revolution ever heard on the English stage. How ironic – and splendid! – that it should be delivered by Larry from the stage of the NT! (During the night I have a dream in which I join a subversive organisation called the Socialist Lavatory League. Its purpose is to bring all private loos into public ownership. Everyone will have the right to use anyone else's loo: which will mean the end of private peeing. The dream wakes me up giggling, but on consideration I don't think it is all that bad an idea.) I have no doubt that the play will be a success. It's maddening that P. Hall's 1974 plans – which have to accommodate new productions by

---

1. Barry Humphries (1934–). Australian comedian and folklorist, creator and populariser of such comic characters as Sir Les Patterson, Barry McKenzie, and Dame Edna Everage, housewife-superstar.
2. 'Barry McKenzie', aka 'Bazza', foul-mouthed, hard-drinking comic-strip character drawn by Nick Garland, written by Barry Humphries, which appeared in *Private Eye*, 1963–73. Subsequently turned into two films, *The Adventures of Barry McKenzie* (1972) and *Barry McKenzie Holds His Own* (1974).

his numerous associate directors – preclude the possibility of giving *The Party* more than thirty-four performances. If it works as well as I expect, this predetermined curtailment will be nothing less than scandalous.[1]

During the morning reading, Larry passes a note to John Dexter. It reads, 'May I go about twelve-forty-five to stand outside Russian Embassy on account of the Panovs, please? (in this mature capitalist society).' The Panovs are the Russian-Jewish ballet dancers who, because they want to emigrate to Israel, have been refused exit visas *and* fired from their jobs in the Kirov company. I like the irony of 'this mature capitalist society' – quoting from the play, Larry is obliquely saying that at least mature capitalism permits one the right of public protest.

12 November

Nicole, discussing future plans: 'I could always go back and work for Plomley's. Plomley has a huge dent in his forehead because of the forceps. He divides Great Britain into bricks and headers and Bleeders and headers. Then he finds out from Tesco's or Scott's a list of the people they supply. And they all get it, whether they're bricks or headers. He has a wife named Pamela. They're all numbered, you see. It's easy when you get to Wales, because the population isn't so thick as it is in London.'

13 November

K.: You don't say many nice things to me.
N.: Mm. But I mean all the things I don't say.

---

1. Tynan to Peter Hall, 29 September 1973: 'The National has never imposed a guillotine on a play's run before it's opened . . . As I'm sure you did at the Aldwych, we always waited to assess the public and critical response before deciding one production's future. It is terribly damaging to Trevor's reputation, not to mention his purse, that the National should write his play off as a flop (thirty-four performances equals a month's run in the West End) before it is even in rehearsal. Has Harold Pinter's widely known dislike of the play got anything to do with this? Or has the play other enemies with other motives? Is the same axe going to fall on *Saturday, Sunday, Monday* when Frank and Larry leave? Is the new regime wielding a new broom or simply a purge . . . All in all, I cannot recall an occasion on which a greater blow has been dealt a talented writer at such a crucial stage of his career. Welcome to the big league, we say, and then slap his face and show him the door. Is there no way of repairing at least some of the damage before the repercussions begin to spread?'

16 November

Peevish and neurotic attack by John Osborne on Larry, the NT and (especially) me, in a new book of interviews called *Olivier*. He calls me 'a disastrous influence' and an example of 'intellectual spivvery' (a typical late-Osborne phrase − vaguely venomous, unsupported by evidence). I reply in the *Evening Standard* and in a letter to the *Sunday Times*; he replies to my reply in the *Standard*. All we are really doing is selling newspapers and (of course) the book. No one is enlightened, no one wins. But it does give me a chance to state publicly that the NT has had a higher percentage of successes over ten years, critical *and* box office, than any other theatre company in English history. It is pleasant to get that on the record. Larry calls to thank me; but of course mud like this does not affect his reputation. It could, however, damage mine.

18 November

Nicole: I'm terrified of stairs. If you'd never seen a flight of stairs and someone showed you one and said: 'Walk down that,' you wouldn't, would you? Have you ever fallen downstairs?
K.: No, have you?
N.: Masses of times.

Paul Getty III, grandson of the richest man in the world, was kidnapped last July in Italy. A ransom of £1,000,000 was demanded; Grandpa, who has roughly 1,000 million dollars, has refused to pay a cent. The seventeen-year-old boy's parents, who are divorced, did nothing. Last week his ear was sent through the post to his mother. We now learn that Grandpa is still holding out, maintaining that to pay up would constitute a precedent. The kidnappers have threatened to send one of the boy's feet next. No doubt Grandpa will continue to resist the pressure; after all, the lad is a prisoner-of-war in the battle of world capitalism, and must learn to take his medicine. What is a limb or two, measured against the loss of face that would be incurred if it were suspected for one moment that capitalism valued human life above property? I have no doubt that Getty will be praised for his grit and courage as, piece by piece, the dismembered carcass of his grandson speeds through the mails. What astounds me is that, although the case has been fully reported, not one word has been printed in criticism of this savage miser. (Later: the boy's parents finally provided the ransom – unaided, however, by Grandpaw.)

26 November

Nicole: My Uncle Willie invented the tap.

K.: What kind of tap?

N.: Like you get water out of. Only somebody got in ahead of him. And he invented a fire escape. Not *the* fire escape. *A* fire escape. He also invented mixing coal and concrete to make it burn longer. He died living in a caravan.

1 December

K. feeling ill, decides to go to the bathroom to try to be sick. Roxana pleads to accompany her: K. demurs. R.: 'Mummy, why can't I see you being sick?' Finally K. lets her in. A minute later R. scurries out and tells me: 'It's a terrible grapey green colour.' She scurries back. More sounds of discreet vomiting; then she returns with a new bulletin: 'Now it's red as well as greeny, with horrible little black spots in the middle.'

6 December

At dinner Gore Vidal bets me $1,000 that Nixon will be out of office by 1 April, next year. Cravenly, I refuse the bet, though I'm sure he can't be right. Gore is fascinating on the subject of E. Howard Hunt, the novelist, CIA man and Watergate conspirator who just may have had a hand in the killing of J.F.K. and the assassination attempt on Wallace. He tells K. a story he got from Princess Margaret about the meeting, at the Duke of Windsor's funeral, between the widow and the Queen Mother, who has always detested her. It seems the Duchess, nowadays a bit gaga, struck up conversation by saying: 'Is your kitchen upstairs or downstairs?' The Q.M., who is completely ignorant of her own domestic geography, replied that she didn't know. For several minutes the Widow Windsor talked about the relative merits of upstairs and downstairs kitchens and then moved away. Later during the wake she reappeared at the Q.M.'s elbow, staring glassily. Then she spoke. 'Tell me,' she said. 'Is your kitchen upstairs or downstairs . . .?'

Mention of bets reminds me of almost my last bet, a disaster that occurred nearly two decades ago. I had been to the opening of *South Sea Bubble* with Harold Clurman[1], a ghastly Coward play starring Vivien Leigh. Afterwards we went to supper with George[2] and Leueen[3] Kaufman, who were then living in London. Harold launched into an attack on the triviality of West End theatre, oblivious of the fact that one of the other guests, Robert Morley, was currently starring in the West End in a particularly trivial play of his own composition, called *A Likely Story*. Morley soon began to be rude about the American theatre in return. After a while I intervened on Harold's side (at that time the US theatre, with Miller and Williams at their best, was streets – or streetcars – ahead of ours). I said English audiences deserved better than they were getting. 'Nonsense,' said Robert. 'All that English audiences need, deserve or want is me and Noël in terrible plays written by ourselves.' Over-reacting, rising like a salmon to the lure, I said: 'I'll bet you a hundred pounds that your play is off inside three months.' (It had only just opened.) After a pause, Robert said: 'I think I shall have to accept that.' Solemnly we rose at the table and shook hands.

£100 then was a vast sum to me, so next morning I decided to do a little checking. I called the box-office of the Globe Theatre, where the Morley play was running, and asked how far ahead I could book seats. 'Oh, we're taking bookings right into the autumn,' said the box-office lady. It was then early spring. Robert had made his bet secure in the knowledge that he could not lose; the race, in fact, was fixed. Sharp practice, I thought, not the kind of thing one expected from 'Honest Bob', the darling of the Turf. I called him and taxed him with gambling on something he knew to be a certainty. 'Not at all,' he said. 'I might fall down and break my neck, mightn't I?' When the time for settlement came, I sneakily decided to pay him in kind rather than cash. I took out in his name (and that of his heirs and assignees, in the event of his death) a postal subscription for eighty-seven years to the

---

1. Harold Clurman (1901–80). Co-founder of the Group Theatre, director and indefatigable drama critic.
2. George S. Kaufman (1889–1961). Master comic playwright and director.
3. Leueen MacGrath (1914–92). Second wife of George S. Kaufman, she co-wrote the musical *Silk Stockings* (1955) with him.

Observer, whose drama critic I then was. As the weeks passed, the regular arrival on Monday morning of a paper he had already read on Sunday began to exasperate Robert, and he eventually telephoned me to protest. With an ill grace, I finally paid up; and it was no real consolation when, in the autumn, his terrible play came off.

9 December

Life on the twilight fringe: Nicole tells me of a girl named Sally Stamp born in the East End but richly married, who goes to restaurants naked under her raincoat. From time to time she opens the coat and tries to twist and bend her nipples, with whose natural conformation she is dissatisfied. Nicole has often gone into the ladies' loo at the A.D.8 restaurant to find Sally and a girlfriend sitting on adjoining seats, chatting about the price of meat as they stuff cocaine up their noses in little silver shovels. Sally's husband filmed the birth of their child, which almost died when the umbilical cord got wound around its neck. They now run the film backwards for friends after dinner. It shows a maniacal doctor apparently strangling a baby and then hastily stuffing the diminutive corpse back into the womb. (N.B. a friend of Sally's, a male tart named Vicki de Something – didn't catch surname – decided a few weeks ago that he needed a new start in life. He therefore changed his name to Louis de Rothschild. The real Rothschilds are livid but can do nothing. Meanwhile the former Vicki is loving it.)

21 December

Reviews of *The Party* are (apart from the *Guardian* and the *Evening Standard*) virulent. Far worse than any of us expected – even taking into account the faults of casting and production on which we had agreed a week or more ago. Once again, as with *Tyger*, one seeks an explanation in the high average age of drama critics, who are, after all, hired watchguards at the gate of a private party. If – like Trevor – you are hoping to conquer a castle, you must not expect too much eager collaboration from those whose life-work is to guard the castle gates. Or, to put it another way, if people are brought up by indoctrination and example to define 'drama' as that which resembles a rissole, there is no doubt that faced with a plate of raw meat, they are going to reject it on the grounds that it is not a rissole.

After the second night, Larry takes K. and me to supper at the Savoy Grill to celebrate my retirement after ten years at the NT. He has secretly planned a vast framed scroll of thankful signatories to mark our decade together (it won't be ready for a few weeks since many of the people involved are in other continents). I am splendidly wined and enormously gratified. He tells many stories of which I recall few (due to excellent drink); also K. has suddenly decided that she would like to write a biography of him and is thus reluctant to share her memory-bank with me. Larry reveals that the evangelical fervour he puts into the playing of John Tagg in *The Party* is based on his father's pulpit manner, while Tagg's clothes (an ageless, aged browny-green tweed suit; a shirt which has had the sleeves shortened to provide material for a new collar) come from his father-in-law (Mr Plowright). The hairstyle is borrowed from James Maxton, the old ILP Leader. The tie – a tattered old silk one – actually belonged to George Ralph, who (Larry tells me to my amazement) was a card-carrying member of the CP.

22 December

Among the classic tastes: bread sauce, Nuits St Georges Les Perdrix 1962, Worcestershire sauce, Toblerone, Bovril.

24 December

Christmas Eve dinner for George Weidenfeld, Min Hogg, John and Miriam Gross. K. and I marinate a saddle of venison for three days and serve it in a rich and complex sauce (with Nuits St Georges mentioned above), preceded by twelve oysters apiece (with Chassagne Montrachet '71) and followed by *Boccone Dolce*, a delicious chocolate-strawberry-meringue layer-cake copied from Sardi's (with Dom Perignon '64). A great success, so much so that George W. who seldom drinks became raffishly drunk, started to talk about pre-war Vienna, and invited us all to change into pyjamas and nighties. He ended by wearing a broad-brimmed and rather sportive summer hat of mine and a nightdress of K.'s slung round his neck. The Grosses were later found on our bed, an exceptionally anti-social thing for a husband and wife to do. There was later a quiz of my composition (identifying famous tits and bottoms, privately recorded voices of the famous and less famous revolutionary quotations) with champagne prizes. A memorable evening.

1974

3 January

Transition from dream to waking:

The new state college, a soaring structure of tinted glass and concrete, overlooks a loop of the river just outside Harper City. On fine days the sun, reflected from the shining towers, turns it into a pillar of fire. What is it called?

'Harper State College.'

'What?'

'Harper State. *Harper State*. Time to get up.'

One input-tube; two output-tubes, of which
One lengthens to assuage the carnal itch.

11 January

Replaying an old Miles Davis LP I recall one of my encounters with this satanic elf, this capricious potentate of jazz. Some time late in the fifties I went to Birdland to hear him. Between sets he joined our table for a drink, and chatted in his rasping whisper quite amiably. Suddenly we were approached by a timid white teenage boy with an autograph album. Nervously he asked Miles for a signature and as Miles obliged he said: 'I've always admired you, Mr Davis. I play trumpet in my high-school band and I think you have a wonderful embouchure. How do you get an embouchure like that?' Miles said casually: 'I got it from sucking off little white boys like you.' The boy absolutely froze. We all did. The words were spoken without passion, but they taught me more about black feeling towards whites than dozens of liberal fund-raising sessions with Sidney Poitier and Harry Belafonte.

12 January

Played the Conversation Game. This is a game of my own invention where – to enliven what promises to be a dull dinner party – you challenge your partners to work a particularly inappropriate phrase into the conversation without arousing attention. For instance, I once challenged George Harewood to say: 'Foolish little me!' and Pat Tuckwell (as she then was and, for me, still is) to say: 'Shiver my timbers.' Last night I thought of one ideally unsuitable thing for Cyril Connolly to say, viz. 'It's good to be back in Blighty.'

Leaden with sleeplessness. Film uncertain (more financing needed); two contracts for books unfulfilled, with heavy advances already spent; no more NT salary to pay tax; reduced royalties from *Calcutta*; inflation eating into savings; £25,000 loan to Markman Securities proving ominously difficult to reclaim.

Elaine's new novel, *The Injured Party*, contains a vicious and vengeful portrait of me as a sadist whose 'vile appetites' (her phrase) compel him to cover his wife with weals, 'some bleeding'. (The last two words are wonderfully horrid: I have never drawn anyone's blood and would hate to do so, as she well knows.)

20 February

Tried to relax by reading Beerbohm[1]. How perverse of him to think that the arch-sentimentalist Maeterlinck[2] was the greatest playwright of his era! I recall playing a lead at Oxford in *Pelléas et Mélisande* (with hair dyed blond and marcelled), ineptly directed by a man called John Boud. The production provoked me to compose a clerihew:

Such treatment of Maeterlinck
Is really most unsettling,
And shouldn't be allowed!
It was bloody, but Boud.

1. Max Beerbohm (1872–1956). Drama critic and essayist, best known for his novel about Oxford in the 1890s, *Zuleika Dobson*.
2. Maurice Maeterlinck (1862–1949). Belgian poet, playwright, essayist and philosopher, won the Nobel Prize for Literature in 1911.

23 February

I spend a weekend at a snug little hotel in Hampshire with Nicole. On Saturday morning we motor to Bournemouth, where I spent most of my summers up to the age of eighteen, and revisit the beaches and chines where I first learned about sex, masturbated to the devoutly awaited weekly magazine *London Life*, worshipped the concert party on Boscombe Pier, experimentally inserted the blunt ends of fountain-pens into the anus of my cousin Betty, contemplated suicide (at twelve) in the belief that I was pregnant, etc.

The trip is less traumatic than I had feared (and hoped): but as we drive along the front I notice that Phil Silvers – perhaps the greatest comedian I ever saw on the Broadway stage, king of the one-line impromptu, last survivor of the last generation of comics who were actually reared in burlesque, is appearing live at the Pavilion in *A Funny Thing Happened on the Way to the Forum*. Phil is an old friend and has never appeared in England: I did not even know he was in the country.

So we go to his hotel and call his room: it's 11.30 a.m. but his voice sounds impenetrably fogged and thick. He arranges to see us after the show (which is on tour in hopes of a London booking), but I conclude that he is hungover – which is odd, considering that when I knew him well in the States, he (like most Jewish comedians) was a teetotaller.

In the evening we see the show. The theatre is only half-full, and Phil, well, his timing is still flawless, his mime is exquisite, his mastery of the audience complete – but he moves haltingly and his voice is hoarse. I explain to Nicole that she has not seen the great man at his best. When we go backstage, he embraces me with real feeling (I'm always moved by the way Americans remember me with far more affection than Englishmen) and asks me what I thought of the show and him. I say that I loved him, and as soon as he recovers from his sore throat – At this his face falls. 'Thought I'd covered that up,' he says; and goes on to explain that two years ago, after a triumphant opening in Los Angeles, he had a stroke and spent ten weeks in the hospital, since which time he has had to learn to talk (and walk) all over again. I am appalled by my gaffe. He adds that he started rehearsal for the current production *on walking sticks*.

Over supper he tells us, with not the least trace of self-pity, that he has lately been divorced, leaving five daughters and an ex-wife to be supported. We reminisce about Jack Benny and Groucho (and the girls

I introduced to Phil when he first visited England – Kay Kendall, Claire Bloom and Jill Bennett were among them: like many of these Jewish non-drinkers, he has total recall). We laugh a lot: but I have the bleak and comfortless premonition that he may not have long to live. I hate the fact that I never devoted a full-length essay to this matchless, whiplash clown, now slowed down so much by infirmity that he might be performing underwater. Even in this shape, however, he is better value than all but a tiny handful of British comics – among them, of course, Eric Morecambe, to whom Phil pays characteristically generous tributes.

3 April

Harper's Bazaar is the Third Avenue *Elle*.

4 April

I have now been working non-start since January.

To Greenwich to see Jonathan Miller's production of *Hamlet* (with Robert Stephens, who wants to play the lead in my spanking film, as Claudius). Once again I reflect how neatly it would fit the play if Hamlet were in fact Claudius' bastard, the fruit of his liaison with Gertrude. The affair has been going on for decades before it finally erupts into murder: and what an edge this gives to Claudius' first line to Hamlet:

And now our cousin Hamlet, *and our son*.

And to the reply:

A little more than King, and less than kind . . .
I am too much *i'th'* sun.

Not to mention the sense it makes of the enigmatic exchange between the two when Hamlet leaves for England and addresses Claudius as his 'mother': 'Father and mother is man and wife, man and wife is one flesh, and so – my mother.' I am not saying that this was the author's intention, but it would not be a *betrayal* of his intention to stage the play in this light.

5 April

J.B. Priestley's *Eden End* confirms Tynan's Post-Decade-of-Dramaturgy principle – i.e. all plays written in the thirties are lousy. The late twenties are fine – *The Front Page, Dangerous Corner* – and in the early forties we get *Blithe Spirit* and *Present Laughter*, but everything in between is virtually unrevivable. Partly this is because the abolition of theatre censorship now makes us aware of all the evasions into which playwrights were forced by the Lord Chamberlain. As soon as the action demands outspokenness on political, sexual or theological matters, the author coyly sidesteps and we notice it. This kind of thing is less obtrusive in earlier plays where candour on such subjects was infrequent in the social circles about which dramatists normally chose to write: but in the thirties, there was a lot of plain talk about politics, God and sex, and the discrepancy between reality and stage fiction is intolerably glaring. Afterwards, in the forties and fifties, the Lord Chancellor began to be more liberal, and the gap, though still visible, is less offensive. It isn't only this effect of censorship, however, that undermines these thirties plays: it's their dreadful, swampy sentimentality – the sentimentality of Odets, Maxwell Anderson, St John Ervine – so soggy after the astringent wit of the twenties. A postscript on *Eden End*: it is as if *The Seagull* had been written by Trigorin. (Priestley is 'a very clever writer – but not as good as Chekhov'.)

6 April

I coin a new Learish name for K. – the Tufty Roo. (Tufty as to the head; roo all the way down.)

My solution to the problem of monogamy: to separate sexual fidelity from personal love and affection. The method: to make marriage permanent and indissoluble, but at the same time, make sexual infidelity compulsory for both partners who would be required to prove that in the course of each calendar year they had slept with a stated number of people other than their spouses. (The number to be determined by reference to the subject's health, intensity of sexual appetite, etc.)

7 April

Nicole: A cunt always reminds me of a blind eye.

8 April

Nicole: You're not a masochist, you're a bum-flasher.

Later: I only flash my bum to pretty people. I never flash it to gross people.

9 April

In today's *Times* Bernard Levin[1] fulsomely congratulates the press on defying the *sub judice* rules and printing follow-up stories on the Wilson[2]-Marcia Williams[3] land-speculation affair. He omits to point out it was the Tory press that led the pack, for obvious political reasons; nor does he mention the fact that when the American press began to expose the Watergate scandal, thus knocking a political figure Levin admired, he wrote a column accusing the *Washington Post* of conducting a trial by newspaper. When Watergate began to break, I went to a lunch at the Hartwells'[4] for Arthur Schlesinger,[5] who answered questions afterwards on the implications of the affair. In the course of the discussion I asked Lord Hartwell: 'If a couple of your reporters on the *Daily Telegraph* had come up with a story like that about Ted Heath, and the Tory Party, would you have printed it?' His reply was candid and succinct: 'Certainly not,' he said. So much for the bold muckrakers of Fleet Street.

---

1. Bernard Levin (1928–). British journalist and author.
2. Harold Wilson, Lord Wilson of Rievaulx (1916–95). Labour Prime Minister 1964–70, 1974–76.
3. Marcia Williams (Baroness Falkender) (1932–). Wilson's secretary, whose elevation to Baroness on the Honours List created a press furore.
4. Lord Hartwell (1911–). Chairman and editor-in-chief of the *Daily Telegraph*, 1954–87.
5. Arthur Schlesinger, Jr. (1917–). American educator, historian.

28 April

A fiasco of a week's holiday in Tunis with K. Gales and rain most of the time, four hired cars (three broke down, surely a record even for Avis), and my luggage deftly sent to Marseilles on the way home. One reasonable pun:

Q.: What do they call members of Tunisian families who go to the bad?
K.: Berber black sheep.

Outlook bleak on all my fronts – the film (out of which I *insanely* and *cravenly* let Kathleen talk me two years ago) seems to be a receding possibility – I can't find the remaining $150,000 necessary to complete the budget of $500,000. (The last time I remember feeling *confident* was two years ago when I returned from Egypt. Now, assurance corroded, energy depleted, would I be capable of directing the film even if the money was there?) The Reich book is hopelessly blocked: I'm stuck halfway through, and have lost control of my material (as well as interest in it). This carries with it debts to publishers and *The New Yorker* in excess of £10,000. Then there are two years back taxes to pay; not to mention the £25,000, and assurance of feminine approbation.

2 May

Last night to the Old Vic for the première of John Hopkins'[1] *Next of Kin*, directed by Pinter – the first new play under the Peter Hall regime. I read it last year, when it was about four hours long, and found it tedious: Peter H. didn't like it either: but Pinter adored it and, true to his policy of letting his associates have their own way, Peter let him do it. It's a bleak and monotonous exposé of suburbia: family life revealed as a hotbed of frustration, infidelity and rat-race competition, hyper-familiar stuff directed by Harold with chromium polish. But how arid and *juiceless*! And also how typical of a Hall administration. Whatever Peter's virtues may be it would be madness to go to one of his productions (or one presented under his aegis) in the expectation of being moved to tears either of laughter or of grief. You will get clarity,

---

1. John Hopkins (1917–98). Playwright known for his taut, bleak TV dramas.

tact, restraint, lucid exposition (*vide The Wars of the Roses*) – all the Cambridge virtues – but you will not be made to *feel*: that vulgar weapon is not in P.H.'s armoury. Look at the people with whom he has surrounded himself: Pinter, Schlesinger, Jonathan Miller, Michael Kustow[1]. I note with some pleasure that Michael Billington in today's *Guardian* expresses serious doubts about the current direction of policy at the NT. I really think Larry and I presided over a golden age. Granted, we started with one let-down, *Hamlet*. But Peter has started with three.

5 May

I read in Alan Watts' autobiography, *In My Own Way*, that alcohol is best taken rectally instead of orally. Since I know this to be true of sleeping pills (suppositories are much healthier than the oral kind), I madly determine to try it. So Nicole and I return from eating a peppery Indian dinner to Emma Gordon's flat, where we are spending the weekend, with a half-bottle of vodka with which to make the experiment. Nicole injects a large wine-glass of vodka into my anus *via* an enema tube. Within ten minutes the agony is indescribable. I am squirming as if Prussic acid had been squirted into my colon. The astringent vodka tightens the rectal passage and inflames the mucous membranes: so that I spend a sleepless night, followed by a tormented day, interspersed with visits to the loo every ten minutes – most of them abortive, since the diarrhoea is denied its natural outlet by the tightly compressed anus. In addition to the pain, I am bleeding copiously from the rectum. Poetic justice is thus visited upon me, anal fixatee that I am, and translated into farce. It takes forty-eight hours for the after-effects to subside (N.B. three days later I am still seeping blood). Oh, the perils of hedonism!

6 May

The only veil between ourselves and the Buddha-nature is our belief that there is a veil. (Zen paradox by K.T.)

---

1. Michael Kustow (1939–). British writer and producer.

7 May

What is my current profession? Drama critic: not since 1963. Impresario: not since *Oh! Calcutta!* four years ago. Nabob of National Theatre: not since last December. Journalist: virtually extinct. Film director: untested (at forty-seven). Author: blocked since January. Thus I have no active professional identity at all – a sepulchral prospect on which to wake up every morning. Were I to commit suicide, I would merely be killing someone who had already – to many intents and most purposes – ceased to exist. These grim reflections have had a markedly depressing effect on my libido. Sex in such a context seems as trivial as reading comics in a cancer ward. (Have today decided to leave some money to Nicole: told K. as much, and was relieved when she received the news without resentment.)

20 May

Nicole (explanatorily): Siss is a twee yuck.

(Explanation: the word 'siss' is used by prim schoolgirls to mean what less inhibited people mean by 'yuck' – i.e. 'how nauseating!')

21 May

> *Nel mezzo del cammin di nostra vita*
> *mi ritrova per una selva oscura*
> *che la diritta via era smarrita . . .*
> *Tant' è amara che poco è più morte.*
>   (*Inferno*, Canto I)[1]

I have been reading Al Alvarez's[2] book on suicide. In it he quotes from a paper by Elliott Jaques, a psychiatrist, on 'Death and the Mid-life Crisis', which deals with the 'male menopause' of the forties and how many artists fail to navigate it. Optimism and idealism give way: 'In the warren of this depression,' Alvarez says, 'all your past work seems trivial

---

1. 'In the middle of the journey of our life/I came to myself in a dark wood/For the straight way was lost . . ./For death itself can hardly be more harsh.'
2. Al Alvarez (1929–). Poet, author, poker-player, best known for his study of suicide *The Savage God* (1971).

or worthless, and your internal resources hopelessly inadequate for the dour task of finding a way through in some new, untested direction. It is a despair not many steps from suicide.'

From Donne:

> Whensoever my affliction assails me, mee thinks I have the Keyes of my prison in mine owne hand, and no remedy presents itselfe so soone to my heart, as mine own sword.

24 May

Nature should be our model. Microcosm reflects macrocosm. As we know, the central fact about the solar system is that, because of the cooling of the sun, it is committing suicide: and are we not bound to follow nature's laws? A powerful argument to hasten the individual's hand as he reaches for the pill-box.

26 May

> Man was born to live, to suffer, and to die, and what befalls him is a tragic lot. There is no denying this in the final end. *But we must, dear Fox, deny it all along the way.*
>
> (Thomas Wolfe)

27 May

I want to sell this house – now declining in value, with a diminishing lease and a collapsing property market – in order to pay my debts (to publishers and the Inland Revenue) and remove that rucksack.

28 May

> He was a slave to his own moods and he felt that though he was capable of recklessness and audacity, he possessed neither courage, perseverance, nor self-respect.
>
> (Amory Blaine in *This Side of Paradise*.)

29 May

I instigate a row with K. about a shirt, new and very expensive, which is sent to the laundry (and ruinously stained) instead of being dry-cleaned as clearly printed on the collar. Roxana watches the developing argument, looking glum, then vanishes and reappears bearing a really devastated pair of school pants, torn and ripped apart. Brandishing these ragged relics, she approaches me and quietly observes: 'Worse things happen to my school knickers.'

5 June

I read that de Gaulle had a mongoloid daughter, Anne, to whom he was devoted. When she died he comforted his wife by saying at the graveside: 'Come, now she is like the others.' Is this the most moving thing ever said by a Great National Hero?

8 June

Information about and comment on and analysis of history can in itself influence history. Reportage can create news. A hunger strike can have no effect on events if nobody knows it is taking place: so the act of reporting it can affect events more than the act itself. In predicting the course of the class struggle, the one thing Marx failed to take into account was the influence of his own work. Capitalism, having digested Marx, responded by creating Keynes to defend and perpetuate itself.

11 June

Blackest day yet. Andy Braunsberg at last admits (what I have lately suspected) that he can't provide the money he has promised to finance my film. He has repeatedly said: 'We'll put up $250,000 if you can find the rest.' Sometimes he has added: 'And if our plan to take over the Gaumont company in France succeeds, we'll finance the whole thing.' So I have spent nine months doing almost nothing but raise the remaining $250,000. First I got it from Bishop, who later pulled out all but $100,000. Then I got it from Stigwood, who finally welched on his commitment. Next I got it from Putnam and Lieberson, whose

Rothschild backers vetoed their participation in an erotic film. Then I got it from Arlene Sellers, who withdrew when I refused to delegate the direction and rewrite the script for Richard Burton. (At present I have it from Israel Katz and Howard Effron, who haven't yet gone back on their word.) Meanwhile there were literally hundreds of other people I wooed and coaxed over hundreds of lunches and inter-continental calls.

Now I find that Andy never had a penny with which to back up his original promises: *everything* was conditional on the outcome of his Gaumont speculation which seems to have collapsed. (He and his partner own only 41 per cent of the shares.) Once having undertaken to supply a quarter of a million, some peculiar code of financial *machismo* forbade Andy to confess the truth. Suddenly all his oddities of behaviour fall into place – his dilatoriness in following up potential investors I discovered, his lack of enthusiasm – amounting to positive discomfiture – whenever I called him to say that I'd found someone who'd given a firm promise to complete the financing. The very last thing he wanted was for the deal to be completed: and only now, when I have come up with an offer nobody could refuse, is he compelled to admit that he has been fooling me all along. I am thus in the position of having to find a new producer and a further $250,000. Back to square one. If I could laugh at the situation, I would compare setting up a film to making a jigsaw out of quicksilver. But I am past laughing. I have only one basket and my one egg, and if that breaks, I can't survive.

11 June

Larry is making a TV film at Pinewood with Kate Hepburn, George Cukor directing. 'Our combined ages,' he morosely remarks, 'come to about 500 years.' *Playboy* asked me to do an interview with him for $3,000. He refused. ('Dear boy, I'm tired of talking about myself.') *TV Guide* offered me $1,000 to describe a visit to the set – no interviews. Both he and Hepburn have vetoed the idea. Thus, while I am indebted to Larry for my year's severance pay, two decisions have cost me over £1,700. I wonder if he realises how much that means to me.

12 June

Tonight Kathleen joined the destroyers. We invited John Bishop to dinner – a property investor who promised to supply $100,000 for the film and is the only person who has shown no sign of reneging on the deal. The idea of asking him to dinner was to reassure him that the film was going ahead and that all was well. After dinner, to my horror and amazement, Kathleen casually remarked that of course nobody could trust the word of Andy Braunsberg and that I would have to seek much more secure financing to be sure of making the film. Bishop's face froze at once; he immediately started to talk about his participation being conditional on absolute assurances, etc. etc. Whether K.'s intervention was deliberate or unplanned I have no idea; in any case it wrecked the one guaranteed investment that the project could still boast. I did not think I could end today more shattered than I began it; but all things, thanks to Kathleen, are possible.

14 June

'We only die if we fail to take root in other people.' Quote from Trevor Griffiths and very exemplary it sounds; noble and unexceptionable. Yet look at it closely, and it reveals itself to be something like a prescription for parasitism. That which takes root in draws sap from: it also invades, imposes itself. The cuckoo takes root in the nest of its unwilling host. The Soviet Army takes root in Czechoslovakia. At the very least, Trevor is saying that invasion of privacy is a condition of survival. Is it only the bourgeois individualist in me that recoils from this proposition? I do not want anybody else's roots embedded in my psyche. Trevor's little apophthegm might be Dracula's family motto.

16 June

At K.'s request, I look back on the entry for 12 June. (She has not read it but knows how I felt about the occasion.) She swears I got it wrong: she wasn't trying to undermine me: my perceptions had turned paranoid through too much wine. Certainly I was part-drunk when I wrote it, which she wasn't when it happened: so I'll take her word that it didn't.

Prediction after the first half-dozen matches of the World Cup: it will be won by Poland or Holland. With saving bets on Yugoslavia and Italy.

17 June

There were happy times with Elaine. Many of them. One in particular, Mike Nichols' birthday party in (was it?) 1960. Mike had been complaining that his best friends were never around when he needed them and, challenged by Dick Avedon to name them, said Elaine and myself. Dick thereupon organised a surprise party for Mike's birthday the following week. He took over Foo Chow's, the Chinese restaurant on 8th Avenue where we all spent a lot of time in those days. The day before the party he flew Elaine and myself across from London. Next evening we were nailed into large crates and carried gift-wrapped into the restaurant just after Mike's arrival. Mike opened the crates with a chisel and out we burst, human presents. Lennie and Felicia Bernstein, the Axelrods, Steve Sondheim, Jule Styne, Betty and Adolph, Betty Bacall, Elaine May, Truman Capote were also among the guests who had spent most of the previous day concocting special fortune cookies for the occasion. I remember one of Adolph's: 'Anna May Wong, and again she may not.'

Mike told me a story of Roman Polanski's first visit to New York, at a time when his command of English was flimsy. He sat in moody silence at a party *chez* the Bernsteins where everyone was playing complicated word games. Suddenly he said: 'There's a great Polish game you ought to play.' 'What is it, Roman?' 'Do tell, Roman!' 'Listen, everyone, we're going to play Roman's game,' said Felicia. 'What do we have to do?' 'Well,' Roman said, 'it's very simple. One person stands in the middle of the room and closes his eyes and bends over. Then somebody else hits him on the ass. Then he has to guess who hit him.' A moment of aghast silence: but by now they were committed.

There followed a tableau I would have given much to see: New York's Upper Bohemia, in its Italian silk dinner jackets and Balenciaga dresses, taking turns to have its ass slugged, led by Felicia, exquisite in her Givenchy, daintily proffering her bottom in what must have been a quite unforgettable frenzy of embarrassment. The story is told against

Roman but as I retell it, I can't help feeling that he won. To *impose* yourself like that.

23 July

Strain of the film situation now continuous and bearable only with constant recourse to pills and booze. Some two weeks ago Paul Getty Jr.[1] (to whom I'd sent a script in March, receiving no acknowledgment or comment) got in touch with me to say that he was willing to invest. This was a godsend, since after weeks of hovering an Anglo-Canadian company called Impact Quadrant had finally decided to go back on its word and pull out of the deal. We needed $150,000 more. I rushed round to see Paul in his Cheyne Walk house (guarded by four locks and closed-circuit TV, formerly occupied by Rossetti). He enthusiastically confirmed his interest and undertook to provide $150,000. A few days later I took one of the American investors, Israel Katz, round to meet him: he repeated what he had told me and, in response to a question from Katz, said he'd be delighted to put up 25 per cent of the money immediately. At last the weight lifted: I felt happy for the first time in months. As the next day passed, doubts began to grow: Paul had said his lawyer would be calling us, and there was no call. Also when I called round to take him out for a celebration lunch, a maid said he had gone out. Another day went by: still no call, and Paul not answering the phone. Next morning I got through to him: everything was fine, we'd meet for dinner that evening, no problems. But the American backers were leaving for New York that day, and needed some tangible assurances that negotiations with Getty had begun. So I waited until a time when I knew they were out and left a message for them with an assumed name and voice, claiming to be a lawyer calling on behalf of Mr Getty. The Americans departed, duly reassured. That evening Getty failed to turn up for dinner and his telephone did not answer. And I learned from Penelope Tree, whom I'd invited to partner him at dinner, that Paul is a notorious speed-freak and drug addict, famous too for making euphoric promises that he never keeps.

That was last Friday: it's now Tuesday, and in the interim I haven't had a moment that wasn't filled with anxiety and dread. I even sent the

1. Paul Getty Jr. (1932–). Oil billionaire.

lease of my house – the only capital I possess – over to Getty's house, as security for his investment. Yesterday he answered one of my calls and said he was seeing his accountants today about the film: but his secretary, Mrs Gadsdon, warned me, when I called back later, against taking his promises too seriously. But it's too late: I'm committed: my producer, associate producer, cameraman, and cast are sitting by their phones, waiting to start work on the preparation that must be done if the film is to be made at all. And all of us are totally dependent on the volatile whims of a well-meaning junkie – who is anyway, I suspect, forbidden to disperse actual money without the approval of his lawyers and accountants.

Of course I have thrashed about calling up bankers and friends in a last desperate effort to find yet another source of cash, but I sense a parallel with the chicken who continues to run round in circles after being decapitated. Tomorrow, Dan (the producer), and Christopher (associate producer) and I were due to arrive in Paris, there to set up the production office and start *work*. Unless the miracle happens and Getty delivers, the trip is off. We can conceivably wait another four or five days: and then the film is off. My plan in that eventuality is simple. A one-way ticket to some far-off place with a phial of sleeping pills. A few days to settle myself and then suicide.

30 July

In the midst of the nightmare of setting up the film in Paris (with a new producer who doesn't really approve of it), physical violence erupts. Last night I was having a drink with some chums at Tom Curtiss's flat under the Tour d'Argent. Otto Preminger is filming scenes from his new movie *Rosebud* in the flat: it deals with terrorism and stars Peter O'Toole. Idly we discussed the possibility of playing a practical joke on O'Toole – perhaps getting a duck from Claude Terrail (before it had gone to *la presse*), stuffing a ticking clock into it, and planting it in the bed where tomorrow's scene was to be played. Finally, I wrote – in mirror-writing – a note addressed to 'the so-called Irishman P. O'Toole'. It accused him in hyperbolic language of being a traitor to the grand old cause of terrorism by appearing in the film, and declared that a terrifying explosive device had been secreted on the premises. I left it on the bed and departed, in no doubt that, although it

IAGO TEMPTS LORD OTHELLO OF BRIGHTON WITH
A LEWD PLAY BY A PERUVIAN MARXIST

might give Peter a momentary start, the extravagance of the language would soon convince him that it was a gag.[1]

At 8 a.m. that morning, however, my phone rang. It was Tom in a state of panic: the production manager had opened the note and *believed* it, the crew (many of them Irish mates of O'Toole's) had fled and were getting drunk in the bar opposite, and the police were clearing and searching the building. Worse, Tom had named me as the culprit (quite understandably, since otherwise he would have been suspected himself). At 10 a.m. Preminger called, cursing wildly: 'My crew have run away, I have lost half a day's shooting, and I am suing you for $20,000.'

4 August

K. and I drive out with Christopher Neame[2] to Chartres for lunch. I pick a restaurant called the Henri IV. As we eat:

K.: I *told* you, restaurants called Henri IV are always dreadful.
K.T.: If there's one thing I can't bear, it's people who are wise *during* the event.

13 August

Nicole: The only thing I mind about being out of work is having to work.

(Translation: she dislikes not acting only because it means taking a job in a launderette, restaurant, etc.)

15 August

If we like people to be emotionally dependent on us – and are prevented by temperament from satisfying our penchant in personal sado–masochistic relationship, I feel no need to invoke the dependence of others and hence have lost the will to write.

---

1. He didn't think it was a gag, and they had what O'Toole describes as 'an animated conversation'.
2. Christopher Neame (1942–). British writer and producer.

London airport is now the most congested, time-wasteful and farcically inefficient in the world – especially by comparison with the new de Gaulle airport in Paris, where all is uncluttered hush and one moves smoothly and uninterruptedly on sliding platforms from arrival at the drum-shaped terminal to the door of the aircraft. London, meanwhile, has evolved a method of embarkation that entails no fewer than *five* queues. (Six if you are foolish enough to want a cup of airport coffee, courtesy of Charles Forte, despot and bane of British catering: at the breakfast counter, where everyone is drinking coffee, coffee alone is not served: you are directed to the self-service counter, a hundred yards away, where a line of twenty people glumly waits.) Queue #1 is the checking-in counter, where baggage is weighed. You then pass to Queue #2 – passport inspection, and from this to Queue #3, where hand luggage is searched for explosives. The most otiose queue follows – #4, at the entrance to a waiting room near the aircraft where we line up to receive numbered tickets indicating the location of our seats. We next sit in the waiting room until a man summons us, number by number, to Queue #5, which gains admittance to the plane itself. It is worth noting that Queue #4 exists solely to provide an excuse for Queue #5: if passengers, when called, went directly to the plane without seat numbers, there would be no need for either 4 or 5. How the British love micro-regimentation!

I dine alone at the Tour d'Argent, noting that Tom Curtiss has notched up an enviable achievement: 'Oeufs Tom Curtiss' is now a permanent addition to the menu. As always at this restaurant, I am overcome with sentimentality. At the Tour d'Argent, on early evenings in summer, even the waiters can be observed staring at the view – the backside of Notre-Dame, held up by that absurd superfluity of flying buttresses, like a fat drunk supported by a crowd of beggars; and the river that bifurcates around it, gleaming in the western light; and across the rooftops to the Sacré-Coeur; and all of it, for me, covered, as with a benison, by memories of summer girls – of Elaine, very long ago, and Evans, and the unexpected, ever-cherished Miss Addie Herder, and Kathleen, of course – and lesser others of no less grateful remembrances. Summer is never summer in London as it is in Paris. Hot nights in small hotel rooms when the city is empty, and the theatres and all but a few restaurants are closed: this is how I remember the city that has given me the blithest, least responsible moments of my life.

18 August

Domini Blythe rings from Canada. She has heard that the film is financially unstable and refuses to return to Europe unless I ring her agent with a firm offer as of Monday (the 19th). Meanwhile Robert Stephens' agent has given us till Tuesday morning: failing a firm offer, his client will sign to do Tony Shaffer's[1] new play. Without the two stars, of course, the film collapses. I recall glancing at my horoscope in *Harper's and Queen*: On 20 August a venture on which you have set your heart will collapse for want of financial support.

Nicole: If you kill yourself you won't be allowed up with Byron and me. You'll be down with the cowards. You'll be with people like Clement Freud.[2] And T.P. McKenna.[3] And Rose Selway (Who is Rose Selway?)

Nicole: I wonder if they ever made Sister Mary Sebastian a saint. [S.M.S. was the founder of her convent school.] You have to perform three first-class miracles and Sister Mary Sebastian had only performed one. Now and again she would perform a *puny* miracle, like making a boil disappear, and everybody would get very uptight.

4 September

In a Sloane Square pub I am drinking with Alan Brien[4] after a performance at the Royal Court. An elderly lady with serene smile and twinkling eyes approaches me. 'You're Kenneth Tynan, aren't you?' she says. I admit it. 'We met at Diana Phelps' villa in Taormina,' she goes on. 'I'm afraid you're wrong.' I reply. 'I've never been to Taormina and I don't know anyone called Diana Phelps.' 'But surely

---

1. Antony Shaffer (1926–). British playwright and screenwriter, author of *Sleuth* (1970), twin brother of Peter Shaffer.
2. Clement Freud (1924–). Writer, broadcaster, younger brother of painter Lucian Freud.
3. T.P. McKenna (1929–). Irish actor.
4. Alan Brien (1925–). British novelist and journalist.

you remember having drinks on her terrace? With that heavenly view?' I shake my head: at the same time I notice Alan looking amazed. 'Excuse me,' he says to the woman. 'I don't know you, but I do know Diana Phelps, and I have stayed at her villa in Taormina.' This seems to me an extraordinary event. Was it just a fantastic coincidence? But in that case why did this woman remember having seen *me* there? Or was she a 'sensitive', who sensed the presence of someone connected with Taormina – someone she wrongly identified as me?

10 September

Last night Ethel Merman[1] opened at the Palladium (her first time there). An ecstatic occasion, standing ovations, and the lady at her militant best (she really made musical comedy a martial art). I love her *defiance*, the feeling that she can survive anything – as with Seneca's heroine, you sense that, if the world collapses, '*Medea superest.*' And her effortlessness: audiences nowadays expect strain and sweat, as provided by pop stars; Merman's golden flow astounds them. America is a democracy and Merman is American to the core; yet she sums up the contradiction of American democracy when she sings, with all her bellicose uniqueness:

Some people
May be content
Playing bingo
And paying rent
But *some people*
Ain't me.

Another deeply American thing about her is that Cole Porter (of all contrasting people) wrote his best songs for her: the dapper upper-class wit inspired by this brassy broad from Queens. This would be inconceivable in Britain – as if Noël Coward had written for Gracie Fields[2]. (Merman incidentally should add a few Coward songs to her repertoire – 'Twentieth Century Blues' or 'Sail Away', for example,

---

1. Ethel Merman (1908–84). Incomparable brassy star of American musicals from 1930–66. Most famous as Annie in *Annie Get Your Gun* (1946) and Mama Rose in *Gypsy* (1959).
2. Gracie Fields (1898–1979). Warm, witty musical-hall legend, famous for her rendition of 'The Biggest Aspidistra in the World'.

not to mention the wonderful 'Sigh No More'. She has, in spades, that gallant rise-above-it quality that so many of Noël's songs celebrate.)

There won't be another Merman because there is no need today for a voice like hers. At sixty-four (or sixty-five?), she used a radio mike last night: but on Broadway she never used anything but the usual mini-mikes in the footlights, and often not even those. Streisand might have been her successor, but she only starred in one Broadway show (*Funny Girl*) before plunging into movies. Streisand couldn't give a performance like Merman's last night because no one's ever written a show for her. Almost everything Merman says was custom-made for her voice and personality: and it shows: the clothes fit like second skins, the colours suit her.

She keeps her distance. What she sells is the song, not herself: you don't miss a syllable. One recalls that never in her Broadway career did she have to address the audience directly, as now: she always played roles in book shows. There are stars you admire and stars you identify with. Merman is one of the former, who have in recent years virtually ceased to exist. The audience called her back for ten minutes, cheering and begging for encores: she thanked them but said, 'I haven't any more music rehearsed.' Professional to the last, she wouldn't insult her admirers by giving them anything unprepared.

11 September

I can't take Robin Blackburn seriously: he takes me too seriously.

I coin a new and needed word – 'dislove' (analogical with 'dislike'). To dislove someone is to feel for them that mixture of resentment and rancour that is left after a love affair ends badly. (I dislove Elaine.) This is not the same as hatred, which one can feel for non-lovers: dislove is specific to those situations where love has turned sour and rancid. (I suppose one could be disloved by one's children and vice versa.)

17 September

With Nicole to see Merman. Perhaps a mistake: she admires but is not overwhelmed, feels the act belongs in a smaller room. (The house wasn't full – to my surprise, for even at a first-house performance on a

Tuesday, you'd expect those notices to have filled the place to capacity.) Part of the trouble is that she, at twenty-nine, has seen so few of the great musicals: that whole era of Broadway's supremacy was over before she started serious theatre-going. She didn't (as I did) wait eagerly and enviously for the first reports of the newest Porter/Loesser/ Rodgers and Hammerstein show. But beyond this I think she is unattuned to the Rolls-Royce *ease* of Merman's style. Just as I would not take a beginner at bullfights to see Antonio Ordóñez[1] (who would seem too facile) or a cricketing tyro to see Graveney[2] or Cowdrey[3] (*ditto*), I should not have taken Nicole to see Merman, expecting that she would recognise perfection at first glimpse. (All the same, I'm glad she admits that she didn't.)

I talk (and write) to Larry, about the huge Theatre Exhibition to be mounted at the Hayward Gallery next spring to mark the opening of the new National Theatre. After discreet consultation with Peter Hall, it has been designed to edit Larry out of the listing of the NT. Fifty-seven display items are devoted to Barry Jackson's Birmingham Rep; only *five* to Larry's decade at the NT. No mention of his *Othello*, *Dance of Death*, *Long Day's Journey* or *Uncle Vanya*. Nothing about the Shaffer plays, the Stoppards, or any of the non-Larry successes (such as *Much Ado*, *The Front Page*, *The Misanthrope*, *National Health*, *Equus*, etc.) in which he took such pride. Nothing but a still from *Three Sisters*; a still from *Flea in His Ear*, and three costume and set designs by Ralph Koltai. Meanwhile room after room is devoted to 'Peter Hall's Stratford' – a regime which lasted eight years, as against Larry's ten. When I inform him of this by phone, his voice is sombre! 'We really didn't understand P.H,' he says. 'I've never known a man more dedicated to self-glorification. He's rewriting the history of the National as if it started with the first reading of his production of *The Tempest*.'

18 September

For use sometime: 'As suicidal as a Grand Prix driver with hay fever.'

---

1. Antonio Ordóñez (1932–98). Spanish bullfighter.
2. Tom Graveney (1927–). England cricketer and television commentator.
3. Colin Cowdrey (1932–2000). Cricketer for Kent and England.

The whole film is now held up by Paul Getty, the hermit millionaire who promised me three months ago that I would have his cheque for $150,000 within a week. The problem is that Paul has been taking a cure to kick the heroin habit; and the rumour from his girlfriend is that he has become addicted to the tapering-off drug that was intended to cure him of his addiction. He now lies in a coma, inaccessible for most of the day, a sleeping beauty waiting, paradoxically, to be awakened by the prick of a needle.

Afterthought: a couple of nights ago David Frost conducted a thirty-minute TV interview with Muhammad Ali on his forthcoming heavy-weight championship fight with George Foreman. Ali was great value, as usual, and plugged the fight with limitless verve. What wasn't mentioned was the fact that the fight has been financed and sponsored by Hemdale, a company owned by Frost. Thus he was paid a vast sum for a half-hour commercial on his own behalf. A fearless, independent, probing reporter gives a fearless, independent probing report on an event he is himself promoting from which he stands to make millions of dollars.

19 September

We go to a big literary party in North Kensington to celebrate Michael Holroyd's new biography of Augustus John. I enter a room full of Antonia Fraser[1], Iris Murdoch[2], Mark Boxer[3], Karl Miller[4], Anthony Howard[5], etc. etc. – and whisper to K.H.: 'I feel terribly shy.' 'Why?' 'I know everybody here.'

From a later conversation:

X: Lord Goodman has a finger in every pie.
K.T.: And a foot in every grave.

1. Lady Antonia Fraser (1932–). Historian and novelist; in 1988 married playwright Harold Pinter.
2. Iris Murdoch (1931–99). Novelist and philosopher.
3. Mark Boxer (1931–88). British caricaturist whose cartoons invented yuppies before the eighties.
4. Karl Miller (1931–). Professor of English Literature at University College London; formerly editor of the Listener and the London Review of Books.
5. Anthony Howard (1934–). British political journalist and broadcaster.

An encounter – the first for more than ten years – with an Oxford contemporary reminds me of my first meeting with Dylan Thomas. The year was 1946, when Dylan was living at Witney, near Oxford. After pub closing-time one afternoon I was walking along the High Street when I saw a tubby, corduroyed man wandering vaguely through the traffic near Carfax. He was obviously drunk and I crossed the road to intercept him. As I approached, he clutched me. 'Can I help?' I said. 'Yes,' he said urgently. 'Have you got any crème de menthe?' I hadn't, but I took him back to my room in Magdalen and procured some from a friend on the same staircase.

By this time I had recognised him from a meeting of the Poetry Society he had addressed the previous term. Swigging the mentholated fluid from a tooth mug, he rewarded me (and a couple of chums) with a thick, gurgling, baleful, boisterous display of bardic pyrotechnics. I recall a parody of those sexually frozen English poets who spoke of 'the terrible caresses in the vast black cavern – which was of course the school boot-cupboard'. And an account of a man condemned to death, whom Dylan knew and who had recently been hanged. 'The night before he died,' he said, 'they gave him his dinner on a tin plate.' What they didn't know was that he had been sharpening the edge of the dish for several days. Half an hour later he gave them back their dish. On it were his cock and balls. And at once, all over the prison, a fearsome clattering noise broke out. It was the sound of prisoners rattling their dishes against the bars of their cells. It went on all night – nobody could stop the terrible lamentation and no one knew how it had started – until the trap-door was sprung and the man died, an event for once unaccompanied by the throes of a final orgasm.

20 September

Description of an undemonstrative female masochist: a wooden O. (*Vide*: *Histoire d'O*).

22 September

I write to *The Times* querying the common but clearly parochial assumption that inflation is 'worldwide'. I point out that it does not exist in the USSR or China, and is only minimal in the Eastern European countries. The conventional wisdom attributes this to 'artificial' devices such as exchange-rate adjustments, export-price levies and import-price subsidies. All the same, the artifice seems to work, whereas our 'realism' doesn't. (The implication, of course, is that if the basic problem is inflation, the basic answer is some form of socialist ownership and planning). Neither of the major parties really contemplates this. The Tories will create unemployment, thereby risking a general strike; Labour will maintain full employment with no income policy, which will destroy the Pound and further discourage investment. Either course leads to economic disaster: neither considers the possibility of abolishing private profit. Three equations suggest themselves: Private profit plus free trade unions (as in UK and USA) = inflation. Private profit without free trade unions (as in South Africa or pre-coup Portugal) = inflation. No private profit and no free trade unions (as in USSR) = no inflation, which leaves one variant still untried, perhaps the most hopeful of all:

No private profit plus free trade unions = ?

27 September

Victoria Brooks rings at 1 a.m. with news of Paul G. (to whose house I delivered a desperate letter last night).[1] He is in the Harley Street Clinic, the explanation of his elusive behaviour for the past fortnight is that he has been suffering from priapism – a rare condition in which you have a permanent erection. At first this seemed funny to Paul and Victoria; but then he developed a bloodclot in the penis, and it became agonising. He couldn't pee and the pain was terrible. He was given only a 50–50 chance of surviving and two days ago made out his will. Yesterday a top urologist was flown in (from France I think). He recommended an immediate operation, which he performed himself a few hours later. It was a success: Paul will live. So another chapter of torture is added to the history of my film.

1 October

Last words of Lear:

---

1. Tynan to Paul Getty, 26 September 1974: 'What is holding us up? My life these days consists – as it has now for many weeks – of sitting idly by the phone awaiting the call that tells me I can start work on our film and redeem the promises I've made to so many people, not least of them you . . . So: I stagnate awaiting a word from you . . . So the ball is in your court – or rather, my balls are in your court . . . Please pick up the phone.'

Pass me the Soneryl –
Goodbye, Goneril.

And a bad-taste poem for America's first lady, lately recovered from a cancer op:

Dear Mrs Ford, avoid self-pity,
Even though you've lost a titty.

Yesterday a bald, deaf, elderly Canadian came to interview me on C.S. Lewis, about whom he is writing a book. Into his hearing aid I bellowed reminiscences of this great man, whose mind was Johnsonian without the bullying and Chestertonian[1] without the facetiousness. If I were ever to stray into the Christian camp, it would be because of Lewis's arguments as expressed in books like *Miracles*. (He never intruded them into tutorials.) Because I stammered, he kindly undertook to read my weekly essays aloud for me, and the prospect of hearing my words pronounced in that wonderfully juicy and judicious voice had a permanently disciplining effect on my prose style.

He was a deeply kind and charitable man, too. Once in the summer of 1948 I came to him in despair: Jill Rowe-Dutton[2] had jilted me on the eve of what was to have been our marriage, and I had spent most of the term in and out of bed with bronchial diseases that I was sure would soon culminate in TB. I brought my troubles to Lewis, asking him whether I could postpone my final examinations until Christmas. To this he at once agreed: after which he got me with the Christian business of consolation. He reminded me how I had once told him about the parachuted landmine which, dropping from a German bomber during an air-raid in 1940, so narrowly missed our house in Birmingham that next morning we recovered some of the parachute silk from our chimney. (The mine destroyed six houses across the road and blew out all our windows). But for

1. G.K. Chesterton (1874–1936). Social and literary critic whose preoccupations informed his conversion to Catholicism.
2. Gillian Rowe-Dutton (1925–). Now married to Sir Peter Parker. Tynan's Oxford girlfriend, to whom he dedicated his first book. Tynan to Jill Rowe-Dutton, 24 September 1947 (undelivered): 'Please SEE me . . . with my face drenched with tears and my eyes red and nearly invisible. And see, too, my ANGUISH at your cool, bloody, hateful betrayal . . . Where O Chum is the vestige of CONSCIENCE . . . Oh, how could you do it? You chum. The you I created in February and shared through March, April, May, June, July, August?'

that hair's-breadth – a matter of inches only – I would already (Lewis gently pointed out) have been dead for eight years. Every moment of life since then had been a bonus, a tremendous free gift, a present that only the blackest ingratitude could refuse. As I listened to him, my problems began to dwindle to their proper proportions; I had entered his room suicidal, and I left it exhilarated.

2 October

Nicole: Keith Waterhouse[1] thought I was three-timing him. I was seven-timing him.

K: Did you ever get paid for going to bed with people?

Nicole: No. I wasn't classy enough for that.

K: Why did it break it up with Keith?

Nicole: He got disgusted with me . . . I didn't learn to think till I was about twenty. I didn't learn to talk till about twenty-three. I would suddenly want to communicate and it was garbage. He would sit there and look puzzled. We used to have lunch at the Caprice and then go to empty cinemas and sit alone in the royal circle because he was *nouveau riche*. That was when it was still nice, before he got disgusted.

3 October

Nicole's way of life is geared to accept and cope with failure – which is why, in my present state of mind, I feel at home in it. But what occasionally nettles me is that failure, to her, is not as exceptional and tragic as it inevitably seems to me. I don't mind failing, so long as the air is filled with cries of incredulity and compassion. What is maddening is when failure is taken for granted.

5 October

I find Claudius infinitely more sympathetic than Hamlet. A pacific diplomat, as opposed to his bellicose elder brother forever smiting sledded Polacks; a man who kills for love, a *crime passionel* of which his thinblooded and misogynistic nephew would never have been capable;

---

1. Keith Waterhouse (1929–). British playwright and journalist, best known for *Billy Liar* (1960) with Willis Hall.

a man of courage (*vide* his response to Laertes' rebellion) and a lover of wine, who would certainly have ruled Denmark with far more judgement, administrative skill and broad humanity than the vacillating, egocentric Prince. It is to be noted that nobody in the play except Hamlet has a harsh word to say about Claudius – which makes him unique among Shakespeare's villains. In a tight corner, or for an evening out on the town, give me Claudius every time.

6 October

Nicole: From the tomato of the past the tomato of today is altogether different. The tomato of today is tasteless. Your wife is a tomato. Your secretary is a tomato. You have nothing in your house but cats and tomatoes.

I have lately been succouring a German girl who is a mentor of an extreme left group of urban guerrillas in West Germany. She was arrested twice three years ago, and has been imprisoned since then without trial, for most of the time in solitary confinement, being subjected to the most favoured form of contemporary torture – sensory deprivation, whereby the victim is kept in total silence and utter darkness for months on end. This produces a total collapse of the personality and complete dependence on the gaoler, and is held to be far more effective than old-fashioned physical torture. Anna (the girl's pseudonym) was released on bail in the spring and fled to England with a false passport. If extradited, tried and condemned, she faces life imprisonment, since she and her group are jointly charged with offences including the bombing of US military camps in Germany.

She is a shy, defensive *hausfrau*, wary (understandably so) to the point of paranoia, ringing always from cash boxes for fear of wiretaps, and unwilling to accept help from members of the British far-left groups, in case they are being watched by the security services. And though I don't agree with the violence her friends employ, I have given her some money and found temporary shelter for her. I have to admit to a certain shameful Le Carré thrill at helping to hide a girl who is, in Germany at least, a notorious public enemy. I discussed her experiences and plight with Robin Blackburn, who said at length: 'I've read a lot about sensory deprivation and how awful it is. But I must say that if I had to choose between going into a dark room and having my genitals burned off with a blowlamp, I think I would probably go into the dark room.'

16 October

We spend a week of *Grande-Bouffe*[1]-ing in France, three-starring it from Paris to La Ferté-sous-Jouarre (Auberge de Condé), Liverdun (Les Vannes), Alsace (L'Auberge de l'Ill, last but one of the Michelin 3-star restaurants I haven't yet tried), and then, after side-trips to Strasbourg, the snowy Vosges and Basle, down to Lyon and Alain Chapel's extraordinary restaurant at Mionnay, Chez la Mère Charles, where we have oyster and scallop *ragout* followed by *ortolans en broche*. Best hotel: La Résidence Les Violettes at Jungholtz in Alsace, where the food is superb (deserving at least one Michelin star) but which belies its listing as one of the most tranquil hotels in France. One is continually staggered by the presumption of the church: the hillside silence of the hotel is shattered, every quarter of an hour, by a clamour of bells from two churches, one of them within half a mile of the hotel and the other chiming exactly twenty seconds later than the first. Moreover, there is a persistent, imperious pealing at 5.30 a.m. that lasts ten minutes and denies sleep to everyone within earshot. The sheer nerve of it, the arrogant audacity, must give pause to anyone who believes that Christianity has lost its power to intimidate. If I sat above the hotel in my car and honked my horn every quarter of an hour, I would undoubtedly be arrested.

18 October

I hear that Janet Suzman[2] frequently pees on stage when feeling nervous. Funny: I always thought people dried.

Rozina passes on a wonderfully improbable rumour: Harold Pinter has left his wife and child and is living with Peggy Ashcroft. Later: not true, alas – he merely had a crush on her when she was in a play of his a couple of years ago.

1. *La Grande Bouffe*. Marco Ferreri's fierce 1973 satire on greed, about a group of French gourmands who decide to eat themselves to death.
2. Janet Suzman (1939–). South-African born actress.

19 October

After two years of bad news, one prospect I felt sure of was the libel action I am bringing against *Private Eye* (for having – quite falsely – accused me of having exposed my genitals in public before a crowd of people, including a twelve-year-old girl). Here, surely, was something even I couldn't lose. But Nicole calls to say that someone has stolen from her flat the album in which we kept photos and letters relating to our spanking exploits. Both pictures and text are totally explicit. Careful checks reveal that nobody whom she knows to have been in the flat could have taken it. The obvious possibility is that *Private Eye* have engaged a private eye to dig up dirt on me to destroy my reputation in court (or in print beforehand). They are quite low enough *not* to have to stoop in order to carry out this sort of trick. The result would be to kill Nicole's parents, injure Kathleen savagely and inflict terrible psychological damage on my children if and when they hear of it. But that would not deter *Private Eye*. It must surely be the most sickeningly nihilistic publication in the Western world. One record it holds against all others: of no other magazine can it be said that it has never printed a word in praise of anybody or anything. (Conversely, it has never printed a word in *dispraise* of Christianity or of the Church. Richard Ingrams[1], the editor, is a fervent believer.)

20 October

Paul Getty (musing over his sliced and shattered but now healing prick): 'God must be very cynical. And very ribald. Otherwise he wouldn't have lasted so long.'

21 October

A solution to the problem of dreams (their origin, and purpose): they fit in very well with the Christian hypothesis: heaven would be the perpetual prolongation of a happy dream; hell, permanent incarceration in a nightmare *from which one could never wake up*. This is a much more credible and daunting hell than the fire and brimstone kind. How

---

1. Richard Ingrams (1937–). Editor of *Private Eye*, 1963–86; Editor of *The Oldie* since 1992.

appalling to be locked up for ever in a world of horrors of one's own imagining. Perhaps one's dreams *are* one's 'soul', and outlive the body: the notion is surely tenable, since we don't know where our bodies are while we are asleep. *Vide* the belief, still widespread, that dreams contain warnings and auguries. Perhaps they literally do; and are themselves to provide the fulfilment of their own prophecies.

28 October

Lytton Strachey, writing about Cambridge: 'It's all or nothing with us. Oxford's the glorification of the half-and-half.' Quite true: and what a condemnation of Cambridge absolutism! I never liked that university of dark-blue suits and dark-blue voices, where a laugh is a judgement passed rather than a moment fulfilled – a place rigorous and extreme, like the east wind that buffets it, as against the gentle miasmic swamps of Oxford. (Why are Cambridge men predominantly dark-haired, Oxonians predominantly fair?) Cam is the home of austerity and certainty; Oxford, of indulgence and doubt. I know where I – a Roundhead in politics but a Cavalier by temperament – inextricably belong.

K: I feel like a shit leaving you like this.

N.: You're a shit for being here at all. But I suppose that makes me a shit too.

K: In that case why don't you refuse to see me again?

N.: I haven't the guts.

29 October

A not untypical evening: 9 p.m.: Meeting with Barry Reckord (West Indian playwright), and Clifford Williams to discuss Reckord's writing a sequel to *Oh! Calcutta!* if Trevor Griffiths fails to deliver. Intense talk about erect penises on stage, the defensibility of incest, the desirability of semen scent being wafted across the audience (does semen smell the same to every man and woman?)

10:30 p.m.: Party at George Weidenfeld's, full of rich smarties, property millionaires (Charles Clore) etc. Mark Littman says we have some *slight* chance of extracting the £25,000 we lent to Markman, the company from which he extracted himself (as a director) without losing a penny. Teddy Goldsmith (last seen at Oxford, some twenty-five years ago) tells me, bearded and foaming with fun, a grisly tale of the death of Stanley Parker's mother. It seems Ma and son were living together on the 3rd floor of a small Paris hotel: one night the 1st- and 2nd-floor residents were awakened by an inundation of hot water from above, where Stanley lived. The police (and Teddy) were called: they found Stanley's apartment feet-deep in water, and his mother – naked, with her hands tied with electric wire – dead in a wardrobe. He explained that she'd had a heart attack and that in a similar situation, some years previously in Australia, he had revived her by putting her in a hot bath. On this occasion he had removed her and forgotten to turn off the bath water. After which it was discovered that she had been dead for a week; and Stanley was unable to account for the tied hands. What had happened? Was he a queer who actually managed to fuck his mother, albeit posthumously? A bizarre episode.

Twelve midnight: We go to see *Emmanuelle*, the French erotic film – pretty, exotic, humourless, and full of pompous lectures about the nature of female sexuality.

2.30 a.m.: Off to the Gaumont Cinema, Kilburn, for a closed-circuit telecast of the heavyweight championship fight between George Foreman and Muhammad Ali. The audience is 90 per cent black (we had to summon a black security guard to eject two blacks, wearing fur coats and hats, from our seats) and Ali does not let them down. He is not only skilled, graceful, arrogant and flamboyant: he is a brilliant strategist and enormously tough. Instead of skipping away from the giant Foreman, as predicted, he leans on the ropes and for four rounds simply soaks up punishment – to the total bewilderment of the champion, who slugs his heart out to no effect. Then Ali counter-attacks with incredibly well-aimed combination bombardments, always hitting the head and chin: and suddenly the looming thug is off balance, tottering and felled. Ali crows in triumph, baring his teeth: what a bitch he is, what a vain, pugnacious bitch!

All the auguries were upset. They said he would run and he stood; they said he was old (seven years older than Foreman) and he looked a stripling; they said he lacked a punch, and he knocked out the heaviest puncher in the world. 'I am the scholar of boxing,' he said afterwards, and rightly. Quite apart from his enormous physical presence and skill, he uses the English language like an Elizabethan. Back home to be in bed at 4.30 a.m. wakeful and exhilarated by what we have seen.

I believe most men feel inferior to women; which is why they have to amass fortunes, win battles, conquer countries, succeed (at least) in *something*, before they feel confident enough, triumphant enough, *un-inferior* enough, to fuck. They have to work like mad to persuade themselves that they are fit for female consumption. In other words, man is an aggressor not because he feels himself superior to the opposite sex but because he knows he *isn't*.

8 November

Liberating extract from an interview with Muriel Spark[1] in the *Guardian*. She . . . is against family loyalties being imposed or friendship loyalties. She feels very strongly about this. 'It's demanding too much of any human to ask them to be loyal to a party, to a system or a person for the whole of their life. To say, "You owe me loyalty," is a terrible thing.'

10 November

An entry postponed from 8 October, when K. and I dined *à quatre* with Jill Bennett and John Osborne, with whom I have been feuding for years (because of his unprovoked attacks on my work at the NT which he called 'intellectual spivvery'). A few nights earlier we had found ourselves sharing a table with Oscar Beuselinck[2] at a Dorchester Hotel party after the première of *That's Entertainment*. It occurred to both of us that, for all our mutual vituperation, we were still more exciting than anybody else present, and that we therefore ought to spend more time in each other's company. The result was a superb Thurloe Square dinner (one of our best, including *Gâteau Marjolaine*) and a lot of happily candid talk about sex. 'I love little pink anuses,' said John at one point; and it was confirmed – what I'd known at second hand for years – that John is as entranced by smacked bottoms and opened bumholes as I am, and – which I already knew at first hand, though twenty years ago – as Jill is. (Jill also revealed that John pees *sitting down*.)

By the end of the evening we were fast friends, and it occurred to K.

1. Muriel Spark (Dame) (1918–). Novelist; caustic books include *Memento Mori* (1959) and *The Prime of Miss Jean Brodie* (1961).
2. Oscar Beuselinck (1919–97). Show-business lawyer.

and me – and, I think to the Osbornes – that here was a couple with whom one could seriously consider wife-swapping. A final sour note: K. refused to demonstrate obedience by removing her knickers. A tremendous fight ensued, after the Osbornes had left: K. had made a very crucial psychological misjudgment, or a very ill-timed display of principled honesty.

Having watched Peter Sellers on the Parkinson show last night I recall the dismal occasion in 1959 when I introduced him (at his own request) to Mike Nichols in New York. Mike arrived with Elaine May (his cabaret partner: he was not yet a director): Peter arrived with his wife and Graham Stark[1], a minor Goon. We dined at Sardi's East. Nothing that Peter said amused Mike; nothing that Mike said amused Peter. The sly, pragmatic, New York Jewish sense of humour meant nothing to Peter; and the giggling facetious, whimsical fantastic Goon-jokes of Sellers seemed merely embarrassing to Mike. I've never been more conscious of the abyss that separates British humour from the specialised world of Jewish Manhattan.

14 November

Last week, Lord Lucan, a millionaire gambler, murdered his children's nanny mistaking her in a darkened house for his estranged wife, and then bashed his wife over the head several times with a length of lead piping. What has happened since then is a perfect illustration of the influence of class on British justice. Firstly: four days passed before the police issued a warrant for Lucan's arrest. (British justice hates to put a nobleman in the dock. And British citizens have a similar reluctance to believe a nobleman capable of violent crime. Kathleen admitted that when she first read about the case she assumed that Lucan must have been insane – a conclusion to which she would never have jumped had he been called Ginger Noakes and lived in Streatham.) Thus Lucan had ample time to leave the country if he chose.

Next, the press reported that many of his friends were 'dedicated men' who would not hesitate to shelter him. Would Ginger Noakes' pals have been described as 'dedicated men'? Or as 'underworld

---

1. Graham Stark (1922–). Comedy actor; appeared in many of the Pink Panther films.

cronies'? Assumption: it is honourable to hide a wanted lord, but squalidly criminal to hide a wanted commoner.

Next: the TV newscasts all used the phrase 'Lord Lucan is still *missing*.' With Ginger Noakes, it would have been 'Noakes is still *on the run* . . .' Several papers expressed fears that Lucan might have killed himself 'to avoid causing distress to his children'. Such a sympathetic diagnosis would never have been made about G. Noakes.

Most significant of all: newspapers and TV shows are full of interviews with Lucan's aristocratic chums, all testifying what an honourable man he is and how unthinkable it is that he should have committed murder. Such treatment would never, of course, have been granted to G. Noakes; it would have been quite rightly regarded as a deliberate attempt to influence potential jurors and to interfere with the course of justice. Meanwhile Lady Lucan has returned home from hospital with a round-the-clock armed guard of police. Would the same protection have been extended to Mrs Noakes?

17 November

André Previn conducts Shostakovich's 5th on TV programme full of closeups of André Agonistes in Michael Fish shirt, his Beatle mop and armpits getting sweatier and sweatier. How he suffered! Through what exquisite torments he passed! As always, closeups of the musicians revealed that none of them was casting the merest glance in his direction. The creative-conductor myth is terribly in need of demolition – as if the alternatives available to the conductor were in any way comparable to those available to a theatrical director! Watching Previn's quiverings and convulsions one couldn't help muttering, 'It's murder to send a boy up in a symphony like that.'

24 November

Last week Jim Haynes[1] sent me one of his mimeographed newsletters. In it he mentioned that in July a man called David Wakefield had been sentenced to three years' imprisonment and fined £7,000 for showing blue films. He told anyone interested in this case to call Mrs Wakefield

1. Jim Haynes (1933–). American-born avant-garde theatrical impresario in London.

at a North London number. I did so and went to see her. I arrived early at a tiny suburban (not working-class) house in Wood Green. In the parlour three small children (not Wakefield's) were noisily romping with a stocky white-haired man who kept bringing them down with playful flying tackles and turning somersaults, while explaining that teetotalism was the only guarantee of prolonged sexual potency. (This was a friend of the family, later identified as sexy Frank.) A middle-aged man with a bulging stomach – Wakefield's uncle – looked on, declaring that he seldom put away less than a bottle of Scotch a night.

This was the Pinterish scene when Mrs W. arrived, a petite wide-eyed Irish blonde in her early twenties, apologising for being detained at her ballroom-dancing class. She amazed me by saying: 'Let's go and have something to eat at a vegetarian restaurant in Hampstead.' (I had expected we were just going to have a few sherries together.) Obediently I drove her about ten miles round the North Circular Road, getting repeatedly lost in what G.K. Chesterton called 'the suburbs of hell'.

On the way this enchantingly open girl told me about herself and her lover. (They are not married but she prefers to use his name.) David runs two very small film clubs in Islington which specialise in sex films. In July he was charged at the Old Bailey with importing obscene articles from Denmark and the US (including *Deep Throat*) and with running a disorderly house. Conducting his own defence (an increasingly popular habit among fringe people), he was acquitted on the latter charge; the jury failed to agree over *Deep Throat*, but they found the Danish films obscene, and David was sent down.

Divina (his girl) was six months pregnant, and the shock of the sentence led to the premature birth of a baby girl, who died three weeks later. David was allowed to attend the funeral – handcuffed and escorted by six coppers. In January he will be retried on *Deep Throat* and, if convicted, faces another sentence. Meanwhile Divina has kept the clubs open (showing only home-grown films) with a sign advising members that *Deep Throat* will be showing at the Old Bailey in January, 'admission free'.

Of course all censorship is monstrous: but what particularly attracts me about the Wakefields is that they aren't the kind of sleazy profiteers that one associates with porn films. They belong to the new, Reich-influenced generation for whom sexual liberty and socialism are inseparable. Sex is just one shade in the libertarian spectrum. (Both, incidentally, are non-drinkers and vegan vegetarians. The authorities at Wormwood Scrubs have refused to supply David with a vegan diet – which forbids eggs, cheese and milk – so he has been existing on cabbage, bread and potatoes.) Both have dropped a good deal of acid: Divina says that it gave her an inner serenity without which she couldn't have coped with the situation.

I should have pointed out that she too has been harassed by the police: once acquitted on a charge of appearing in obscene movies (made before she met David and not shown at his clubs), twice fined for possessing hash, and regularly subjected to house searches by cops allegedly looking for dope and dirty movies. Divina's parents, strict Ulster Protestants, have refused to speak to her since she began to live with David two years ago: her fifteen-year-old sister, ostracised by all her friends when David's case came to trial, attempted suicide.

As a matter of socialist principle, David uses most of the earnings from his clubs to finance – among other things – East End community groups, Kids-Aid (which gives help and advice to children under fifteen in trouble), strike funds and organisations supplying legal and medical aid to drug addicts. He also pays the rent of *Up Against the Law*, an outspoken underground magazine that exposes bent coppers and biased judges. Over our rice rissoles and vegetable stew, Divina tells me she is toying with the idea of charging the Bank of England under the Obscene Publications Act. After all, she argues, it wouldn't be difficult to prove that bank notes have a tendency to 'corrupt and deprave' (in the words of the Act) 'those into whose hands they are likely to fall'.

I'm very taken with this spunky girl (apart from anything else, she's very sexy), so I tried to get the *Observer* to print something about the case. They refused on the usual cowardly grounds that it was still *sub judice*, but Tony Howard of the *New Statesman* was more responsive. He's agreed to take it up in his 'London Diary', and I've today sent him an account of the background.

25 November

Papers still full of the case of Lt.-Col. Brooks, the former Lord Mayor of Kensington and Chelsea who is suing *The People* for calling him 'a menace to young girls' because he likes to spank female bottoms. (He used to advertise for girls to spend weekends on his yacht and then paid them to be smacked.) The enormous publicity, which reflects the passionate English interest in the subject, cannot but be a good thing: it brings spanking out into the open: and although Brooks is obviously a diehard Tory squire, I can't help admiring the ebullience with which he admits that he adores spanking. Ten years ago he would have been in the dock, probably accused of indecent assault: alternatively, he would probably have submitted to blackmail rather than admit to his proclivities. It's nice – and indicative of greater sexual openness – that in this case he should be the plaintiff.

26 November

Dreamed of reading in the *Guardian* an article about the probable timing of Edward Heath's resignation. It was headed: 'The Politics of Ta-ta'.

27 November

'When old men decide to barter young men for pride and profit, the transaction is called war.' (Len Deighton)

28 November

If we conceive of Western Europe and the Middle East as a vast aircraft, it is possible to cast the Arab states as hijackers who are holding Israel hostage and threatening to destroy the economy of the West unless the West abandons the hostages. Last night James Mitchell, my half-Israeli lawyer, passionately maintained that, if threatened by the Arabs with defeat, the Israelis would use the atomic bomb to destroy all the major Arab cities. And what (I asked) if this triggered off a nuclear war that demolished Western Europe? So much the worse for Europe, said James: we aren't looking for anyone's approval, this is simply something we *must* do. If I am asked whether I am prepared to sacrifice Western Europe on the altar of Israeli nationalism, I must say no. George Weidenfeld agrees with me that it will not come to this, that the Americans will probably use 'coercive military measures' against the Arabs, and that in any case the Arabs and Israelis will sooner or later work out a balance of terror that will operate as effectively as the

Russo-American equivalent. But do I want European civilisation to be permanently dependent on a balance as volatile and precarious as this? (Later Kathleen tells me that very few people suspect that there is a connection between the increase in oil prices and Arab hostility to the State of Israel, and that if the West gave up its support of the latter, the Arabs would take a softer line on the former).

30 November

Unexpected gaps department: not since Michael White said to me, some five years ago: 'I have never eaten a banana,' has there been such a blinding flash of ignorance as today's. K. and I were driving along the King's Road when she said: 'What's that funny thing over there shaped like a drum?' 'What thing?' I said. 'Over there, behind the houses,' she said. 'Made of metal, very big thing.' I looked and said unbelievingly, 'You mean the gasometer?' 'The what?' 'The gasometer. Thing that holds gas.' 'Oh,' she said, with a small blushing giggle. 'Is that what it is? I always wondered what those things were for.' She later admits that she had hitherto believed that gas came up from underground, through tubes.

2 December

Alan Beesley has killed himself. On Saturday night he told his mother (with whom he was living) that he was taking some new pills which would put him to sleep for thirty-six hours, and that he mustn't be disturbed. After twenty-four hours his mother became worried and went into his bedroom. He had drunk a bottle of whisky and taken an overdose of sleeping pills. He left a note asking that I and Russell Enoch should be informed. K. and I are aghast. Alan's book is to be published in the spring and the American rights had just been sold – although he had not yet received the money. Why could he not have waited? We are painfully aware that, although it was I who got him to write the book and found him a publisher, we did not do all we might have done to save him. We could have spared him more money than we did: and during the last year our own domestic troubles have made us unwilling to have him as a guest. I know he must have felt this; I did not realise that his need for love and companionship was as great as his need for money. K. says we must do something to help his children, and she is obviously right. For all his despair the words that spring to mind when I think of Alan are words like buoyancy, verve, resilience, and an insane indomitable optimism. 'Don't worry, Tynan,' I hear him braying with a convulsive flourish of his cigarette. 'Next year is going to be our year.' What a waste of a talent! I pray the book does well.

5 December

At a health farm near Ipswich, I apply for a colonic irrigation, hoping for a ravishing nurse to part my shaved and shyly proffered globes, assuming at least that the administrator will be female. It turns out to be a male nurse with bad teeth. A highly indecent experience.

6 December

I note with interest that W.H. Auden wrote in his last book, 'Wilde, Kierkegaard, Williams and Lewis guided us back to belief.' (C.S., of course.) Will he finally guide me?

In the last poem of the book (by Auden with Chester Kallman[1]), the celebrated line from 'September 1939' is revised thus: 'We must love one another and die.'

Did Auden know that I proposed this revision – in print – over a decade ago? If so, how unkind of him not to mention it.

One reason why I cannot write nowadays is that I no longer have a *stance*, an attitude, what Eliot called in a letter to Lytton Strachey, 'the core of it – the *tone*'. I used to have a sign by my desk: 'Be light, stinging, insolent and melancholy.' But I am no longer any of these things, except melancholy. Can one have a stance without a cogent moral or political philosophy? Or is it emotional wholeness that one needs – the quality I sacrificed when I divided myself between Nicole and K. ? Or is that cart before horse? Could I have split myself if I had not already lost my entireness?

---

1. Chester Kallman (1921–75). Poet, translator, librettist; collaborated with W.H. Auden on five opera librettos including Stravinsky's *The Rake's Progress*.

7 December

On the Parkinson TV show Muhammad Ali loses his cool when Parkinson quotes Budd Schulberg[1] to the effect that Ali, though he professes to hate white men, has many white friends. Ali launches an intemperate near-paranoid attack on Parkinson, accusing him of laying traps, of behaving like the typical white devil. Later he says something revealing: that if he had had an education, he would never have been a rebel, because education induces conformity, especially in blacks. This is true: but the tragedy is that the only form of rebellion accessible to him is one of the most fanatical and intolerant religious cults in the world. In other circumstances, what a socialist crusader he could have been! (His ferocious puritanism is another enormous pity – he rants proudly of his wife as a chattel, his face contorts with contempt when he talks of miniskirts. He covers his mouth when he talks about sex: it's hard to tell whether his religion has made him neurotic on the subject, or whether his neurosis inclined him towards that religion.)

10 December

Lytton Strachey writing in a letter about his work in progress on Queen Elizabeth: 'If only she could be reduced to nonsense – that would be perfect. The whole of Art lies there. To pulverise the material and remould it in the shape of one's own particular absurdity. What happiness to do that!' Can I do that with Reich? Am, by the way, enormously pleased to read that Strachey wrote nothing at all (except a mediocre piece on Disraeli for a woman's magazine) between August 1919 and May 1923 (age thirty-nine – forty-three).

What to learn from the Bloomsberries? Their insistence that friendship comes before all other passions, from patriotism to sex, and must never be sacrificed on account of the latter. Also their attempts (never *quite* successful, but more often so than one would have thought) to extirpate the wasteful emotion of jealousy. One marvels at Strachey's Ham Spray household – with Ralph Partridge[2] loving Carrington[3], who loved

---

1. Budd Schulberg (1914–). Novelist and screenwriter, won an Academy Award for *On the Waterfront* (1954).
2. Reginald Sherring 'Ralph' Partridge (1894–1960). Husband of British diarist and translator Frances Partridge; had a *ménage à trois* with Lytton Strachey and Dora Carrington.
3. Dora Carrington (1893–1932). Painter, diarist, committed suicide after the death of her beloved Lytton Strachey.

Strachey, who loved Partridge, surrounded by Gerald Brenan[1] (fucking Carrington), Henrietta Bingham[2] (fucking Carrington), and Frances Marshall[3] (being fucked by Partridge). That all this went on with no bloodshed and so little agony is a tribute to a group who, however anaemic their writing may have been, were not bloodless in their private lives.

11 December

Splendid last verse of a strange hymn, addressed to God, which Strachey wrote on his deathbed.

Fill with a golden clearness
My crowded hours of light;
And hallow with thy nearness
My most abandoned night.

15 December

Nicole at least confesses that, contrary to earlier protestations, she has had several brief affairs in my absences during the past two years. This news, on top of what I already know (and suspect) about Kathleen's affairs, leads to a curious conclusion: though accused on all sides of infidelity, I am the only one of the principals in this situation who has remained sexually faithful throughout.

16 December

Definition of lyricism in the English cinema: a solo woodwind against shots of hilly greensward, overlooking a vista of smoking factory chimneys.

21 December

Conversation in a pub in Suffolk between myself and fat properietor:

1. Gerald Brenan (1894–1987). Writer, became friendly with several members of the Bloomsbury set.
2. Henrietta Bingham (1900–65). Lover of Carrington, who made several erotic drawings of her.
3. Frances Partridge (née Marshall) (1900–). Wife of Ralph Partridge.

F.P.: Did you come in a car?

K.T.: Yes.

F.P.: Well, for God's sake, don't go back through Snape. The police jump out from behind hedges and put the bag on your head whenever you cross the bloody white line.

K.T.: Thanks.

F.P.: You'd think they'd have better things to do. Ought to be out hunting these Communists and Irish. [Pause. Then the sublime non-sequitur.] Sometimes I wonder why we fought the last war.

At the NFT I see a brilliant 1939 movie, written by Billy Wilder and Charles Brackett[1], directed by Mitchell Leisen[2] and called *Midnight*. Archetypal thirties plot, set in Paris, of penniless lady gambler (Claudette Colbert) and cab-driver (Don Ameche) posing, respectively, as a Hungarian baroness and baron. John Barrymore, Mary Astor and Francis Lederer also present. The Wilder wit at its inventive best – e.g.: 'I should have suspected your father was insane when he gave us as a wedding present one roller skate covered with Thousand Island Dressing.' Or this – Colbert bitching Astor, who is trying on a hat: 'It does something for your face. It gives you a chin.' One of my favourite lost paradises is the vision of European high life conjured up in Hollywood during the thirties by European refugees. I can't think why *Midnight* isn't regarded as a classic.

1. Charles Brackett (1892–1969). Former drama critic of *The New Yorker*, became Hollywood producer and screenwriter, collaborating with Billy Wilder on *The Lost Weekend* (1945) and *Sunset Boulevard* (1950), winning Oscars for both.
2. Mitchell Leisen (1898–1972). Hollywood film director with a gift for witty romantic comedy.

1975

13 January

A visit to Munich last week opens up a new possibility for the film – a German pornoflick producer offers me his technicians and crew in return for German distribution rights. But this creates complications at the British end: if the picture is to be German-based the British investors cannot get Bank of England permission to transfer their funds. These delays (and the eggs-in-one-basket nature of my commitment to the film) have frayed my nerves to shrieking.

Two TV programmes last week reinforced my belief (which sometimes seems a sentimental evasion of responsibility) that in a socialist world I could flourish: I would not be as bereft of purpose, energy and ambition as I feel now in a world whose creed of personal fulfilment and gratification I have so lovingly embraced. One of the programmes was a study of Cuba after fifteen years of Castro's Communism. It showed that, in spite of restrictions on political freedom, a new kind of man is being evolved by life in a system where the common weal has replaced personal pleasure as the primary focus of existence. (cf. Milton: 'To the public good, private respects must yield' – the creed of Dagon's followers in *Samson Agonistes*, which I have hitherto regarded as dehumanising when in fact I now suspect it might better be described as super-humanising.)

The other programme was a documentary about the workers at the Meriden motorcycle factory who, when the company decided to close the plant fifteen months ago, responded by occupying it and announcing that they could run it themselves. They have kept the place picketed twenty-four hours a day; they have worked on improved designs and more economic production methods, all the time pressing the government for financial aid, which has been repeatedly promised but not yet delivered. For fifteen months they (and their solidly loyal families) have survived without pay, and they swear they can survive another fifteen months if necessary. Listening to these vigorous, inventive, dedicated men, who radiate conviction and contentment despite their privations, I had a new surge of certainty that this was the answer to the collapsing West; cursed the newspapermen who deride worker-control of industry; and cursed myself for being too old, unskilled and lost in self-indulgence to help them build the new society. As recent entries in this journal indicate, I have even lost the ability to write well. Without self-approval, there is no self-confidence, without self-confidence one has no secure identity; and without a secure identity one has no style.

'Prolonged stress will cause sterility, impotence and even death' (a professor on TV, talking about the problems of breeding wolverines in captivity). *Vide* K.T.

14 January

Just before Christmas, quite insanely, I bought a Jaguar XJ12, mainly on hire purchase. The loan repayments (£25 a week,) the insurance (£6 a week,) and the petrol consumption (8 miles per gallon, at the new extortionate prices) are far beyond my purse; and the timing of the purchase, when nobody is buying huge cars that can do 150 m.p.h. (since the British speed limit is 70 m.p.h. and may be reduced to save fuel) is definably dotty. Yet I love the silently lumbering giant, I love the velvety smoothness of its motion, I love creeping through traffic jams with the stereo radio blasting the overture to *Cosi fan tutte* from all four speakers; above all, I love bowling along motorways in the sun. The sense of *cushioned escape* is complete; I feel utterly protected, totally truant, and get that glowing, illusory sensation of being in control of my own life, of knowing where I am going, at least until the petrol runs out. Yet all the time I am aware that XJ12 is a doomed species, shortly to become extinct because of the increasing unavailability of its natural diet (four-star petrol): I am at the wheel of a dinosaur. Meanwhile the smaller indigenous species – especially the once-mighty Mini – are threatened with extinction at the hands of the invading hordes of Datsuns from Japan. It is all very evolutionary.

15 January

Last night to the Coliseum for six hours of *The Mastersingers*. I come virgin to Wagner, never having seen any of the operas before. It's not an experience I shall soon repeat. Have I been spoiled for Wagner by long exposure to the Hollywood school of epic background-music composers (e.g. Max Steiner,[1] Dimitri Tiomkin,[2] Alfred Newman[3]) who are his true heirs? Many of the great Hollywood movies were in fact operas without singing: mood and atmosphere was always established (and action unfailingly underlined) by the composer, precisely in the manner of a Wagner music-drama, where everything is accompanied by (when not drowned in) a sonorous backwash of explanatory sound. Banal and prolix as this may be, it is not in itself boring (though how it could be described as Shakespearian in its infinite variety entirely escapes me). What eventually grates is the paucity of the content in which such orchestral extravagance is lavished. A young nobleman defeats a scheming critic in a very uneven battle for the heroine's hand, and ends up winning a sort of Eurovision song contest with Fasching trappings. Matter here for a couple of hours at most: but *six*? And what a resolution, with the hero safe in the embrace of bourgeois nationalism.

20 January

I suppose there is no doubt that I hastened the death of my mother. By leaving her to live alone in Birmingham and visiting her rarely while I lived in London, I condemned her to the isolation that eventually – combined with the anaemia that dried up the blood supply to her brain – led to her inability to live without constant supervision. If she had come to London and lived with me in the fifties, she could have been sustained by human contact: but I never invited her, and, lacking it, she degenerated until there was no alternative but to consign her to the palatial but heartless home in Northampton wherein, appallingly emaciated, she died. I could have

1. Max Steiner (1888–1971). Austrian-born composer and arranger, won Academy Awards for *The Informer* (1935), *Now, Voyager* (1942), *Since You Went Away* (1944).
2. Dimitri Tiomkin (1899–1979). Hollywood composer; Academy Awards for *High Noon* (1951), *The High and Mighty* (1954) and *The Old Man and the Sea* (1958).
3. Alfred Newman (1901–70). Hollywood composer; won nine Academy Awards including one for *The Song of Bernadette* (1943).

,postponed her death at the expense of my own absorption in self-advancement; I chose not to.

Tonight I felt this old, self-accusing wound all over again when I watched a TV play starring Elizabeth Bergner[1] as a dotty old *émigrée*, widowed and intolerably eccentric, who is evicted from the bed-sitter in which she has built herself a nest for decades, and who dies within a year, despite the superior comfort of the alternative accommodation that is provided for her. We deplore the existence of over-mothered sons, and label them neurotics: but perhaps they are essential to the salvation of bereaved or deserted mothers.

21 January

I find in Moore's *Principia Ethica* this following remark: 'Verbal questions are properly left to the writers of dictionaries and other persons interested in literature: philosophy *as we shall see*, has no concern with them.' That was in 1903: and it was, of course, precisely what we did *not* see. Rather the contrary: in the light of subsequent developments, it seems that philosophy has no concern with anything *other than* verbal questions.

On BBC-2, a programme about Roman Britain reminds me of a similarity between the Roman gods and the Far Eastern religions, and the basic difference between both and Christianity. Neither in pagan Rome nor in Buddhism (Zen or orthodox) is a man condemned because he behaves badly: there is no moral sanction: he is condemned only (by the Roman reckoning) if he fails to carry out the correct acts of worship at the prescribed times. What we would consider immoral behaviour would have been considered merrily anti-social. Similarly, Zen lays down no rules about conduct: that is left to Confucius. Such concepts as sin or guilt are unknown, since neither the Roman nor the Zen Buddhists believe that the creator of the universe and the moral legislator are one and the same. The Judaeo-Christian God, in other words, is the criminal who imported into civilisation the crippling notion of sin.

1. Elizabeth Bergner (1900–86). Austrian-born actress who became a star in Britain and America.

Nobody – on TV – has to be funny any more. All laughter is canned, pre-recorded, *fixed*: the art of comedy is in the hands of backroom engineers, matching laughter tracks with jokes: and so infectious is laughter that home audiences laugh along with the mechanised euphoria. This is perhaps the most hateful thing about TV: that it removes from the audience its great prerogative of deciding which performers are good and which are not. So subtle is the manipulation that when the comic pauses, the engineer will dub in a tiny audience cough to indicate that the pay-off line has not yet arrived. Instead of making the spectator laugh, the comic tailors his gag to fit the most enthusiastic available burst of pre-recorded laughter. In other words, it is impossible for all but the most critical audience to decide for itself what is funny or what is not.

24 January

My XJ12 continues to drive me, instead of the other way round, and quite often I have the impression that it is very kindly giving me a lift. Its waltzing (whenever there is a drop of rain on the roads) has improved in verve and abandon, and I am considering entering it in the Formation Dancing Contest for Saloon Cars that is to be held in Woolwich Car-park on the next wet Sunday.

25 January

To the Old Vic for a preview of Peter Hall's production of *John Gabriel Borkman* with the sort of cast that Binkie Beaumont would have given it ten or fifteen years ago (Ralph Richardson, Peggy Ashcroft, Wendy Hiller). P. Hall has now had a year at the helm and one has a frantic sense of a ship that has run hopelessly aground: a few oars swing furiously in their rowlocks, beating at air, and there's no breeze around to fill the sails. Why *this* Ibsen, anyway? Today we just can't accept the late capitalist as a tragic hero, as Ibsen just could: when Borkman declares that it was he who brought the minerals from the mines, he who awakened them from their subterranean slumber, we want to say: 'No, it wasn't: it was the miners.' We no longer feel awed at the fall of a banker, or shocked when his son departs for the Mediterranean with not only a mistress but a female companion to replace her, should need arise. To make this very elderly play work, we need either (a) a Borkman of tremendous brooding magnetism (such as Frederick Valk brought to the part), not a dotty, whimsical old buffer like Ralph, or (b) a production that recreates – in word and gesture and atmosphere – the late nineteenth century instead of one (like P. Hall's) which could be a Pinter play dressed up in frock-coats and bombazine. The last act (with Borkman and Ella out in the snow) was frankly hilarious. What a mess P.H. has made of our theatre! – and when will someone say so in print?

About four years ago I stopped doing two things – eating potatoes and working hard. Which prompts a reflection: may it not be that the world should be divided into the potatoed and potatoless countries? How much has the creativity of Europe and North America to do with their vast consumption of potatoes? (And their neuroses, too, perhaps). Isn't it possible that the decisive alien-ness of the Japanese, Chinese and Indians derives from the fact that they have been denied the benefits (and ill-effects) of the magical tuber? I can take a high-protein diet with no problems, envying nobody his sugar or sweetmeats: but I die with desire for a crisp mouthful of hash-brown potato.

26 January

Having discovered that Frin Mullin has never eaten either oysters or pheasant, I order an elaborate oyster-and-pheasant lunch at Gravetye Manor and drive her and Nicole out to eat it. This partly to celebrate the birth of her daughter (Mikayella) last month, and partly a farewell treat, since she goes back to her boyfriend in India next week. Lunch a great success (with the biggest oysters I have ever eaten – shells about 5 inches in diameter, so vast that we have the last six packed in ice and take them back for Mullin *mère* and *père* to eat). Then a horrendous scene as I drive Nicole alone up to London.

She has been offered a flat at the ridiculously cheap rent of £7.50 a week: but a tacit part of the deal (unspoken but extremely operative) is that in order to get it she must go to bed with the owner. This she has now done (he's a personable chap, it seems, around thirty) and it's clear that further favours will be expected of her. I said this saddened me, and asked why she didn't take an evening job so that she could afford to take a flat without prostituting herself. (She takes singing lessons during the day and at present lives on the dole, which is approx. £12 a week.)

This provokes a ferocious outburst against people who float around in their Jaguars spending more money on a lunch than she has to live on for a month, and presume to tell poorer people that they ought. And then, when her anger dies down, she begins to fear that she has alienated me: and after a long pause, looking at the floor, she mutters: 'All right. I won't go to bed with him again and I'll get an evening job.' What I wanted to say was: I'm sorry for what I've done to you: why should you get an evening job if you don't want one? All I said was. 'It doesn't matter. Make up your own mind.'

That evening K.H. and I go to dinner to meet David Wakefield, husband of Divina, whom I met before Christmas. He is out of prison pending the result of his appeal against conviction: he will know the result in a fortnight. The Wakefields live in a third-floor flat, quite comfortable and roomy, in Clapham. There is a great rattling of bolts when we press the doorbell: David peers warily out with the chain still on (he's a shock-haired, bubbling, vivacious chap in his early thirties, with a strong Cockney accent). He explains that on Friday night three burglars with stockings over their heads broke into the flat, tied him and Divina up and held razors to their throats while they ransacked the place, obviously expecting to find some of the money David makes out of his film clubs. But there was no money on hand, and although they left the flat a shambles all they took was a watch. David seems unperturbed by the experience, but it has clearly upset Divina, who is very shaky and *piano* all evening.

We talk for a while about censorship, socialism, the need for radical change, etc. and then David reveals his real obsession: he believes that the world can be changed by LSD. He explains that he has taken hundreds of trips (he still takes two a week) and that each has given him new insight and enlightenment: there are, he says, no problems LSD cannot solve. He talks with infectious verve and enthusiasm. As for many acid-heads, 2001 is his favourite movie, and he venerates Kubrick. Some of his ideas are freaky: he believes that LSD has already infiltrated the Establishment and that top people in the CIA are secretly pushing the drug at high government levels to prepare for the day (probably imminent) when LSD rules the world. He even suggests that Nixon was a devout acid-dropper who deliberately engineered Watergate in order to discredit power politics and its machinations.

Although he sometimes skids into fantasies like these, David does not come across as a maniac: just as a man with generous (even visionary) impulses and enthusiasms who simply lacks the information and education to restrain his wilder flights of wish-fulfilment. He is a nice man: you don't feel you're in the presence of a fanatic. He is in fact a missionary, and his ebullient optimism corresponds exactly to that of the early Protestants, who were – as C.S. Lewis points out – not in the least what we mean by puritans: 'Whatever they were, they were not sour, gloomy or severe.' Thomas More complained that the Protestants were drunk with 'lewd lightness of mind and vain gladness of heart'. 'Protestantism was not too grim, but too glad to be true,' as Lewis put it. Protestants were 'not ascetics but sensualists'; More remarked that they practised 'more sensual and licentious living than ever did Mahomet'. So there is no anomaly in David Wakefield's showing sex films and wanting to purify the world: and no hypocrisy either.

Rereading Lewis on what it felt like to be an early Protestant, I'm powerfully reminded of Wakefield on LSD:

The experience is one of catastrophic conversion. The man who has passed through it feels like one who has waked from night-mare into ecstasy. Like an accepted lover, he feels that he has done nothing, and never could have done anything, to deserve such astonishing happiness . . . He is not saved because he does works of love: he does works of love because he is saved . . . Relief and buoyancy are the characteristic notes. In a single sentence of the *Tischreden* Luther tosses the question aside for ever. Do you doubt whether you are elected to salvation? Then say your prayers, man, and you may conclude that you are. It is as easy as that.

Except that in David's case it isn't 'say your prayers' but 'take your trip'. He has asked me to drop some acid with him next week. I've never done it, and am tempted.

29 January

(1) Appalled to read three glowing reviews of the NT's *John Gabriel Borkman*. P. Hall's mastery of public relations surges relentlessly on: for weeks now it's been impossible to turn on radio or TV or pick

up a paper without reading something radiant about his film of *Akenfield*.

(2) Last night to Greenwich for John Osborne's new play, *The End of Me Old Cigar*, all about a wealthy whorehouse madam plotting to destroy male supremacy by releasing to the world her collection of films and tapes of prominent male citizens in bed. Play full of culture references, yet on the whole strangely uneducated. Dialogue in first act mostly bitchy monologue by Rachel Roberts as the madam; odd phrases stand out from a swamp of unfiltered venom. Most of Act 2 is a bed scene in which, amid the moral squalor, Jill Bennett and Keith Barron 'find love'. Perfunctory curtain. Main interest consists in lengthy first-act attack on me, described as lilac-trousered Oxford trendy with a passion for inflicting 'dangerously painful spankings'. God knows I'm used to being attacked, but there are two aspects of this tirade that leave a shitty taste.

(1) Sickening to find J.O. resorting to the old puritan trick of knocking people because of their sexual habits; quite like old Queensberry vilifying Wilde. And why *'dangerously'* painful spankings? He must know this is a lie. If not, he should ask his wife, whom I spanked to our great mutual delight nearly twenty years ago.

(2) The programme says J.O. wrote the play last summer. Since then he has accepted my offer of renewed friendship and twice visited the house for dinner. I don't see how he could have done that, knowing that he was about to savage me on stage. In a similar situation, I would either have turned down the invitation or – if the renewed friendship worked – revised the play. What is particularly craven is that he never mentioned the subject: fearful, I imagine, that to admit the character was myself would be to lay himself open to a libel action. K.H. more upset by this than I am. Am dismayed to reflect how much distress has beset this golden girl on my account.

Footnote: am reminded that long ago J.O. wrote a ferocious attack on gossip columnists who invaded people's private lives – *The World of Paul Slickey*. Ironic that he should now have turned into Slickey himself.

2 February

C.S. Lewis says: 'Surely no genius is so fortunate as he who has the power and wish to do well what his predecessors have been doing badly. He need neither oppose an existing taste nor create a new one: he has only to satisfy a desire which is already aroused.' Perhaps it is under such conditions that the perfect work comes, ripe and not over-ripe: a Jane Austen following on a Fanny Burney, a Racine on a Corneille – and an *Alex and Sophie* on a *Deep Throat*. (I am *bursting* with frustration.)

3 February

Use the word 'unpurchasable', borrowed from C.S.L.

5 February

The anus of Marie Corelli[1]
Was vast and repulsively smelly.
One morning it tore
On a nail in a door,
And out fell her guts and her belly.

7 February

(Spate of scatology continuing, these poems being the products of morning twilight sleep.)

It was the Bugger's birthday,
And all the sods were there,
And each man held his grimy prick,
And every bum was bare.
The Bugger rose up slowly,
And bowed to left and right,
And said: 'I'll fuck the lot of you
Before the morning light.'

9 February

Supper at Parkes with Joan Plowright. She fills me in on Larry's state of mind and health. His hatred of P. Hall is now ineradicable and borders

1. Marie Corelli (1855–1924). The pen-name of Mary Mackay, best-selling British author of twenty-five books including *A Romance of Two Worlds* (1886).

at times on paranoia. Last October, perhaps psychosomatically, he went down with a rare disease causing progressive muscular degeneration; it could have been fatal but was happily arrested and he has been back at home for several weeks, apparently fully recovered and hoping to return to work soon. He now passionately regrets ever having given his backing to P. Hall as his successor; several times he has drafted letters to Max Rayne resigning from the NT planning committee and from the figurehead job of 'President' that has been thought up for him. He has been appalled by what P.H. has done to the good will created by his regime, to company spirit ('It's like a morgue backstage nowadays,' says Joan) and to relationships with the audience.

Joan sums up P.H.'s approach to theatre by an anecdote about Robin Philips' Stratford production of *Two Gentlemen of Verona*, which I didn't especially like but which was a tremendous success. P.H. and John Barton saw a dress rehearsal and were appalled, so much so that there was talk of cancellation. But the audience at the first preview were rapturous: so P.H. and Barton summoned Philips for a chat. 'What was your concept in this production?' asked P.H. Philips looked puzzled. 'What was your governing idea?' said Barton. 'Oh,' said Philips, 'I didn't have one. It just – happened between me and the actors.' P.H. and J.B. simply could not understand: how could anyone stage a play without first writing a 1,000-word programme note 'reinterpreting the play for contemporary audiences', etc. And this is typical of the RSC method.

I saw it in action at the Aldwych the other evening in *Twelfth Night*. Here the basic concept is Narcissism: the backcloth is dominated by a painting of Narcissus contemplating himself in a pool. All the performances are scaled down to fit the mould. Nobody objects to a basic idea: what is tedious is when it becomes so obtrusive that the production is nothing more than a lecture-demonstration. The actors are so busy fitting the interpretation that they forget to be *interesting* or *charming* or *funny*. It is just not enough to be *right* in the theatre, to be lucid in exposition and loyal to the author's subtext. You must also be *exciting*, and this is what the RSC (since P. Brook's departure) has totally forgotten. The first job of a director is to get the maximum amount of appropriate vitality out of his actors: *vide* the revolution caused by the Zeffirelli *Romeo* at the Vic in 1958 – he did not ask what the governing idea of the play was, he asked himself: 'Let's make these people come alive and watch them behave – and if we do that with enough truth and expressiveness, the play's meaning will speak for itself.' A simple formula, one would have thought: but how rarely repeated!

To return to Joan: she says none of the younger stars with whom she grew up ever wants to work for P.H. again. Nor will they tolerate the servitude of long commercial runs. Joan is therefore trying to set up a company of all the talents, unsubsidised, its home to be a converted cinema in Notting Hill Gate, where people like Maggie Smith, Tony Hopkins, Frank Finlay, Alec McCowan, Diana Rigg and herself would work in a repertory system that would be based on a mutual agreement to take over each other's parts after productions had run for two months. There would be financing provided by a contract with TV companies both here and in the States. It sounds a bit pipe-dreamy (I can't see all those stars happily understudying each other) but I agree to help if I can, and propose that Joan gets together with Michael White.

10 February

Further to last entry: Paul Scofield and John Dexter are also interested in Joan's project. Tentative company title: 'The NT Rejects'. I must say the whole thing would be a splendid slap in the face for P.H. Joan confided in me, by the way, that Max Rayne and the Board have also been shaken to the core by the Hall regime, not least by the appalling cost of it all: in addition to his own vast salary and perks (including a flat in the Barbican and chauffeur-driven car) he employs two assistants to whom he delegates authority, over the heads of the associate directors; and his astounding decision to take over the TV arts programme *Aquarius* – an act of bizarre effrontery with the NT in such a fragile condition – was taken in the face of unanimous opposition from his associate directors.

13 February

Talking to someone about witty impromptus, I recall one of Gore Vidal's musings as we drove out together to Elstree in the long-gone days when I was head of scripts at Ealing Films and he was working on the screenplay of *J'Accuse*: 'I have just been reading,' he observed, 'Somerset Maugham's book on the great novelists of the past. A fascinating exercise. He fits them into a private pantheon of his own

– chopping off Hardy's wrist, lopping off Conrad's legs – in which, in a prominent central position, there is a *gap*, which can only be filled by a certain, well-known, wizened little figure.' This paragraph was delivered with exemplary phrasing and not a trace of hesitation – not bad at any time, but quite remarkable at eight in the morning.

A letter arrives from John Bishop in South America. He has been unable to raise the money he promised for the film. On this we were absolutely counting. Even I must now admit that it's all over. At 7 p.m. I have to go on the Russell Harty TV show and sparkle. (I can't cancel because I did that last month at the last moment.) The mouth dehydrates at the prospect. The pill bottle is going to be hit very hard today.

14 February

Managed the Harty show: but it was a long interview and I fitfully glimmered rather than sparkled, making do with well-tried anecdotes. Georgia Brown[1] also on show. She lives in Los Angeles now and advised me strongly against living either in New York or California – the cause that Kathleen is now urging on me by long-distance telephone. Sent Kathleen – now in Hollywood – a Valentine telegram advising her to read Shakespeare's 109th sonnet – 'O never say that I was false of heart.'

To Brighton with Nicole to see Michael White and his new show, Tony Shaffer's *Murderer*. Michael strongly advises me to forget the film for three months: he is setting up a film-investment group with some millionaire backers and promises me that, if it comes off, he will back the film. *Murderer* is a play with one brilliantly grisly gimmick – a silent twenty-minute opening sequence in which Robert Stephens apparently strangles a girl and chops her body up into fragments. Unfortunately the rest of the play doesn't work. It's clearly in my interests that Michael should have as many hits as possible to encourage his investors, so I closet myself with Clifford Williams and we try to doctor the plot so that it will work. At present it's all hook and no fish.

---

1. Georgia Brown (1933–92). British actress and singer.

15 February

Lunch with Michael, Clifford and Tony Shaffer to discuss my suggested improvements. Not all are accepted, but Tony – not the most energetic of rewriters – at least realises that radical revision is necessary.

16 February

I call K.H. in Beverly Hills and find with chagrin that although she has received my cable, she has not bothered to look up the relevant sonnet. She begs me to come to New York at the end of next week to gauge the scene and investigate the opportunities she claims to have found for me. But even if they are all she says, have I the will and spirit to take them? I remain very low, turned in on myself, unready for new ventures. It's clear with all the lack of ambition that that implies and all the bouts of self-accusing gloom that it entails; K. wants what I was and what I could be. Meanwhile my debts mount (I was really counting on the money from the film); and I get a letter from Michael White asking me to agree to royalty cuts on *Oh! Calcutta!* until the present theatre slump ends.

Fine reviews for John McGrath's new play with music, *Fish in the Sea*, which I saw last week at the Half Moon Theatre. I'm delighted, as I was when I saw it: a strong, warm, socialist saga about a Liverpool family and the lives of its three daughters – the kind of committed theatre one looked for, but never quite got, in the wake of the Royal Court revolution of the late fifties. I hope it transfers to the West End and a wider audience.

A fifty-minute TV interview with Kingsley Amis. His face a sedately controlled sneer, the nostrils flaring with contempt, which he tries unsuccessfully to soften into the semblance of a smile; the voice costive and smug; the general manner that of a less seedily Byronic Peregrine Worsthorne.[1] Nothing remains – in Kingsley's frigid xenophobia, his special loathing of American (and above all American-Jewish) writers, his paranoid distaste for the Left – of the open-minded, wickedly funny, jazz-loving drinking companion I knew and liked at Oxford.

1. Peregrine Worsthorne (1923–). Journalist and Editor of the *Sunday Telegraph*, 1986–89.

17 February

Felled by flu – my hoodlum ambusher, who always chooses low moments to step out of the shadows and zap me. So: sleepless nights with raw throat and a day (the first of not a few) spent coughing the endlessly rattling phlegm up out of my left lung. Meanwhile a party is being given for K.H. in Beverly Hills, a poolside wing-ding with Tony Richardson, Warren Beatty, Billy Wilder and cast of surely hundreds. I don't wish I was there: but can she really wish she was here? Feel powerful need to fly to some sunny island, perhaps in the Seychelles, and damn everything and everyone, including Kathleen and the expense.

20 February

Useful word unearthed by Paul Johnson in the *New Statesman*: 'eirenic', *M · K?* meaning 'tending towards peace'.

28 February

Reading Brendan Gill's book on *The New Yorker*, I come across a reference to Irwin Shaw[1] that brings vividly to mind the last time I saw him. The occasion was a publisher's party in Paris last summer. Tousled, half-drunk and amiably blinking, Irwin had asked at least a dozen of the guests (including me) to go on with him to dinner at the Pactole. No good pointing out that the Pactole was *chic* and would be crowded: he insisted that the patron would find room, which of course he didn't: so Irwin led us, a straggling drunken rout, from café to café along the Boulevard St Germain, each as full as the last, until finally we came to rest, gasping, in a dim *bistro* near Notre Dame. Here Irwin rapidly became lachrymose. 'I used to be the darling of the Left,' he mumbled. 'That was in the thirties. Then I moved to *The New Yorker*, and the Left said I'd sold out. Then I was the darling of the literary set because of my short stories. But when I began to write best-selling novels, the literary set said I'd sold out. And when they started to buy my novels for movies, *everybody* said I'd sold out. So now all the bastards hate me,

1. Irwin Shaw (1913–84). Author, dramatist, *New Yorker* contributor.

every goddamn one of them.' He was led off into the night by his extremely tall girlfriend. I saw them crossing the road, Irwin slouching like a clothed penguin, making great whirling gestures of disgust with his stubby arms.

7 March

Am in Brompton Hospital for week of lung-function tests to see how my emphysema's progressing. (Answer: no deterioration, but of course no improvement either.) Sharing a National Health ward with five other victims, I'm overwhelmed once again by the efficient courtesy of the doctor, the patient niceness of the (mainly Filipino, black or Irish) nurses, the sheer indispensability of the NHS: for all its faults, what an advertisement for socialism. Atmosphere in the ward one of uneasy conviviality, each man privately seeking evidence to support his necessary conviction that he is less mortally stricken than any of the others. But the camaraderie is genuine: being in this kind of ward is like being in an air-raid shelter during the Blitz.

I remember when I first guessed that I had emphysema. It was at a party at William Styron's on Martha's Vineyard in c. 1967: the table was candle-lit and after dinner the male guests competed in blowing out the candles without pursing their lips (i.e. just forming an open 'O'). Jimmy Baldwin, Terry Southern, Johnny Marquand Jr., George Plimpton, Philip Rahv[1], Lillian Hellman among the company. Of the men, I alone couldn't perform the feat, even at a couple of inches' distance from the flame. 'Aha,' said someone (was it George?) 'that means you have emphysema.' When I got back to London, I checked, and learned with a little shudder that he was right. The party was held just before the publication of Bill's *Confessions of Nat Turner*, already guaranteed (the grapevine always knows in advance) to be a huge best-seller, although with the imminent growth of the New Left ideas and black militancy among the Manhattan intellectuals, it was soon to be written off as a WASP bourgeois travesty of black aspirations. However, it made Bill a heap of money (not that he was short of cash, since his wife Rose is rich: but the kudos was badly needed): and as Rose was soon to be saying with immense satisfaction: 'It's Bill's turn.' Rose used this expression whenever a member of the Quality Lit. set had a big

---

1. Philip Rahv (1908–73). American literary critic, co-founder and editor of *Partisan Review*.

financial hit. A year or so later, with *In Cold Blood*: 'It's Truman's turn.' Presumably in 1969, after *Oh! Calcutta!*, it was Ken's turn.

Characteristic dilemma arises over Patrick Lichfield's wedding tomorrow. It's a shatteringly posh affair, with 1400 guests from the Queen downwards, and only today do I discover that morning dress and toppers are being worn. Possessing neither, I am faced with a choice between (a) turning up in an ordinary suit and being sneered at in the right-wing press for pathetically cocking a 'snook' at the affair, and (b) renting the gear and being accused in the left-wing press of having sold out to the upper classes. So it looks as if I can't go at all, much to the chargrin of K.H. who has bought a grand new hat for the occasion.

8 March

K.H. called Patrick Lichfield and established that dark suits were acceptable, so we motored up to Chester anyway. Whole city lined with flag-waving crowds, many of them having waited since 6 a.m. Charabancs take us from car-park to hotel for buffet lunch (Patrick Garland, Anthony Haden-Guest[1], David Bailey, Quentin Crewe[2] among people we know), and then to the cathedral to await arrival of bride and groom, Queen, Queen Mum, Margaret, Mountbatten and assorted minor royalty. After the ceremony (during which the best man fainted and Margaret had to retrieve the ring, which he dropped) we are bussed off to Eaton Hall, the ramshackle and spectacularly hideous seat of the Duke of Westminster. Here we queue for nearly an hour before gaining entrance to a vast marquee. No reception line, no music, two speeches (by best man and groom) which were as brief as they were boring, champagne and hot sausages, and back to the car-park. Not one of the peaks of my social pilgrimage. We delivered a promised piece of wedding cake to the owner of a Chester pub where we'd stopped for a drink *en route*, and sped south again.

22 March

Can it be true – as I sometimes suspect – that only unhealthy people are sexual deviants? (*Physically* unhealthy, I mean.) Am I wrong in assuming

1. Anthony Haden-Guest (1937–). Anglo-American journalist.
2. Quentin Crewe (1926–98). Journalist and author.

that all athletes are straight fuckers? Is it just indoctrination – *mens sana in corpore sano* – that makes it impossible to imagine George Best[1] wielding the birch or Ken Rosewall[2] downing the knickers?

23 March

Fly via Tangiers to Agadir, hideously rebuilt since its earthquake a decade or so ago, and thence by car to Taroudant, a pink-turreted town fifty miles inland. (I travel with Robert Morley and his wife, by coincidence bound for the same place.) I'm here in a last-ditch attempt to rid my lungs of the bronchial spasms that have shaken me for the past five weeks: if the sun won't do it, I give up. The last time I made a similar desperation trip was to Tunis, two and a half years ago; then the sun worked its miracle, and I went home breathing freely. But I am older now, with less stamina, less to live for, weighed down by a deep and leaden depression. Yes: a sequel to *Oh! Calcutta!* is on the stocks, and I've commissioned Clive James[3] to adapt Willie Donaldson's brilliant autobiography for the stage[4]: but these are marginal entrepreneurial anxieties: they don't really involve me. And the film seems as far off as ever: Michael White told me on Saturday that the financial support he hoped to provide looks like melting away. So I wonder if there is much point in returning to London. Am reading a book called *Hemingway in Spain*, by a Spanish novelist, about the years when I knew him, and in his arid, despondent, written-out condition I see a giant mirror-image of my own *accidie*.

25 March

The Morleys drive me on a picnic across this parched landscape of scrub and mesa. We eat at an oasis and give the remains – a dribble of wine and a few slices of sausage – to a young Moroccan who guided us to the

---

1. George Best (1946–). Tempestuous Irish soccer super-star; as striker for Manchester United scored one hundred and thirty-five goals in over a decade.
2. Ken Rosewall (1934–). Australian tennis champion.
3. Clive James (1939–). Australian-born author and broadcaster; television critic for the *Observer*, 1972–82.
4. Tynan to Kathleen Tynan, 25 June, 1975: 'Clive James has called to say that he can't continue the Donaldson adaptation, doesn't like what he has done and is giving it up. Won't be dissuaded and is coming over to apologise. Just another day in the sun-drenched life of K.T. . . .'

picnic-ground and refused our offers of food and drink until he saw we had finished. As we drive back (via a little drab village in the foothills of the Anti-Atlas which Robert hails as: 'Ah! The Malvern of Morocco!') Robert quizzes me about Hemingway, Spain and bullfighting, revealing only when I have spilled my beans that he regards *toreo* as something only slightly more lovable than child-murder.

The more I read of *Hemingway in Spain*, the more I realise that most of the climaxes of my emotional life – the glooms, the exhilarations, the guilts, the explosions – took place there, as did Hemingway's. 'You bullfighting people must have something in common,' Robert muses aggressively. 'You and Hemingway and John Huston. I wonder what it could be – some kind of insecurity?' I protest that most people are insecure in some way or other. 'Nonsense,' says Robert crisply. 'I know *hundreds* who aren't.'

I suppose it is awareness of death that separates us from Robert. 'How can we live, seeing we have to die?' Thus Hemingway: I can't imagine the question bothering Robert. I must go back to Spain, even without Antonio's presence in the plazas: I miss the late-afternoon anguish of the *corrida*, without which holidays in other Mediterranean countries are like vegetarian diets. Perhaps I can justify a trip to San Isidro in May?

Reading the correspondence between Scott Fitzgerald and his editor, Maxwell Perkins, I find myself wincing at the latter's smugness (and at the way in which Fitzgerald filially deferred to him). Two points of dislike: Perkins asks Fitzgerald to omit from a book a short story in which Shakespeare commits a rape, 'a crime . . . associated with Negroes'; and shortly afterwards he describes the guests at a party he didn't enjoy as 'a rather Semitic-looking crowd'.

31 March

Robert Morley recalls a meeting with Lord Longford at which pornography was discussed: 'I told him that if somebody liked to dress up in chamois leather and be stung by wasps, I really couldn't see why one should stop him.' Robert and Joan are staying at the posh, Frenchified hotel (the Gazelle d'Or) while we are at the cheaper but more atmospheric Salom. I smugly pass on to Robert the information (gleaned from the owner of the Salom) that the Gazelle d'Or has to close during the summer months because the town sewers overflow at that period into the hotel gardens, bringing with them thousands of poisonous serpents. Robert is gratifyingly appalled: I could not have guessed that sewage and snakes are two of his pet phobias.

6 April

Robert tonight pooh-poohed (or rather pooh-bahed) the idea of my directing a film. 'Far too difficult for you, darling,' he said. 'Why don't you try directing a play? You might be able to manage that.' And more in the same dismissive, and hurtful, vein. He claims not to be an aggressive man, but there is tremendous hostility at work beneath the *bonhomie*. The other day he introduced himself to a middle-aged Dutch lady staying at his hotel and invited her to take coffee with us. No sooner had she sat down than he subjected her to a virulent cross-examination on the Common Market (which he hates) and the danger of Communism (at which he scoffs, embarrassingly insisting that the Russian people are freer than we are). Next day, when the Dutch lady nervously approaches our table, Robert rudely freezes her out.

  His trouble, I suspect, and it explains why he repeats that he is only in show business for the money and despises subsidised theatre because it is uncommercial – derives partly from the fact that he has never appeared in a good play in his life. (I can remember only three of the dozens of plays he has starred in: *The Little Hut*, *Edward My Son*, and of course *The Man Who Came to Dinner*, which introduced him to sophisticated comedy in 1941.) More than that, however, he has not only never joined one of the great subsidised companies, *he has never even been invited*: and that must rankle. Alec Guinness has never worked for the National or the RSC but at least he has been asked. Robert – alone among the Shaftsbury Avenue stars – has not. Hence the fat boy sulks, excluded from a party he would dearly have loved the chance to boycott.

9 April

K.T. (watching the glacial Grace Kelly in a TV rerun of High Society): She looks as if ice-cream wouldn't melt in her mouth.

'Fishes are underwater birds' (remark attributed to Peter Scott, the naturalist).

12 April

Man in a restaurant: Excuse me, Mr Tynan, is it possible to get hold of a copy of *He That Plays the King*? I lent my copy to Jill Rowe-Dutton and never got it back.

K. T.: Funny. I once lent Jill Rowe-Dutton to someone and never got *her* back.

13 April

Why is it that most of the pop songs sung by men have to do with women leaving them – and most pop songs sung by women have to do with men leaving them? Why are there no songs about men who have left their women – and vice versa? This is just as common a situation, and one that ought to produce just as many memorable songs.

14 April

Mel Brooks, who is in town to publicise his new film *Young Frankenstein*, comes to tea, stubby self-confidence radiating from every pore. I remind him that I first saw him performing at one of the great Broadway jamborees of the fifties, Moss Hart's fiftieth birthday party at an Italian restaurant off Times Square. He and his partner improvised a brilliant sixty-minute routine in which Mel played Moss Hart's analyst, being interviewed by Reiner. The brilliance lay in Mel's basic premise, which was that the analyst was a raving puritan. Though it's over twenty years ago, I still remember whole sections of the dialogue – e.g:

C.R.: What does Mr Hart talk about during your sessions?

Mel: He talks smutty, that's what he talks, he talks filth and smut.

C.R.: And how do you deal with that?

Mel: I say: 'Don't talk like that, don't give me that filth and smut,' and I slap his wrist a little.

C.R.: Would you say that Mr Hart had an Oedipus complex?

Mel: A what?

C.R.: An Oedipus complex.

Mel: What is that?

C.R.: That's when the patient wants to make love to his mother.

Mel (outraged): What kind of filth is that? Listen, Moss Hart is a nice Jewish boy. Maybe, of a Saturday night, he'll take his momma to the movies and on the way back home he'll maybe give her a little peck in the back of the cab – but making *love* to the mother! Get outa here!

C.R.: Have there been any special difficulties in dealing with Mr Hart's problems?

Mel: Yes. There have been outbursts of great violence, emotional outbursts.

C.R.: And how do you cope with these situations?

Mel: I stand outside the room on a ladder and toss aspirins in through the transom.

He's certainly the funniest impromptu comic I've ever heard, with a gift of free-wheeling vocal fantasy that outdoes even Lenny Bruce. He tells me, however, that his new film will be a *silent* comedy. 'I first knew you on records as a disembodied voice,' I said. 'And now you're going to be a disemvoiced body.' The movie will consist of about 5,000 insane sight gags, of which about 2,000 will be chopped in the cutting-room. Mel says he has an infallible technique for soothing actors whose scenes have to be dropped. 'I say to them: You're only thinking of one individual tile. I have to look at the whole mosaic.' Mel, like many great comics, is the cause of wit in others, and his remark prompts me to imagine a producer coming up to Charlton Heston and saying: 'Chuck, I want you to be a tile in a Mosaic mosaic.'

15 April

I hear on the radio that Michael Flanders[1] had died on holiday in Wales. He was in the Brompton Hospital a few weeks ago when I was there, having a check-up and recovering (so he said) from an ulcer. We had a brief chat, in which he said it puzzled and saddened him to think that all the things he was, and had been brought up to be proud of – solid

---

1. Michael Flanders (1922–75). British actor and lyricist, wrote memorable revues with Donald Swann.

professional middle-class, well-educated at non-snob public school, liberal with a small 'l' in politics and morals – had suddenly become bad things, to be ashamed of. He said he couldn't really adjust to this new image of himself. A nice man, who surely had no idea that he had such a short time left to live.

16 April

I cannot bear to sacrifice the envy other men feel towards me because of my marriage to K.

18 April

Saw a private showing of the new Warren Beatty film, *Shampoo* – a sensational success in the States. Found it a unique, self-erected (he co-wrote the script) monument to narcissism: every shot is an act of salivating homage to the incredible loveliness, the tousled charm, the innocently puckered brow, the tentatively parted lips, the unassuming *muscle* of W.B., the hayseed whoremaster. All other men in the picture are either ugly, middle-aged clowns or raving poufs. *Everyone* in it is corrupt except Beatty, a randy hairdresser whose only crime is that he enjoys fucking. Sure, at the end he loses the girl he really loves (Julie Christie) because – in a sudden and belated bow to conventional morality – he has spread himself too thin: but to whom does he lose her? Why, to a corrupt multimillionaire who is *fat* and *combs his hair forward*, for God's sake.

So although Julie quits, she'd have done better to stay with Warren, wouldn't she? Because whenever Warren and a girl go walking together, the music gets pure and exquisite and lyrical, which it doesn't when anybody else does *anything*. The action of the picture takes place concurrently with Nixon's election as President in 1968: and we are supposed to be gulled into believing that there is a valid parallel between the moral hypocrisies of the characters in the movie and the hypocrisies of the political world outside. This pretentious attempt at 'extra resonance' isn't for an instant credible. On the credit side: beautiful photography of Beverly Hills (by Kovacs).

22 April

Preview at the National of the new Pinter play, *No Man's Land*. How little I like nowadays. This is a pale piece, extremely discourteous in its disdainful treatment of the audience. Two old men confront each other in an opulent Hampstead house (circular in construction, and compared to a lighthouse: the host sitting on a central throne: the plagiarism from Beckett's *End Game* is blatant); yet not until the second act does Pinter deign to tell us who they are and how they met, thereby dispelling the needless aura of mystery. Now mystery is fine when we discover, with the clearing of the clouds, a retrospective shape and purpose that could not otherwise have been revealed. Here we don't: it's gratuitous obscurity, in other words padding.

One of the men is a famous, moribund writer: the other a failed writer, equally aged. The dialogue is full of surprises, but empty of purpose: everything is unexpected, nothing is inevitable. It's like a series of eccentric jottings from the commonplace book of a brilliant beginner: in fact, it sounds like a very promising first play, and if the author were unknown, one would predict a fine future for him once he had learned about structure and development and how to write poetic speeches that carried an emotional charge.

As it is, the funny bits are often *very* funny; and the poetic bits are very boring. Two sinister Cockneys (guardians of the famous writer) intrude from several earlier Pinter plays; and all of the four characters affect a mixture of pedantically baroque language and slang that pays diminishing returns. I can't imagine anyone begging to play these parts in twenty years' time. Ralph Richardson (the celebrity) and John Gielgud (the failure) play with total aplomb: rather like the great instrumentalists reclaiming from oblivion some forgotten eighteenth-century concerto by Josef Foerster. But how one would prefer to see them performing Mozart – or Telemann.

John G. has a wonderfully seedy, Third-Programme-producer manner and wig; and Ralph R. moves about in his usual, unique, split-level gait – from the waist downwards he walks; from the waist upwards he rolls as if on casters. It would be nice to think that the play will not be acclaimed: but I fear the critics will be overawed. It isn't often, nowadays, that they dare to dent an established reputation.

Robert Stigwood has expressed renewed interest in backing the film, and I have sent him scripts and lists of casting suggestions, together with a two-week option on the script. Hope is sluggishly reborn.

23 April

Buffet dinner at Boty Baker's for John Huston, whom I hadn't seen for years. Flatteringly he came straight over to me beaming and spent most of the evening chatting to us. He's about seventy, suffers from emphysema, and still turns out a film a year: he was just back from Marrakesh where he's been shooting a Kipling story with Sean Connery and Michael Caine. He was wonderfully encouraging about my film, assuring me that of course I could and must direct it, and promising to give me a whole evening of practical advice when he returns to London next month. John's charm increases with age: the hooded eyes, the rangy, stooping gait, the incredibly winning smile. He shares my passion for Orson, and told us how Orson had talked him into playing the lead in his last movie. Shooting, as always with Orson, was spread over several years, with sudden and protracted suspensions of activity whenever the money ran out. John, having accepted the part, didn't hear from Orson for a year or more, and assumed the project was cancelled. One day Orson summoned him to Arizona, where he explained that the picture was completely finished except for Huston's part which was the lead. Orson had managed to 'shoot round' the Huston character so that nothing remained but to cut in solo shots of John himself. 'And so,' as John put it, 'I can boast that I have starred in a movie without meeting anyone else in the cast.' (Huston's advice on direction: 'Always shoot each scene as if it was the most important scene in the picture.')

24 April

At the ICA: a production by Bill Gaskill[1] and Max Stafford Clark[2] of *Fanshen*, a documentary play by David Hare based on a book about the

---

1. William Gaskill (1930–). Stage director; Artistic Director of the English Stage Company at the Royal Court, 1965–72; director, Joint Stock Company, 1973–83.
2. Max Stafford Clark (1941–). Artistic Director of the English Stage Company at the Royal Court, 1979–93.

conversion of a Chinese village to Communism in the middle and late forties. Nine actors each playing about three parts: no decor apart from a few agricultural tools and slogans on red banners. The theme: revolution as a continuing process of persuasion, action, criticism, self-criticism, reappraisal, more persuasion, new action – all presented with total objectivity and no attempt to rouse us with rhetoric. The cadres make as many mistakes as the villagers. They are trying to instruct; and the party leaders from whom the cadres get *their* instructions are shown to be fallible, too. The endless patience required by a successful revolution is wonderfully demonstrated: after each failure, the slate must be wiped clean and we start all over again from zero. No one is flawless and no theory: but no one is irreclaimable: and, as one of the cadres almost casually says: '*Everybody* can face *everything*.'

By sheer understatement the play achieves, by the end, enormous power and moral authority. This is the first native offshoot of the Brechtian tradition that seems to me to stand comparison with the parent tree. Despite excellent notices, the small theatre was only half full. If I were a critic today, I would guarantee to have it packed. Beside this, the Pinter play is simply frivolous: as well as far less gripping.

25 April

N.B. Nietzsche's belief that dreams are the origin of all metaphysics, the source of the idea that body and soul are separate. Note also Nietzsche on Christianity:

A god who begets children with a mortal woman; a sage who bids men work no more, have no more courts; but look for signs of the impending end of the world; a justice that accepts the innocent as a vicarious sacrifice; someone who orders his disciples to drink his blood; prayers for miraculous interventions; sin perpetrated against a god, atoned for by a god; fear of a beyond to which death is the portal; how ghoulishly all this touches us, as if from the tomb of a primeval past! Can one believe that such things are still believed?

27 April

Roxana, fired by a film about Helen of Troy, has been looking up the story in a book of Greek legends. I ask her what happens at the end. 'Ah,' she says, 'Ackles gets hit in his venerable spot.'

28 April

K. and I go to Strand-on-the-Green for a riverside drink, a place we haven't visited since 1966. There are high-rise flats everywhere, dwarfing the Queen Anne cottages.

K.H.: This place has come down in the world since 1966.
K.: The world has come down in the world since 1966.

TV runs a wartime film starring Eric Portman. I knew this ferocious, self-loathing, sporadically brilliant actor in the fifties, when I was asked to write a short biography of him. Since I'd never met him, we arranged a supper at his Chelsea flat to get acquainted. (He was starring in Terence Rattigan's *Separate Tables* at the St James.) He lived alone, attended by an Irish valet. At first he was scrupulously polite to Elaine and myself: 'How about a bijou gin-ette?' was the phrase he used to offer us a drink, but during the first course, and after a few drinks, he suddenly said: 'You know, of course, that I was born in the same town as Christie?' (The necrophile and mass murderer.) I said I did. 'And that I knew him when I was a boy?' I said I assumed so. More long swigs of Scotch. Then: 'You needn't think that I don't know what you want to do to me.' I said I didn't know what he meant. 'I know,' he said, his eyes bulging and voice throbbing with hostility, 'that you were responsible for having John Gielgud arrested, and that you want to do the same to me. You're going to worm out my secrets and pass them on to the police, aren't you? *Aren't you?*' (This was just after John G. had been fined for soliciting in a Chelsea loo.)

I was utterly silenced by this load of paranoid balls. Elaine sprang to her feet and said she wasn't going to listen to any more crazy insults. I stood up as well. But so did Portman and he *pounced* towards us and chased us upstairs – the only escape route open to us – until we took refuge in his bedroom, where Elaine locked the door. 'What are you doing in there?' he bellowed. 'Reading your mail!' Elaine rather splendidly shouted back. At length he retreated and the Irish butler smuggled us out of the house, with proper apologies. As we left, he said: 'He's always like that. Every weekend we go down to his cottage in Cornwall. He gets tight and the first thing he does is to smash every mirror in the house. I have to replace them every Monday morning. Good-night, sir.'

A TV show on Ed Murrow[1], its climax being his 1954 TV show on Senator McCarthy, which led to the latter's downfall. I remember watching that famous show at George Cukor's house in Hollywood. Elaine and I were the only guests, but when it was over, I recall Cukor's reaction. Elaine and I were openly cheering, and Cukor said: 'Jesus Christ, I'm surrounded by a bunch of pinkos!' He was smiling: but my God he was also nervous. 'We must not confuse dissent with disloyalty . . . we are not descended from fearful men,' said Murrow. I'm proud that he knew and seemed to like him. (Irrelevantly, I remember Marlene telling me about her affair with him. It ended – or began to end – one afternoon when she was naked in bed awaiting him and he stripped and, sitting on the edge of the bed, lit a cigarette which he insisted on finishing before he joined her between the sheets. Noting his priorities, Marlene felt her passion cooling.)

29 April

Badgered by Clifford W. and myself at a party two weeks ago, Antonia Fraser sat down and wrote a sketch for *After Calcutta* embodying what she insists is her favourite sexual reverie. A girl in a Victorian nightie lies in bed reading Proust. A man enters and they engage in desultory but barbed dialogue, the man reiterating that Kafka is better than Proust. Finally, with silent, deliberate ferocity, he slowly tears up all the sheets and blankets on the bed, followed by the girl's nightie. Throughout all this she continues to read. It's obviously almost impossible to stage (the cost of all that nightly destruction would be vast): but the shape and style – two people talking at cross purposes, conversation that is a mask for real meanings, a climax of unexpected violence, a menacing

---

1. Edward R. Murrow (1908–65). Broadcaster, journalist, director of US Information Agency, 1961–64.

intruder – all suggest one influence: Pinter. It was satisfying to learn (via Kathleen) from Edna O'Brien today that Antonia has in fact been having an affair with Pinter for the past few months.

3 May

We take Roxana to Stratford for her first Shakespeare (an excellent *Henry V* by Alan Howard) and my first visit, shamefully, to Shakespeare's tomb. In the church I buy three C.S. Lewis paperbacks. On returning to London via Oxford (where we show Roxana all that beauty, too: I hope it's been a really *imprinting* weekend for her) I finish reading Richard Findlater's admirable biography of Lilian Baylis,[1] an eccentric of the oddest kind, but a passionate believer, not so much in the theatre, or the opera or the ballet, but in the use of the arts as instruments of Christian enlightenment, bringers of instruction and beauty. And so to C.S.L. and *The Problem of Pain*. As ever, I respond to his powerful suggestion that feelings of guilt and shame are not conditioned by the world in which we live but are real apprehensions of the standards obtaining in an eternal world.

I mark passage after passage for recollection – e.g. this on why Job subjects man to such tribulations:

Over a sketch made idly to amuse a child, an artist may not take much trouble. But over the great picture of his life – the work which he loves, though in a different fashion, as intensely as a man loves a woman, or a mother a child – he will take endless trouble – and would, doubtless, thereby *give* endless trouble to the picture if it were sentient. In the same way, it is natural for us to wish that God had designed for us a less glorious and less arduous destiny: but then we are wishing not for more love but for less: When we want to be other than the thing God wants us to be, we must be wanting what, in fact, will not make us happy. These Divine demands which sound to our natural ears most like those of a despot and least like those of a lover, in fact marshal us where we should want to go if we knew what we wanted.

---

1. Lilian Baylis (1874–1937). Set up in 1914 and managed for twenty years the Old Vic Theatre, devoted to the production of Shakespeare plays.

The chess player's freedom to play chess depends on the rigidity of the squares and moves.

We forget that our prehistoric ancestors made all the most useful discoveries, except that of chloroform, which have ever been made. To them we owe language, the family, clothing, the use of fire, the domestication of animals, the wheel, the ship, poetry and agriculture.

C.S.L. works as potently as ever on my imagination, but this book, though it effectively explains the Christian uses of pain in the salvation of adults (and even the higher animals), entirely omits the most inexplicable and unforgivable kinds of pain – e.g. agonising illness in babies and young children. What is the Christian purpose here? Or would C.S.L., taking his cue from certain hints in the New Testament, evade the issue by claiming that disease was brought into the world by Satan?

Odd how often C.S.L. thinks of himself (*qua* Christian) as a child in need of a fiercely loving father: and how impossible it is for him, never having had children, to think of himself as a parent.

5 May

More Lewis. He defends the right to kill under authority – i.e. in just wars or at the behest of properly appointed magistrates. As for 'Thou shalt not kill', he points out that, in Greek as in Hebrew, there is one word for 'kill' and another for 'murder' and that the word from which the Biblical injunction is translated is the latter.

On sex: 'This appetite is a ludicrous and preposterous excess of its function' (i.e. if we give way to gluttony, we shall eat too much but 'not terrifically too much', whereas a healthy young man, indulging in sex with contraception whenever he felt like it, could populate a small village in a couple of years). But he is fair:

The old Christian teachers said that if man had never fallen, sexual pleasure, instead of being less than it is now, would actually have been greater. Christianity is almost the only one of the great religions which thoroughly approves of the body . . .

nearly all the greatest love poetry in the world has been produced by Christians.

Reading him, I see without any doubt that I should stop seeing Nicole: there are journeys it is necessary to undertake even with the loss of an eye and an arm, not merely because we are so instructed, but because the end will be happiness greater than if we had tried to undertake them with too much baggage. But can I stand the immediate loss, especially as I have no certitude of the ultimate gain? In other words, even if I leave Nicole, I may already have undermined K.'s. love for me so completely that in the end I shall lose her too. I know I should not think in this squalid, profit-and-loss manner: but I am too weak to help doing so. (And I must stop congratulating myself on being able to admit that I am weak. And also on my strength in recommending myself to stop congratulating myself.) Is it too late now for me to unravel myself back to the first dropped stitch and knit the garment all over again? Signs and portents surround me.

I should have recorded, thankfully, that my bronchial infection re-treated, under massive assault from antibiotics about two weeks ago, after holding out in my lungs for about ten weeks. I doubt if I could withstand another siege like this.

J.L. Barrault[1] talking on TV about theatre: 'Society is domination and domination provokes and artists are there to provide the *riposte*.' (Proud to be this man's friend, too, as I always am to be the friend of a *devotee*, even if my own devotions are not made to the same altars.)

On TV, Georges Brassens'[2] first and only concert in England. He sings the great love song I first heard him sing twenty years ago and should have acted on: *'J'ai honneur de ne pas te demander ta main.'* A man introducing the programme acutely says that, whereas English popular music was overrun and conquered by America in the thirties, forties and fifties, France remained immune; hence the pure tradition represented by people like Brassens.

1. Jean-Louis Barrault (1910–94). French actor, director and producer.
2. Georges Brassens (1921–81). French cabaret singer and songwriter.

11 May

The new *Oxford Book of Literary Anecdotes* yields a wonderful story about Jowett of Balliol. There used to be a tourist guide in Oxford who would address his groups as follows when they reached the Broad: 'This, ladies and gentlemen, is Balliol College, one of the very oldest in the university, and famous for the erudition of its scholar. The head of Balliol College is called the Master. The present Master of Balliol is the celebrated Professor Benjamin Jowett, *Regius* Professor of Greek. *Those* are Professor Jowett's study windows and *there*' (here he would pick up a handful of gravel and throw it against the panes, bringing Jowett, livid with fury, to the window) 'there, ladies and gentlemen, is Professor Jowett himself.'

Astaire again on TV in a programme in celebration of Irving Berlin. I recall what I said to the Panovs (Jewish ballet dancers recently allowed to leave the Soviet Union) when I met them at the party after the London première of *That's Entertainment*. The Panovs had never before seen Astaire and when they asked me what I thought of him, I said, half-jokingly: 'He's the poet of late capitalism.' The more I see of him – always in top hat and tails, against settings of grandeur and glitter, the more I take my own joke seriously. Whatever can be salvaged by art from the greed and oppression of the thirties is contained in the elegance of that tapping and twirling little gentleman. He is the froth thrown up by the maelstrom of a condemned era, and miraculously, he has outlived it.

17 May

The greatest films are those which show how society shapes man (cf. *The Godfather 1 & 2* – we saw Part 2 tonight). The greatest plays are those which show how man shapes society. Probably not strictly true, but worth defending as a stepping stone to the truth.

After *Godfather 2* with its brilliant exposition of the Sicilian ethos (defend the family, kill enemies and traitors, compel respect, demand return with interest on favours granted) we go to a Sicilian restaurant, where we are given a free meal on the (tacit) understanding that Kathleen will get *Vogue* to write about it. We were invited, and did not buy this favour; but it was granted, and we must now, in true Godfather style, return the compliment.

18 May

To Madrid to write about the city for *Esquire*. Bullfight in a rainstorm. We leave halfway through. Previous night: a dream in which a tall, beautiful pin-headed black girl enters my bedroom, wearing a white satin wedding dress, with her face covered in icing sugar and shaving soap – I haven't time to find out, because she produces a gun and shoots me, I think dead. Before her entrance I have been gnomically warned by amplified voice: 'An exit is open to you, but not in this building.'

20 May

Another Madrid dream. I attend one of the rare performances of a celebrated amateur troupe called the London Chinese Niun Theatre Group of Great Stepney. Underlit, with a certain lack of cohesion due to under-rehearsal, the company perform traditional Chinese dramas of extreme length, dealing with anguished widows, brutal war-lords, betrayed maidens, etc. Their leader is Michael Croft.[1] The main trouble with the performance is that (a) there are no costumes and (b) each actor is given complete freedom to establish, in his own way, that he is Chinese. Croft, for example, adopts a shuffling gait and shambles around the stage with his hands inserted into the sleeves of his familiar baggy tweed suit. He also effects a long Fu Manchu moustache. In the case of David Pryce-Jones, on the other hand, Oriental origins are suggested by a coolie hat bearing a sign reading 'Hello, Sailor! I'm a nice bit of take-away Chinese.'

These performances are gravely reviewed by the critics, some of whom, however, doubt whether the company manages at all times to achieve full mastery of the nuances involved in this ancient art form. It was also obvious that several members of the large cast had been unable to attend many rehearsals and therefore had a very imperfect grasp of what was going on. These, wearing hacking jackets and flannel trousers,

---

1. Michael Croft (1922–86). Oxford contemporary of Tynan's. Founded the National Youth Theatre in 1956.

would content themselves with slowly hopping and skipping about the stage, following their leader – Croft – in the matter of stuffing hands up sleeves. Quite clearly, the company had not found time to rehearse with sound effects. When a gong was suddenly struck off stage, they all jumped towards the wings with looks of absolute astonishment. There was no scenery, though one or two stage hands could be dimly seen leaning against the back wall, puffing fags and looking puzzled.

30 May

Theatre gives an object lesson: film shows the object lesson.

6 June

The Common Market referendum has locked us into the crumbling fortress of Western captitalism. Roy Jenkins, interviewed on TV after the result was announced, made an unguarded remark that summed up the tacit elitism of the pro-Marketeers. Asked to explain why the public had voted as it had, Roy Jenkins (the wild man of the Tory Left, as I sometimes think of him) smugly replied: 'They took the advice of people they were used to following.'

7 June

Saw the new Antonioni,[2] *The Passenger*, raved about by critics, especially P. Gilliatt. Oh dear. In any other hands, this would have been a banal but interesting TV thriller (with pseudo-philosophical overtones) about an alienated journalist who assumes another man's identity. In Antonioni's hands, it certainly isn't interesting. It's a guided tour around some picturesque locations – Gaudí's[3] Barcelona, Mojacar, North Africa – about which the critics write as if Antonioni had built or even *created* them, not merely hired a cameraman to photograph them. The only cliché about identity that isn't in the script is: 'Why are you running away from yourself?' – and the only reason for its absence is that it is inherent in the basic situation. Worst of all is the acting. Jenny Runacre is an actress

1. Michelangelo Antonioni (1912–). Italian film director, notably of *Blow-Up* (1966) and *Zabriskie Point* (1969).
2. Antonio Gaudí (1852–1926). Spanish architect.

so bad that I actually thought her too incompetent to be in *Oh! Calcutta!* (in which she appeared for six months). Maria Schneider and Jack Nicholson are under-directed to the point of extinction. One doesn't mind (one can even tolerate) bad acting: but *slow* bad acting is insupportable. The only point at issue after this film is whether Antonioni *really* cannot handle human beings, or deliberately chooses to *look* as if he cannot handle human beings (apart from Italians, of course: I liked *The Eclipse*). Yet the critics laud this portentous drivel:

> Into the room the women come and go,
> Talking of Michelangelo.

The critic's job – at least 9/10ths of it – is to make way for the good by demolishing the bad. Antonioni is at present blocking the street. He almost makes me wish I were back at work bulldozing.

11 June

> If your wife does not love Goya,
> Instantly consult your lawyer.

K.H. has given me a £21 book on Goya, including a *catalogue raisonné* of his entire work. I've never had a more exciting gift. After revisiting the Goyas in Madrid last month, I've decided to add his name to the guest list at my ideal dinner party, which now consists of: Shakespeare, Byron, Wilde and Goya. How nice to reflect that the arch-mandarin Berenson[1] ('Modern anarchy begins with Goya') disliked him.

13 June

Reception at Marlborough House to celebrate Commonwealth Day. Sunlit lawn full of dark beauties in garish saris. Am introduced to diplomats of both sexes who have translated Hebbel, invented new methods of mixing cement, worked for the Royal Bank of Canada, played party games with me ('but of course you won't remember') in

---

1. Bernard Berenson (1865–1959). American art historian and connoisseur of Italian Renaissance painting.

1956, and investigated civic corruption in Malaysia. Heath present: and argument develops as to whether he uses a sunray lamp to preserve his year-round Bermudan tan. (He *must*.) Queen also there, looking pasty in green. Three glasses of warm champagne, and away.

15 June

Realisation of a fantasy that has nagged at me all my life. A few months ago I answered an ad in *Time Out* that said: 'Pliant girl seeks order in her life.' Scenting a submissive, I wrote back telling her to reply to my letter immediately and at length, or she would be spanked. Three months later she replied: 'Immediately!' Three months later: 'At length!' about twenty words. 'I did it on purpose. Send for me.' I did: we met in Sloane Square and had a drink. My first question to her was: 'What do you deserve when you are disobedient?' 'A good spanking.' 'Where?' 'On my bare bottom.'

Her name is Sally; she's pretty and dark-haired, in her early thirties, with a husband and two children. She had nearly 500 replies to her ad; out of the handful she answered, she has entered into serious spanking relationships with four men. (She only discovered that her greatest happiness was to be under discipline when she read *L'Histoire D'O* two years ago. It doesn't enter into her relationship with her husband.)

I asked her how she would like to be disciplined by a man and a woman simultaneously. She said that would be ideal. So last night, on the dot of 8 p.m., she rang the doorbell of 14 Pindock Mews, where Nicole and I were waiting for her. I told her she could ask us any questions she liked. It was soon obvious that we were all on exactly the same sexual wavelength. I produced a bottle of champagne and we drank a solemn toast: 'To spanking.' The atmosphere of happy anticipation was intoxicating.

Then Nicole and I played the roles of a count and countess whipping a new housemaid for theft and drunkenness. Sally wore Victorian knickers with a slit at the back, Nicole a pair with a rear-buttoned flap. After lecturing Sally (or Sophie, as we named her), I put her over my knee, opened the slit of her knicks and gave her chubby bum twenty-five smacks. Nicole sat two yards away, staring at the reddening globes. She then replaced me and gave Sophie twelve stingers with the hairbrush, making her count after each stroke. Sophie opened her bum well as Nicole instructed, and we noted an exquisite, hairless little pink anus.

Now came the reversal of fortunes: I revealed that the Countess, too, was to be chastised, for having spent £500 on a new dress without permission. So it was Nicole's turn to bend over my lap. I unbuttoned the flap and Sophie got her first glimpse of my darling's bare bottom. I gave her twelve hard strokes with the brush. Sophie watched, riveted. (Both girls afterwards said that they found this episode the most exciting of all; Sophie humbly said that one day she hoped to be granted the privilege of spanking Nicole.)

Then both girls were sent to the bedroom to prepare to be whipped. When I joined them, Nicole was already in the whipping position, her bum well spread; and Sophie demurely sat at the foot of the bed, her eyes fixed on Nicole's anus. I gave her six stripes, very hard, with the white whip. Sophie then took her place: Nicole and I both noticed that she spread her globes much wider apart than we do, so that the flesh around the anus was pulled as taut as a drum. She got six, too, after which I left the whip resting between her outstretched cheeks.

After a few minutes standing in the corner for their red bums to be on penitential display, the girls joined me on the bed to have their weals inspected. I made both of them kiss each other's whipped globes. They held my prick, I gently squeezed their corrugated bums, and we quietly and passionately reminisced about every detail of an experience that had already eaten its way into the deepest recesses of our minds.

'Did you like Nicole's bottom?' – 'What does she think of mine?' – 'We both adore your anus.' – 'Did the hairbrush hurt more than the whip?' – etc. etc. on into the night. On this occasion we didn't fuck in Sally's presence (she had to get home to North London): but next time Nicole will surely end up on top of me, being whipped by Sally while I fuck her and at the same time stroke Sally's already glowing bottom. A milestone! If it were now to die.

16 June

Further note on Antonioni's film: Tynan's Law of Responsible Cinema: *all* films that seek seriously to diagnose the Contemporary Human Predicament are *bad*. Only historical films, comedies, satires and thrillers are any good. I do not know why this is so: but it is (N.B. *Citizen Kane* is partly historical, partly a satire).

17 June

Robert Stigwood's office calls to say he has been unable to raise money to finance my film. So another roof caves in, another escape route is blocked. Add that to my health (another bad chest infection has just sent me back to bed); the tax debts; the fact that nobody wants to buy the house (and even if they did, it would be at a price 40 per cent less than two or three years ago); my writing block; the unrepaid publishers' advances; the *impasse* of my private life – put all these together, and you have, I would say, a pretty fair prescription for suicide.

18 June

Ben Sonnenberg,[1] Brendan Gill and the Jonathan Millers to dinner plus of course Edna O'B. I make two good remarks. Brendan G. asks me about the current state of English letters. 'The English literary scene,' I reply, 'is all wasps and no honey.' Later Brendan G. becomes extremely drunk (having earlier congratulated me on being the only *New Yorker* drama critic who did not become a drunk) and I drive him and Ben back to Claridge's. Ben, a rich man who loves literature but is given to flights of embarrassing hyperbole, says to Brendan as I switch on the ignition: 'You realise, Brendan, that this is like having your shoes shined by Picasso.' 'No, Ben,' I interpose, 'like having your boots licked.'

19 June

A telepathic moment. I am awaiting a visit from my old friend Harold Clurman on his annual summer trip to Europe. Rebecca, aged four, our nanny's daughter, sits watching TV. I tell her she will soon have to go up to the nursery, as I'm expecting an old friend for a chat. 'Oh yes,' she says brightly, 'he always wears a big black hat.' Now it is true that Harold always wears a jaunty, broad-brimmed, black-velour boulevardier's hat on his European trips. But Rebecca has never met him, nor have I ever mentioned him to her. Explanation, please.

---

1. Ben Sonnenberg (1936–). American founder and former editor of the literary magazine *Grand Street*.

23 June

'It would be more profitable for the farmer to raise rats for the granary than for the bourgeois to nourish the artist, who must always be occupied with undermining institutions.' (Chekhov)

'Brancusi declared that to make art is easy but that the difficulty was to be in a state to make it.' (Harold Rosenberg)

'If you can't get a woman, get a clean old man.' (Nathaniel West)

1 July

Back from nightmare weekend in Geneva with my accountant and sheet-anchor, Pat Kernon. Kathleen and I had been invited to a party there by an Italian millionaire we had never met, who was taking over the Hotel Réserve for the weekend and would pay all our hotel expenses. This seemed an ideal opportunity, if properly exploited, for me to take Kernon to meet Pierre Sciclounoff, my Swiss lawyer – a thing I'd never hitherto been able to afford to do. So I accepted the invitation and took Kernon instead of Kathleen. The party itself was stupendously dull: five hundred guests, mainly rich tax exiles, of whom I knew about three (including Sciclounoff but excluding, of course, the host, Signor Giori, who – I later learned – makes his fortune by the manufacture of machines on which banknotes of all nations are printed. As Pat K. pointed out, there at least is a man who is making money – in two senses – out of inflation. The appropriateness of Geneva as a setting for this gentleman's jamboree could not have been improved on by Evelyn Waugh). The canapés were exclusively caviar, and there was nothing at all to drink except Dom Pérignon and Mouton-Rothschild '64. Sedated out of my mind to avoid screaming with boredom, I lasted till about 1:30 a.m. before sliding off to bed. The other guests danced (Victor Sylvester[1] style) till 7.30 a.m. The police tried to persuade them to abate the racket at about three-thirty, clear evidence (as one of the guests mysteriously told me next day) that Switzerland was falling prey to 'creeping socialism'. I don't know about the socialism, but I can testify to the creeps.

On Sunday Pat and I rented a little car and drove to Talloires for

---

1. Victor Sylvester (1900–78). Popular British band leader.

lunch at Père Bise (memories of my disastrous stay at that gorgeous village with Elaine and Gore Vidal some fifteen years ago when we all got drunk and Elaine and I put on a spectacularly unimpressive *exhibition* of S-M for Gore's benefit; memories, too, of a more recent visit – halcyon vintage – with K). Monday was to have been the gala meeting with Sciclounoff, when Patrick would look at the books and confirm that Sciclou's Swiss company had indeed been delivering the promised goods and that I could at least pay my income tax for the next year or two.

The upshot was disaster. Sciclounoff failed to show up at his office for the meeting: a secretary explained that he had been in bed all weekend with bronchitis – an obvious untruth since I had seen him in the pink of condition at Saturday's party. Clearly he was ducking the meeting. We got one of his assistants to show us the books. By diligently questioning (conducted through me, since Pat speaks little French), Pat discovered that Sciclou had made investments on my behalf which had lost *at least* £15,000. In this, of course, he was perfectly within his rights, since the company belongs to him: what was shattering was that he had never told me about these (by my standards enormous) losses. Nor were we able to discover how much cash remained in the company's current or deposit accounts.

Pat rightly insisted on telephoning Sciclou at home, which we did: he sounded hungover rather than ill, promised to supply the figures we needed, and said he would come to London next week to discuss the situation. Pat's impression is that he is not crooked but simply careless. This, however, does not diminish my gloom; on first hearing the news about the £15,000 deficit, I experienced, for the first time in many years, the sensation described in the phrase: 'The blood drained from his head.'

This, *à part*, my bronchial virus rages unchecked; and I must rush from Sciclou's office to the plane for London, where Kathleen will be waiting to celebrate, since today is our wedding anniversary. (Also waiting for me at home is the news that I have no hope of gaining any libel damages from *Private Eye*, who said I had exposed my genitals to a twelve-year-old girl. Their defence is that, in a recent article in *Punch*, I said I had made love to a girl in the first-class compartment of a transatlantic airline, which proved that I was given to indecent exposure in public places. Apparently it doesn't matter that the compartment was darkened and empty, that the lovemaking took place under blankets, and that the girl was an enthusiastically consenting adult: the jury will not even give me a farthing's damages.

I point out to my lawyer that if *Private Eye* accuses me of running over a child while drunk, it is no excuse to say that I have in the past been fined for speeding and that I occasionally drink too much wine. He agrees, but still says I haven't a chance – and might even be charged with sexual assault and indecent exposure! (Shades of the Wilde case!) This means, in effect, that even if *Private Eye* accused me of prostituting Roxana and buggering Matthew, I wouldn't have much hope of winning an action against them. From now on it is open season on K.T.

2 July

I read more impassioned praise of Antonioni's *The Passenger* in the American press and I recall the *echt* sixties party that we gave in (or around) 1967 and that he attended when he was gathering material for *Blow-Up*. Our theme was the work of Clovis Trouille[1] and we peopled the Mount Street flat with fibre-glass models of girls dressed like the creatures of Trouille's imagination. In the living-room stood one of them in a picture hat, suspender belt, black stockings and a bat spreading its wings across her cunt; in the bedroom reclined the *Oh! Calcutta!* girl, her body swathed in Indian silk, arranged to frame her bare bottom; and sitting on the edge of the bath was a girl in nun's garb, a cigarette in her hand, and her habit tucked up to reveal silk stockings with red silk garters.

The guests included Gore Vidal, Richard Harris and Marlon Brando, the latter pair drunk on arrival; Marlon joined me in the bathroom, locked the door, and dared me to kiss him on the lips as a proof of friendship. (I did.) Earlier in the day Antonioni, whom I'd met only once before, telephoned and asked whether he could come to the party, of which he'd heard advance rumours. I agreed, and he turned up in a dark business suit looking grave and stricken, rather like Paul Lukas as a decent liberal in an anti-Nazi film. So politely did he efface himself that several guests took him for the butler and asked him to get them

1. Clovis Trouille (1889–1975). French artist whose 1946 painting *Oh! Calcutta! Calcutta!* gave Tynan an image and title for his erotic revue.

gin and tonics, which he decorously did. From this party I later heard, he got his image of 'Swinging London'. It wasn't, in fact, especially depraved; nobody stripped, not a Beatle, or Stone, was present, and no drug except pot was ingested. It was, however, a pretty swaggering affair, and I remember it with pleasure and some pride.

4 July

The phrase to remember is: 'The necessary tinge of wham.' This is how Peter Sellers (I think it was) summed up, tonight, the salient quality of Terry Southern. We have just come (rushed?) home with him from a party given by Evelyn de Rothschild. I had just bought a large cake of hash from Nicole, and we zoomed away as soon as *politesse* permitted to share it with him and Joy, who was still awake. Peter taught us how to get the best out of pot by spreading tinfoil across the top of a wine-glass, prodding holes in it (and a gash) with a needle, then crumbling the pot over the holes, igniting it, and sucking the fumes in through the gash. (What a brilliantly lucid exposition, only a couple of hours after the event!) Thus primed, we spoke of Terry S. and the immortal phrase was uttered. But by whom? And why?

The Bugger's Birthday (2nd version)

> It was the Bugger's birthday
> And all the sons were there,
> And each man held another's prick
> And every bum was bare.
>
> The bugger rose up slowly;
> The whole assembly cheered.
> Some cried: 'See how his ancient cock
> Peeps through his long white beard . . .'

5 July

Last night's pot-inspired word-play brings to mind a small verbal triumph from my *New Yorker* days. I was having a drink with

Peter de Vries[1], who was getting slightly nervous because, on the last two occasions he had been in the office, Mr Shawn had passed him in the corridor without noticing him. This reminded me that I, too, had had no personal contact with the editor for over a month. Next day I sent him the following letter:

> Dear Mr Shawn,
> De Vries and I
> Are saying with a sigh
> That you
> No longer care . . .

6 July

We are invited to a play staged in the restaurant of a new London hotel called the Tara; entitled *Another Bride, Another Groom*. It's an English adaptation of an Australian farce about a disastrous wedding reception where the bride is eight months pregnant and the families collide in a drunken brawl. Actually quite funny in its rowdy, tearaway way; but what was funnier was the presence in the audience (mainly showbiz) of Lord Hailsham of Marylebone[2], reacting with frozen astonishment to dialogue like:

A. Doctor Silverside cured Valerie's itch.
B. Then let's all watch her scratch.

7 July

More reminiscences of the pot-smoking night with P. Sellers. As one sucks the smoke through the gash in the tinfoil, the hash embers glow, and the close-up view is exactly like that of a burning city seen from the air. This led me into an improvisation, accompanied by Peter, of a Bomber Command navigator, talking to the rest of the crew as they go in through the flak to prang Dresden. 'Coming in at twelve o'clock, sir. Firestorm raging in the western suburbs.' (Suck.) 'Think we got the

---

1. Peter de Vries (1910–81). Novelist and *New Yorker* writer.
2. Lord Hailsham of Saint Marylebone (Quintin Hogg) (1907–). Barrister; Lord Chancellor 1970–74; 1979–87.

cathedral that time, sir. Hell of a blaze on the starboard side.' (Suck.) 'Art gallery's bought it, sir, or I'm a Dutchman. I don't think Jerry'll be gloating over his ruddy Cranachs tomorrow morning.' (Suck.) 'M. for Montague's gone for a Burton, sir. 'Fraid it's C for curtains for Wing Commander Wimbush . . .' (etc.)

24 July

Josh Logan gives a lecture on his work at the American Embassy, and I contribute introductory speech, pointing out (a bit fulsomely) that if Josh did not exist, it would be necessary for Broadway to invent him; indeed, it would almost be necessary to invent Broadway. (He has directed ten shows that ran more than a year, including three that lasted more than 1,000 performances.) I call on my dim memories of the Logan machine in action, after the Boston opening night of William Inge's *Picnic* in 1953. (Josh directed and co-produced it.) Josh invited me to have a drink with him after the show in his suite at the Ritz-Carlton. I went expecting a quiet chat, a little mutual congratulation between author and director, perhaps some talk of a lighting rehearsal the next afternoon. Was I (as they say) ever wrong.

At the Ritz-Carlton that night I learned what it felt like to be among a group of nuclear physicists working against the clock to beat Hitler to his atom bomb. S.N. Behrman[1] was in one bedroom, putting laughs into Act I. Tennessee Williams was in another bedroom, taking laughs out of Act II. Josh took me into the bathroom and said: 'Ken – what's wrong with Act III?' I said it somehow seemed to belong to another play. Josh thought for a while and then said: 'There may be a reason for that. You see, I wrote Act III.' (He nowadays denies saying that; and no doubt he was exaggerating.)

In the living-room, Lawrence Langner[2] of the Theatre Guild was addressing an empty piano stool on the dangers of trusting audience reaction in New England. The phone rang. It was Leland Hayward[3], calling from California. He proceeded to give a detailed critique of the

1. S.N. Behrman (1893–1973). Playwright; wrote memorable memoir of Max Beerbohm, *Portrait of Max* (1960).
2. Lawrence Langner (1890–1962). Producer; one of the original Board of Managers of the Theatre Guild.
3. Leland Hayward (1902–71). Hollywood agent and film producer.

Boston opening, totally undeterred by the fact that he had not seen it. Meanwhile a young woman in blue was making some extremely intelligent suggestions for improvements, many of which were subsequently incorporated into the text. Nobody knew who had brought her, and she left without giving her name. I suddenly realised that there was one notable absentee. 'Josh,' I said. 'Where's the author?' 'Oh, Bill,' said Josh. 'He's in Palm Springs, I think.'

After we had all worked for an hour or so, the first review arrived. It was a rave. Work stopped, corks popped. Half an hour later I recall seeing Josh entering the suite with a crushed newspaper in his right fist and his face the colour of an oyster. He had just read the second overnight review, by Elliot Norton, and it was a stinker. Within a minute everyone was back at work. The extraordinary thing is that out of this madhouse there emerged a play which (though I never particularly liked it) ran for 476 performances, won the Pulitzer Prize and the Critics Award for the Best Play of the Year. The chaos of the Ritz-Carlton that night taught me more about Broadway than I could have learned in a decade of drama criticism.

27 July

General depression – due to still-persistent bronchial infection (which now allows me only about three–four hours' sleep each night, preceded and followed and interrupted by prolonged coughing fits) which desperate visits to three acupuncturists have failed to alleviate; due also to increasing despair over financial situation.

6 August

Up in Arms on TV – Danny Kaye's first film, made in 1944, which I saw six times in my teens and which *defined* American comedy for me. His 'Lobby Song' and 'Melody in 4F' are as dazzling as I remember them (and so, as I'd forgotten, is Dinah Shore singing 'Tess's Torch Song'). Nobody has ever rivalled that laser-beam precision of utterance. Of course, Kaye's *attitudes* are all clichés: but I was into technique, not attitudes, then: which is how we all start loving performers. Conclusion: D. Kaye is the square Lenny Bruce.

8 August

Destiny is moral. See how it has conspired to prevent me from spending any significant time with Nicole during two weeks when I am alone in London:

(A)   Nicole is offered a stage job, which means she is occupied every night until 11 p.m.

(B)   Her sister Frin arrives from India with baby daughter for two–three weeks' stay. Naturally she must stay with Nicole while in London, which, because there is only one bedroom, means that I cannot sleep at Nicole's.

(C)   Reg announces that he will be coming to Thurloe Square early every morning to work on Roxana's nursery. This means that Nicole cannot stay at Thurloe Square, where there are about two dozen beds.

(D)   We cannot stay at a hotel because I cannot afford it. So: celibacy.

I had arranged a spanking trio with Sally for Sunday evening and was annoyed when she wrote to say that one of her professional clients had summoned her to a 'contract' that same night, and that of course business came before pleasure. I phone to remonstrate with her, but without success: 'If Nicole had to act on Sunday night,' she said, 'wouldn't that take precedence?' She's right, of course; if I object, I'm saying that fucking for fun is morally superior to fucking for money, and that whoring is a different *kind* of profession from acting – neither of which I believe. So I'm reduced to a sort of accusing silence, the more foolish for having no moral grounds on which to base the accusation. Yet I am annoyed and do feel cheated. I suppose it's injured ego: that she should prefer anyone to me as a reddener of her bottom!

9 August

Arthur Askey,[1] reminiscing about music-hall days, names Robb Wilton[2] as the funniest ad-libber he ever knew. Wilton (he says) once went to a funeral and found himself at the graveside standing next to an aged

1. Arthur Askey (1900–82). Popular British comedian.
2. Robb Wilton (1882–1957). British radio comedian.

fellow-vaudevillian named Charlie Edwards. After the ceremony Wilton turned to his friend and said: 'Er – how old are you, then, Charlie?' 'Ninety-four,' said Charlie. Wilton looked at him for a moment and then said: 'Hardly worth your while going home, is it?'

11 August

Nicole revisits Hastings, where she went to school at the Convent of the Sacred Heart. As we approach the seafront she says: 'That's the beach where I went to collect pebbles.' 'What did you want pebbles for?' 'To put under my sheets and sleep on as an act of penitence. I'd been reading about St Mary – she was into that trip.' Of her relationships with boys: 'I wouldn't let anyone pull me, so I had to pull them. But I couldn't do it directly, because I was too afraid of being rejected.' 'So what did you do?' 'Same as I do now. I hang about. I fool around. I tread on their heels.'

Two consecutive massive courses of antibiotics leave me exhausted, deeply depressed and still coughing all night. Sometimes I think of the upper lobe of my left lung as an insane but dedicated little sputum factory where a round-the-clock work-in is in progress, diligently turning out a product (phlegm) for which no other part of my organism has need. If they would only cancel the midnight shift, it would be *something*.

13 August

The bug still rages in my chest. In a way it is like living with Elaine in the bad later years. After a week of furious activity (sleepless with coughing, every breath during the day drawn in expectation of a cough) there will be a tapering off, enough to fill me with thanksgiving: at which point another night of paroxysms will rack me. Followed by a day of total respite and more.

15 August

Whenever we solve the problem of dreams, we shall not be far from solving the root problems of human identity and creativity. Has anyone noticed the really inexplicable thing about our nightly narrative tapes? *They have suspense.* This occurred to me last night, when I was involved in a Hitchcock-type chase dream – in which, I suddenly realised, I did not know what was going to happen next. I did not know who would be lurking behind the next door; and I wanted desperately to know. What part of one's mind is it that harbours secrets unknown even to the unconscious? (For in dreams we are surely privy to the unconscious in full flood.) The theory that in dreams we tap a source of energy outside the individual psyche is powerfully reinforced by the presence of suspense.

I recall a recurrent dream from Oxford days. I am following Philip Warner, a dapper little Wadham man with pebble glasses and a briefcase, as he picks his way through the steep and cobbled streets of a city where every building is a cathedral – some Gothic, some Romanesque, some baroque, some modern, all enormous in the misty evening gloom. At each massive portal he halts. We enter. He peers around and, shaking his head, says, 'No, I'm afraid he isn't here.' I shake my head back, not wanting to admit that I don't know what he's talking about, and say: 'Too bad.' This is repeated a dozen times in a dozen cathedrals. Once we even penetrate a crypt, but Philip is again disappointed. At length we enter this largest cathedral of all, on top of a hill. This time he says: 'I think it's here!' 'Good!' I say, and follow him up a long winding staircase to the belfry. Great bells hang between oak rafters. Exhausted, I slump into a chair at the end of the room. Philip carefully puts his briefcase on a table. 'Well,' he says, 'here it is.' I smile and say: 'Now that we've found it, Philip, would you mind telling me what it is.' He is padding quickly towards me, smiling. He stops in front of me and then (he is a small man) climbs up on to my lap. He lifts his hands and 'It's *you*, Ken,' he says, as he begins to strangle me.

17 *August*

From Gavin Lambert's *The Dangerous Edge*: a story of how John Buchan, meeting T.E. Lawrence a few weeks before the latter's death, told his wife that he thought T.E.L. was ready to return to a life of action and power. Lady Tweedsmuir disagreed. 'He's looking at the world as God must look at it,' she said. 'And a man cannot do that and live.' Not a bad description, *mutatis* very much *mutandis*, of how I feel these doldrum days.

19 August

Have been at the Spiegel villa in St Tropez for four days with K. and the children. Infection worse than ever as one dreads the moment of lying down at night, aware that whatever position one adopts the bronchial beast will strike. Days are drained: I wander slowly about like a wheezing zombie. After four insupportable days we consult the local doctor. Dourdou by name. He asks acute questions and prescribes various pills, suppositories and cough mixture plus massive injections of penicillin and streptomycin. He also says: keep out of the sun, because it intensifies infections.

That night (last night) I have my first cough-free sleep since May. Indeed I lie awake for much of the time, filled with gratitude and making various vows to the deity. Three times in the night the beast growls, but does not attack. At dawn I feel a curious sensation in the left lung, lair of the beast: as if three needles were being driven into it, one after the other. Like stakes into a vampire's heart. It's now midday on the following day: still no paroxysm. Begin to feel life is a rational possibility. I pray I'm not speaking too soon. Has the exorcism really taken place?

23 August

From '*Toro*', a poem by Neruda, this superb phrase about a *torero*: '*Debe danzar muriendo, el soldado de seda.*'[1]

26 August

Back to London after a week free from infection. No sooner do I reenter the house than wheezing recommences: the cats are back – to which (according to the Brompton Hospital's spring tests) I have a virulent allergy. K. has always refused to – what? – *believe*

1. 'He must dance, dying, the silken soldier.'

in such tests (or to get rid of the cats), and now asks me to go through the allergy experiments again to prove that the doctors were not lying.

28 August

I go with K. to a party for Studs Terkel[1], and hacking – come rattling recurrences. Among the guests: Doris Lessing, James Cameron,[2] Michael Frayn and Victor Spinetti.[3] Victor tells me that he has spent the last two years as the lover of an American millionairess. She was so rich, he says, that Tony Shaffer advised him to marry her *for the wine*. Their apartment was 'Windsor Castle' on the corner of 56th Street and Sutton Place.

7 September

Dominic Elwes has killed himself. An outsider like Alan, whom he never knew but some of whose dynamic gusto he shared. Nobody has made me *rejoice* more. The aristocracy elected him its court jester (a role he embraced) but never really accepted him because he didn't have money. Nor had he much more than skill and facility as a painter: and I think he knew it. All he had was the most ebullient and fantastic raconteur's flair I've ever encountered: and he would spill it as readily in a chance encounter in the street as at a dinner party. But the sage exclusive Bloomsberries who make the rules that determine who's in, who's out, ruled that Dominic was unstable, a bit of a bounder, without the money or background that can palliate such faults. (There is a Bloomsbury of the social and political as well as of the artistic world: its grail is good taste, its watchword sensitive restraint, its armoury the civilised sneer.)

At his best he was truly radiant, his face bubbling with life like the sun, his laughter a triumphant yelp of victory. He was forty-four. Four years his senior, I sat happily at his feet. (Another outsider of brilliantly fertile wit, prematurely dead: Harold Lang.[4])

1. Studs Terkel (1912–). American interviewer and oral historian.
2. James Cameron (1912–85). Doyen of British foreign correspondents.
3. Victor Spinetti (1933–). British actor.
4. Harold Lang (1925–75) British actor and director.

Later K. learns from the Wigrams that Dominic's Establishment pals were especially outraged by his behaviour in the Lucan case. Although a buddy of Lucan's, he broke the *omertá* of clubland by giving interviews to the papers on the subject, painting an impression of 'The Lucan Set' for the *Sunday Times* magazine, and similar misdemeanours. For these offences he was expelled from Annabel's, bolthole of the Establishment, and ostracised by dozens of former chums. He had nowhere to go.

9 September

The revulsion occasioned by the atrocities of the demagogues, and the re-establishment of successive tyrannies in France, was terrible. Could they listen to the plea of reason, who had groaned under the calamities of a social state, according to the provisions of which one man riots in luxury while another famishes for want of bread? Can he who the day before was a trampled slave, *suddenly* become liberal-minded, forbearing and independent? This is the consequence of the habits of a state of society to be produced by resolute perseverance and indefatigable hope, and long-suffering and long-believing courage, and the systematic efforts of generations of men of intellect and virtue. But on the first reverses of hope in the progress of French liberty, the sanguine eagerness for good overleaped the solution of these questions. Thus many of the most ardent and tender-hearted of the worshippers of public good have been morally ruined, by what a partial glimpse of the events they deplored appeared to show as the melancholy desolation of all their cherished hopes. Hence gloom and misanthropy have become the characteristic of the age in which we live, the solace of a disappointment that unconsciously finds relief only in the wilful exaggeration of its own despair.

Shrewd analysis of the bitter and reactionary pessimism of lapsed Leftists like the R. Conquest gang. It comes from Shelley's preface to *The Revolt of Islam*.

A reporter from the *Sun* calls. He has got hold of Dominic's suicide note and tells me I am mentioned in it: Dominic requests that I should read the Apologia (whatever that is) at his burial service. I am touched.

'For writers it is always said that the first twenty years of life contain the whole of experience – the rest is observation; but I think it is equally true of us all.' (Graham Greene, *The Comedians*.)

10 September

In a dream the manager of the Restaurant Pic in Valencia whispers in my ear: 'When we cut off the head of our king, we distributed the crown jewels – and they are the great restaurants of France.' (I have been on a diet for a week: hence the gastronomic obsession.)

11 September

At a publisher's party to celebrate Shirley MacLaine's book on China, I sit with Shirley for dinner and listen to Lew Grade[1] talking about his forthcoming *Life of Christ*, to be directed by Zeffirelli with an all-star cast. Christopher Plummer passes by and Grade hails him with: 'Glad to have you in my Christ picture, Christopher.' 'Oh, yes?' says C.P. 'What am I playing?' But Grade, to his embarrassment, can't remember. After an awkward pause I came to the rescue by saying: 'You're playing Pilate in the pilot.'

12 September

Disc jockey on BBC: 'And now here's a record for Beverly who works the twilight shift at the suppository factory.'

I interview Larry for TV at Thurloe Square, not having seen him for over a year, during which time he has suffered (and nearly died) from a muscular degenerative disease that has robbed his voice of its bass notes, leaving only a light tenor. He is frailer than

1. Lew Grade (Baron) (1906–98). Entertainment impresario.

I remember him and has difficulty climbing the stairs to the living-room; his Rolex watch hangs loosely round his wrist; and he has unwisely grown a little suburban moustache which makes him look slightly pathetic, like a boring retired major in a Sunningdale saloon bar. He will never appear on the stage again, though he has several big film parts lined up.

Over lunch he chats unhappily about the National, underlining how he laments the fact that under the Hall regime all sense of company solidarity has gone: 'It isn't a company any more. They just cast each production from scratch out of *Spotlight*. That wasn't what this National Theatre was created for. That wasn't what we fought for all those years.' His contract with the NT expires next month, and he won't be sorry; several times he has dictated intemperate letters of resignation, only to be dissuaded from posting them by Joan.

My general impression is that in the past year he has somehow faded. He seems to be talking to one from a long way off; that overpowering physical presence has irrevocably waned. Still, he talks for the cameramen for an hour, never boringly though sometimes forgetfully: it was a kindness on his part to do this for me, since he is getting only a token payment. At one point, rather oddly, he says that he regrets not having imposed more of his own ideas as a director on the NT company: whereas one of the things on which I prided myself during our association was that I was able to protect him from doing just that!

13 September

Dominic Elwes' funeral: high mass at Arundel Cathedral, followed by motorcade to Protestant graveyard at Amberley, five miles away, where he is buried next to his father. About sixty friends and family in attendance, with hundreds of wreaths (one card reads: 'Hope you're OK – Olly'): not a bad turnout for an unmarried suicide. Helen Jay, Dominic's mistress for two years until she left him to get married to someone else, is there, looking more beautiful in pink-eyed sorrow than she ever looked in her carefree days with Dom.

I have never been to a Catholic funeral before and the priest's props and business – covering the chalice with white damask, flourishing black-velvet squares, transforming wine and wafers into the blood and body of Christ – take me back to the conjurer at children's parties, who likewise works miracles of transformation while distracting our attention with brandished handkerchiefs. Which came first – the conjuring of spirits or the conjuring of tricks? Is the children's magician ape or forerunner of the priest?

The weather is balmy, warmly autumnal. Hugh Millais points out how appropriate it is that Dom's death should coincide with the publication of the last volume of Anthony Powell's *Dance to the Music of Time*. With Dom's passing, one especially spirited variation of the social gavotte will never be danced again. I weep, as usual, and pointlessly sprinkle holy water over the coffin. I have never attended a funeral more sincere, at which it was so clear that the deceased would be intimately and urgently missed by everyone present as long as they lived. The sound of Dominic's laughter was in my ears all day. K. asks why he killed himself. There is no use looking for complex answers. He simply did not have money enough to support his way of life; had lost the knack of earning it; could not pay his bills, could not even pay for tomorrow's breakfast; and so, surrounded by rich friends, extinguished himself. I truly loved him, and I think he loved me, though we did not know each other very long or deeply.

Entering a boring party, we would spot each other across a crowded room, and literally begin to jump up and down with delight: the occasion might be tedious, but at least (I knew) there was someone present with whom to relieve the sheer outrageous dullness of it all, and make it hilariously memorable. Those who attended his graveside were all people on whom he had breathed fanciful and exuberant life in his descriptions of them. Without him, they seemed drab and bloodless spectres, transparent ghosts, marionettes without a puppet-master. The source of their energy was the man nailed down in the coffin.

14 September

We invite a few friends of Dominic's for drinks and a Siamese dinner at a nearby restaurant (Hugh Millais, Peter and Virginia Blond, Mark

Boxer and Emma Soames[1]). Hugh assures me that money was not the prime cause of D.'s death: he would have inherited enough from his father (who died a month ago) to tide him over his debts. So it was – as the papers said – ostracism by the Lucan clan that did it. Hugh adds that he was almost equally shattered a few years ago when he was proposed for membership of White's and blackballed. How could so remarkable and gifted a man have set such store by the opinions of people so vastly inferior to him in every way?

Incidentally, Hugh confirms that Peter Ustinov once said that Dominic was the only person with whom he could not compete at a dinner party.

15 September

One of the emptiest occasions of my life: the American Embassy invites us to the opening at the British Museum of a travelling exhibition dedicated to Benjamin Franklin and Thomas Jefferson in honour of next year's Bicentennial celebrations. Because of last week's assassination attempt on President Ford, the streets around the museum are closed to traffic, so we have to circle the district before parking. Once inside the museum, we were seated behind the speakers (US Ambassador, Nelson Rockefeller and Harold Wilson) in privileged positions from which we cannot hear a word because of museum acoustics and gale-force air-conditioning. There follows a half-mile walk to the exhibition itself – a disappointing collection of reproductions, housed in one smallish room – where there is no alcohol on offer. Elbowing our way through brush-cut security thugs in their best suits, we thankfully flee.

16 September

Third change of heart on the reason for Dominic's death. Dinner with the Wigrams – much closer friends than we were – reveals that he did in fact lack money, that he would have received very little from his father's death, and that he could not face more borrowing from rich chums. To my question: 'Would he be alive

1. Emma Soames (1949–). Editor *Telegraph* magazine since 1994.

now if he had inherited £100,000 last Monday?' the Wigrams' answer is – thoughtfully but decisively: 'Yes.'

20 September

Another death: Pamela Brown, at fifty-eight. I had worshipped this pop-eyed, tawny-haired, ferally attractive actress since my teens: indeed when I was under twenty I burst into her dressing-room after a performance of *The Giaconda Smile* and fell on my knees before her. She was witty, kind and waspish; and although she was a semi-cripple, with one leg partially withered and visibly thinner than the other, she had great sensuality and could look at you with a wonderfully predatory gleam in her eye. I gave a party for her and Trevor Howard and the Old Vic company when they visited Oxford with *The Taming of the Shrew*: that was when I officially met her (self-introduced a year or so earlier, as explained above).

In the late fifties she came to New York, where I was unhappily married; and I remember a memorable day we spent together in her hotel suite. I confessed all my (then horrible secret) sexual desires, and she happily indulged them; yes, I spanked the lovely cripple; and we fucked and tenderly talked and giggled and knew we were friends for life, even if we never met again. Sadly, we didn't meet much thereafter: but had she been ten years younger, there was – as I think we both divined – a distinct possibility that we might have been in love.

Susceptible to both good and bad interpretations. Good: the English regard nobody as their superiors and will not surrender the fast lane to the rich. Bad: the English are determined to make everyone move at their own plodding rate, and take a quiet vindictive pleasure in holding back the overtakers. Leftists identify the plodders as the bourgeoisie, holding back the working class. Rightists identify the plodders as socialist levellers, holding back the entrepreneurs. Either way, in this country, the brakes are on. Politically and economically, we are demonstrating the impossibility of running what is euphemistically known as 'a mixed economy' where organised labour is strong and militant. The Tories have no way of controlling the unions; the socialists will not use the power of labour to bring about radical social change. Results: deadlock and stalemate, until economic disaster and social breakdown make genuine socialism imperative. Which will be a long and painful process. Better to admit now that revolutionary change is inevitable, and to plan for a peaceful transition to the new, non-capitalist way of life. But this won't happen: the party leaders don't want it and the media won't let it.

21 September

A Tory thesis commonly heard these days is that, just as the aristocracy and the bourgeoisie in their respective eras wielded exorbitant power, so nowadays do the trade-union leaders, who must similarly be cut down to size. Nobody on the Left has so far noticed the flaw in this argument. The aristocracy controlled the wealth of the country by force of arms. After the industrial revolution, the bourgeoisie succeeded in sharing it with them. But, then, as now, it was the working class who *produced* it; and it is the working class that is now – rightly – claiming it. In other words, the new ruling class belongs in a different category from its predecessors. To what they merely stole or annexed, it has an unassailable title.

Ball of Fire on TV – a 1941 film directed by Howard Hawks and written by Billy Wilder and Charles Brackett – I remember as simply a 'crazy comedy' about seven professors who get mixed up with a gangster's moll. After thirty-four years, it reveals itself as something much more interesting; a statement by the anti-Nazi refugee, Billy Wilder, of the importance of siding with the intellectuals against the book-burners. (The film was made while America was still neutral.) None of the professors is guyed: they are affectionately mocked, no more: and their standards are wittily upheld against those of the totalitarian mobsters.

And what a cast! Gary Cooper, wonderfully strong and ingenuous as the leading encyclopedist; and Barbara Stanwyck as the stripper – quite irreplaceable now, although there were at least fifty actresses in Hollywood then who could have played this part better than anyone today. And when one considers the weight of expressive talent among the supporting professors – including S.Z.

Sakall, Richard Haydon, Henry Travers and Oscar Homolka – one has to end up giving thanks once again for the only place – Hollywood – and the only epoch – 1930–50 – in which the art of entertainment at the highest level was truly international.

22 September

Afterthought on *Ball of Fire*: we no longer go to the cinema for comedy. (By which I mean full-length narrative scripts designed to be intelligently funny: I exclude *Carry On* films and TV situation comedy.) Comedy nowadays belongs predominantly to the theatre – e.g. the vogue for Neil Simon on Broadway and Alan Ayckbourn in London. We go to the movies for spectacular thrills, sex and violence: very seldom for laughs. This represents a really radical change from the thirties and forties, and one that nobody seems to have noticed. Why has it happened? Largely, I suspect, because movies are obsessed with the battle against TV; they have withdrawn their troops from the comic sector, where TV is strong, in order to concentrate on the areas – viz: spectacular thrills, sex and violence – where TV is relatively weak. By adopting this strategy to defeat TV they have left comedy open to the theatre as well; and the playwrights have seized the opportunities. I congratulate them on their good luck: but how sad that modern moviegoers are deprived of education in comedy that I and my generation received from the marvellously gifted Hollywood craftsmen – many of them lured from Broadway by the loot – of the thirties and forties. Brackett, Wilder, Perelman[1], Hecht[2], MacArthur[3], Parker[4], Lubitsch[5], Mankiewicz (H.), Kaufman (G.), Ryskind[6] *et al* – wherever their contemporary equivalent are working, it certainly isn't in the cinema.

1. S.J. Perelman (1904–79). *New Yorker* humorist and satirist; also wrote films for the Marx Brothers and plays for Broadway, including *One Touch of Venus* (1943) with Ogden Nash and *The Beauty Part* (1963) for Bert Lahr.
2. Ben Hecht (1894–1964). Prolific American playwright and screenwriter, most famous for the hard-bitten iconoclastic comedy *The Front Page* (1928) with Charles MacArthur.
3. Charles MacArthur (1895–1956). Playwright.
4. Dorothy Parker (1893–1967). Poet, short-story writer, known for her scathing wit.
5. Ernst Lubitsch (1892–1947). German-born film director who brought sophistication to Hollywood in such films as *Ninotchka* (1940), *The Shop Around the Corner* (1941), *To Be or Not To Be* (1943).
6. Morrie Ryskind (1895–1985). American playwright and journalist; collaborated with George S. Kaufman and the Marx Brothers on several plays and films. In 1931 he shared the Pulitzer Prize with Kaufman and Ira Gershwin for *Of Thee I Sing*.

Nashville, the new Robert Altman film, which I saw a couple of days ago, and *They Shoot Horses, Don't They?* on TV tonight, jointly convince me that America would much rather show us what is colourfully wrong with the state of society than what could possibly be put right. (cf. *Rollerball* and thousands more.)

25 September

The third episode of *Days of Hope*, Tony Garnett's[1] series of four TV films set in working-class England between 1916 and 1926, is the most explosive so far. It dealt with the disillusionment of a young Labour MP in 1924 who discovers, when the party is voted into power for the first time, that the purpose of Parliament is to make capitalism work, not to dismantle it. I've never seen a more truly subversive work on TV. The thesis being that parliamentary democracy is the shop-window sugar on the bitter, perennial pill of property and profit, and that true power will reside in ownership of land and industry, backed up by the armed forces, the civil service, the educational system, the law and the information media, until such time as the working class takes over. Jim Allen's[2] script and Ken Loach's[3] direction are a seamless marriage, and the recreation of period is as precise as the revolutionary fury that the programmes evoke. The Tory press is up in arms, I note with delight.

27 September

Having reason to suspect that Nicole has found a new lover, I send her the following telegram: 'Please ask your boyfriend to report to us urgently – Outpatients' Department, Chelmsford Leper Colony.'

---

1. Tony Garnett (1936–). British television producer, his influential TV productions include *Cathy Come Home* (1966).
2. Jim Allen (1926–). British screenwriter, often teamed with Ken Loach.
3. Ken Loach (1936–). Left-wing British film director and screenwriter; his work includes *Kes* (1969) and *Raining Stones* (1993) which won the Jury Prize at Cannes.

28 September

The English reviews of Burt Bernstein's[1] biography of James Thurber have all had that nauseating mixture of crocodile tears and relish with which the British Lit. set greet damaging accounts of the private lives of their dead superiors, especially if the latter are American. Burt's portrait of Thurber, as reported in the press, is simply not the man I knew: who wrote me a fan letter out of the blue in the early fifties; who entertained me whenever he stayed at the Stafford Hotel; who gave me lavish and valuable advice on the ins and outs of New York journalism; and with whom I spent many blissful hours drinking at the Algonquin. In the very last years he tended to ramble and repeat himself (the obvious signs of an undiagnosed brain tumour) and he was wryly bitter over the number of rejection slips he was getting from *The New Yorker*, but I remember him with fondness, admiration and gratitude as a man who never grudged his respect to anyone who could construct a shapely English sentence, and also as a man of considerable courage – not only in facing his private afflictions but in standing up for liberal values at a time when McCarthyism was in full cry.

When Larry Adler[2] reappeared in New York in the late fifties after years of blacklisting, Thurber volunteered to make an introductory speech welcoming him back. Elaine and I went down to the Village Gate with James and Helen on that occasion, which turned out to be sadly embarrassing: James went on too long, often lapsing into a barely audible mumble, and embarrassed even Larry – not the humblest of men – with the fulsomeness of his eulogy. But for a sick man to risk public obloquy by praising an alleged Red was a gesture of enormous generosity. I hadn't realised until that night how sick he was: and his death, not long afterwards, did not come as a surprise.

---

1. Burton Bernstein (1932–). *New Yorker* writer, brother of Leonard Bernstein.
2. Larry Adler (1914–). Virtuoso American mouth-organist.

30 September

To Max Wall's one-man show at the Shaw Theatre. Although he's often called the last of the great music-hall clowns, Max really belongs in a more specialised category: he was (and is) what used to be called an 'eccentric comedian', a loner with a funny walk and a rubber face, unthinkable with a stooge (the audience is his stooge) or any other intermediary between his random musings and the outside world. A slight man, usually wearing a black suit ('I'm in mourning for my material') with overpadded shoulders, a small grey trilby with upturned brim and white tap shoes, physically resembles an inverted triangle with a smaller inverted triangle – his turnip head – balanced on top of it. The voice is wanly resonant (he needs no mike), speaking volumes of disenchantment except when lighting on an exotic word, italicising it, isolating it for spellbound inspection: 'We can't leave that in abeyance.' (Pause) '*Abeyance*.' (Pause) 'I don't even know what *country* that's in.' Or again, discussing boils and their habit of appearing in embarrassing places, 'Such as the nose-holes. Lovely word, nose-holes. Earthy. The other word's a bit camp' – his face screws up into a mask of contorted gentility – '*nostrils!*' That face! It's a condemned playground, a fever-chart of intense but utterly unfelt emotions: the jaw swivels in cartooned disgust as a gag fails, or the lips project in a totally false V-shaped smile that shades into a conniving wink before collapsing into a nauseated scowl. It isn't that he resents the audience, far from it. 'I told the manager,' he says bluntly, with the air of a man unafraid of expressing revolutionary views, 'I see no reason why those good people who are sitting in the auditorium shouldn't be entertained.'

So he gallantly consents to take on the job; giving a thunderous tap-danced imitation of an express train; accompanying himself on the guitar as he sings strange little songs of his own invention ('Does a carrot think a turnip is anaemic? Does rhubarb ever sigh, when we place it in a pie?'); assuming the gait and features of a lascivious ape, and extending to the audience a horribly beckoning finger (though he fails, as he admits, to put the wind up as much as he would like: 'I don't frighten people any more,' he mysteriously explains, 'since I had the nut and bolt taken out of me neck') trying anything, in fact, to keep us from dropping off; for what he is essentially doing, like the tramps in *Waiting for Godot*, is whiling away the time – time that we would probably waste anyway, if left to our own devices, and might just as well waste in his company.

He dares us to be bored: lacking such artificial aids as plot, suspense or *dénouement*, all solo performers are tightrope walkers without a net, and what grips us is the possibility that they might fall off. Often Max pretends to slip: after each particularly ancient gag, he leans forward, insanely beaming, and snaps his fingers at us, demanding the laugh that doesn't come. '*That* was a dead loss,' he then calmly observes (failure never surprises him): but his face is stricken, and his body becomes a walking wince. He has the stoic assurance of a man who mistrusts everyone and whose worst misgivings are constantly being justified. He claims, now and then, to be absolutely crazy about himself: 'I look at myself in the mirror. "What is so magical about you?" I ask, kissing my wrists. Yes, narcissism is creeping up on me.'

But doubts always undermine him: he confesses that once desperately seeking a new opening for his act, he toyed with the idea of entering in a dense mist, first having had all his bones removed from his body. He would thus *slither* into sight – 'completely filleted – if such an operation could be performed'. But he never found a co-operative surgeon, and the gimmick was stillborn. He strikes wonderful plastic poses, embodiments of grace under pressure, and recommends them for use when confronting creditors: 'The fist raised, the foot forward, and the *stentorian* voice – "One moment, *please!*" – that's the way to handle a threatening landlord.' In slack moments he draws on a vast store of backstage anecdotes – concerning, for instance, a pantomime Dick Whittington who strode across the stage in the Highgate Hill scene and asked a peasant who was sitting on a milestone: 'Canst tell me how many miles to London?' 'No,' said the peasant, subtly segueing into his specialty act, 'but I *can* give you our impersonation of Frankie Vaughan.'

Max Wall is a true original, whose roots, paradoxically, are in the banalities of traditional vaudeville. He sums up the paradox in a single gag. 'I'm the only comic,' he boastfully confides, 'to whom nothing funny has ever happened on the way to the theatre.' He then pauses, flashes his gleaming grin, and adds: '*Until tonight.*' His mimetic suppleness and physical agility are astounding in a man of sixty-eight. But what gives him his title to greatness is the fact that he never fails, even in his most familiar routines, to take us by surprise.

2 October

Days of Hope ended last night with two and a half hours on the rise and ignominious fall of the General Strike. Perhaps it's a bit too obsessed with the backstage manoeuvring and betrayals that went on and too little concerned with what was happening in the streets (so that one suspected a slightly unhealthy interest in corridors of power, 'the story behind the story', etc.): even so, it remained riveting throughout, and one realised how rare – in any medium – it is to see a work based on the assumption, passionately held, that the workers are the blood and muscle of the body politic, while the great majority of the intelligentsia are merely frayed nerve-ends. The use of detail was masterly – e.g. when Birkenhead casually calls J.H. Thomas 'Jimmy', we know that the latter's capitulation has begun. There was a superb scene in which Baldwin uses a strike by the typesetters of the *Daily Mail* (in protest against an anti-worker editorial) as his excuse for breaking off negotiations with the unions – the point being that the TUC men all take it for granted that failure to assist the propaganda activities of a Tory press lord constitutes an intolerable interference with freedom of speech.

Time and again one grits one's teeth as the workers' representatives – in parliament and in the unions – tacitly accept, in the name of 'fair play', a state of affairs which is transparently loaded against them. Predictably – but none the less powerfully – the film ended with the reformist Labour MP who believes in social democracy breaking with his wife and brother-in-law, who have decided that direct action is the only road to radical change. (As happens very rarely these days, the enemy was correctly identified as the employing class, the class that lives on others' labour. Failure to understand this is responsible for the familiar, irrelevant gibes at socialists like myself who enjoy good food and drink. Socialism is *not* opposed to material pleasures: indeed, as a professedly materialist doctrine, it could hardly adopt that stance without severe internal contradictions. What it opposes and seeks to withdraw is the class that pays for its material pleasures with wealth produced by the labour of others: and to this class I do not belong.)

3 October

Gore's fiftieth birthday party – forty guests at Mark's Club, including Princess Margaret, Tennessee, Diana Cooper, Jonathan Miller, Claire Bloom, Sidney Bernstein, etc. (Pinter and Antonia absent through illness.) I spend most of dinner making outrageously obscene conversation with Miriam Gross, not I think altogether to her displeasure.

I make a brief speech, addressing the guests as 'Comrades', since this is also the last day of the Labour Party Conference at Blackpool, and fraternally congratulating Brother Vidal on having chalked up half a ton and on having brought together – and kept together in unity – 'this great party of ours' for the better part of two and a half hours. Then Clive James – the pride of the outback, the scourge of the networks, the Sultan of Shine – delivers an ode to Gore which we pressured him into writing: too clever, and delivered (because of nerves) too fast, but much appreciated. We drive Princess Margaret home and return tipsily to fuck, for the first time in many weeks.

4 October

Post-party lunch at Marguerite Littman's: Tennessee, Maria St Just, Martin Amis, John Huston, Anouk Finney, Claire. Tennessee enters blandly euphoric on speed (I observe, perhaps too candidly: 'There is panic in your laughter,' to which he replies, 'There always is') and – as often when speed is in the bloodstream – makes huge gaffes with his face wreathed in smiles. Describing a party at Maria's, he says, 'What a beautiful man Jim Dale is! I do so love his songs. He's just the man to rescue a really *disastrous* party. When everything is really boring and *disastrous* he comes along with his songs and saves the day.' All this blithely to Maria's face.

Then he turns on Marguerite: 'You did a terrible thing to me last night. You know what she did? She told me to sit beside Princess Margaret and give her a bit of a giggle – that's what she said. I don't know Princess Margaret, and anyway I expect she's quite a stupid person – so how could I give her a giggle?' We asked what he had said. 'Well, I told her I was vaguely connected with *la vie de bohème*. And she said: "What is that?" And I said: "I believe it's an opera!"'

Maria and I discuss Dominic Elwes and she recalls an occasion when she went with him to a night-club where the other customers included Lady Docker, who then had a gold-plated Rolls-Royce. Dominic suddenly left the table and was afterwards discovered flat on his back under the Rolls-Royce, chipping away bits of the gold plating into a handkerchief with a penknife.

5 *October*

P. Hall starts his stewardship of *Aquarius*. (*Arena*, BBC 2's arts programme, started last Wednesday, my contribution being a eulogy of Lilian Baylis and an interview with Larry about her.) The programme includes a funny but undeniably unserious film of Gore in Rome, which ends with Gore remarking: 'Just think − if Remus had killed Romulus, we would be sitting in Reme.' But P.H. goes 'out of his way to avoid being associated with such trivia': opinions expressed on the show, he gravely informs us, are not necessarily his. As if we would otherwise have assumed that Gore was playing dummy to his ventriloquist. The man's subfusc pomposity knows no bounds.

At the end of the programme, looking like a society priest, he returns to the theme, referring to a young Irish poet as an artist who 'unlike Gore Vidal is still living in his own country and struggling to interpret it'. Coming from P.H. this takes the breath away: exactly what he − the director of *The Wars of the Roses*, grand opera and an intergalactic musical comedy on Broadway − has done in the way of struggling to interpret the problems of contemporary England is a question I have advised Gore to raise in a terse Evelyn Waugh-ish letter to the newspapers. He has a sitting target, since P.H. seems unaware that Gore − apart from running for Congress − has devoted a good deal of his writing life to polemical analyses of the American political scene.

From E. Waugh's diary, August 1943: 'I don't want to influence opinions, events, or expose humbug or anything of that kind. I don't want to be of service to anyone or anything. I simply want to do my work as an artist.' For 'artist' read 'writer', and E.W. expresses my own feelings exactly. I must get off my shoulder the censor of what I-ought-to-be-saying and pay heed instead to what I-really-felt, however discreditable. My persona and myself have never properly matched, with the result that they have drifted apart and I have lost touch with (and faith in) myself. (E.W. always had Catholicism to act as an inner compass, which steers only by God. I have had to steer by socialism, which unluckily but inevitably involves one in a less personal, more objective approach to writing – and makes one suspect anything too idiosyncratic. Godly people are allowed to be frivolous at times; socialists never.)

6 October

Go to Berlin to write for *The New York Times* about present state of Berliner Ensemble. Day of typical disasters. Baggage staff at Heathrow are on strike so I have to tote two heavy cases about half a mile to Gate 24, puffing like leaky bellows. As plane starts to descend over Berlin, small girl on my right turns smiling towards me and sends copious flood of vomit all over my lunch tray and trousers, returning with interest what she has just ingested from her own tray. Later in the day I go by taxi to Checkpoint Charlie, the only entrance to East Berlin other than the S-Bahn. Here uniformed bureaucrats keep me waiting for forty minutes where passports are vetted and currency statements checked: after which I have to run (or stagger) nearly a mile before flopping just in time into my seat at the Berliner Ensemble (for *Mrs Warren's Profession* – with superb performances by wide-eyed, thin-lidded, forthright, vulnerable and highly sexy girl named Jutta Hoffman who plays Vivie).

Deciding to return by *S-Bahn* I struggle up and down many ill-chosen flights of stairs before being told that if one enters *via* Checkpoint Charlie, one must exit there, too. So I hunt for a taxi, go through repeat performance of bureaucratic hangup at the border only to find myself back in West Berlin too late to hope for a passing taxi, in an icy wind, with a persistent-looking rainstorm starting. I plunge desperately into a pizzeria, pretend to be slightly iller than I am, and beg the owner successfully – to phone me a cab.

8 October

The Ensemble, four years after Heli's and nineteen years after Brecht's death, is like a haunted house – part enslaved to, and part trying to break away from, his great ghost. Trying to avoid rigid Brechtian procedures, it has plunged into a capricious eclecticism that is either no style at all or (at times – e.g. in the new production of *Die Mutter*) a strange throwback to expressionism. To rewrite the Communist Manifesto: a spectre is haunting European theatre – the spectre of Brechtianism. He is still the major influence not only on German theatre but in France (Planchon[1]), Italy (Strehler)[2], and England (Gaskill *et al*) as well. Nothing new has taken his place after nearly two decades. Perhaps the Ensemble needs a new *coup d'état* to overthrow Ruth Berghaus, the present director, and restore the old order under Manfred Wekwerth.

10 October

Finished C. Sykes' biography of Evelyn Waugh. Full of odd, unnoticed facts – E.W., who abhorred theatre, saw *Kiss Me Kate ten times* (was he a spanker? apropos of the Profumo scandal, he said that 'a pound a swish' was a highly inflated price); and he insisted, later in life, on having all his teeth extracted *without an anaesthetic* – an ordeal that, according to Auberon W.,[3] hastened his death. Sykes gives us this amazing piece of information with no comment or explanation. Perhaps Waugh feared anaesthetics as a kind of rehearsal for death: if so, the fact that he preferred the agony of multiple extraction tells us something of the terror death must have held for him.

I have gone on to the life of another hard-drinking obstreperous melancholic, James Thurber, who seems by contrast a very pallid figure. A description of Harold Ross – untutored, rough-tongued, parsimonious, earthy yet puritanical creator of a remarkable artistic product who didn't see the point of art, a genius who worked entirely on instinct – suddenly puts the notion into my mind that you could describe him very fairly as the Lilian Baylis of American letters.

11 October

In his Thurber book, Burt Bernstein says James was so incensed by my cool review of his book on Ross that he wrote to his English publisher

---

1. Roger Planchon (1931–). French theatre director, actor, and manager.
2. Giorgio Strehler (1921–97). Italian stage director; co-founded the Piccolo Teatro della Citta di Milano.
3. Auberon Waugh (1939–2001). Curmudgeonly journalist and author; edited the *Literary Review*, 1986–2001; son of novelist Evelyn Waugh.

about the 'snarl of [my] ego and psyche'. He also calls me, along with Rebecca West and J.B. Priestley (who also didn't like this book) 'sick and insulting'. That was in the summer of 1959, and gives the impression that James had broken with me for good. In April 1960, however, Bernstein quotes at length from a warm letter to 'a friend' – without revealing that the 'friend' was me. To have done so, of course, would have required a much deeper analysis of Thurber's many-levelled roller-coaster friend-ships than E.B. cares to provide. (Incidentally, the letter quotes something I'd forgotten. I'd written to James saying that Truman Capote would probably expand if dropped into water. I called him: 'Instant Woollcott[1]'. 'Which' says James, 'is exactly what he is.')

Alone in Berlin on a Saturday night, with no theatre to attend, I ought to go out gaily in search of adventure. But age has struck: I scan the list of night-clubs, restaurants, massage parlours without a flicker of inter-est, my only concern being whether I shall have enough of the *New Statesman* left unread to last me through a Chinese dinner. Even if call girls were half their present price (100 marks plus cab fare), I wouldn't pick up the phone: the language barrier, over which I used airily to skip, now seems insuperable. (If the girls were 25 marks a throw, of course, I might just exert myself.) Part of the trouble is emphysema, which now makes even walking a block in cold weather as exhausting as running half a mile used to be, twenty years ago.

12 October

Back in hotel at 2.45 a.m. after grisly tour of Berlin night-clubs. Choice of colour films of fat women sucking cocks or fat women sucking themselves, seldom on the sexy side of forty-five. One sings to a room lined with twenty impassive men with folded arms in leather jackets:

Ich bin eine San –
Eine Hüre, ein Nutte –
Ich bin eine San –
Aber eine gute!

1. Alexander Woollcott (1887–1943). American theatre critic and personality. Tynan on Woollcott, *Profiles*: 'His fine and illuminated intellect grasped, held, and assessed; little indeed was beyond his wit, the wise and jetting laughter of a corkscrew of a brain.' (July, 1943, *King Edward's School Chronicle*)

Weighing in at 16 stones, looking like Mrs Thatcher grotesquely inflated, she is introduced as 'INES EVENING'!

Politics is serious in Europe in a way that it never is in England. We tinker; we quip; we are bright dilettantes; but we have never had a real live Communist regime across the border. As long as we prospered, we could afford to stay aloof. But now we are poor, the game we have played in our hothouse becomes pathetically vulnerable to storms and cold blasts from outside. Because socialism as a political fact has never been nearer to us than – what? 1,000 miles, we have never had to take it seriously, as a real and immediate possibility. Other capitalist countries in Europe – France and Italy, for example – have adopted homeopathic remedies; they have inoculated themselves against the dreaded disease by tolerating strong Communist parties within their borders. Thus they have become familiar with what the party believes and how it behaves. By contrast, the English are totally and complacently ignorant. The presence of powerful Marxist parties provokes the social democrats and right-wingers to genuine thought. Lacking such provocation, our twin parties have no ideological foundations: they are like opposing attorneys playing a game in court, after which they will share a bottle of wine at their club.

19 October

The most powerful influence on the arts in the West is the cinema. Novels, plays *and films* are filled with references to, quotations from, parodies of – old movies. They dominate the cultural subconscious because we absorb them in our formative years (as we don't absorb books, for instance); and we see them again on TV when we grow up. The first two generations predominantly nourished on movies are now of an age when they rule the media: and it's already frightening to see how deeply in their behaviour – as well as their work – the cinema has imprinted itself on them. Nobody took into account the tremendous impact that would be made by the fact that films are *permanent* and *easily accessible from childhood onwards*. As the sheer number of films piles up, their influence will increase, until we have a civilisation entirely moulded by cinematic values and behaviour patterns.

Last night at a restaurant K., appalled to see me smoking a cigarette, blurted out to the friends present my doctor's warning that unless I gave up the habit I would be dead in five years. I understand her concern, but I wish to God she hadn't made that bit of ultra-private knowledge public. It will be all over London within a day or two: and anybody wondering whether to employ me as a film director will conclude that I am uninsurable and abandon the idea.

While capitalism prospered in this country, under the benevolent protection of the law courts, the police, the civil service and the armed forces, the façade of democracy could be permitted to exist, charade though it was: a Labour party could be tolerated, in Punch and Judy conflict with the Tories; because the foundations of the building were secure. But now that the edifice totters, the Establishment's faith in the superstructure is beginning to collapse. Strikes are unpatriotic; Marxists are subversives; the Labour Party is a hostage in the hands of left-wing militants, etc. Political realities have at last destroyed the game by exposing its artificiality. Cleaned so often it's threadbare.

22 October

To Covent Garden for the debut of Baryshnikov, the reputedly sensational new Russian dancer, at Covent Garden: he plays Romeo in the Prokofiev ballet. An affecting little chap with wide eyes but not much in the way of presence or personality: two spinning jumps, tilted sideways, made the house gasp: but nothing happened to alter my view of ballet as an entertainment that preserves much of the best of silent screen acting, accompanied (often) by excellent music and occasionally thrilling gymnastics. Dickie Buckle[1] says that when he re-choreographs the ballet, it will have a happy ending: 'Friar Lawrence, having been unfrocked for futility, will marry the Nurse.'

25 October

Ballerinas are nurses. Athletic, poker-backed nurses. Brisk, energetic, scrubbed, antiseptic and pure-souled. (If not nurses, then nannies, governesses, perhaps. But I would choose nurses.)

---

1. Richard 'Dickie' Buckle (1916–). British ballet critic.

Q: There have been sexy male dancers (mostly queer) but why has there never been a sexy ballerina? No one ever went to see Pavlova, Markova, Ulanova, Fonteyn, to look at their legs.

26 October

'I'm taking up parachuting.'

31 October

A useful word previously unknown to me: 'ergophobia', meaning 'fear or hatred of work'. At last I can define myself in one word.

3 November

A golden autumn weekend with K. and children at a Cotswold hotel in the village of Upper Slaughter. Matthew's vocabulary grows apace and he now qualifies as a person with whom conversation is possible. Roxana long since passed that test. Both are simply breath-bereaving in their prettiness. Watching Matthew eating pâté (for which, at four, he has developed a connoisseur's fondness) and being asked by Roxana to explain the meaning of democracy, I caught K.'s eye across the lunch-table (roast beef and burgundy) and felt for almost the first time that we were a family – i.e. that each had tough and durable wires of sympathy connecting him/her with the other three that he/she would never feel for any other person.

6 November

I learned that Harold Pinter was incensed when I said on TV a few weeks ago that the English theatre was preoccupied with the minor emotional crises of the urban middle class, and never opened its eyes to analyse society as a whole or the world outside England. I named *No Man's Land*, *Otherwise Engaged*, and *The Ayckbourn Trilogy* as examples of the kind of thing I meant, and summed up the plot of the Pinter play as a rich middle-class writer has a wary confrontation with a poor middle-class writer. Pinter's comments were that it would be easy to write of *Hamlet* and *Coriolanus* in similarly glib sentences. But of course it wouldn't: because *Hamlet* is about Denmark, not just Hamlet, and *Coriolanus* is about Rome. In both plays, whole societies are under scrutiny, not just individual temperaments.

11 November

I read Eileen Kaufman's biography of her husband, Bob,[1] the black poet, whom I knew in San Francisco in the fifties, when he, Kerouac[2], Ginsberg[3] and Neal Cassady[4] were the leaders of the beat generation. Though it's naive in its hero-worship of Bob (whom she describes as the Villain of North Beach), the book brings vividly back those free-wheeling days – the period that spawned the hippy-flower-power protest movement of the sixties. Bob's addiction to speed (which he mainlined into every available vein, sometimes needing as many as thirty jabs a day) is described in horrific detail. After Kennedy's assassination in November 1963, Bob lapsed into total silence: he literally did not utter a word for ten years; simply lived like a Trappist zombie, getting more and more dependent on amphetamines. Then, on the day the Vietnam War ended, he broke his silence: sitting with Eileen in a café, he suddenly began to recite poetry – the whole of 'Prufrock', *The Waste Land* and most of the *Four Quartets* – in an uninterrupted flood. Since then he has been talking freely and has begun to write again. (I never knew that his mother was a voodoo priestess from Martinique and his father a Jew, or that he ran away to sea.)

15 November

Nicole: I never give myself, because I'm afraid I shan't get myself back. I live in constant fear of being stolen. (*Said with mock gravity*)

---

1. Bob Kaufman (1925–86). Beat poet; described in France as the 'Black American Rimbaud'.
2. Jack Kerouac (1922–69). Novelist, a founder of the Beat movement for whom he was an icon; most famous for his semi-autobiographical novel *On the Road* (1957).
3. Allen Ginsberg (1926–97). Poet; his epic poem *Howl* (1956) is one of the best pieces of writing the Beats produced.
4. Neal Cassady (1926–68). Writer and creative inspiration for the Beat movement; in the late fifties, Tynan visited Cassady in San Quentin Prison where he was serving time on a drug charge.

16 November

How much of theatre has to do with imposture! Walter Kerr¹, in his brilliant book *The Silent Clowns*, points out that Chaplin's genius lay in his ability to assume any identity at the drop of a hat – to become, in a split second, according to the demands of the plot, a great lover, a great gymnast, violinist, skater, thief, gourmet, conjurer, etc. etc., while having, at bottom, no true identity of his own. This leads me to reflect how much of world drama concerns people pretending to be what they aren't. Hamlet feigns madness; the noble King of Thebes is an incestuous patricide; Kent pretends to be a serving-man, Edgar to be a mad beggar. In *Too True to Be Good* (which I saw last week in Clifford's excellent production) nobody is what he seems – the humble Private Meek is in fact the military commander, while the commander himself is a frustrated water-colourist; the confidence trickster is a priest; his henchwoman poses first as a nurse and then as a countess. Throughout Shaw, burglars turn out to be philosophers, and villainous exploiters turn out to be heroes; even Saint Joan dresses up as a man. Mistaken identity is not only what the craft of acting is all about; it is what much of drama is all about. An actor is a man who pretends to be someone who is usually pretending to be someone else.

21 November

Went last night to see Jacques Tati's new film *Parade*. Tati himself appeared afterwards to answer questions: tall, dapper, beaming, ever ready to disconcert his interlocutor (an NFT official) with sudden pieces of irresistible mime, as when the chap turned away from Tati for a moment to listen to a question from the audience, only to be confronted when he turned back by a huge pot of yellow flowers that Tati had picked up from a floral display in the footlights and was gravely proffering – as in a ceremonial presentation – just beneath the official's nose. I should have included Tati (and Bruce Lee) high in the list of great performers in my new book.

---

1. Walter Kerr (1913–96). Distinguished American theatre critic who with his wife Jean wrote musicals.

24 November

At rehearsals of *Arena* programme, Deborah Norton was talking about Martin Amis and said: 'Good heavens, I've known him since he was eight inches.' 'Oh,' said David Cheshire, 'not long?'

My own contribution apropos of Peter Hall, I said: 'At last the National Theatre has a director with ash in his belly.' Incidentally I keep reading newspaper articles asking us to pity poor beleaguered Peter Hall with all his financial problems (at the NT) and postponements (positively not his fault, etc.). Another stroke of brilliant PR: we seem to have moved from acclamation to commiseration without any intervening period of *criticism*.

26 November

Yesterday I delivered an address at memorial service for Dominic Elwes held at Farm Street Church. I had taken trouble over it and think it was a good evocation of his personality and qualities. John Aspinall[1] also spoke, very eccentrically: after rightly comparing Dominic to an Anglo-Saxon bard whose job was to celebrate the day's doings in the great hall after supper – to 'unlock the word-hoard' as it says in *Beowulf*, he went on to read a letter in which Dommie said his life had been one of total unhappiness, and then lectured the dead man for his inability to cope with the realities of life. Not perhaps the most tactful thing to say to an audience including Dommie's family and children. Afterwards a dotty rugby-playing cousin of Dominic's rushed up to Aspinall and slugged him in the chin, shouting: 'That's what I think of your bloody speech, Aspinall!' Instantly press cameras clicked and the fracas was all over the headlines. How sad that a tribute to Dominic should be remembered mainly as the occasion for an upper-class punch-up!

1 December

People who call *Mairzy Doats* art should not waste their time on Mozart. Alternatively: the staggering thing about Mozart is that everything he ever wrote is art.

---

1. John Aspinall (1926–2000). Wealthy British zookeeper, casino owner and eccentric misanthrope.

2 December

Entranced by TV appearance of the eighty-nine-year-old playwright Ben Travers[1]. Very joyful old gentleman. He says that for him the hub of Edwardian London was the gents' lavatory in Leicester Square. He remembers it as entirely made of marble, with a plate-glass tank above each urinal. In every tank swam twenty goldfish. When the flush was released, the water-level would sink to a couple of inches. 'The fish would huddle together with consternation written all over their faces.' But then, as the tank refilled, 'You could see their relief – life was beginning again.' Travers says: 'I often think – isn't that a perfect image of human life as a whole? Disaster's about to strike, and then life goes on, and we all breathe again.'

4 December

Unutterably bored by Russian film at National Film Theatre. Called *The Invocation*, it's about obscure blood feuds and heroic love in medieval Georgia and looks as if shot on a fourteenth-century film stock. Unbearably slow and accompanied by sepulchral readings from the works of a great Georgian poet. In the darkness I compose a parody of the subtitles, to be read in sluggish, guttural voice-like English played backwards:

What is life but a
    bowl of goat-fat?
Let us burn down the
    Giaour's uncles
Until the yeast-churns
    run with blood.
Truly he is a Kaftan
And no true-born Shashlik,
Nor will he ever return,
Not even in a great trice.
It is said we have toothpicks
But the oxen have no toothpicks
Thus does a man learn

1. Ben Travers (1886–1980). British farceur; the National Theatre revived his *Plunder* (1928) in 1975.

That only when the sun has risen
Is it daylight, nor ever else
    shall be.
Do not lend thy bed to swine
For pigs may sleep in it.
The snow alone is unchanging,
Save when it is shovelled
    in the fireplace.
Unlock snow! Then no more is it
    changeless.
It is but a puddle.
Or so the currish
    Gnashvilis say
It occurs that when they
    shave not,
They do not grow beards.
Such traitors are ill-met by
    fools.
Does a shoemaker prod
    pomegranates?
If so, how else?
Behold the Giaour, if Giaour
    he be,
For he is out of focus.
Done for, destroyed is he,
Had it he has.
Not for him now the toothpick.
Only one thing is eternal
    under Allah
And that is accursed footage
Of hairy men in filthy weather,
See, there is grim boding in
    the hills
For if a man's teeth fall out,
Where shall he put his
    toothpick?
Lo! the borscht is on
    fire!

And never more shall the
  Shashlik
Make peace with the Shish
  Kebab.

6 December

His chest wheezed like the mew of a cat trapped in a distant cupboard.

14 December

Summit of achievement for an artist: to reach that level of reputation at which audiences come to believe that failure on their part to appreciate your latest work points to a flaw in themselves. (E.g. Pinter, P. Hall and now Stanley Kubrick, whose new film *Barry Lyndon* – which seems to be a stately bore – has been received by most critics with the kind of unconvincing acclamation that springs from self-doubt.)

15 December

Remark on seeing a bad movie performance: 'She's such a lousy actress they even have to dub her footsteps.'

21 December

A lavish dinner party for Tom Stoppard and wife, Bill Davis and wife, George Weidenfeld and friend and Kingsley Amis and wife. Superb wines (Cordon Charlemagne '68 and Chambertin '64), fine Christmas food (oysters, Magdalen venison and *Gâteau Marjolaine*) followed by fierce debate between Kingsley and myself about the future of socialism. K. believing that socialism is identical with fascism, while I propose that with Kingsley's support England could become the first country to achieve a bloodless transition to democratic socialism. We part on terms that allow no transition to any kind of political agreement. At Oxford Kingsley was an instinctive Leftist, utterly opposed to authority in all its forms. Now he is the most ferocious intransigent right-winger I know. Wish he would realise that one does not fight illiberal Leftism with Rightism: one fights it with liberal Leftism.

31 December

Bedridden since Christmas day with usual bronchial infection, back with renewed venom. Martin Landau's debt of £25,000 and 12 per cent still unrepaid, though it fell due on 30 November. Have been offered job as drama critic of *New York* – a proposal countered by Mr Shawn of *The New Yorker* with an offer of $44,000 for six profiles per year (of 4 to 10,000 words each). May take either, if I can prove between now and the summer that I can still write well enough. (Cannot take both, since each insists on exclusivity.) Morosely reading a book on prehistoric animals, I concoct this:

The fossilised remains of Tynanosaurus Thurlovi-ensis (the so-called 'pseudo-lizard of Thurloe Square') are unique survivals of the late pre-holocaust era. The penis, in retraction a paltry object, seems to have been capable of monstrous extension, and there has been speculation that it was used as an offensive weapon or as a 'truffling snout' to dig up tasty tubers. The thoracic cavities were thickly lined with the characteristic layers of nicotine and tar with which many vertebrates of this epoch armed themselves against anxiety. The arms (or 'wings', according to the eccentric and largely discredited hypothesis of Ricqwihr) are tenuous and brittle, scarcely capable of supporting any manual exercise more demanding than self-abuse. (Was the Tynanosaur *homo masturbans*, as Guddle posits?) The cerebral hemispheres, though relatively huge, were filled with rust, used stamps and bird droppings, suggesting that the creature's brains had been 'picked' by members of his peer group (a not uncommon feature of life in the *genus journalisticum*), or that they had somehow fallen out of his ears (*vide* Ricqwihr's curious monograph: 'Braindrip by Aural Seepage'), or that the Tynanosaur had fallen into such general atrophy and disuse that, by a process of accelerated natural selection, his brains had been eliminated altogether. All these features point to a remarkable conclusion: for the first time in the history of palaeontology, we have here a creature which, long before physical death overtook it, had already become partially extinct.

31 December

It is a dangerous fallacy to assume that being a perfectionist is the same thing as having good taste. Those who are reverent about Kubrick's new film *Barry Lyndon* (which I haven't yet seen) all whisper: 'He's such a perfectionist!' But perfectionism without taste is far worse than sloppiness without taste, because it guarantees that the tastelessness will be perfectly and totally expressed. (De Mille was a perfectionist after all, but . . .)

1976

3 January

Birthday telegram to Nicole's baby niece, Mika:

> Fill a foaming birthday beaker!
> Here's a health to little Mika!
> After truth a doughty seeker,
> Lithe of limb, but not a streaker.

15 January

Landau has repaid £25,000 after weeks of pressure and broken promises: *but* although the loan was made in dollars he has paid it back in pounds, which means (because the pound has slipped so badly in the past two years) that he has cheated me out of nearly £5,000. And he has not paid the interest. So there must be more legal hassling.

Last night: *The Ik* at the Roundhouse, Peter Brook's[1] first London production for five years, and a crushing disappointment. Using six actors of different nationalities, he and his collaborators have dramatised Colin Turnbull's book about an African tribe who, forcibly removed from their traditional hunting ground, declined into a state of brutalised amorality in which the mere possession of food (by whatever means, including snatching it from aged parents and babies) was the only criterion of virtue. In other words: remove the necessities of life and people behave badly. Something of a truism, one would have thought, yet Peter gravely presents it as a horrific revelation of human depravity. (Analogy: if you close down the traffic lights at a crossroads and remove brakes from all cars, there is a distinct possibility that collisions will occur. This proves that all drivers are innately homicidal.)

---

1. Peter Brook (1925–). Theatre director, whose distinguished productions include *Marat/Sade* (1964), *A Midsummer Night's Dream* (1970).

Peter has in fact seized on Turnbull's book as yet another piece of evidence to support the thesis that has increasingly obsessed him in the past two decades – namely, that people stripped of social conventions are rotten to the core. This vein of ritualistic misanthropy, first visible in his Theatre of Cruelty season at the LAMDA Theatre, runs right through his productions of *Titus Andronicus*, the *Marat/Sade*, *Lear*, the Seneca *Oedipus*, *Timon of Athens*, *US* (which was not an attack on American involvement in Vietnam but a comprehensive plague-on-both-your-houses indictment of the US army and the Viet Cong alike) and of course his film of *Lord of the Flies*, a novel which has an unfailing appeal for facile pessimists.

As for the production: well, the actors certainly transform themselves into African natives with the conviction of long practice: but throughout the short evening one keeps reflecting how much more effectively a filmed documentary could do exactly the same job. There is no specifically *theatrical* excitement in the show: it's a series of short realistic scenes linked by straight narration. And it appears curiously detached about the present fate of the Ik tribe: a programme note tells us that 'as far as anyone knows', they still exist. But couldn't someone have troubled to find out? I was bored by the lack of theatrical inventiveness and by the intellectual shallowness of it all.

While Peter has been away in Paris, the Fringe theatre in Britain has overtaken him: *Fanshen*, for instance, was an infinitely more compelling and informative documentary, conceived in terms that made it a purely theatrical event, not a film *manqué*. I began to invent a documentary of my own, as my attention wandered from *The Ik*: it would demonstrate how, if you deprive a theatre audience of food, drink, tobacco, theatrical stimulation and intellectual sustenance, they slowly go mad with boredom and rage and begin to contemplate acts of violence on the cast and director, reverting in the end to a condition of total savagery, culminating in the terrible ceremony known as 'demanding the money back'.

How I wish Peter would stop tackling huge philosophical problems and return to the thing he can do better than any other English director – i.e. startling us with stage magic. I don't want to hear Peter on anthropology any more than I would have wanted to hear Houdini on spiritualism. It's as if he had come to despise his real gifts, to regard them as superficial, whereas in fact the shocks he was capable of inflicting on an audience's susceptibilities set up vibrations that linger permanently in the memory. His theories, on the other hand, dissolve overnight like melting snow. (I wickedly recall the famous exchange between Max Beerbohm and Harry James, after they had attended one of William Poel's[1] spartan exercises in Elizabethan stagecraft. 'It's all done with great economy of means,' ventured Max. 'And – ah, of *effect*,' said James wearily.)

16 January

Tracy has spent the last three weeks here, and we have been much closer than ever before. She has survived beautifully, and at twenty-three every horizon is open to her sweetness and energy. Whatever my sins, I can certainly sire exquisite children. She tells me a lovely story apropos of the *auteur* theory of cinema: a guide showing film buffs around Hollywood says: 'And that is Otto Preminger's house – I beg your pardon, a house by Otto Preminger.'

21 January

A letter informs me that for the past eight years Sidney Franklin – the former American matador and buddy of Hemingway – has been lying in a Lower East Side hospital bed unable to move, see or speak – the result of a stroke. His only contact with the outside world comes when his brother reads letters to him. (It is impossible, of course, to know whether he understands them.) Sidney is seventy-two. I knew him in Spain in the fifties, a garrulous little man full of outlandish stories about the bulls ('Then I did seventy-five linked *naturales*') and Papa ('I looked at his prick in the toilet and realised his problem. *Nature had short-changed Ernest*'). He was running a bullfight school outside Seville with very little success: indeed, when I was there his only pupil was an American junkie. His fate – not so uncommon, I suppose – appals me.

Later in the day my cousin Alan rings with further proof that God is alive and busily going about his business. Alan used to design motor cars until he developed epilepsy a few years ago. When his condition

---

1. William Poel (1852–1934). British actor and director; founded the Elizabethan Stage Society (1894) and greatly influenced Shakespearian staging in the first half of the twentieth century.

was diagnosed, he was instantly fired and has been unable to find regular work since. (He's nearly fifty, married, with two children.) He's a dull, stoical, cheery man who seems – perhaps fortunately – unaware of how desperate his position is. He told me on the phone: 'I think I'm going to have to leave my wife, Kenneth. She keeps sneering at me because of my epilepsy, and making remarks about it in front of the children. I think that's a bit sadistic, don't you? So I'm seriously considering a divorce. About three years ago I had a mistress in Sweden, for a couple of weeks. I wish now I'd stayed with her. And what's your news? Has your chest been playing you up again? Are you getting any exercise? I've been doing a lot of hitch-hiking lately, all over the place. You meet some very interesting people that way, you know. And I can tell you something – there are an awful lot of lonely men on the roads of England these days, Kenneth. Well, I'm sorry you haven't time to get together – my fault really, I should have let you know I was coming to London. Next time, perhaps? Anyway, take care of yourself.'

To see Stanley Kubrick's *Barry Lyndon*, which the critics have almost universally panned, calling it a beautiful bore. Apart from one curiously sentimental episode (the death of Barry's son in a riding accident), I admire it enormously. No: this isn't the eighteenth century of ogling oyster wenches and sexy young rapscallions and bottom-pinching squires, it isn't a headlong rush of picaresque incident, swarming with Academy Award-seeking cameos. Kubrick doesn't attempt to make the eighteenth century 'relevant' to us: he expects us to be relevant to it. Because what he has done is to recreate the 1760s on their own terms, at their own pace, inevitably more leisurely than ours, letting performances establish themselves quietly with no attempts at playing for easy laughs, quaintness or lens-hogging charm. With infinite care for detail (the passionate precision with which he reconstructs the past becomes almost an aesthetic value in itself) he builds up a picture of the immovable, impenetrable English Establishment – the landed aristocracy with its supporting pillars, the Army, the Law and the Church. The indictment is the more devastating for being totally implicit. And Ryan O'Neal as Barry, the Irish outsider who tries to con his way into wealth and title, never makes the character into the usual charming rogue of costume epics (e.g. *Tom Jones*): we are invited to pity him not because he is a sexy and sympathetic swashbuckler but because he is a (rather thick) human being, quite unaware of his own pathos.

The entire film is breathtakingly beautiful, but it is never merely pretty: the beauty is always functional, building up shot by shot a social panorama, a portrait of a way of life as complete as any that the cinema has ever achieved. It sucks you into the past: as Jonathan Miller put it to me a few days ago, Kubrick is the filmic equivalent of Lewis Namier[1]. A piece of instruction comes quietly but indelibly, across: if you wished to breach the privileged citadel of the eighteenth-century ruling class, the only way to attempt it was by chicanery, fraud, bribery or double dealing. And the attempt would fail.

2 February

Shirley MacLaine opens at the Palladium. A staggering success, and a triumph of H.D.P.: she dances like Zizi Jeanmaire,[2] has ten times the looks of Streisand and the charm of Minnelli, and a voice to match either. Moreover, she can act. For an hour and a quarter she goes through really complex and taxing Broadway dance routines, effort-lessly singing her heart out; and all this at forty-two. I hug her afterwards and tell her that she is a credit to the species.

10 February

Life for the past two weeks (apart from an ebullient lunch with lovely Shirley at the Waterside Inn last Sunday) has been a depleting experience. When the jury acquitted Linda Lovelace's autobiography of obscenity, The Times ran a thunderous leader headed 'The Porno-graphy of Hatred' in which it singled me out as a writer who had himself been 'depraved and corrupted' by the pornography of cruelty, of the concentration camps, of rape and the rapist. This flabbergasting charge has stunned me and inhibited all action since it appeared. I can hardly reply to it myself since it accuses me of having had my character perverted by exposure to pornography: independent witnesses are needed to attest that I'm not irreclaimably sunk in depravity. Letters

1. Lewis Namier (1888–1960). British historian, instrumental in introducing stronger empirical methods and social analyses into the study of eighteenth-century politics.
2. Zizi Jeanmaire (1924–). French dancer and choreographer.

from John Trevelyan[1] and Eric Hobsbawn appear in my defence: but mud like this will stick. (It's no good my saying that spanking between consenting adults is a little different from what went on in Auschwitz: it will all look the same in print.)

The day this vicious attack appeared, Michael White summoned Clifford and me to his office and announced that he couldn't agree to finance the sequel to *Oh! Calcutta!* (now called *Carte Blanche*) until the original show has closed, which may not be for two or three years. He says that I have an obligation to the bankers of *Oh! C!* not to risk their investment by opening a rival show. I point out that, having poured £600, 000 of profits into their pockets over the past six years, I consider my obligation fulfilled. And when I think that I cancelled my plans to spend a tax-free year out of England on the strength of Michael's promise to stage the show this summer: his change of mind will have cost me at least £8,000–9,000. I decide to offer the script to another producer, after discussion with Clifford (who is part swayed by Michael's argument), and it has today gone to Richard Pilbrow.[2] Were Michael and his backers influenced by *The Times* leader, with the clear indication of an impending puritan backlash?

11 February

It occurred to me last night that my recent deep melancholy may be due to the fact that for the last month or so I have been using Mandrax instead of Soneryl as sleeping pills. (Mandrax has a fearful reputation for turning people into zombies, but the doctor who prescribed them assured me this was bogus.) Last night I returned to Soneryl. Result: a dramatic lightening of mood. So it wasn't – wholly – my chest, after all.

The main practical purpose of acquiring wealth is thermostatic – i.e. it enables people to control the temperature in which they live. In cold weather the rich follow the sun. In cold houses the maids rise at dawn to light the fires, and in the evening put hot-water bottles in the bed. Servants cook the food (i.e. expose it to the right amount of heat) and

1. John Trevelyan (1903–86). Head of the British Board of Film Censors, 1958–71. Steered it on a more tolerant and permissive course; his *What the Censor Saw* (1973) argued for its abolition.
2. Richard Pilbrow (1933–). British lighting designer and producer.

serve it at the proper temperature. Central heating is among the first luxuries that the poor man buys when he acquires a little money. Fur coats may have snob value, but their principal virtue is that they are warm. To be bronzed is the visible evidence of wealth. We may have ceased to be sun-worshippers: we remain heat-worshippers.

12 February

Lunching at Le Carafe, where nothing but fish is served, I notice at the next table Michael Heseltine – Tory Shadow Minister of Industry – with a pretty American girl. The menu arrives and he asks what she would like. 'Anything at all,' she says with a sparkling smile. 'Anything at all, except fish. I can't eat fish.' A nice quandary, and I wait with interest to see how Heseltine will get out of it. Instead of offering to take her elsewhere (there are dozens of good restaurants in the neighbourhood), he decides to be stubborn. Still smiling, she reiterates her position: she has hated fish *since childhood* and positively cannot stomach a mouthful. 'Very well,' he says, 'if you don't mind having a drink while I eat.' And thus the problem is solved. I see in this a symbol of British industry's attitude towards the foreign buyer. 'If you don't want our product, please don't imagine that we're going to change it to suit you. You'll take what's on the menu or you'll go hungry.' But of course the foreigner has no intention of going hungry. He buys elsewhere.

15 February

Depressions expand in direct ratio to the amount of leisure time available to accommodate them.

Thought – God knows why – of Paul Senft, the Austrian analyst to whom I went, about fifteen years ago, with the request: 'Please lighten the burden of guilt that now makes it impossible for me to leave my wife.' He succeeded, pointing out on the way that he had performed a similar service for his own wife, who was immobilised by guilt feelings connected with her mother. 'I was able,' said Senft, 'to demonstrate to her that her mother was in fact an exceedingly unpleasant woman whom she had been quite right to reject.' One day as I was turning into Senft's garden path (in Hampstead, of course), an extremely pretty dark-haired girl roared up on a motorbike in a flashy white-leather siren suit and opened the front door for me. 'I expect you've come to see my husband,' she said – astonishing me because the good shrink was a plump, diminutive, physically unmemorable man of sixty plus.

A few weeks later he was escorting me downstairs after a session when the same girl emerged from what was probably the kitchen. I smiled and bade her good morning. As Senft opened the door to let me out, he said in his quiet, tentative, lightly accented voice: 'Mr Tynan – that young woman you just spoke to – do you know who she is?' 'Oh,' I said airily, 'I assumed it must be your daughter.' Senft smiled. 'Mr Tynan,' he said a little wearily, 'you know perfectly well that it was my wife. She introduced herself to you several weeks ago.' 'Oh yes, of course,' I said, feeling oddly ashamed, as if caught in some mildly unworthy act. 'I forgot.' 'But do you know *why*,' Senft persisted, 'you told me you thought she was my daughter?' 'No,' I said honestly. 'Why?' 'Because at that moment,' he said with that faint infuriating smile, 'she entered for you the realm of sexual availability. Good morning, Mr Tynan.'

27 February

Why not a film about sleep? Or rather sleeplessness. Six actors in a locked studio simply staying awake, filmed by a crew who also have to stay awake; and possibly a second crew to film the first crew. The point being to see what happens when human beings are deprived of sleep for an indefinite period. And then challenge the *audience* to stay awake – through a film that might last a week: since we know that people can stay articulately insomniac for quite as long as that, I would find it fascinating.

In New York for the first time in four years to discuss new job with Mr Shawn. Intimidated by such a long absence: will I still get a table at Sardi's? (Nowhere else on earth would this matter.)

29 February

Exhaustion total: the icy New York air hits my lungs hard, so that I dread the thought of living here again. Extreme loneliness: for succour and reassurance I twice phone K., staying with Dirk[1] in France. I lunch with Marion Capron, a girlfriend of my New York days, whom I haven't seen for twelve years. We used to travel a lot together – to Chicago once, and even to Vienna, where I filmed an interview with John Huston (then working on his 'Freud' film) and she was working for André Deutsch, into whose Soho office we broke one night and fucked on his desk. Marion looks fine – a tall, chirpy, gallant girl – but has a terrible story to tell of the past decade. She had a child which was born deformed, whereupon her boyfriend left her: and soon afterwards the child died. She then fell in love with someone else: three days before they were to marry, he died of a heart attack. She went heavily on to pills and liquor, but has since straightened out. I note that she drinks only Coke at lunch.

2 March

Barely able to tote my hand-luggage from cab to checking-in desk, I fly to Miami in search of recuperative sun (my usual spring pilgrimage: cf. Taroudant last year). I have never felt more fragile: my last two nights in NY were sleepless through coughing. My ambition is zero: no will or wish to do anything but lie down, and when I do *that* I cough. Sidney and Gail Lumet[2] invite me for drinks on my last day in NY and Adolph and Phyllis join the party: all say how glad they are that I'm coming back, and promise parties and help with schools: but somehow I can't see it happening. I can't face the spontaneity, the free-flowing energy, the high spirits of these excellent, enviable people.

4 March

In Miami, I sit in my room in a 'family hotel' while high winds wail in the palms outside, deterring nobody but me from lying on rows of mattresses around the pool, and rising from time to time when a cheery 'social director' summons them by microphone to do some exercises. I am too scared to leave my room except for meals, and anyway the walk

---

1. Dirk Bogarde (1921–99). British actor and author.
2. Sidney Lumet (1924–). American child star and prolific film, theatre, television director; among his nearly forty films are *Twelve Angry Men* (1957), *The Fugitive Kind* (1960), *Dog Day Afternoon* (1975); Gail Lumet (1937–), his second wife, daughter of Lena Horne.

to the lobby leaves me gasping. So I watch daytime TV – a mad market on which, all day long, carefully chosen, eager-looking, attractive (but not *too* attractive) Americans leap up and down, clutch their heads, roll their eyes, hug their MC's in carefully rehearsed frenzies of delight at the news that by correctly stating that Henry Kissinger's wife is named Nancy they have won a mink coat, a Chevrolet convertible and a Caribbean cruise.

I read a fascinating book by Martin Green called *Children of the Sun* about the English 'dandies, rogues and naïfs' (as he calls them) of the 1918–1950 period – Waugh, Connolly, Harold Acton,[1] Brian Howard,[2] Quennell, Auden, Isherwood, Philby,[3] Burgess, MacLean, etc. I am struck by this 1955 extract from Brian Howard's diary:

> In a month I shall be fifty. What has kept me from writing hitherto, was – first – too much self-criticism, perfectionism. Secondly, a swelling guilt: I have it as others have elephantiasis . . . Once I had not only talent, but what English people call 'character'. By which they mean the power to refrain. Now I have neither. Will has left me, and the capacity truthfully to imagine – vision – is leaving. I consider myself damned.

Subtract one year exactly from Howard's age, and this could be me – '*ce moi haïssable*'.[4] Howard killed himself shortly afterwards.

Even the weather, here, is falsified for money. As the palms bend outside my window in the gale, I turn on TV to hear that it's another sweltering day for Miami Beach, with cloudless skies and temperature in the 80's. Because of course the tourists must not be discouraged. As posters remind the citizens: 'Visitors are vital.'

Using push buttons, 100 members of the audience at the Merv Griffin TV show are asked who would get their vote for President if the

---

1. Sir Harold Acton (1904–94). Poet and self-styled aesthete.
2. Brian Howard (1905–58). Aesthete, thought to be model for Evelyn Waugh's Anthony Blanche and Ambrose Silk.
3. Kim Philby (1912–88). British spy; defected to Moscow in 1963.
4. 'This detestable me.'

election were today – Teddy Kennedy, Ford, Humphrey or Reagan. The results, according to Griffin, are 49 per cent for Reagan, 46 per cent each for Kennedy and Humphrey, 43 per cent for Ford. Griffin doesn't explain how 184 per cent of 100 people managed to vote. Obvious answer: the results are falsified to avoid alienating viewers (and advertisers) of either party. Does *everyone* cheat and lie in America?

I read Tennessee's *Memoirs*. Conclusion: there is a sensitive and poetic girl called Rose Williams, confined to asylums since 1939, who writes plays. These are performed and published under the name of her wastrel brother 'Tennessee', a raffish low-life homosexual addicted to dope and drink.

5 March

Last night's cab-driver tells me he came to Miami from New York two years ago and now feels like going back: 'They don't pay enough down here.' Tonight's cab-driver also migrated two years ago from New York and says he wouldn't dream of going back: 'In New York I earned $500 to $1,000 a week, I drank too much, I was into drugs, I was miserable. Here I earn $300, I live in the open air, I swim, I sail, I run around the track chasing girls, I'm happy.' He's a big, moustached man around forty.

7 March

Two nights ago on TV I saw a documentary about a club in California called Sandstone where people with sexual/marital problems go and where open sex is practised. One of the directors was interviewed with his two girlfriends, one of whom was asked if she ever felt jealous: 'If I feel jealous,' she said, 'I know it's because I'm insecure. So I face it head-on and involve myself – emotionally, sometimes physically – with the other person.' Today I start to read a book about Watergate, and almost at once I find that Daniel Ellsberg[1] and his wife Patricia attended group-sex sessions – at Sandstone.

1. Daniel Ellsberg (1931–). Economist and former government employee; leaked the Pentagon Papers to *The New York Times* in 1971, which detailed the extent of US military involvement, deception and incompetence in prosecuting the Vietnam War.

KT: Can you take me to the Café Chauveron?
Cab-driver: They have good food there?
KT: Pretty good. And at $30 a head it had better be.
Cab-driver: How are the wines?
KT: Expensive.
Cab-driver: I guess a Lafite or a Mouton–Rothschild of a good year
   would run around $500?
KT: Probably.
Cab-driver: Personally I'm just as happy with a decent Beaujolais.

(Where else outside France?)

14 March

I write to Mr Shawn, enclosing a list of twelve people from whom to
choose the six I shall write about for *The New Yorker*. They are: Pinter,
Stoppard, Shirley MacLaine, Irving Lazar, Bob Kaufman, Peter Sellers,
John Curry, Mel Brooks, George Burns, Johnny Carson (No. 1 on my
list), Robert de Niro, and Ralph Richardson. (When I asked Mr Shawn
why the magazine no longer published critical profiles, he said (a) that
although it had published 'playful' or satirical profiles, they had never
been really hostile, and (b) that he simply shrank from the idea of
destroying people in print and would rather leave that to other magazines.
For him, merely to be ignored by *The New Yorker* is punishment enough.
It's interesting that he wouldn't think of publishing pieces about people
whose careers were in decline: and that he refused to consider Gore Vidal
a worthy subject for a *New Yorker* profile.)

15 March

At last able, after many months (almost a year) to make love to Kathleen
again. But my potency abruptly vanishes after she spends another night
with her lover Dan Topolski.[1]

Shits never die young. Cyril Connolly once said to me that longevity
was the revenge of talent on genius. It's also the revenge of shits on nice

---

1. Daniel Topolski (1945–). Writer and former coach of the Oxford Boat Race eight.

people. Look at the list of the prematurely, unforgivably dead from among my own acquaintances – Kay Kendall,[1] Dylan Thomas, Harold Lang, Pauline Boty[2], Alan Beesley, Dominic Elwes (how I hope the last two have met in some uproarious afterlife, as they never did on earth!), Steve Vinaver, Gerry Raffles[3] . . . Yet all around me the bastards survive and flourish. Surely there is a dark undertow to the life force that drags pure spirits under. It's enough to make a Manichaean of me.

Gala opening of the National Theatre – *Plunder*. Very expensive way of getting a dozen laughs: and frankly too trivial a choice for the occasion. But the Lyttelton Theatre works smoothly, the vast lobby is a triumph of cosy convenience, and I note with pleasure a photo of myself on the wall. Another twinge of pride: leaving the auditorium during the interval, I hold the swing door open to let a middle-aged man through. He insists on holding it for me, saying: 'This is your night.' I see Denys Lasdun, who promises the Olivier Theatre will be ready by June. Gaia Mostyn-Owen tells me during the interval that P. Hall is earning £18,500 basic plus rent for his huge penthouse, plus chauffeur-driven car, plus his London Weekend Television fee – in addition to which he has just signed to do two operas at Glyndebourne. When will the first breath of criticism blow through the press? It looks as if Michael Blakemore was right when he said that P.H.'s major flaw was not love of power but 'simple greed'.

18 March

On the analogy of Benny Green's Swiss vocalist, Heidi-Ho, may I present the French Victor Sylvester – Charles-Louis d'Ince?

19 March

Victor Spinetti tells me that Joan Littlewood is talking about killing herself with fifty Nembutals on the anniversary of Gerry Raffles' death in April. I must write to her and insist that she change her mind: she must learn to be less presumptuous and to go on suffering like the rest of us.

1. Kay Kendall (1926–59). Theatre and film actress.
2. Pauline Boty (1938–66). Pop Art painter; wife of Clive Goodwin.
3. Gerry Raffles (1922–75). Joan Littlewood's partner and Theatre Workshop colleague.

20 March

Since I was prevented from making my film, I have been like a child who sulks in his room when forbidden to play with his new train set: 'If I can't do what I want to do, I won't do *anything*.'

27 March

Debts now mountainous: yesterday the telephone was cut off because of non-payment, and the same will happen to the gas next week. Kathleen says we must put on merry faces and appear to enjoy ourselves. My comment: 'I don't enjoy *enjoying* myself any more.'

30 March

Booking to see Peter Darrell's ballet, *Mary, Queen of Scots*. I reflect why Mary, *Queen of Scots*? We don't say 'Elizabeth, Queen of Brits'. If the aim was to avoid confusion with the late Queen of England why not Queen Mary of Scotland? 'Q. of Scots' can't be a traditional Scots form of address, or we would have James, King of Scots. I note, too, that we don't refer to Louis, King of Frogs. So: why Mary, Queen of Scots? (No doubt there's a simple answer).

I remember one day long ago driving down Park Avenue on the way to Penn Station with a sheaf of notes for a Harvard lecture in the right-hand pocket of my raincoat, and in the left, a celluloid packet containing twelve photographs, with accompanying text, of one girl model spanking another on her bare bottom with a hairbrush. Given a choice, I would far rather have jettisoned the contents of the right-hand pocket: with this dichotomy I have spent my life. (Note the fearless candour of this amazing revelation.) (And note, too, the self-deprecating irony – '*fearless* candour', '*amazing* revelation' – with which I have phrased it, thereby showing what a self-critical person I am.) (And if you think *that* sounds self-congratulatory, let me answer you that I am well aware of my faults, which are numerous.) (And if *that* implies too much self-knowledge, may I add that, in fact etc. etc. etc.) Such is the art of autobiography.

31 March

After seeing the *Mary, Queen of S.* ballet: no characterisation in classical ballet is possible that does not entail one or other of the adjectives 'jaunty', 'noble', or 'sinister', i.e. you can be *romantically* sinister or *tragically* noble, or *triumphantly* jaunty, but such are the limitations of the physical vocabulary of traditional ballet that you cannot – whatever you are expressing – avoid the three obligatory epithets altogether. My favourite moment was when John Knox appeared, bristling in black, to warn Mary against the perils of sensuality. He made terrible faces and wagged his finger at her, like the Wicked Fairy in *The Sleeping Beauty*: and then launched into a *pas de deux* with her, so that within a few moments the great puritan had his arms around her waist, and was whirling her round in the air, one hand firmly gripping her thigh. Having thus made his point, he wagged his finger again and marched off.

1 April

Interview with Dirk Bogarde on TV. I annoy K. by describing his highly artificial performance in *Death in Venice* as 'A middle-aged man pretending to be a young man made up as an old man'.

3 April

To Leicester, where I've been unexpectedly offered a job as artistic director of the excellent local repertory company for eight months, starting in September, while the present incumbent, Robin Midgely, has a holiday. This is what I should be doing – what I always wanted to do until the dread morning in 1952 when I was fired by Fay Compton on the second day of directing her at the Arts Theatre in *Les Parents Terribles*. Also the pay wouldn't be more than £125 a week. I shall turn the job down (having already accepted the job with *The New Yorker* for the same period), but I shan't congratulate myself on having done so.

4 April

The car radio plays. I realise that, during World War II, the focus of everyone's nostalgia was South America. 'That Night in Rio', the whole Carmen Miranda cult – these reflected our yearning for the one reasonably sized area of the globe where nobody was being bombed or invaded, and where nothing was more important than rhyming 'you and I' with 'under a starry sky'.

A newspaper photo of Edward Montagu[1] (imprisoned for homosexuality in 1954 along with Peter Wildeblood[2]), reminds me how very much life has been improved and civilised by the abolition of the law against adult queerness. How desperately all one's queer friends were terrified of blackmail and the law! I think of James Agate,[3] blackmailed for decades by a vicious guardsman. And how beastly it seemed when Beverly Baxter wrote a snide article in the early fifties attacking those theatrical 'bachelors' – Coward, Rattigan, Gielgud, and Novello – who had never known the ripe fulfilment of marriage and family life. Shall we ever know the terror that must have gripped John G. when he was arrested for soliciting in that Chelsea lavatory, not much more than twenty years ago? This is one respect in which life today is unequivocally freer and better than it was when I was at school. In retrospect, I don't think I ever did anything of which I'm prouder than having stood bail for Peter Wildeblood.

I see in the papers that the singer, Frank Ifield, popular in the fifties, is planning a comeback. I remember reviewing his debut at the Palladium under the insane misapprehension that he was blind. (I had him confused with a blind vocalist who bore a similar name.) I watched agape with admiration while he strolled around the stage with every appearance of knowing where he was going, and I burst into spontaneous applause as he strode down to *within a foot of the orchestra pit* without the least sign of fear. By the end of his act I was misty with tears at the thought of his courage. I often wonder what he thought when he

---

1. Lord Edward Montagu (1926–). Tried, along with Peter Wildeblood, in 1954, for 'acts of gross indecency' with two RAF servicemen; the highest-profile gay trial in England since Oscar Wilde's a half-century earlier with both men sentenced to eighteen months in jail.
2. Peter Wildeblood (1923–99). British journalist, playwright; his *Against the Law* (1955) galvanised the movement against laws which persecuted homosexuals.
3. James Agate (1877–1947). Drama critic of the *Sunday Times*, 1923–47; met Tynan for the first time in July, 1945. 'Are you homosexual, my boy?' 'I'm a-f-f-fraid not,' said Tynan. 'Ah, well,' Agate said, 'I thought we'd get that out of the way.' On 30 May 1947, in *Oxford Viewpoint*, Tynan published a review of Frederick Volk's performance of *Othello* and sent it to Agate, who quoted an excerpt in his diary which concluded: 'In other words, here is a great drama critic in the making.'

read the review in which I congratulated him on the gallantry with which he had overcome the handicap of sightlessness.

5 April

A programme of Gershwin songs on TV. When is someone going to take a deep breath and declare that, at some time in the thirties, the 'serious' music tradition finally withered, curled up and died of sterility and malnutrition; and that the greatest composers of the twentieth century are Berlin, Rodgers, Porter, Kern, Gershwin, *et al*? The songs were sung by Steve Lawrence and Edie Gorme: Even with middling American talents like these, one feels such a glow, such a pressure of *bonhomie*, such an unforced, unservile wish to please, that one is disarmed and conquered. In this field the British don't begin to compete.

It is too simple to think of the narcissist as someone in love with himself. One can detest oneself intimately and still be a narcissist. Mailer on Henry Miller:

> The narcissist suffers from too much inner dialogue. The eye of one's consciousness is forever looking at one's own action . . . The narcissist is not self-absorbed, as much as one self-absorbed in studying the other. The narcissist is the scientist and the experi-ment in one . . .
>   It is not love of the self but dread of the world outside the self which is the seed of narcissism.

I recognise this in myself; the less confident I am, the more intense my narcissism becomes.

6 April

Portrait of oneself as a stricken, blotchy, corpse-pallid, double-chinned, river-veined wreck – the image that stares back at one from the changing-room mirrors in men's clothing shops. (Why is this uni-versally true? Is it the harsh strip lighting? And if so, can't they improve it?)

7 April

Jemima perches on the loo;
Sir Henry tells her what to do.
And while he watches every move,
She opens wide her sepia groove.
Her bottom swells, rotundly sweet,
Framed by her guardian's toilet seat.
She strains and presses, close to tears,
Until the chestnut trunk appears,
And falls with a resounding plop;
Whereat Sir Henry murmurs: 'Stop!'
For Kleenex now Jemima gropes
To use between her nursery slopes,
And so she wipes her silken bum,
He fills her lovely mouth with come.

8 April

Two Irish gypsy crones come to the door and K. uncharacteristically gives them £10 for a palm-reading. She is deeply impressed by the results, which she has sworn not to reveal to me. Although she insists they are not unpleasant I'm slightly perturbed – and annoyed at myself for being perturbed.

I remember a story Peter Brook once told me about a woman he knew. He used to go to a clairvoyant who lived near a garage in Ealing; he made her acquaintance through Binkie Beaumont, a passionate fatalist who would never announce the opening date for one of his productions without consulting her. Peter recommended her to a friend named Judy who duly paid a visit. The lady inspected her palm and promptly refused to reveal what she saw. Judy implored her saying she could take any news, however bad, but the woman wouldn't budge. Judy then begged Peter to intercede for her, which he did, and at length the lady relented. Steeling herself, Judy returned to Ealing, ready to know the worst. 'All right,' she said. 'Let's have it. What is going to happen to me?' The clairvoyant looked at her in silence and then said, 'Nothing.' 'Nothing?' 'Nothing is going to happen to you. You will wake up every morning, eat three meals a day, and then go to bed. And one day you will die. *But nothing of any consequence will ever have happened to you.* Good morning.'

And so it turned out. Judy's life (she died a couple of years ago) was entirely without incident or significance, a flat panorama without peaks or valleys. No wonder the palmist shrank from warning her of so ghastly a prospect.

9 April

Seductive dream of Egypt and the ecstatic winter month I spent at Luxor so long ago – was it five years? – the last period of uninterrupted happiness I can remember, when I was just finishing the film script and a new horizon seemed to be opening up. Karnak and the Valley of the Kings and Hatshepsut's temple – these for me are images of bliss, in a climate that flattered my lungs like no other I've encountered. And the little temple of Amun, with an erect prick surprisingly sprouting from the god's official regalia; and the boatman who took us by felucca to have lunch in his mud hut, and gave us a huge parcel of Kif as a farewell present.

And my theory about Akhnaten, a figure who has fascinated me since childhood (he was the frontispiece of my first book): the heretic Pharaoh who worshipped the sun's rays and married Nefertiti. Why did he so suddenly transport the court from Thebes to El Amarna, thus abruptly shifting the centre of an entire civilisation? My suspicion: that he was either queer or androgynous (the curiously realistic statues and reliefs of him suggest as much: he looks effete, curvaceous in the wrong places, something of a loller: in addition, he frequently lacks male genitals. And that Nefertiti was not a woman at all but his boyfriend. (Why, in the Berlin portrait bust, alone among Egyptian women, does she wear that strange headdress that fits her as closely as a skull-cap? Because 'she' had the close-cropped hair of a boy.) Akhnaten had to get out of Thebes to avoid what must have been a huge scandal – i.e. when he announced his determination to 'marry' his boyfriend – whose name, incidentally, means 'the beautiful woman is come'.

It's interesting, too, that Nefertiti appears literally out of nowhere (her background and origins are unknown); and that immediately after her supposed death, Akhnaten's brother, Smenkh-Ka-Re, became his co-regent. There's a *stela* in Berlin that implies a queer relationship between the two men: and there's the further fact that, on assuming the co-regency,

Smenkh-Ka-Re adopted the epithet 'Beloved of Akhnaten' into his title, and also took over the name 'Nefer-neferi-Aten,' which had formerly been borne by Nefertiti: I can't avoid the conclusion that Smenkh-Ka-Re had *become* Nefertiti at the behest of his incestuous brother, the Pharaoh.

11 April

With family to spend Easter in an ancient barn near Burford, expensively refurbished by Diana Phipps. A vast stone-flagged living-well, with a huge gallery around it, from which a carpeted alcove recedes, containing beds or baths. Ideal place for an orgy or a very discreet affair: for which latter purpose it was in fact used by Harold Pinter and Antonia, who did their heavy courting here.

Peter Parker, my Hamlet at Oxford and the man who filched Jill Rowe-Dutton from me (now his wife) is appointed head of British Rail. I hope he makes a success of the job (and his charm, energy, intelligence and determination suggest that he will). I can see him in the Cabinet within three years; and after that, even as Prime Minister – for where else will Labour find a man whose proven mastery of big business impresses the Tories?

14 April

Dream about Antonia and Harold Pinter, in which they are living in Sam Spiegel's New York penthouse, a garish leather-padded pleasure dome full of marble grilles and priceless art-work. (I went to Sam's house-warming party there and when he asked me what I thought of the place, I said: 'It looks like the men's room at the Taj Mahal.') In my dream, Pinter and Antonia hold a press conference:
Q.: Lady Antonia, can you confirm that you are a convert to Judaism?
Antonia: Yes. But as Dr Jonathan Miller once said, 'I'm not a Jew. I'm Jew-*ish*.'
Q.: Mr Pinter, are you aware that this apartment was once likened to the men's room at the Taj Mahal?
Pinter: Yes. But it's not a lav. It's lav-*ish*.

15 April

Dinner with Jane[1] and Kingsley Amis at their palatial home in Barnet (recently sold: they move in July to Hampstead because Kingsley wants proximity to urban life – i.e. pubs). Food splendidly prepared – my former mistress Jane is a classic cook – and wine flatteringly chosen – Kingsley anxious to vie with the wine we gave him in Thurloe Square (his choice: Haut Brion '60 – costly but rather past its best). The other guests include George Gale, and Paul and Marigold Johnson.[2] Kingsley gets progressively more paranoid in his loathing of socialism, and even of social democracy; I try to avoid an open quarrel, but it's no use; even the well-meaning intervention of G. Gale, a rogue Tory who tries to persuade Kingsley that his beliefs are dotty, doesn't help.

Over liqueurs, Kingsley calmly says that I am a lover of tyranny and that I propose to turn England into a vast prison. 'That's the rough scenario, isn't it?' All I can do is smile the tolerant smile, shrug and murmur that I'm a libertarian socialist. He goes on to say that he isn't deceived by this for a minute: it's merely a cloak for my true intentions (me and my 'fellow Lefties') which are the establishment of a police state in which he will be executed, probably after a spell on the Gulag Archipelago. What's more, he says, I would unhesitatingly connive at his execution; might, indeed, be garnering evidence against him at this moment.

When, unable to believe my ears, I challenge him to repeat this alarming statement, he does so (even more explicitly), there being no doubt in his mind that anyone sympathetic to socialism is capable of deliberately murdering a friend. It is chilling to have an otherwise intelligent man uttering opinions like these. At this point I quietly leave the party, since there is no way of accepting hospitality from someone who is sincerely convinced that one is involved in a conscious plot to destroy him!

In the car on the way home I get involved in a pointless row with K., whom I always suspect (quite wrongly) of taking sides against me in situations like this. To my horror, I find myself slapping her face: the first time I have struck her in anger in our twelve years together. (Next

---

1. Elizabeth Jane Howard (1923–). British novelist; second wife of novelist Kingsley Amis.
2. Paul Johnson (1928–). Author. Editor *New Statesman*, 1965–70.

day she denies this and says I once assaulted her before. I ask when. 'You threw a pair of trousers at me,' she says, rather diminishing the high drama of the occasion.)

Footnote: has Kingsley got what the analysts call a monosymptomatic neurosis? i.e. he is rational on every subject except one and on that subject he is barking mad. (cf. the young doctor I met during my Reichian researches who was charming, amusing and highly intelligent, but who just happened to have in his garden a construction of long aluminium pipes, pointed at the sky, with which he said he could cause rain.)

The first big edition of Brecht's poems in English is about to be published. I am sent an advance copy: 500 golden pages, and at least four-fifths of them previously unavailable in English. This is not word-play: it is a form of word-sculpture in granite: and the book should belatedly force the Anglo-Saxons to admit that B.B. is the greatest poet of the century they thought theirs. His style echoes in one's mind: over dinner tonight I composed a pseudo-Brechtian poem:

> There are faces which look
> As if they have been used
> And been useful.
> There are faces which look
> As if they have resisted use.
> Proud and petulant,
> They have resisted living.
> Life has no use for them.

I am a habitual dog-earer of books: but this one seems to me so holy that, for the first time I can remember, I find myself marking memorable pages with strips of paper. I have used up a lot of paper.

18 April

Having finished the monumental Brecht volume in which the poet, while remaining very much a private man, bears witness to, and participates in, the public history of his century – I pick up Robert Graves' *Collected Poems*. Although Robert has long outlived B.B., their birth dates were not far apart and both lived through the two great wars. Yet from his published poetry you would think Robert spent most of his adult life in bed. Or, if not *in* bed, then inviting someone *to* bed, or reminiscing *about* bed. What a cocoon he seems to inhabit! And how narrow his horizon, compared to B.B.'s – how confined to self-gratification!

Lunch at Diana Phipps' house near Lechlade. Among the guests: George Weidenfeld, Peter Quennell, Diana Cooper. I toy with the idea of playing my Garment Game with this sedate assembly. The rule: everyone takes turns to guess the total number of garments worn by all present. (Jewellery and watches don't count: shoes and gloves count two each: tights count one.) A winning score usually depends on one's skill at guessing how many people are wearing knickers, underpants, vests and bras. (Or, of course, surgical trusses.) A photograph of Peregrine Worsthorne, curly-locked and grinning toothily above an article in which he explains what far-sighted chaps the White Rhodesians are, prompts me to reflect that he looks exactly like Ken Dodd made up as Margaret Thatcher.

21 April

John Lilburne[1], the puritan whose tenacity and contentiousness finally compelled the British government to accept the principle that no man can be compelled to bear witness that may be used against him, is celebrated in a splendid *New Yorker* series about the origins of the 5th Amendment. Exile, floggings, trials on capital charges, and numerous imprisonments did not deter this amazing man, known to the London crowds who loved him as 'Freeborn John'. He defied Star Chamber and the Stuarts just as he later defied Cromwell, when the Protector tried to impose on him the same compulsions (i.e. to answer all questions, whether or not they incriminated himself or others) as Charles I's courts. 'From his time on,' wrote Professor Leonard W. Levy, 'the right against self-incrimination was an established, respected rule . . . of English law.' Richard Harris, the author of the *New Yorker* pieces, adds that: 'The concept of the individual as a being whose self-respect and

1. John Lilburne (1614–1657). Pamphleteer and Leveller.

dignity and privacy were inviolable had been born.' He questions the historian Margaret Atwood Judson, as saying that this was 'the first great outburst of democratic thought in history, with John Lilburne . . . leading the way'.

On an impulse I consult Antonia Fraser's biography of Cromwell to see what she has to say about Lilburne. In no way to my surprise, I find that she describes him as 'this egregious nuisance'. Under the US Constitution, a citizen has no *duty* to the government; if the government wishes to proceed against him, it must shoulder the entire burden of proof itself. It is irrelevant whether he is a 'good' or 'bad' citizen: either way, he cannot be compelled to speak and has the right to conceal the truth. A dutiful citizen is a deferential one, who speaks when he is spoken to (and only then); of such citizens, not of mutinous nuisances, Antonia's world-picture is composed.

22 April

Apropos deference: I recall Alan Beesley's story of how he went one year to the State Opening of Parliament and, standing in the crowd just as the Queen approached, preceded by Black Rod, he saw on the other side of the procession an old Oxford chum named Neil Finlay. To attract his attention, Alan yelled, 'Neil!' *And immediately everyone in the crowd knelt down.* Ageing tourists muttered to their wives as they sank to the pavement: 'Daisy, the guy said, Kneel, so for Christ's sake *kneel . . .*'

23 April

The *Daily Mail* says the unions – by rejecting Healey's[1] proposal for a wage increase of 3 per cent – are destroying Britain, and with it their own standard of living. It seems they have failed to realise that 'the foreign creditors and bankers . . . hold the whip hand'. As of course they do; it's perfectly true that if they don't like what we are doing, they can bring down the pound. But what a strange admission from a Tory paper. The usual Tory line, after all, is to complain that in modern

---

1. Lord Denis Healey (1917–). Chancellor of the Exchequer in Wilson's Cabinet, 1974–9; Deputy Leader of the Labour Party, 1980–83; resigned from Shadow Cabinet, 1987.

Britain it is the *unions* who hold the whip hand. Quite apart from this, however, wouldn't it be more appropriate for a true-blue patriotic organ to argue that when threatened by an unrepresentative minority of bullies (and foreign bullies at that), we should resist their intimidation at all costs? After all, appeasement is the coward's way, and if we flinch at these whip-cracking outsiders now, they will treat us with increasing contempt in the future. Yet here is the *Mail* haranguing the unions for their *failure* to bend the knee to foreign tyrants. (But of course one recalls, looking back on its record in the thirties, that the *Mail* has always had a soft spot for appeasement.)

24 April

To Stratford with Roxana to see *Much Ado* — an Anglo-Indian production with Dogberry in a turban; well done, though Judi Dench, by making Beatrice a muted spinster, too obviously in love with Benedick from the word go, loses much of the comedy of the egotist deflated, there being so little ego to begin with. On the way we visit Warwick Castle, where Roxana insists on inspecting the torture chamber, which disappoints her greatly — no thumbscrews, not even a rack left behind. I dream up a limerick at dawn next day:

'Look *what* I've received in this parcel!'
Said a torturer in Warwick Castle.
'A serrated brass prick,
Which shortly I'll stick
Up many a historic arsehole.'

27 April

Am amazed to find, in C.S. Lewis's *Reflections on the Psalms* (which I hadn't read before), a long reference to Akhnaten and his remarkable poem, 'Hymn to the Sun'. C.S.L. says that Akhnaten's monotheism is the first prefiguring of Judaism in world literature, the first proposal that there is an *author* of the universe. (The pagan gods are actors in the cosmic drama; they did not *invent* it.) A. did not identify God with the sun; the latter was merely God's manifestation: 'It is,' says C.S.L., 'an astonishing leap,' and he suggests that although his religion died with him as far as recorded history is concerned, it may have formed part of the Egyptian 'wisdom' in which Moses was brought up.

He goes on: 'In the verse [of the "Hymn to the Sun"] "Thou didst create the earth, according to thy desire," Akhnaten even anticipates the New Testament.' And he concludes: 'What gentle heart can leave the topic without a prayer that this lonely ancient king, crank and doctrinaire though perhaps he was, has long seen and now enjoys the truth which so far transcends his own glimpse of it?'

All this is extraordinary. Can it be that what has always fascinated me about the heretic Pharaoh is not, as I used to think, his alleged status as 'the first individualist in history' (or his putative sexual deviance, at which I recently made a guess in these pages) but the fact that he was an early prophet of Christianity? C.S.L. would certainly hold the view that, by drawing my attention to this passage in his book, God was offering me yet another signpost pointing towards acceptance of the Christian faith. (Just as it was Satan who prompted my ribald speculations about Nicole's sex life.)

4 May

Back from my first trip to Copenhagen, where I talked to Flemming Flindt, director of the Royal Danish Ballet, about the possibility of his contributing a dance item to *Calcutta* 2. (He's very interested: I wish his strikingly pretty wife, Vivi, were also available to take part.) The shrinking pound makes Denmark ludicrously expensive – far more than Miami Beach! – but K. and I find the Danes exemplary people: free-hearted, open-minded, tolerant, humorous, with all the virtues you expect to find in a small civilised country and none of the vices (power mania, corporate greed, over-ambitiousness, hyper-competitiveness) that breed so rampantly in big countries. The visit confirms my feeling that life in countries where the population exceeds about 50 million is incomparably nastier than in their less imposing neighbours: small is getting more beautiful every day.

I'm especially attracted by the large military encampment in a Copenhagen suburb which, vacated a few years ago by the army, has been occupied ever since by a community of about 1,000 drop-outs of all ages, who have renamed it Christiania and turned it into a sort of working model of Utopia – a non-coercive commune where goods and services are held in common and nobody makes a profit out of anyone else's labour. Danish politicians are divided over whether to close the experiment down, since the Christianias refuse to pay income tax, electricity bills or water rates: but even the right-wing realises the advantage of having a tolerated ghetto for dissenters. We also tour the celebrated streets of porn-shops and live sex shows: even on a Saturday, they are deserted. So much for the 'flood-gates-of-filth-are-opened' school of thought.

Antonia Fraser and Harold Pinter came to look at the house with a view to renting it while we're in America. Harold meets Roxana and is spellbound, instantly asking whether we would let her play the little girl in *The Innocents*, William Archibald's[1] adaptation of *The Turn of the Screw*, which he is directing on Broadway in the autumn. (The idea appeals to me but appals K.) Both Antonia and Harold tell us how delighted they are by Jimmy Goldsmith's[2] criminal libel action against *Private Eye*, which has been printing repellent slanders about them for years. Hearing news of the impending case in Yugoslavia, they instantly ordered a bottle of champagne and drank to the magazine's downfall.

Harold looks lean and dapper and beautifully organised. His face has two expressions, which replace each other with disconcerting rapidity. One of them, his serious mask, suggests a surgeon (or dentist) on the brink of making a brilliant diagnosis: the head is tilted to one side, the eyes narrow shrewdly, the brain appears to be whirring like a computer. By contrast, his sudden smile – revealing long sharp teeth with a good deal of air between them – is quite unmistakably a *leer*, and turns his face into that of a slick, bespectacled stand-up comedian who has just uttered a none too subtle sexual innuendo.

A quote from Leavis[3] once more arouses the never-dormant self-critic in me. He is talking about the Bloomsbury set:

'Articulateness and unreality cultivated together; callousness disguised from itself in articulateness; conceit casing itself safely in a confirmed sense of high sophistication; *the uncertainty as to whether*

---

1. William Archibald (1917–70). Playwright who adapted Henry James's *The Turn of the Screw* in the fifties, which chilled Tynan who found it 'a bestial dramatic exercise in artificial fright'.
2. Sir James Goldsmith (1933–1997). Financier.
3. F.R. Leavis (1895–1978). Influential Cambridge literary critic; co-founder and editor of *Scrutiny*.

one is serious or not, taking itself for ironic poise: who has not at some
time observed this process?'

Recognising much of myself in this, I recall the moment when my own
unseriousness lost me the trust (long enjoyed and much cherished) of
Marlon Brando. *Playboy* had asked me to approach him with a view to
interviewing him for the magazine. I called him in Rome, and made
the request. 'I'd rather be boiled in urine,' he said softly. I pointed out
that the questions would be mine, not *Playboy's*, and that I was merely a
contributor to the magazine, not a part of its publicity machine. 'I've
never even been in a Playboy Club,' I said rashly. There was a pause.
'Ken,' Marlon said. 'Why did you say that? Because I've got here in
front of me a picture of you and your wife drinking in a Playboy Club.'
And he was right: I *had* attended the opening-night party of the London
Playboy Club. He had caught me in a lie, and I squirmed like Steiger in
the taxi-cab in *On the Waterfront* when Brando turns towards him and
says, in a voice full of commiseration, bewilderment and moral rebuke:
'It was you, Charlie – it was *you*.'

I used to be a close chum of Marlon's (we once read Act III of *Othello*
together, me playing the Moor and imitating the intonations and
emphasis Larry was amazing us with in rehearsals, with Marlon, reading
Iago, interrupting to say: 'Jesus Christ, he can't play it like that, it's
impossible'). And I think of the occasion when, at Marlon's express
request, I took him to dinner at Parkes with Princess Margaret, and for
the only time in my experience saw him over-awed, literally unable to
address her except through me: 'Would you ask Princess Margaret what
she thinks of . . .' etc. HRH said next day on the phone that this wasn't
an uncommon reaction. 'People just clam up. I'm told it's like going on
television for the first time.' Since the *Playboy* gaffe, we have drifted
apart, to my great regret.

Reading a piece on Thornton Wilder[1] in *Books and Bookmen*, I think of a
lunch at Claridge's in the fifties with Thornton and Ruth[2] and Garson

---

1. Thornton Wilder (1897–75). Playwright and novelist; won Pulitzer Prizes for his novel *The Bridge of San Luis Rey* (1927) and for his play *Our Town* (1938).
2. Ruth Gordon (1896–1985). Actress; wife and screenwriting collaborator of Garson Kanin (1912–99) on such urbane romantic comedies as *Adam's Rib* (1949), *The Marrying Kind* (1957), *Pat and Mike* (1953).

Kanin. Thornton was delivering one of his galvanic, impromptu literary lectures, halting after ten uninterrupted minutes to observe that the head waiter was standing at his elbow, pencil poised to take our orders, as he had been for some considerable time. He looked, for all his professional impassivity, the least bit fed up. Thornton stared at him for a moment and then enquired: 'Are you annoyed with us, or are we annoyed with you?' (I used a variant on this in 1967 at the première of Peter Brook's *US*. It ended with the house lights up and the entire cast standing on stage staring accusingly at the audience, the intention being to arouse our guilt-feelings over the Vietnam War. My reaction, since I felt no guilt, was one of mounting irritation. The audience docilely stayed in its seats, shifting a little uneasily (not out of self-accusation, as Peter later declared, but out of sheer uncertainty as to whether the show was over). I finally decided to break the deadlock from my seat in the third row. 'Excuse me,' I said to the actor nearest me, 'but are we keeping you waiting or are you keeping us waiting?')

8 May

The millionaire hero of Terry Southern's[1] *The Magic Christian* says that his life's ambition is to 'make things hot for people'. For my part, I enjoy *testing* people – exposing them to ideas and/or experiences that will for them reassess the values by which they live, either politically, theatrically or sexually. Hence, *Oh! Calcutta!* and *Soldiers*: hence my penchant for disrupting suave dinner parties.

9 May

Ulrike Meinhof – one of the co-defendants in the trial of the so-called 'Baader-Meinhof group' of urban guerrillas – has hanged herself in prison. I wonder what happened to the other female member of the group who escaped from Germany and came to me about eighteen months ago in search of money and refuge? She pretended at first to be approaching me on behalf of a friend and only admitted that it was she herself who needed help after I had agreed to provide it in the shape of cash, a short sojourn at Nicole's Islington flat and a longer stay with

---

1. Terry Southern (1924–95). Novelist and screenwriter, including *Dr Strangelove* (1964) and *Easy Rider* (1969).

Robin Blackburn. She was lesbian, militant and deeply suspicious of my apparent affluence. Should I have helped her – since the activities in which she took part were undoubtedly violent and based on the theory that innocent lives must sometimes be sacrificed (as in Algeria) if the revolutionary cause is to succeed? I'm not sure: but I'm quite sure, on the other hand, that I could not have turned her over to the authorities. Perhaps one has a special instinctive sympathy with anyone who wants to overthrow the established order in Germany.

On TV I see for the first time Spencer Tracy's last film, *Guess Who's Coming to Dinner?* – the one in which Sidney Poitier wants to marry his (white) daughter. It was held at the time to be a slice of sentimental middle-brow hokum, since Poitier is so obviously a respectable bourgeois black; but watching it tonight, I ask myself how many racially mixed marriages I know, and the answer is: very few. Johnny Dankworth[1] and Cleo Laine;[2] Lena Horne[3] and Lennie Hayton[4], and Lena's daughter, Gail, and Sidney Lumet. Blacks and whites still intermarry rarely, far more rarely than they should; and although the film is full of verbal schmaltz, its message remains potent and timely. (If Black Power entails Black Separatism, I'm against it.) And Tracy is superb, carved out of rock, exuding moral authority as few actors ever have. I ask Kathleen if she would have liked him as a father. She says: 'Yes, even if I'd hated him.' There's an unforgettable two-shot in which Tracy, who was already known to be dying, describes his love for Kate Hepburn, from whose eyes, as he speaks, tears start to descend. Larry may have greater power than Tracy in the portrayal of monsters; but he can't play *nice* men with anything like Tracy's monumental authority.

11 May

Jeremy Thorpe[5] resigns. The newspapers who hounded him are today claiming that the real issue was not his sexual tastes but his veracity; but

---

1. Johnny Dankworth (1927–). Alto saxophonist, composer, conductor.
2. Cleo Laine (1927–). Jazz singer, married to Johnny Dankworth.
3. Lena Horne (1917–). Afro-American singer and actress.
4. Lennie Hayton (1908–71). Pianist, composer, musical director, most notably for his wife Lena Horne.
5. Jeremy Thorpe (1929–). Leader of the Liberal Party, 1967–76, forced to resign after allegations of a relationship with Norman Scott.

the truth, of course, is that he was brought down by a moral climate in which (despite 'permissiveness', despite even changes in the law) it is still impossible for a politician to admit that his anus has ever been fingered by another man. So another insane anal scandal goes into the books alongside Byron, Wilde, Casement, etc. (I see that the *Daily Mail*, which led the pack, has the insolence to compare its grubby smut-hounds to Woodward[1] and Bernstein[2], who toppled Nixon! Interesting, too, that nobody in the Tory press has pointed out the clear political advantage the Tory party stands to gain from the collapse of the Liberals, who have always taken more votes from the Tories than from Labour. I don't say the Tories egged Norman Scott on to say Jeremy was a poof; but I've no doubt that the subsequent press campaign was politically motivated.)

George Davis has been released from prison by Roy Jenkins. I feel a surge of pure delight at the news, which seems to indicate that there *is* a point to campaigning and demonstrating in a good cause and that the good chaps do occasionally win. Tell me what your immediate, instinctive, unreflecting, *visceral* reaction was to the news of Davis' release, and I will tell you what your politics are. If it was 'Thank God!' 'How marvellous!' etc. you belong to the true libertarian Left. If it was 'They've let that bastard loose,' 'Dangerous precedent,' 'Giving in to the mob,' etc. you belong to the true authoritarian Right.

20 May

Went with K. (in the Garbo dress from *As You Desire Me* which I had copied for her) to a twenties ball, at which I wore a feathered blue lurex peignoir, sequinned knickers, suspender belt and black stockings and a wig modelled after the hairstyle of Louise Brooks. And a six-inch ivory cigarette-holder. Introduced myself, to people who asked who I was meant to be, as Lord Baden-Powell. I also shaved my legs for the occasion. Although I wouldn't want to be a woman, I love the idea of making love to a woman while dressed as one; and I much prefer the

1. Bob Woodward (1943–). *Washington Post* journalist and author; co-wrote *All the President's Men* (1974) which uncovered and chronicled the Watergate scandal that forced President Richard Nixon from office.
2. Carl Bernstein (1944–). Journalist and author, co-wrote *All the President's Men*.

feel of my own legs when they are hairless. This doesn't make me a transvestite; but it does mean that I enjoy exploring more sexual possibilities than those available to *macho* males in jeans and T-shirts. (I regard it as a gap in me that I've never been turned on by the sight, touch or thought of a man.) Sadly, the other guests were mostly rich bores.

Contentious business meeting with Michael White and Richard Pilbrow over the *Calcutta!* sequel. Michael claims that he thought the agreed percentage of royalties to be paid to the writers, composers, Clifford and myself also included the choreographers, who will doubtless want $1\frac{1}{2}$ per cent or 2 per cent to share among them. Since his own lawyer drew up the draft contract, which makes no mention of choreographers, this is simply a lie: he knows quite well what was agreed and is trying to cheat us. Depressing when friends behave like this. Coincidentally, I came across an appropriate quotation, attributed by Orson Welles to Molnar: 'Never touch shit, even with gloves on. The gloves get shittier; the shit doesn't get glovier.' Since he became a millionaire, Michael hasn't got any glovier.

25 May

Visit from Robert Wilson, the extraordinary young American *animateur, auteur, metteur-en-scene*, what have you, who invents and stages marathon theatre events loosely based on images suggested to him by the lives of the great – including Sigmund Freud, Queen Victoria and (in his latest work, to be called *Einstein on the Beach*) Albert Einstein. He is lean, composed, has well-trimmed dark hair and wears a business suit: he speaks with immense politeness and a quiet but absolute assurance. He has one of the essential attributes of a first-rate director: one is inexplicably anxious to impress him. I found myself going out of my way to be entertaining, intelligent and helpful (he had come to see if I knew anyone who could put up £30,000 to bring *Einstein* to London in October).

Producing a sketchbook, he made a series of exquisite little drawings to show how the images – visual leitmotifs – of *Einstein* presented themselves to him. It's a five-hour opera, entirely sung; and what is sung – by the cast of twenty-six – is *numbers*. There are three dominant images: a train, a trial ('but then a *bed* appeared in the courtroom', he says, swiftly sketching in the bed) and a field. Between the four acts are shorter scenes which he calls 'Knee-plays' because their function, as with the knee joint, is to act as connecting pivots between longer parts of the skeleton. All this might have sounded mad if uttered by a man less composed and serenely persuasive – by, in fact, anyone other than a supreme imposer. His earlier works have split their audiences into two camps – those who find them protracted essays in tedious and pretentious quietism, and those who regard them as manifestations of genius. He certainly left me with a great desire to go to Avignon in July, where *Einstein* has its première.

With characteristic meticulousness, he has already been rehearsing it for six months; and he has talked the Italian government into paying for the elaborate scenery. During our meeting I had to leave the room for a minute or two; as I returned, I heard him quietly chatting away to what I took to be an empty room. When I entered, I found him engaged in conversation with our Abyssinian cat. One gets very quickly on to fairly intimate terms with people like this (another mark of good directors). To indicate what I mean: sitting beside him while he made his sketches, I made a mildly amusing comment: he stopped drawing, turned towards me, and, *inclining his head so that it rested on my shoulder*, laughed soundlessly in appreciation.

28 May

Attacked again in *Private Eye*, this time because of wearing drag at the twenties ball. I have just identified the distinguishing feature of the magazine's style. It is written *as if by a collection of teachers at public schools,* viz. the constant use of phrases like 'the wretched Wilson', 'the appalling Rees-Mogg', 'the vile Haden-Guest', etc. which exactly capture the tone of the sarcastic beak[1] rebuking the errant pupil. (And of course all *P. Eye's* standards of conduct derive from Victorian public schools.) Odd how *Eye* contributors, like many other right-wing journalists, develop from inky schoolboys into middle-aged schoolmasters without any intervening period of young manhood.

---

1. British public-school slang for schoolmaster.

After going to the première of *Robin and Marion*, Dick Lester's new film about Hood's declining years, I'm struck by two things (1) the indestructibility of the legend: one can't help being moved when the dying Robin shoots his last arrow out of the window to mark his grave, and (2) the influence it must surely have had on Barrie when he was writing *Peter Pan*: the lost boys in the Never-Never Land are Robin and his band of outlaws in Sherwood Forest; Captain Hook is the Sheriff of Nottingham; and Wendy, the den-mother, is Maid Marian.

2 June

Two visits, on consecutive nights, from men with secrets to tell, accompanied by their mistresses. George Weidenfeld (and Ingrid the German publishing lady) explains the fuss over Wilson's Honours List which has so embarrassingly devalued his peerage. It seems that Bernard Donahue (a member of Wilson's staff) saw on the PM's desk a list of pencilled *suggestions* for honours written by Marcia Williams. It included David Frost and Jarvis Astaire, the sports promoter, as well as robber barons like Hanson and Goldsmith. Incensed at being denied a title himself, Donahue leaked the list to the *Sunday Times* as if it were Wilson's final selection. Thus the fuss began. Poor George looked quite pale from the effort of explaining the situation to all his friends, adding of course that the real reason for what he calls his 'preferment' is to be sought in various secret political missions he has carried out, in America and elsewhere, on the government's behalf. On the details of these, he is, of course, sworn to silence: classified information, you know.

Then last night Michael Blakemore came to dinner with Dona (his actress girlfriend) to tell me how and why he had resigned from the NT. He says that whereas Larry's rule appeared to be autocratic but was in fact democratic, Peter's regime is the other way round. The 'associate directors' are mostly Peter's creatures, employed to rubber-stamp decisions previously and privately made by himself and his two assistants, Michael Birkett and Peter Stevens. (Exceptions to the rubber-stamp rule: Harold Pinter and John Schlesinger[1], neither of whom is in Peter's pocket. But Schlesinger, of course, is very seldom in London.)

---

1. John Schlesinger (1926–). British film and theatre director, Academy Award for *Midnight Cowboy* (1969).

Anyway, Michael prepared and read a paper at an associates' meeting, distributing copies to all present. It was seriously critical of P.H.'s policy and methods, and specifically criticised the case of *No Man's Land*. Pinter allowed the NT to do the play only on condition that after a certain number of performances it would transfer to the West End on normal commercial terms. Thus the NT was being used as a try-out theatre; the taxpayers were the investors who would get no recoupment; and the result was that a play was staged at public expense and immediately transferred for private gain. Gielgud and Richardson were both on vast salaries and percentages; and P.H. got 4 per cent of the gross as soon as the play transferred (an unprecedented royalty for a director in this country; but of course P.H. was awarding it to himself). Michael's paper was received in cold silence, and discussion was inhibited by the fact that none of P.H.'s placements cared to criticise his boss. Finally P.H. made the brilliant tactical suggestion that anyone who thought the subject had been fully enough discussed should return his copy of the document to Michael. One by one everybody capitulated; the pile of papers in front of Michael slowly grew. By this device P.H. made sure that the contents of the paper could not be leaked to anyone in the organisation, and that if they leaked to the press, only Michael could be responsible. Larry would never have had the foresight to think up a brilliant self-protective trick like that.

Michael's dispute with the NT was over money, not principle. I think Michael should directly publicise the contents of his paper. For his part, he feels disinclined to make trouble for the NT at such a difficult time. But (I point out) unless there is a public debate on the subject, P.H. will get his contract extended to ten years and then we shall be stuck with him until 1984.

11 June

To Paris with Clifford to look at the new erotic theatres (six or seven of them) which have lately been prospering there. They are all tiny, seating fifty or sixty people, and most are simply *exhibitions* of the kind formerly available in brothels – a nude girl masturbates and pushes a vibrator into her cunt; two girls lick each other's crotches and anuses; a man joins them and, after ten minutes of frenzied fellation, gets a limp erection which subsides before he can squeeze it into place – all this

accompanied by simulated orgasms and watched by spectators paying
100 or 150 francs (not excessive when compared with normal theatre
prices, which can run to 70 francs or more).

Only one show, at the Théâtre des 2 Boules, shows any imagination:
a split-level set, with a net extending from the upper storey out over the
audience, so that the cast fuck as in a hammock two or more feet above
one's head. The cast here have charm and attractiveness, and I'm
momentarily stirred when the blonde heroine spreads the bum of an
Indo-Chinese maid and licks her delicious and spotless anus. One of the
two men in the show achieves a respectable erection, but I notice that it
is triggered off only when his partner thrusts her finger into his anus.
Cliff and I agree that the great disadvantage of sex shows is the male
inability to achieve stiffness to order; one is distracted by worrying
about whether or not he will make it. Better to equip the men with
false phalluses and let artifice take its course.

The high point of the trip is a lunch at the Tour d'Argent which
costs an amazing 727 francs, not much less than £90 for three, a
stunning price when you consider that we drank two of the cheapest
wines on the list. Bizarre coincidence: on arrival we went to the
Coupole for lunch, where we were immediately greeted by my old
pals Phyllis and Eberhard Kronhausen, the sexologists, who told us
they had just completed a documentary film on – the sex shows of
Europe.

14 June

Drinks with Ralph Richardson, about whom I'm going to write a piece
for *The New Yorker*. He gravely offers me his favourite drink – a large
helping of gin, followed by a dash of Italian vermouth and a dash of
French vermouth, topped off with a huge slug of vodka. He then sits
down (in his stately Nash house overlooking Regent's Park) and says, 'I
don't know what we're going to talk about. After all, where did we
come from? Did you ever have visions of the place you came from
before you were born? I did, when I was three years old, and I used to
draw pictures of it. It looked like Mexico.' The man is a poet: who else
would start a conversation like that? His voice reminds me of onion-
skin, cf. the onion-skin image in *Peer Gynt*, R.R's great part, who peels
himself down to what he hopes will be the kernel of himself, only to

discover that the last onion-skin, when removed, leaves behind it nothing, or the transparent shells of prawns. I barely knew him before entering the room; when I left, after listening to an hour of his fantastic musings (and ingesting a steady flow of that murderous cocktail, which he replenished whenever the level fell more than an inch below the rim of the glass), I felt I had known him all my life.

22 June

During the boring last afternoon of the Lord's Test against the West Indies, Fred Trueman[1] says, apropos of the allegedly dangerous driving of Brian Close: 'After the match 'e will be 'ome in Taunton in one hour and a quarter flat, provided that a telegraph pole does not leap out into the road and savage 'im.'

I read *Steppenwolf* for the first time and find the following:

> His whole life was an example that love of one's neighbour is not possible without love of oneself, and that self-hate is really the same thing as sheer egoism, and in the long run breeds the same cruel isolation and despair.

(Remember that the Steppenwolf is a man of fifty who lives alone in rented lodgings.)

23 June

On 4 July an American spacecraft will land on Mars, with equipment delicate enough to establish whether or not there is visible life on the planet. Already the split among scientists is instructive. Conservatives believe no life will be found; radicals believe the opposite. The reason for this line-up is of course that the former tend to have religious hankerings, while the latter are agnostic-to-atheist. And if there is life on Mars, then – as an American physicist has said, life itself becomes not a miracle but a statistic.

---

1. Fred Trueman (1931–). Cricketer for Yorkshire and England.

26 June

Thought about novelists: how unfair it is that the greatest insights into other people's suffering should be given to the self-centred! (But perhaps the supreme egoists are precisely those people who can identify with *everybody*.) Second thought: that insulting, condescending Olympian passion for defining and judging others, which is the wellspring of all good prose, seldom makes its possessors agreeable people to live with.

1 July

Ominous warning: a painful sore throat. Can this presage another virus attack?

2 July

Yes, it can. Sputum gushing up, primrose yellow, even tinted with sepia. Temperature up to 101°. I go to Thurloe Square to take K.H. to see *Blithe Spirit* at the NT but am simply too ill to make it, and spend a cough-racked night at home. *Ça recommence.*

4 July

I re-enter Brompton Hospital under doctor's orders. The first night – in a ward full of ancient emphysema victims – is hell, because I have forgotten to bring sleeping pills (and thus lie hacking until dawn) and because the nocturnal sounds of my fellow-sufferers would probably have forbidden sleep in any case. I listen to the falsetto, gibberish moans that are the audible half of the dialogues in which old men take part while they sleep: the other speakers are heard only in their dreams.

5 July

Nobody not facing a possibly mortal operation and not undergoing great pain really minds being in hospital. In my ward middle-aged men play house and doctors (with real blood, of course), happily reverting to the nursery, with teenage Jamaican and Oriental girls standing in for their mothers. They enjoy the submission of it all, the abolition of responsibility. As before, I bow in admiration of these efficient, good-tempered girls, coming as most of them do from societies where looking after the old is still a primary obligation and one which they do not resent. Indeed, they seem to enjoy it.

The best cure for anyone who is tainted with Enoch Powell's racialist notions would be to spend a week in a National Health hospital. (The private wards at the Brompton, incidentally, are nowadays full of Arabs, and are referred to by the staff as 'the Kasbah'.)

6 July

In the bed next to mine is a septuagenarian – sombre, expressionless, taciturn – who every morning rises, dresses himself in a neat brown suit and trilby hat, packs his belongings, wishes us goodbye, and leaves the ward. Half an hour later he is brought trudging back between two nurses, who gently explain to him that he must wait until the consultant sees him. But when the consultant sees him, nothing is prescribed except a new course of pills; so next day the charade is repeated – except that this time he managed to get out into the Fulham Road before being apprehended. Why do they keep him?

7 July

Success at last. The old man made his daily dash for freedom; was caught; but at lunchtime bureaucracy caved in; and his doctor, sighing, gave him permission to go home. I felt like cheering.

A minor triumph for me: after days of mounting pressure (exerted by me from the coinbox phone in the corridor outside the ward) Martin Landau has sent over a cheque for £4,000 – which leaves him owing me only £4,000 more. This means that I can stave off at least the most menacing of the twenty-odd creditors who are threatening me with legal action. A breathing space – though the phrase has its irony, since it is precisely for lack of breathing space that I am in this goddamned hospital.

Last night in sleep I improvised a riddle: what did the Jamaican patron say to the famous eighteenth-century composer when commissioning

from him a series of choral works? Answer: He, Mr Telemann, tally me
cantatas.

22 July

Devastating disarray. No sooner had I managed to force Martin Landau
to repay the £25,000 he owed to Sciclounoff than Sciclounoff gambled
it *all* on buying gold – and the price of gold, the papers tell me today,
has lately slumped to its lowest for years and looks like going lower still.
I feel shell-shocked. All that strain and legal battling to get the money
back to Geneva; and Sciclounoff instantly throws it away.

25 July

After spending months debating titles for the *Calcutta!* sequel, we are
reduced to this selection for the final choice: *The Last Partouze, Queen
Kelly's Secret Circus, Xanadu, Second Skin, Blanket Bay, Soft Anvil* (from
Rochester's line about the cunt: 'On this soft anvil all mankind was
made'), *Congress, Flirt, Indigo Blue, The Blue Revue, Vertical Smile, Follow,
Follow, Looking Glass, Tightrope, The Gamut, Projections,* and *Carte
Blanche,* we finally settled on the last because it is nobody's first choice
and everyone's second. And Michael White likes it because, as he says,
'It's got my name in it.'

28 July

Reading Jean-Louis Barrault's memoirs, I came across this: 'Liberty . . .
is the faculty of choosing the constraints one will accept.'

4 August

To the National Theatre to see the first new play P. Hall has presented
there – Howard Brenton's *Weapons of Happiness.* An insulting evening
which moved me to boo for the first time in a decade. This offensive
piece purports to be an analysis of the possibility of revolution in
England. Its microcosm is a family-owned factory where the workers
are all mindless, illiterate, sex-crazed yobbos (the owner, though silly, is
charmingly silly) with the exception of Frank Finlay, who plays a Czech

exile, purged in the Stalinist era and now a despondent onlooker as the numbskull English workers attempt (unsuccessfully, of course) to take over the factory in which they work.

The whole history of the Left – the great movement which has made life tolerable and tenable for working people over the last two centuries – is reduced to a choice between despotic Stalinists and idiot children whose idea of revolution is to shit on the factory floor. The message, loudly and clearly proclaimed, is: how dare the working class complain about its lot, since the only alternative is tyranny? As if we hadn't heard again and again, ever since *Darkness at Noon*, that Stalinism was a bad thing. The mixture of arrogance and condescension was impossible to stomach: it almost made me long to be a critic again, since this rubbish has been praised by people as disparate as Billington of the *Guardian* and the berserk H. Hobson, now in the twilight of his loony reign on the *Sunday Times*.

16 August

To lunch at Tom Stoppard's with Kingsley Amis and Jane. Politics are thankfully eschewed. Later in the day I'm to be interviewed by Robert Cushman[1] about the opening night of *Look Back in Anger* twenty years ago, a subject so staled by repetition that I determine to do a little myth-making. With help from Tom and Kingsley I concoct a little mis-information that will, if Cushman swallows it, take its place in the files to confuse future historians. As with the premières of *Hernani*, and *Le Sacre du Printemps*, it's amazing how many prominent people were present at the Royal Court on that celebrated night. Amis, for instance, had dropped in, and observed to me in the first interval, apropos of Jimmy Porter, 'Chap plays trumpet. Can't be all bad.' While Binkie Beaumont, maudlin drunk, was heard moaning: 'We can roll up the map of Shaftesbury Avenue . . .' And who was the bewhiskered, purple-faced, choleric gent in a corner of the bar, banging a brandy glass and muttering to himself: 'The rough beast has come slouching home at last . . .' None other than Evelyn Waugh. These and similar snippets are duly fed by me to Cushman later in the day. It will be interesting to see how many of them appear in print.

1. Robert Cushman (1943–) Then drama critic for the *Observer*.

Later in same year: they all did. Thus are legends born.

24 August

If you are a writer the best way to cope with the father figure is to follow the example of P.G. Wodehouse (whom I've been reading greedily of late). In creating Jeeves, he internalised Father while at the same time keeping him firmly under control. Jeeves is Bertie's guide, philosopher and father-surrogate: but he is also Bertie's servant. The ideal solution. No wonder P.G.W. went on repeating it; and that we go on reading it.

Shocked to hear from K.H. that she is planning to send the children to Los Angeles a week before she arrives, accompanied only by Sheila (the cook). The reason: she needs another week in England to do research on her Agatha Christie film script. How could she conceive of sending two kids to a strange country, a strange house and a strange school with neither parent to look after them? (I have to stay here for the opening of *Carte Blanche* on 30 September.) I protest strongly, and she will no doubt change her mind. Which won't remove the stain left by the fact that she even considered the idea.

25 August

Casting about for a possible poster for *Carte Blanche*, I think of Pauline Boty's *Bum* which hangs in the dining-room framed in the proscenium arch of a Pollock's Toy Theatre. I remember Pauline's temperamental quickness and openness. (She was Clive's wife and died ten years ago of a rare form of cancer.) In the Mount Street flat I covered one wall of my study with wallpaper I had made up of a huge enlargement of a detail from a nude photo of La Goulue – the detail being the cleft of her bottom. Multiplied thousands of times, it was of course unrecognisable, and I used to challenge guests to guess what it was. 'A smoker's lung', 'part of the spiral nebulae', 'a snow crystal', were typical answers. Nobody got near it till one day I showed the wall to Pauline. 'That,' she said instantly, 'is a girl's bum' (which gave me the idea of commissioning the painting).

Back from a weekend in Cornwall with K.H. spent at a tiny peaceful place, the Danescombe Valley Hotel, on a bend of the river Tamar, in a valley spanned by an elegant Victorian viaduct. We visit the Woolly Monkey sanctuary on the coast near Looe, where a colony of these pretty South American apes – rapidly dying out in their own continent – is being reared by a dedicated preservationist named Leonard Williams (father of the guitarist John Williams). He and his devout young associates treat the seventeen monkeys as a separate but equal species: they have large acres of living space ('territory') indoors and out, and are free to swing in the trees if they wish. Williams has managed to breed a second generation of Woollies, something never before achieved in captivity.

He introduces himself to us and gives us sherry. Noting the sunken eyes, the steady rattling cough, the breathlessness that follows even the crossing of a small room, the hunched shoulders, the shoulder blades projecting like vestigial wings, I recognise a fellow sufferer from emphysema. Williams, at sixty-six, has had the disease for only two years: he is myself a few years hence. We exchange commiserations. He asks me whether I have trouble putting on weight, and speaks of a friend of his, dying of emphysema, who weighs barely six stone. This chills me. I thought my weight, steady at something like ten stone seven pounds, was a tribute to my diet (no sugar, no carbohydrates except in potatoes). I flattered myself that I was slender. I now see that I am simply wasting away. What I took as a source of pride has become a source of fear

30 August

A couple of nights ago the BBC re-ran Peter Watkins'[1] astounding film of *Culloden*. At a second viewing it seems even more stunning than when I first saw it – easily the most memorable account ever filmed of a battle and its aftermath. The parallels with Vietnam (e.g. the 'pacification programme' of savage repression undertaken by Cumberland's army after its victory) are uncannily prophetic when you remember that the film was made in 1963. Watkins went on to make *The War Game* and last year's *Edvard Munch*. That makes three masterpieces, more than

---

1. Peter Watkins (1937–). British filmmaker, won an Academy Award for *The War Game* (1967).

any other living English director can boast. I know his ventures into feature movies (*Privilege*, *Punishment Park*) have been over-ambitious and hysterical. But merely on his TV record, he is the finest film auteur we have.

Two days ago I went to Lord's for what (in my present state of health) I seriously feel may well be the last time. A one-day match between the invincibly brilliant West Indies team (Richards destroying our bowlers, Roberts destroying our batsmen) and England. Rain and wind at first: then grey cloud: and at last sun: a typically wayward British summer's day, quite untypical of this steaming summer. How I shall miss Lord's on days like this! The green pitch shaded with porridge-grey cloud; the stick figures in white loping and trotting and diving; the occasional fierce leather crack and the sputter of applause. The patience of the game! I love the way it brings together so many kinds of human knowledge – of the weather and its vagaries, of the behaviour of turf and the earth beneath it, of human temperaments under stress, of human reflexes and their preferences, of time and how to use its passing. All these things interact in the course of a three-day match – better still in a four-or-five-day game. No wonder so many English writers love it to the point of fanaticism: like Pinter, and Tom Stoppard (whom I saw playing – very well – for Pinter's XI against the *Guardian* in a West London park some weeks ago) and Terry Rattigan and Wodehouse and Amis – the list is endless. Not many socialists are on it, I notice with a qualm: their game tends to be soccer; and working-class cricket fans tend (like Fred Trueman, to take an example of many) on the whole to be Conservative. I hope this analysis is not as correct as I suspect it is.

12 September

'What is Zen pornography?' I am asked. Answer: 'The sound of one lip smacking.'

13 September

Rehearsals of *Carte Blanche* have moved into the Phoenix and have reached the critical phase. Everyone wants my 'Triangle' out but cannot insist, since I have taken care to write it into the contract that the number cannot be excluded. The strain is great: I shall be told that (a) it's a superb one-act play but doesn't belong in a 'revue', or (b) you'll be damaging a first-rate piece of work if you cut it to the extent necessary to fit into a 'revue'. But the truth will be that spanking and all that it implies are still unpresentable topics on the English stage: 'It will drive people out of the theatre,' says Richard Pilbrow in an honest and unguarded moment.

17 September

Iller than ever. Coughing all night and feeling like a grey ghost all day. Rehearsals of *Carte Blanche* exerting immense pressure: the first preview is next Monday, and my worries mount as nothing seems to be both right and ready.

Kathleen's lovers during past four years: Michael Blakemore, Christian Marquand, Bernardo Bertolucci, Warren Beatty, Gay Talese, Topolski, and others unadmitted. My record is slimmer: Nicole.

7 October

The show opened: predictable notices – 'boring', 'disgusting', etc. Not quite as bad as for *Calcutta!*, but in the same vein.

Business, however, is good. I am suing Michael White for breach of contract, since he removed from the show the longest item in it, my sketch, 'Triangle', which was intended to be the foundation stone of the second half. My contract stipulates that this sketch is an integral part of the show and cannot be cut without my consent: but the rich can break solemn contracts with impunity; and Michael knows quite well it will be two years before the case comes to court. Five days before the opening I appeared on the Parkinson TV show; returning home after a little BBC hospitality, I got into a row with Kathleen and deliberately let myself fall off a chair on to the stone kitchen floor, where I badly bruised my ribs so that breathing (and even more, laughing) has ever since been extremely painful. The infection continues to prosper, mucus varying from emerald green to primrose yellow. Kathleen left for California with the children on 4 October.

21 October

Back from trip to Oxford, where Tom Stoppard and I were Freddie Ayer's guests at High Table at New College. Food lamentable; drink varied and excellent (sherry; Moselle; Bonnes Marcs '62; Sauternes; Madeira; port; brandy). Either Tom has done some quick homework (not beyond the realm of possibility) or he is cleverer than I thought; he shows himself capable of arguing philosophy with Freddie on equal terms. I sit largely silent while they debate whether or not it is logically possible to hold, that (a) Wagner's music is better than it sounds or (b) there are *fewer* things in heaven and earth than are dreamed of in philosophy. I interject a tentative reference to Oriental philosophy, but Freddie pooh-poohs it, dismissing the whole of Taoism, Confucianism, Hinduism, Buddhism and Zen with a simple barking laugh. cf. Hegel, who rejected Hindu philosophy as no philosophy at all. 'It's of some psychological interest, but no more – mainly it's a device for reconciling people to a perfectly dreadful earthly life. I believe there were one or two ninth-century Indians who contributed a few ideas to mathematics – but that's about all.'

Over brandy a young postgraduate student tells me he is writing a thesis about sex and philosophy, intended to demonstrate that philosophy has castrated itself by refusing to consider sexual behaviour or the sexual impulse as part of its province (or, indeed, itself as part of the sexual province) and to point out certain passages in Aristotle which stress the role of physical contact in the formation of moral ideas. I mention this young man to Freddie afterwards. 'Nice fellow,' he says briskly, 'but obsessed with sex!' Thus might a medieval monk dismiss a Biblical scholar who took *The Song of Songs* literally.

22 October

I invite Willie Donaldson round for a drink. He says he'd love to come, but his son has just been expelled from Eton and the day of my invitation will be his first day home. (He's sixteen.) I urge Willie to bring him along, but he sounds doubtful, so I tell him not to worry: no orgy is planned, and no bad influences will be there to corrupt the young shaver. 'It isn't that,' Willie says, 'I'm more worried about him being a bad influence on you. You see, he's a sort of walking supermarket of illicit substances.' He's been expelled, it seems, in the hope that exposure to Willie's paternal example will be beneficial to his moral health. I am not clear whether the authorities at Eton are aware that Willie is a pimp.

In passing, Willie asks me whether I ever take my elder daughter out to parties. I say, 'Of course, and people are always mistaking us for brother and sister. It's very flattering.'

Jonathan Miller remarks of Peter Hall: 'It will be said of him that he rose without trace.'

I have achieved sexual fulfilment. People who have not done this sometimes pick up boys, tie them up in chains and drug them – and then write brilliant songs to seek my applause and affection. Or they find themselves unable to get erections and seek the love and admiration of people like me by means of TV productions or comedy routines. What bothers me is the question: Why should I take the trouble to write, except of course for money?

25 October

The pound drops a record 7 per cent because the Arabs and other foreign speculators are selling. One of the bitterest paradoxes of these unpleasant times is that when the trade union leaders succeed in influencing the actions of the government, the Tory press erupts in righteous outrage, complaining that a pressure group with no responsibility to the electorate is interfering with the democratic process; whereas when another irresponsible pressure group – the foreign speculators – force the government's hand, their activities are hailed as representing a victory for economic sanity and common sense.

Duke Magenta and the Rowdy Lizards: cryptic title for a pop group.

The Queen opens the National Theatre. Larry makes a typically florid speech on the stage of the theatre that bears his name, singling out a dozen politicians for praise and not one playwright, actor or director – except of course P. Hall. The choice of play is perverse to the point of madness – a minimal Goldoni called *Il Campiello*: devoid of wit or warmth or any kind of excitement. The company shouts, stamps and runs about betraying all the signs of panic. The whole evening was what Noël would have called 'sheer sauce'. The most significant performance was given by a drinking fountain that played throughout the action – quietly pissing on everything we expect of a National Theatre. During the second half, Larry, who was sitting beside the Queen, dropped off to sleep. HRH instantly noticed and directed a beady glare in his direction, fearful lest he should topple forwards into the acting area. The glare lasted for five minutes until Larry, galvanised by some particular noisy piece of business, returned to wakefulness. During the interval Ben Travers said to me, 'If they had to open the theatre with a thoroughly rotten play, why couldn't they choose a thoroughly rotten English play?' He summed up what was felt by most people present. What a disaster! But will the press record it as such?

THE HOLLYWOOD YEARS

On 30 October 1976, Tynan flew to Los Angeles, and, for all intents and purposes, left England for ever. 'Life in Santa Monica is very curious,' he wrote to Marlene Dietrich. 'Every morning a large golden orb appears in the sky. People remove their clothes and jump into pools of water. It's all very curious.' Tynan could be droll about LA, he just couldn't be happy there. 'Interesting symptom: a journal is the last refuge of whatever ego one has, and I have made no entries in mine for months,' he wrote within a year of his arrival in America. Tynan called himself a 'climatic émigré', but he was choked both by the air and by the intellectual entropy of the place. The Coast only exacerbated Tynan's general sense of drift and self-loathing. 'As my father's health declined, his sado-masochistic sexual escapades became more extreme,' Tracy Tynan said. 'Kathleen told me some of these details – details I did not particularly want to know and which frankly appalled me. I think she was so desperate and hurt, she felt she had to tell someone. Then my father would discover Kathleen had told me something, and he would reveal one of her infidelities. It was rather sad.'

Nevertheless the Tynans put up a plucky stylish front, living beyond their means in one over-priced rented house after another. Tynan still hoped to get funding for a film based on his screenplay about a ménage à trois, which he wanted to direct. In the manner of the town, he hustled, putting himself about with neither relish nor resolve. The New Yorker had thrown him a lifeline by paying him $44,000 for six profiles (and, more important, the magazine covered his medical expenses). Despite his increasing decrepitude, Tynan produced his classic study of Louise Brooks and fine appreciations of Johnny Carson, Mel Brooks, and Sir Ralph Richardson. He also accepted a commission to write his autobiography and began making notes. The work gave him both cash and cachet. But, to write, Tynan had to smoke; and, according to his doctor, by 1977, he had the highest level of carbon-dioxide in his blood ever recorded at the hospital, and the lowest oxygen.

Regardless, the Tynans had entered the Hollywood sweepstakes, and they were playing to win. (Kathleen sold her screenplay about Agatha Christie which was filmed as Agatha with Dustin Hoffman and Vanessa Redgrave.) In the aristocracy of success there are no strangers, and the Tynans had the distraction of the famous company they were in the habit of keeping: Tony Richardson, Joan Didion and John Gregory Dunne, Gore Vidal, Jack Nicholson, Christopher Isherwood, Orson

*Welles, among many. Tynan's high-amperage social whirl helped to bolster an ego
that had been made even more fragile by the increasing precariousness of his health.
('Bankruptcy, emphysema, paralysis of the will – and now this!' Tynan wrote, in
1977, after discovering that there was pus in his penis, which added to his list of
calamities. 'Feel that God is making his point with rather vulgar overstatement.')
Tynan was, according to his eldest daughter, '. . . invited to every celebrity bash. He
was both fascinated and repulsed by the gaudy displays of wealth. He was wickedly
cruel about these events, yet rarely turned down an invitation.' At one celebrity
scrum, Tynan chatted up the fourteen-year-old Tatum O'Neal, who had been an
Academy Award winner at the age of ten. Later, he recounted to Sir Laurence
Olivier the conversation between himself and 'Miss Tatum O'Neal (who cannot be
a day over 38)':*

K.T. (breaking the ice*): Good evening, Tatum.*
Tatum: *Mnnh.*
K.T.: *I suppose you know everyone in this room, don't you?*
Tatum: *Yrnnh.*
K.T.: *Is there anyone in the world that you don't know who you'd like to meet?*
Tatum: *Nah.* (Pause.)
K.T.: *Maybe Laurence Olivier?*
Tatum (ponders deeply for a moment. Long pause. Then she shakes her
head): *Nah.*

*The Tynans, who were habitually strapped for cash, could not entertain their
Hollywood friends with comparable lavishness; what they could offer – in
addition to the wit of their conversation – was dinner with British royalty.
Despite Tynan's outspoken views on the monarchy – he wanted it abolished – he
had frequently hosted Princess Margaret over the years. Tracy Tynan was present
at the last of these dinners, where the Tynans, skint as usual, had decided to try a
new black caterer who served soul food. 'As the hour for the party approached,
there was no sign of the caterer or the food,' Tracy said. 'My father threw up his
arms in despair and said he was going to the bedroom to "kill himself".' At the
last minute, the caterer rolled up; the party began. 'It was quite a sight to see
Hollywood royalty scrambling over each other's backs to get to the real royalty.
People were literally shoving each other aside to get the Princess's attention.' The
next day Tracy overheard Kathleen in Palace protocol talking to Princess
Margaret. 'Yes, Ma'am, I am so glad you enjoyed it, Ma'am. Thank you,
Ma'am. We'll see you at Sue Menger's tonight, Ma'am.'*

Tynan quickly fell into step with the Hollywood confidence trick; that is, every aspect of life was mobilised to give confidence. It was crucial for the Tynans to keep up the appearance of well-being and to keep their glamour burnished. They flew to a Swiss clinic to be injected with sheep hormones which promised 'to keep them young for ever'. They promoted the public illusion of vigour. 'I was constantly told not to tell anyone about my father's illness, as this could jeopardise his work situation,' Tracy said. Even in the last months of his life, Tynan was outraged to read about his condition in a clipping from the British tabloid press. The final, undated, entry of his 1980 journal reads:

Returned to LA from PV [Puerto Vallarta]. I find sickening Hickey column in Daily Express for 8 Jan. It says I am dangerously ill, living entirely on oxygen, suffering from a terminal disease; also that one shred of one lung is all that remains to me. It adds that I have taken brief (and by implication, final) holiday with wife and children and that mother-in-law is flying to my bedside. (She is in fact coming to spend a few days en route to visiting friends in Canada.) These grotesque exaggerations and lies are couched in terms of praise for my pluck in fighting back. The damage to me, professionally, is incalculable: what publisher or editor would commission a work from a dying man? And – worst of all – suppose Matthew and Roxana had happened to read the piece? I shall have to take legal action. How I despise English journalism! Even if the story was true, no American newspaper would publish it, for the simple reason that it would cause needless suffering.

The sightings of Tynan in hospital during his LA stay are infrequent and unhappy. After one 1978 intubation, Tracy had to be called to the hospital to calm her hysterical father, who kept trying to rip the tubes out of his throat. On that occasion, unable to speak, Tynan scrawled a series of notes. 'From what I could decipher,' Tracy said, 'he claimed that the doctors and nurses were trying to torture him.' The notes, which he scribbled then tore off the pad, and pushed immediately into his daughter's hands for fear they would be intercepted by the hospital staff, said things like 'Call the British Embassy and get help!' 'Save the notes. This is proof of what they are doing to me.' 'If it were not for the wild, desperate look in his eyes, I might have laughed,' Tracy said. Tynan's paranoia was a side-effect of the level of carbon-dioxide in his blood; when that stabilised, so did his mood.

But not his rebellious spirit. He continued to sneak cigarettes in his hospital bed, despite the fact that the tubes in his nose were connected to enough oxygen to blow him and some part of the hospital wing to smithereens. 'What's the difference?' he said sheepishly. 'I'm going to die anyway.' He instructed Tracy to look into the Hemlock Society. He didn't want to live, but he was angry about dying. At one low point, the hospital sent a psychiatric social worker to talk to him about preparing for death. Tynan sat through the meeting in a stony silence. 'He took great pleasure in watching the man become increasingly nervous and fidgety,' Tracy said. ' "I showed him!" said my father proudly. "How dare he presume to talk to me about dying. What can some young punk tell me about dying?" '

A few days before he was discharged from the hospital for the last time, Kathleen reports in her biography hard words between them. Throughout his long dying, Kathleen had been by Tynan's side; her generosity was not always repaid in kind. 'He was so unbearable to her often, in and out of the hospital, that she would be reduced to tears,' Roxana Tynan said. On this day, Kathleen records Tynan saying to her, 'If you don't come down to the bottom with me, I don't want to go anywhere with you.' She added: 'I recall very clearly his look of rage and fear, and even more sharply my own swift, evasive response, my awful absence of feeling.' The following day she recounted this exchange: 'He said after a time, "I have no lifeline." I said, "You have me." "But I don't feel it," he answered.'

The last time Tracy saw her father was at a small luncheon Kathleen gave after he'd been sent back to die in the verdant calm of their rented home on Westgate in Brentwood. Tynan was pale; he'd shrunk to a hundred and seventeen pounds. To his daughter, he looked more like seventy-three than his actual age, fifty-three. 'When I arrived there was some music playing,' she said. 'I asked him what it was, he said it was the slow movement from the Mozart Clarinet Quintet. He was planning music for his funeral. He said there was so much to choose from it was hard to make a selection.' At one point, the doctor dropped in. She joked with him about his wine intake; he complained about feeling lethargic and tried to panhandle some speed. Kathleen had to leave early on an errand, and Tynan went into a monologue about feeling like a character out of a bad Tennessee Williams play. 'I'm the doddering old man that everybody is waiting to snuff it,' he said. 'That's my glamorous wife, going off, gallivanting God knows where.' 'It was all very light and gay and sad,' Tracy Tynan said.

4 November

After four days in California am still disorientated. K. has rented a huge movie-star-type house for us in Santa Monica. The sun pours down at a daily 90. What have I done – more ominously, what am I going to *have* to do to deserve all this?

A joke for which I must find a funnier context. Asking whether Martin Landau had yet paid me the promised £1,000 still outstanding (he hasn't) K. says: 'I wish he'd put his money where his mouth is.' I reply, 'In that case it would be up George Weidenfeld's arse.'

7 November

In California I live in an oasis surrounded by used cars, and go to hilltop parties where middle-aged women talk about masturbation. I think: what is this man doing in this set-up and who is going to pay the rent?

10 November

In New York (icy blasts freezing my lungs) to see Ralph Richardson, whom I shall write about for *The New Yorker*. To the first night of *No Man's Land* I take Ellen Holly, a beautiful black actress I've known for years, who is perhaps my closest girlfriend in New York. (We've never fucked, not for wanting of trying on my part; she lives alone with her great Lena-esque beauty and talent, and suffers, I fear, from severe sexual hangups.) Several years ago she wrote a brilliant, poetic film script about a black concert pianist (female) who goes to Haiti and discovers her racial origins by falling in love (symbolically) with Henri Christophe, the black dictator and visionary who ruled the island in the early nineteenth century. I tried without success to persuade Joe Losey to make the film. For the past eight years she has been starring in an afternoon soap-opera, and I'm amazed to find, at the Pinter première, that the target of the autograph hunters is not Betty Bacall or any of the other big names who are present, but my lovely Ellen. They *queue up* for her signature; and as we walk the four blocks to Sardi's, people constantly stop her in the street, ask her to smile, tell her how they've grown up with her. Ellen explains, with amused bitterness, that she's a major celebrity to 25,000,000 Americans, but not to the media since critics never watch soap-operas.

Bianca Jagger, who has never done anything, is a media star; Ellen, after eight years of TV exposure, five days a week, is not. Hers is one of the so-called 'adult soaps' – i.e. abortion and pre-marital sex can be mentioned in it – and she argues persuasively that soaps of this kind are as close, in their development of character and exploration of social groups over long periods of time, as America has ever come to epic. (Ellen has other causes for bitterness. Her skin is pale enough to pass for white with a little make-up; and she has frequently been offered parts in shows on condition that she pancakes her face and tactfully refrains from mentioning to the sponsors that she is black. Being a brave and militant girl, she has never yielded to such temptations. Yet – mysteriously to me – she is a passionate supporter of Jimmy Carter, on the grounds that white Southerners 'understand' blacks more deeply than Northern liberals.)

11 November

Lunch with Ralph Richardson; drinks with John G., garnering material about Ralph. Then I rashly join the crazy Howard Effron,[1] who promised to back my film two years ago and suddenly went broke. Curiosity prompts me to accept his manic invitation to come to an orgy. I meet him in the bar at the Regency with a nice but unlovely girl in her late thirties, whom Howard E. describes as 'one of the foremost packagers of cosmetics in New York State'. She leaves us to do some late work, and Howard takes me down to the Village, explaining as we go how traumatic it was for him to lose all his money (if I remember rightly, he was indicted for embezzlement). I interpolate that it was pretty traumatic for me, too, since he had signed a contract to finance my movie, and didn't bother to inform me that the deal was off. 'Oh, I didn't talk to *anyone*,' he yells (he always yells), 'for over a year. For Christ's sake, where are we going? I'm a guy from out-of-town but I

1. Howard Effron (1928–). Broadway theatre producer.

damn well know where 4th Street is!' (This is bellowed at the driver.) He tells me that his mother is still very rich: 'She can't even spend the *interest* on her investments. She's seventy-nine years old and her husband is in his sixties. I gave her a ticket for a round-the-world cruise and would you believe it, she cashed it in and kept the money! When I complained, she said she didn't dare to renew her passport because then her husband would know how old she was.'

We finally arrive at East 4th Street and an elevator the size of a barn takes us up to an attic full of tropical plants, middle-aged men and oddly assorted girls. 'Just wait,' says Howard, his eyes popping. 'This will develop into *some orgy*! Do you have any spare money on you? The banks were closed today.' I have no money to spare and invent a dinner date with the editor of *The New Yorker* to extract me from what promises to be a spectacularly unappealing scene! 'Quite understand,' says Howard. 'Business comes first.' He has frog eyes and may be forty.

13 November

Drive 260 miles to Las Vegas in resplendent new car, a Buick Riviera on lease. We stay with Shirley MacLaine and Pete Hamill.[1] Shirl is performing at Caesar's Palace. I haven't been to Las V. for about eighteen years and am knocked out by the leaping, loutish, shameless, shattering, gargantuan folly of the city as it now is. Grand Hotel, the huge MGM hostelry, with its 2,000 rooms, the largest on earth, is like an outsize realisation of the hotels Bunchmans used to caricature; its gigantic silver-glittering awning is deliberately designed to dwarf the three or four hundred people who can shelter under it. We dine before Shirley's show in the new French restaurant at Caesar's Palace – beginning with some superb beef marrow in pastry with a truffle sauce, followed by a pair of plump quails *en casserole*. Wines equally good; although all the food is flown in, the chefs are from Maxim's and the results show it.

During dinner we are entertained by the finest card manipulator in the world, Jimmy Grippo, a squat little man aged eighty-five with horn-rimmed glasses, a thick black wig and barely a line on his face. He has played Buckingham Palace eight times, but never seeks publicity: he

1. Pete Hamill (1935–). Journalist and author, editor of the *New York Daily News*, 1996–7.

is content that people who can command the best know that he is the best. His tricks combine fantastic fingertip delicacy and a unique visual memory with a brilliant and disturbing use of hypnosis and ESP. This is his true originality. For instance, in one of his best numbers, he hands a sealed pack of cards to a male member of our party, bidding him open it, pick a card and return it to the pack (which he has not touched). He then asks Kathleen to concentrate, to close her eyes, to focus her mind on his shirt front, to think of it as a mirror and to imagine what card it might be reflecting in his inside pocket. She thinks for a moment and says, slowly but not hesitantly: 'The three of hearts.' He then reaches into his pocket and produces that very card. This is the most inexplicable piece of manual magic I have ever seen, and it makes everything that follows seem doubly mysterious.

K. tells me afterwards that as soon as she closed her eyes, a vivid picture of the three of hearts appeared before them. Grippo has grandiose dreams of curing the world's neuroses through hypnotism, and of creating a super-scientist by amalgamating the mental capacities of the top ten living scientists in all disciplines. He reminds me of the medium in Gian-Carlo Menotti's opera, who in the midst of her vast repertoire of duplicity is capable of genuine extra-sensory perception. It is possible to be fraudulent and authentic at the same time. (Footnote: in the lobby of the Grand Hotel, chained to a rostrum, sits the MGM lion, with whom, for a small fee, you can be photographed.)

23 November

In London I wear a dinner jacket roughly once a year. Here, in casual, informal California, I have worn a black tie three times in the past week. (The première of *The Last Tycoon*; Sunday's wedding of Marisa Berenson[1] to an extremely unappetising young man named Randall – all in a circus tent festooned with fringes, with the service performed by a highly non-denominational clergyman who sounded like a Greek Orthodox Zen Buddhist; and, last night, dinner at Swifty Lazar's[2], which I tried to cancel during the afternoon, only to be told that I *had* to come, since it would ruin Mary's seating arrangement if I didn't. I went. It was a scene of great

1. Marisa Berenson (1947–). American model and actress.
2. Irving 'Swifty' Lazar (1907–93). Hollywood agent of note.

provincial splendour, with a pianist playing ('Swifty ordered a tenor sax player as well,' Mary told me, 'but I threw him out') and *le tout Hollywood* present – Jack Nicholson, Anjelica Huston, Warren Beatty, Ray Stark[1], Sue Mengers[2], Dinah Shore[3], Merle Oberon[4], Danny Melnick[5], Liza Minnelli, Valerie Perrine[6], Peter Bogdanovich[7] (nice) plus a couple of transients – Lew Grade and Cole Lesley, whose biography of Noël Coward has been a great source of comfort and delight in the past few weeks. The plump Miss Mengers sits seething on a sofa. 'That goddamn Swifty!' she says between gritted teeth. 'I'm giving a party tomorrow night and he's asked the *exact same people*. He swore to me he wouldn't ask Warren and guess who just walked in the fucking *door*! I could spit. Well, fuck him, I'll show the bastard, I'll get *Streisand* tomorrow, so help me.' She is perfectly serious. Later she sidles up to me and hisses: 'And *Johnny Carson too*, goddamnit!' It is all very strange.

24 November

Half as good as her word, Mengers strikes back with Streisand (though she arrives too late for the stuffed squab – resembling a scrotum filled with wild rice – which passed for dinner). The supporting cast includes: Warren Beatty, Swifty Lazar, Peter Bogdanovich (still nice), Ray Stark, Ryan O'Neal, Tatum O'Neal, Steven Spielberg (who directed *Jaws*), James Coburn, Dudley Moore, Tuesday Weld, Angie Dickinson, Tina Sinatra and introducing Ken Tynan, who smoked too much.

Dudley, pleasantly jet-lagged from the Polar flight, was a welcome relief in a room criss-crossed by mutually hostile emanations from so many warlike egos. Sue, a nervous hostess to the point of paranoia, buzzed from table to table, anxiously asking whether we were enjoying ourselves. Her hilltop house is like a spacious and virulently modern art gallery without any art in it.

1. Ray Stark (1909–). Hollywood producer.
2. Sue Mengers (1938–). Hollywood agent.
3. Dinah Shore (1917–1994). Popular singer of forties and fifties.
4. Merle Oberon (1911–79). Australian-born beauty and Hollywood movie star.
5. Danny Melnick (1906–79). Hollywood producer.
6. Valerie Perrine (1944–). Actress.
7. Peter Bogdanovich (1939–). Film director and writer, his *The Last Picture Show* (1971) won the Oscar for Best Picture.

Another sleepless night of coughing. I see myself as a threatened species, Mucus Melancolicus doomed to extinction not because of ecological imbalance but because of sheer unpopularity. There used to be others of me; now there is only one, snarling, wanking and retching.

25 November

Thanksgiving dinner *chez* Billy and Audrey Wilder, guests include Louis Malle[1], George Burns, Mary Benny, the Boy Moffatt[2] (Ivan, so called because Evelyn Waugh refers to him in a diary entry describing his visit to Hollywood in the forties), and of course Sue Mengers. Sue is sourpussed again for unexplained reasons; just as inexplicably, I start to grope her during dinner. Sliding my hand down the back of her backless dress to squeeze her enormous bum. Have no idea why I did this; she responds with happy moans and intimate work with her knees. Her daunting size would of course be a deterrent if it came to the crunch; but on the other hand there would be a lot of sheer buttock to whip.

George Burns talks to her about the price of fur coats and is shocked to hear that a good sable coat can cost $40,000. 'For that kind of money I'd expect a coat that would serve me hot soup and a cold martini.' Questioned by me, he insists that the legendary vaudeville act, Swain's Rats and Cats, of which I've heard from many sources (including Groucho) but in which I've never quite believed, actually existed: 'The rats were dressed as jockeys, and rode around a little race track on the cats' backs.' (I *still* don't believe it.)

I remind him of a story Jack Benny once told me about how he watched a French Marquis kissing Mary's hand and, when Jack asked why the man was paying such an elaborate compliment, replied: 'He's finding out whether he'll have to bite her fingers off to get at the rings.' Burns denies the attribution, on the grounds that the remark is too crude: 'If I'd said that, I'd have said he was wetting her fingers to get off the rings.'

---

1. Louis Malle (1932–95) French film director.
2. Ivan Moffatt (1918–). British-educated Hollywood screenwriter, wrote *Giant* (1956).

28 November

Going through some old sixties notebooks I find this remark, made over luncheon by Dinah Brook's schizoid father, a hearty, tweedy, rubicund little man. 'I'm told that the Navy knows how to deal with moose.' (Does he mean 'mousse'? The context revealed nothing.) 'No less a person than Rear Admiral Lambert told me that. But while I'm convinced of the Royal Navy's ability to deal with moose, I'm not altogether persuaded that they can cope with hippopotamus.'

Also this exchange with Cyril Connolly: apropos of E. Dundy:

C.C.: Was Elaine a trial?
KT: No, more of a jury.

Also: in Britain employers quite often fraternise with workers. Contempt breeds familiarity.

Also: McLuhan on Twiggy, proving himself the windiest hand of the sixties: 'She is a programme in which people can become involved. She is not escapism. She is involvement.'

Also: Larry and John G. used to be compared to burgundy and claret. With the passage of time, they have become Milk Stout and PLJ.

Also: George Jessel[1] talking about a big-breasted starlet: 'She has a nipple like Eartha Kitt's head.'

Beardsley: 'Genius it was; that immediate access to some world outside our own, that perfectly clear conviction, which creates its own skill, that a thing must be thus and thus and not otherwise.' (Less persuasive as a definition when one reflects that it could easily be applied to Mabel Lucie Attwell[2].)

13 December

Man, please thy Maker and be merry,
And give not for this world a cherry.
(Dunbar) – quoted in an essay on C.S. Lewis by J.A.W. Bennett.

---

1. George Jessel (1898–1981). Actor, MC; dubbed 'Toastmaster General'.
2. Mabel Lucie Attwell (1879–1964). British artist and children's book illustrator.

Back from a weekend in San Francisco. Drove there by the coast route, stopping to see San Simeon, an important pilgrimage for me, since *Citizen Kane* was the crucial artistic experience of my life and San Simeon was in many ways its inspiration. The place is awe inspiring, not just because of the mountainous setting (one might be in a sun-baked part of the Scottish Highlands) but because the incredible eclectic jumble of styles and tastes – the façade of the Casa Grande, for instance, which contains bits of Far Eastern temples, medieval monasteries and Ronda Cathedral – does hang together, does achieve an unvulgar unity, thanks to the extraordinary talent of Julia Morgan, the architect who planned it all with Hearst. The swimming-pools – the indoor even more than the outdoor – have a genuine antique splendour.

In a sense San Simeon is a humble creation. When Louis XIV builds a monument to himself at Versailles, everything about it must be of his time, reflecting his era and its aesthetic. Whereas Hearst collects from all periods and places and builds a monument not so much to himself as to the history of civilisation. I buy from the gift shop an ashtray in the shape of a foot, with the following inscription: 'I get a kick out of the Hearst Castle at San Simeon', which I propose to send to Orson. Driving north I wonder why nobody has written a musical about the place. Possible titles: *The Folks who Live on the Hill*, *Simeon's Rainbow* or simply: *His and Hearst*.

In San Francisco, one superb French meal at L'Etoile, and a sad lunch with Bob Kaufman, my old friend, the former Beat poet who, hooked alternatively on alcohol and amphetamines, fell into a virtually complete silence that lasted from J.F.K.'s assassination to the end of the Vietnam War. His wife Eileen had assured me that he was now recovered and off dope and drink. That he is off stimulants I can believe; but he looks like a man struck by lightning – not an inept image, because Eileen tells me that he had massive doses of ECT in a state mental institution. These have turned him into a zombie. He speaks little, and then only as if we were living a decade ago. 'How are the Beatles coming along?' he asked me. Moreover, he's extremely deaf. I cannot possibly write about this shattered man. He used to be a demonic lord of mischief and misrule: now, meek and muted in his best suit, he looked like a punch-drunk boxer at a wedding.

A review of *Carte Blanche* by Sandy Wilson, so venomous that K.

refuses to let me read it – after that the phone rings and the cheery voice of a child – who starts by announcing that she attends a local school whose seasonal project is to make similar calls to everyone in the Santa Monica neighbourhood – wishes me a very merry Christmas.

21 December

Dinner at Christopher Isherwood's with Gore Vidal and Tony Richardson. Asked by me to name the twentieth-century figures whose letters and/or journals he would be most excited to read, Christopher says E.M. Forster (many of whose letters he received); and later adds, to my delight, that if there were anything unpublished by Cocteau, that would come a close second. Blue-jeaned, closely grey-cropped and dapper, Christopher admits that his literary generation avoided the French: Germany was where the boys were; and he always regrets never having met Cocteau. I notice that Gore, such a show-off in other company, is restrained and un-bossy when Christopher, whom he much admires, is around. I congratulate Christopher, whose new book I've seen reviewed but have not yet read (although it's on order at the Brentwood Bookshop), on contributing to the literature of testimony – i.e. eye-witness accounts of significant events – which I suspect will prove to be the most lasting of our time. He surprises and pleases me by saying that he agreed with my view of this kind of literature when I first expressed it more than a decade ago.

I further please him by recounting (and liking) the film script he wrote for MGM on the life of the Buddha some twenty years ago: I read it for Ealing Films and recommended it for production, although I was well aware that a historical epic which was entirely without bloodshed and did not endorse the tenets of Christianity stood very little chance of being made.

(Over dinner Gore confides that Noël Coward invited him to bed in Italy. When he entered the bedroom Graham Payn was already naked between the sheets. Noël bustled in and stripped; Gore buggered Graham, and Noël masturbated with his prick against Gore's bottom. Having rapidly come, he rose and dressed within seconds and went off to work, leaving Gore and Graham to share the post-animal *tristesse*.)

28 December

Went to an 'enema clinic' advertising spankable girls. The sweetheart
assigned to me turned out to be a huge black girl built like a Watusi
warrior with an Afro hairdo like a geodesic dome. She was under the
impression that I wanted to *wrestle* with her, and opened the conversation by menacingly informing me that she cycled twenty miles to work
every day and twenty miles back home. I swallowed hard and went
through the motions of putting her over my knee, but it was about as
enticing as spanking King Kong. (Her buttocks were like black marble.)
Apart from anything else, I have never derived any pleasure from
spanking black girls: it conflicts with my belief in civil liberties. Now
there's a situation for a Feiffer sketch . . .

1977

1 January

Two New Year's Eve parties – to Billy Wilder's beach house for a fairly frugal buffet (no champagne), and guests including Deborah and Peter Viertel,[1] Jack Lemmon and William Wyler,[2] who is deaf. Then on to Peter Bogdanovich, where the cast is larger, younger and in general duller, though enlivened by Gore and Isherwood, whose phone numbers Peter B. had extracted from me earlier in the day. I think of a title for a biographical film about a failed agent: *The Days of Wine and Grosses*. Also: why doesn't someone make a sequel to the current successful *Bad News Bears*, which features a children's baseball team, about a football team of miniature *apes* – twenty mini-Kongs in one movie.

5 January

> The world is so full of a number of things,
> I am sure we should all be as happy as kings,
> Though, when you consider the Greeks and the Dutch,
> Not to mention the Spanish, that's not saying much.

Read a magazine quiz, compiled by experts on geriatric subjects, which purports to predict your life expectancy on the basis of your answers to questions about habits and general way of life. I answer with scrupulous accuracy and discover that I shall be dead in May.

16 January

Useful line to describe ham actor expressing grief: 'He turned away, risibly moved.'

---

1. Peter Viertel (1920–). German-born novelist and screenwriter.
2. William Wyler (1902–81). Film director, Academy Awards for *Mrs Minniver* (1942), *The Best Years of Our Lives* (1946), *Ben Hur* (1959).

Just back from two days in Santa Barbara with Tom Stoppard. The university there is holding a sort of Stoppard festival, producing about nine of his shorter plays, organising student expeditions to LA where *Travesties* and *The Real Inspector Hound* are playing. Tom also gives a lecture (which, as he rightly says, 'consists of a series of free associations with an infinite regression of parentheses'). It is rapturously applauded by a packed auditorium.

The head of the English department, introducing Tom, calls him 'the most Shakespearian playwright in the English language since Webster' – a confusing assessment, but all in all I think it could be said that there is quite a Stoppard cult in Santa Barbara.

19 January

Dinner with Donald Cammell[1] and Andy Braunsberg. We discuss whether we should contemplate a biographical movie about Sue Mengers. My first title suggestion: *Pigs Can Fly*. My second: *Swine Flu*.

Go to Paramount where a producer named Jerry Bick says he can promise me a quite fantastic deal if I can come up with an idea for 'a Thing picture' – which means, I gather, a horror movie in which men either turn into or are menaced by Things. (Such as ants, lice, lichen, Venus' fly-traps, etc.) Bick says he has unearthed a forgotten novel by Bram Stoker with a title that is money in the bank. If I can find a plot to fit that title, he declares, we shall both be able to retire. It is *The White Worm*. Can't I see it (he asks) – a gigantic white worm causing panic and devastation in downtown Los Angeles?

Visit a journalist who lives on a hilltop in Bel-Air. Across the valley he points to a vast hotel of a house, owned by a millionaire who made his fortune out of Barbie dolls and atomic missiles. He has seventy-five telephone extensions, none of which rings like a normal phone. He is a keen ornithologist, and each telephone is tuned to emit the call of a different American bird.

---

1. Donald Cammell (1934–96). British film director; co-directed *Performance* (1970) with Nicolas Roeg.

20 January

To see *Network*, the Paddy Chayevsky[1] film that is supposed to be the final destructive analysis of TV as the medium that dehumanises us all and sensationalises the world in which we live. How ironic – and how bitterly appropriate – that Peter Finch[2] (who plays the newscaster-turned-guru who twice collapses during the film and is finally murdered on camera because his ratings are slipping) – how ironic that he should have collapsed and died of a heart attack in the Beverly Hills Hotel a few days ago – so soon after appearing in a film that purports to attack those who exhaust and exploit human beings for sensational purposes.

Some good scenes (a network boss explaining that the world is no longer made up of nations but of corporations; a well-observed dialogue between a middle-aged Ed Murrow type and the wife he is leaving for a younger woman), but the usual gaping flaws you always find in major-studio movies that pretend to indict 'the system', i.e. the newscaster who goes 'mad' does *not* offer a rational and/or socialist analysis of the American way of life; instead, he talks of energy fields and spiritual rebirth like any evangelist on LA radio stations. (Socialism is represented by a black power group who are interested only in money and who, in the end, consent to assassinate Finch to please the network managers.)

The biggest cop-out of all, however, is that when Finch's ratings fall, it is not the sponsors or the bosses who order his death: on the contrary, the latter give explicit orders that his show must continue. It is the *hirelings*, the managerial class, who plan and authorise the killing. Conclusion: it's a mad, brutal, cynical world, but the bosses oppose what the blacks commit – deliberate murder. The film is an attack on the rats in the rat-race, but not on the owners of the racetrack; and it reserves much of its spleen for those who would like to take the racetrack away from those to whom it currently belongs.

---

1. Paddy Chayevsky (1923–81). American dramatist best known for the screenplays *Marty* (1953), *Network* (1976), for which he won an Oscar.
2. Peter Finch (1916–77). Australian-born actor; subject of a biography by Elaine Dundy.

28 January

Gore gives birthday party for Howard, Paul Newman and Kathleen. Present: George Cukor, William Wyler, Billy Wilder, Peter Bogdanovich, Ryan O'Neal, Bianca Jagger, Swifty Lazar, Sue Mengers, Tony Richardson, Johnny Carson, Christopher Isherwood, George Segal, various heads of studios, and paltry self. B. Jagger and I idly discuss possibility of sexual threesome with K.H. to whom Mrs. J. confesses herself much attracted. I get slightly drunk but thank God there is no grass to produce the deadly effect of a few nights ago when, departing from a party at Tony Richardson's, I drove the Buick into a bunker on a miniature golf course, and then reversed it straight into a parked sports car.

30 January

Reading *Zen and the Art of Motorcycle Maintenance*, I wonder whether the author, Robert Pirsig, could be a pseudonym for my old friend Harold (Doc) Humes, who disappeared about ten or twelve years ago. So many of Pirsig's ideas – so many of his philosophical flights – bring back the sound of Doc's voice, the confident rationalist talking about things beyond the reach of reason. After the J.F.K. assassination he began to have morbid fantasies of being assassinated himself, and brought his wife and children to live in London. He was already an established novelist (*The Underground City* was his best-known book), spoken of in the same breath as Mailer, James Jones, Philip Roth, etc. He was fascinated by physics, and one day brought me a handwritten book full of diagrams, purporting to demonstrate what he called *The Vortical Theory of the Creation of Matter*. (Odd, said a scientist to whom I showed the document, how often the vortex appears in the work of people who are going off their rockers.) Doc claimed to have seen CIA men with guns in restaurants that we frequented; and although this seemed clear evidence of paranoia *then*, I doubt whether it would seem so now that we know a little more about the way the CIA works. Doc also used to insist that the CIA were involved in the opium traffic in Vietnam – which we now know to have been the case.

One night he came to my flat in Mount Street at about 3 a.m. His voice was a whisper and I assumed he had laryngitis. He shook his head:

didn't I know that my flat had probably been bugged by the CIA? He went on to explain his latest discovery – that Universal Aunts, the organisation from which he (like many others) obtained his cleaning lady, was a CIA front, used to gain access to the homes of people under surveillance. (Again: it sounded mad then, but now has a distinct ring of plausibility.) I said: 'Doc, do you realise you're talking like a paranoid schizophrenic?' 'Of course I do,' he said, smiling broadly. 'I am a paranoid schizophrenic, and I go to an analyst regularly. But what good is he doing me?' He picked up the phone and called his analyst, who can't have been best pleased to be awakened at about 4 a.m. 'God-dammit,' Doc was soon shouting into the mouthpiece. 'I'm a classic case of paranoid schizophrenia and what the hell are you going to do about it?'

Shortly afterwards, his wife left him and took the children back to the States; I tried to help by introducing Doc to Ronnie Laing, whose brilliant work on schizophrenia was just beginning to be published, and for a while Doc lived at one of the 'open houses' run by Laing for disturbed psycho-social misfits. Later I heard that he had been seen in Indian clothes, wearing a long beard, a sort of imported Yankee *guru*. Then silence. He had an extraordinary mind, and a real gift for lucid exposition; one evening, on the paper tablecloth of a restaurant in Greenwich Village, he explained to me the theory of atomic fission in five minutes flat. I miss him and wonder what became of all that vagabond, unharnessed, intellectual energy.

6 March

Music for my memorial service: slow movement from Mozart Clarinet Quintet. Adagio from Vivaldi's Second Sonata for Trumpet and Organ, The Beatles' 'A Day in the Life'.

Am still immobilised by flu germ which struck me down a week ago in Madrid, ruining a research visit there with Nicole most of which was spent in a hotel bed, while Spanish doctors used me as a target for the *banderillas* they call hypodermics. Am now a month behind with my *New Yorker* work; debts pile up in LA and income is nil. On the last day in Madrid I crawled out of bed, rented a car and took Nicole off on a jaunt to La Granja (first visit: exquisite, and deserted in the snow of the

Guadarrama) and Segovia, which I last saw with Elaine twenty-five years ago (had forgotten – if I ever knew – how beautiful it was: the hilltop town, crowned by the cathedral, with the Alcazar at one end and the aqueduct striding across the valley at the other). Of course the hire car starts to stall every time we stop, and the return to Madrid in the rush hour ('*la hora del rush*' as modern Spain calls it) is a nightmare of accidents missed by inches, culminating in my attempting a U-turn, stalling halfway through, and remaining thus becalmed while four lanes of high-speed traffic bear down upon us. All this and coughing, too. I eventually flew back via London, resorting to a wheelchair at Heathrow and again at Los Angeles. Great times, great times.

30 March

Back in LA. I read that Nunnally Johnson[1] has died at seventy-nine. I last saw him just before I left for Europe: he too had emphysema, though it's some consolation that he survived to such a splendid age. Nunnally was a laconic deep Southerner: his most famous one-liner was his comment on Jeeter Lester's family in *Tobacco Road*: 'Back where I come from, we'd have called them the Country Club set.'

Reading *The Hidden Years* (story of Howard Hughes' last decade, spent in darkened rooms and almost complete nudity, seldom getting out of bed, eating virtually nothing, while his nails became six-inch claws and his hair straggled down below his shoulders), I think of myself in the darkened hotel room in Madrid and of the insidious temptations of the semi-invalid life. Perhaps I am the Bankrupt's Howard Hughes.

Into Hughes' life, I decide, the whole history of autocracy of individual rule – is compressed. He starts out inheriting a fortune, his patrimony being the Hughes Tool Company: he is the son of the Old King. He then proves himself by performing deeds of heroism; and we have Hughes the airman, breaking world records and risking his life. He then enters into a period of wielding absolute power over a large empire, flourishing like a Caesar or a French Bourbon. Then he gradually withdraws into an egomaniacal trance, cutting off all contact with reality, losing touch with the world; one thinks of the Spanish kings after their empire collapsed. Finally, to save him from himself (and his empire for themselves), a group

---

1. Nunnally Johnson (1897–1977). American producer, director and screenwriter.

of hard-headed businessmen take over effective power – as the bourgeoisie took over after the French revolution – and run the organisation
while Hughes himself dwindles to an impotent cipher. At his death, they –
the so-called 'Mormon Mafia' – rule in his stead.

Madame Flanner[1]: 'Some en-Janetted evening.'

1 April

K.H. thinks I should dispense wisdom on a TV show to beguile my
declining years. What Oral Roberts is to religion, Anal Tynan could be
to philosophy.

2 April

> He sat down on a sunlit heath
> And took the gun between his teeth,
> He pressed the trigger; felt the shock.
> Wet brains splashed on the Inchcape Rock.

'I have acceded to the hierarchy of good scribes, and rather like my
niche.' (Max)

Two wrongs don't make a right; but two rights often make a wrong.
(e.g. Mark Antony – ruined by two right impulses: his love for
Cleopatra, and his desire to rule the Empire well.)

14 April

Still feeble, unable to restart work on Stoppard profile, due for delivery
end of February. Finished Christopher I.'s *Christopher and His Kind*.
What a buggers' banquet Eng. Lit. was between the wars – Christopher, Wystan, Stephen, John Lehmann,[2] Ackerley,[3] Morgan Forster,

---

1. Janet Flanner (1892–1978). Journalist and novelist; as 'Genet' contributed 'Letter from Paris' to *The
   New Yorker* from the magazine's inception in 1925 to her death.
2. John Lehmann (1907–87). Poet, editor, founding editor of *London Magazine*.
3. J.R. Ackerley (1896–1967). Literary editor of the *Listener*, 1935–59, and author of such well-
   regarded books as *My Dog Tulip* (1956) and *My Father and Myself* (1968).

Strachey, etc. all busily swapping tales about each other when they weren't actually swapping boyfriends. (As bad as the heteros, very nearly, in the clannishness.) The book is excellent, full of Christopher's strict candour – and the classlessness that he shares with almost no other British writer of his generation. (I've seen him in cabmen's pull-ups and grand mansions, with no change in manner or accent.)

Am reminded of one of the more *outré* parties I threw in Mount Street in the fifties (which were my twenties). Christopher was one of the guests, and Dizzy Gillespie[1] was another; they had never met, but got along famously, talking about oriental religions. I was especially impressed when Dizzy, who was playing with Cagney, a ginger cat I had at the time, suddenly seized one of the animal's front legs and plunged it into his mouth, right up to the shoulder. He then slowly extracted it. We all craned forward, expecting blood from claw-scratches to come pouring from his mouth. Amazingly, there was none. 'That's how much animals trust me!' said Diz, smiling broadly. That, in fact is how much *everyone* trusts him. I remember Christopher's astonishment that anyone could render himself so vulnerable to a strange creature, and escape unscathed.

18 April

> An enjoyment that is shared is enfeebled. This is a recognised truth; if you try to give enjoyment to the object of your pleasures, you will soon have to recognise that you are doing so at your own expense. There is no passion more egoistic than lechery; there is none that must be served more severely; one must absolutely think only of oneself. (De Sade.)

This is absolutely true if the partner is a masochist. Her pleasure comes precisely from the knowledge that her partner is not concerned with arousing it. She is completely at his disposal and *therefore* not *responsible*. No true masochist would ever *ask* to be whipped: it would be a presumptuous usurpation of her master's prerogative, and would destroy the pleasure (which is in part a thrilling dread of the unknown)

---

1. Dizzy Gillespie (1917–93). Trumpet maestro, one of the most influential players in the history of jazz.

of being a wholly passive object. A masochist will enjoy being made to *repeat* the words: 'Please spank me.' She will never *volunteer* them.

19 April

In 1789 the Marquis de Sade was released from the Bastille and sent to a mad house at Charenton, from which he was liberated in the following year. He was fifty years old. He started an affair with an actress aged thirty named Marie-Constance Quesnet. She remained loyal to him until his death, twenty-four years later. 'It was the only successful relationship,' Edmund Wilson notes, 'in Sade's life.' She even went to live with him in Charenton when he was locked up again, there to spend his last ten years, half-blind and increasingly ill. At fifty, who will join me in Charenton?

22 April

Afterthought on de Sade's view of sexual enjoyment: a pleasure shared is a pleasure halved.

A season of Jean-Luc Godard films is about to open in Los Angeles. It would be a graceful gesture if they made the first night a charity show for victims of emphysema. (The season opens with *Breathless*.)

A friend on the *Evening Standard* writes congratulating me on my Noël Coward piece in *The New Yorker*. He tells me an anecdote to demonstrate that Noël's wit really was impromptu. He was talking to Noël on the phone when he heard the death of General de Gaulle announced on the radio. He passed the news on to Noël, and said: 'I wonder what he and God are talking about in heaven.' 'That,' Noël replied, 'depends on how good God's French is.'

Forgot to record that on 19 April Kathleen gave a large dinner party (over thirty guests) in honour of George Weidenfeld. The thing was planned and the invitations were sent out before I was even consulted. Because of this, and because we are nearly broke, and because if I want to honour someone it would not be a gossip entrepreneur, I refused to attend, despite strident and reiterated entreaties from K.H. (Instead I went to the première of an indescribably boring and bogus play by Robert Wilson.) To my annoyance, it seems that my gesture went unnoticed – K.H. said I had to write about the play; everyone believed her and apparently had a splendid time. What is particularly vexing is that during the evening I announced via the Citizens Band radio in my car that Jack Nicholson (one of the guests) was giving away autographed photographs at 765 Kingman Avenue – and nobody believed me.

A few facts about California to temper my initial rapture: it has a higher suicide rate than any other state. One Californian in three is employed in the manufacture of weapons. (The GNP of California places it fifth among the *countries* of the world: it produces 46 per cent of America's missiles and space systems, 44 per cent of military building supplies, 33 per cent of military research and development; 27 per cent of petroleum products for the Department of Defence; etc. etc. (Statistics from Kenneth Lamott's book, *Anti-California*.)

29 April

With K.H. and Tony Richardson to see a sad and inexplicably praised film, *The Late Show* (one of those movies based on other movies that are going to form the staple diet of world culture in the future as the towering mass of available film footage increases). At supper – a repulsive fish restaurant chosen by K.H. – Tony asks me about *Carte Blanche* – will I bring it to the States? I explain that I am suing Michael White for removing 'Triangle', which was a clear breach of contract, etc. etc. Here K.H. breaks in (and I recognise the signs from a thousand previous rows: wife determined to show guest that she is independently intelligent and capable of uninhibited disagreement with husband) to argue that, after all, compiling an erotic review is very difficult, and who can say whether my choice of material would have been preferable to Michael's. I say: that isn't the point: he signed a contract that specifically included 'Triangle' in the show, and *he broke the contract*. She reiterates that my taste might not necessarily have been better than his. I reply that what I wanted to see was *my* show, on which I worked for two years, and not his; and in any case his show demonstrably hasn't worked. A depressing evening: so often before, she has compulsively attacked me in public on issues on which she has professed to support me in private. (And this for many reasons, including the subject-matter of 'Triangle', is quite an important issue.)

25 April

My delightful doctor, Elsie Giorgi, has prescribed an anti-depressant pill which will, she says, lift me out of my despondency and fill me with energy. I take it, and am instantly poleaxed with a leaden lethargy that forces me to spend the whole day in bed. Am caught in web of real despair.

30 April

Bizarre dinner chez Sue Mengers, who greets us with monologue about the horrors of water conservation (there has been a drought in California and legislation against waste is being enacted): 'What's going to become of us rich Jews and our swimming-pools? And what about the toilet? I'm so fucking clean that every time I *pass* the toilet I flush it, just on principle.' Other guests: Ryan O'Neal (whom at last I appreciate and find very funny), Sammy Davis and his ravishing wife, Barry Diller (head of Paramount), somebody von Furstenberg (an expensive seamstress who irritates me by taking flash pictures all evening), and Truman Capote, with whom I haven't spoken since our famous altercation twelve years ago. I am slightly apprehensive, but need not have worried; as he arrives he whispers to Sue that the two people who hate him most in the world are here – the other being Sammy, whom (I learn) he described on the Carson show as an untalented nobody.

Conversation at dinner is spotty, to put it mildly: Ryan and I use each other as springboards and are quite funny, but Truman talks only to Sue and nobody else talks much to anybody. Sammy laughs nicely at Ryan and me. Meanwhile the seamstress flashes away. Sammy and wife leave (escape) early. Sue declares jovially to Ryan and me: 'Boy, did I make a ballsup!' A colourless young model whom Truman brought with him is captivated by Ryan and stays, presumably to go home with him.

We drive Truman back to the Beverly Wilshire, where he insists on inviting us in for a drink. Either he is on a mind-paralysing drug or he has fallen prey to some form of sleeping sickness. The vivacity of old has gone completely: 'Is this,' K. wonders later, 'the court jester of the Beautiful People?' His voice is a sluggish whine, and his gestures now move at a pace that would make a slow loris look like a bush baby. For an hour he treats us to a repetitive and barely audible aria of narcissism: it seems that he has been having an affair with a banker, but has lately transferred his affections to the banker's daughter, who is the model Ryan has snared. 'You mean you actually *fuck* her?' I ask with Dexamyl-induced candour. 'Yes,' he snarls torpidly (and incredibly). Our quarrel, it seems, is made up.

9 May

I learn on the 11 p.m. news that Jim Jones[1] is dead. So another friend is gone from the group of Americans who made Paris in the fifties so much fun to visit: gruff, gentle Jim, with the big chin and bashful smile, shorter than he would have chosen to be, and perhaps less belligerent, too: uxorious towards his busty and beloved Gloria as few husbands I have known have been towards their wives: always keeping open house in his apartment opposite the Tour d'Argent (where I once heard him benignly say to a snobbish young girl who asked him: 'What are you doing this summer, my dear fellow?' – 'I'm having my asshole sewed up to see if I can shit through my armpits'). There was the hot summer in the fifties when I went alone to Paris, met the Jones' closest girlfriend, Addie Herder, started fucking her the same night, and spent the next six weeks with them as a quartet – partly in the emptiness of off-season Paris (which I have ever since adored) and partly in Berlin, where I introduced Addie, Gloria and Jim to the Berliner Ensemble. Then there was that later summer when Elaine and I (our last summer abroad, I think it was) went on a quick gastronomic spin through France with Gore (who peeled off at Lyon) and then went to Pamplona with the Joneses. Jim, a worshipper of Hemingway, had never been to Spain, and I remember how he would self-mockingly strike Hemingway attitudes in the Café Choko, hoping that people would challenge him to a fight. (Nobody did.)

It was during that trip that Elaine confessed she had had an affair with Kingsley Amis: I caned her, one stroke for each letter of his name, and made her confess to the Joneses that she had been whipped. (They were

---

1. James Jones (1921–77). American author of among others *From Here to Eternity*.

intrigued but unshocked.) Kathleen, I recall, was waiting in the South of France on the strength of a half-promise that I would leave Elaine and join her; at the last moment I backed down, postponing the amputation.

Not the greatest of writers; but a great friend and companion, full of classless curiosity. I miss him already.

14 May

To New Orleans with K. The Vieux Carré much more beautiful and formal than I'd expected – precisely square, the streets forming a rectangular grid – and everywhere the complex wrought-iron balconies (seen so often in pictures) leaning over the sidewalks. Dinner at Antoine's – Oysters Rockefeller (the bi-valves buried under a spicy carapace of sorrel and other unidentified greens) followed by *Poulet Rochambeau* (which is like two mad chefs let loose on one dish – ham in *bordelaise* sauce and chicken *béarnaise* – either of which might separately have been good, but both of which together are intolerably pungent). We spend the night at a (historically listed) house in the Garden District – white pillars and verandah, and (that supreme test of hospitality) absent hosts. They also give us the use of a vast stationwagon. A drink after dinner with Louis Malle, who is making a film called *Pretty Baby*, about a child prostitute in New Orleans in 1917.

15 May

We board the *Daphne*, a cruise ship carrying the first boatload of American tourists to Cuba since 1961. (Anti-Castro Cubans picket the pier where the boat leaves.) The sleek Greek ship carries about 400 passengers, featuring jazz music as its theme – exemplified by Earl Hines[1], Dizzy Gillespie, Stan Getz[2] and David Amram[3]. I wonder whether the anti-Fidelites will seek to blow up the boat in Havana (were I of their persuasion, I would certainly do so) in order to ruin the prospects of tourism between Cuba and the US. Nearly a third of the passengers are in the communication business, all three TV networks, plus numerous radio stations, magazines and newspapers are repre-

1. Earl Hines (1903–1983). Pianist and bandleader.
2. Stan Getz (1927–91). Jazz saxophonist.
3. David Amram (1930–). Composer and French horn player.

sented. (K. is covering the cruise for American *Vogue* and the London *Sunday Times*.) One observes reporters interviewing one another. I invent a personality for myself – Emilio Fracaso, the Riot Correspondent of a leading Mexican newspaper. 'I began by covering – what is your word? – hubbubs, where just a few grenades kill a few students, but from the hubbub I graduate to the – how do you say? – hullabaloo – the *autentico* riot. But I am not sure whether this will have authentic riot.' Fracaso is seen lurking around vulnerable parts of the ship bearing inflammable objects so that he can clear the front pages of Mexico and scoop the world. 'This is Fracaso – give me the riot desk.'

Earl Hines (aged seventy-one or seventy-two) gives a fabulous concert on the first night – with a fixed grin, a peach-coloured suit and a jet-black wig. His fingers are as steely as ever.

16 May

Second concert: Dizzy, his cheeks distended like an inflated owl, plays Israeli, Moslem, Baha'i and half a dozen other sorts of ethnic music – his technique as pyrotechnical as I remember it twenty years ago, his muted work as moving. We greet each other with emotion. 'Hey,' he asks. 'Did I bring Noble Sissle[1] to that party of yours in London? And is Noble Sissle dead?' At a press conference he pays a tribute to me (quite unsolicited) that touches me a lot – about how wittily I wrote, etc. the kind of thing that means all the more because it comes from a man of another discipline, who has nothing to gain from my friendship. At the press conference, someone asks Diz his age. He hedges and mumbles. I interrupt: 'He's *almost* old enough to be Fatha Hines' son.' (Big laugh.) I wish, however, that he could bring himself to include in (or restore to) his repertoire some of the American-Jewish songs – by Kern, Berlin, Gershwin, Rodgers, etc. that were the staples of the jazz repertoire before jazz discovered its roots.

17 May

Havana. Not at all what the Western tourist expects underprivileged tropical islands to be – none of the usual amenities: no prostitution, no

---

1. Noble Sissle (1889–1975). Bandleader, lyricist, singer; with pianist Eubie Blake wrote the first African-American Broadway musical *Shuffle Along* (1921).

begging, no gambling, no illiteracy, no malnutrition, no picturesque squalor. (One tourist had brought a trunk full of old clothes, persuaded that the Cubans were threadbare and barefoot; he had to be politely informed by the customs people that his charity was not needed.) None of the expected personality cult: in two days I did not see one picture of Fidel. Where, in 1959, there were mud huts, one now sees high-rise housing estates, schools and clinics, garishly painted in primary colours. Of course there are plenty of fifties cars in a state of dilapidation but there are plenty more spick-and-span new Fiats and other small cars.

I go to the Hemingway house and see on its shelves copies of two of my books, one of which I brought to him, abjectly inscribed, in 1959. The Floridita is unchanged (I drink several '*papadobles*' – double daiquiris without sugar) except for the clientele: no beautiful people, no *señoritas*. The man next to me at the bar is an assistant electrician from a local theatre: in 1958, he said to me, 'I would not have been allowed in here. Some American would have shouted: "Get out of my way!"' And this man was not uncritical of Fidel: he expressed his disagreements quite openly, with none of the nervous sidelong glances you associate with a police state.

Dizzy is a big success with the crowd on the quay as we embark: he bustles across the road and is cheered and embraced. But though we are all welcomed with friendship and *politesse*, we are not hailed as liberators, which I think was what some of the tourists expected. We are received (and this is the big change) *as equals*, not as superiors. Diz, Hines and Stan Getz take part in a four-hour concert at the Teatro Mella: together with David Amram, Diz rustles up a dozen Cuban jazz musicians, who join the Americans on stage in a cacophonous impromptu collaboration.

K. and I nip off for half an hour during the concert to see the multi-level open-air floor show at the Tropicana, where there are stages and lifts and treetop catwalks on three sides of the audience. It is like an insane memorial tribute to Carmen Miranda; no bare tits or bottoms, and a smaller cast (perhaps fifty instead of eighty) than I remember last time; otherwise, the same.

In Vedado some of the once-grand houses look a bit shabby (their owners are in the States, Spain or South America): the big change is in the poor districts, where all is new and vivid. With all the authority of a two-day visit behind one, I can't see much wrong with Cuba that a lifting of the US blockade wouldn't cure. (There are, according to reliable estimates, about 2,000 political prisoners, tried for plotting to overthrow the regime. Ninety miles from a country militantly dedicated to the overthrow of Cuban ideology, the Castro government cannot be accused of overreacting. And there have been no suggestions of torture.) I disembark at 2 a.m. on Thursday. K.H. stays behind to research her pieces, in (slim) hopes of meeting Fidel.[1]

21 May

Back in LA I buy two magazines devoted to colour pictures of female anuses and assiduously wank.

22 May

Footnote on Cuba: rent is restricted to 10 per cent of one's earnings, and there is no income tax.

Cammell on *Jack the Ripper* was finished, so I'll be getting around $3,000 soon from Columbia to match the $3,000 I received on signing the contract. But I still can't finish the Stoppard profile for *The New Yorker*, which is now three months overdue. Unless I can knock off three *New Yorker* pieces in the next three months, my European plan is jeopardised. Ironically, it is now Kathleen who wants to stay in California, because of her newly burgeoning career as a screenwriter. This conflicts with the children's educational needs: both Roxana and Matthew (especially the former) are far better suited to English schools and are longing to go back home. So (a) since for tax reasons I can't return to England till April, 1978, my preference in (and after) August is for Spain, (b) the children, from all points of view, would be better off in London, and (c) K. is determined to stay in Los Angeles. God knows what will happen, or to whom.

29 May

Peaceful Sunday afternoon. Get up from nude sunbathing on lawn to discover viscous yellow fluid oozing from tip of prick. This, considering

---

1. She did.

I have had no sexual contact with anyone or anything (except my own right hand) since I was in London, is really too much. Bankruptcy, emphysema, paralysis of the will – and now this! Feel that God is making his point with rather vulgar overstatement.

New monthly magazine (with newspaper format) has just been published here. With bashless simplicity, it is called: *NATIONAL BOTTOM*, and deals exclusively with events in and around the anus. Decide to take out life subscription, which should cost me, if my present condition persists, roughly $4.50.

30 May

A blood test some weeks ago at UCLA revealed that I have a genetic enzyme deficiency (quite rare: about .001 per cent of the population has it) which renders my lungs specifically vulnerable to tobacco. If I smoke, they degenerate far more swiftly than other people's, and death is immensely hastened. Now I can do almost anything without smoking, except write. Thus if I write as I have always written – cigarette in hand or mouth, it is likely that I shall die relatively soon. On the other hand, if I do not write, I shall be broke (at present I have $300 in the bank, an overdraft in excess of £5,000 in London, and am living on what remains of the cash available from remittances from Geneva). Not an easy choice. So I opt for writing self-pitying, self-exonerating journal entries like this. (The fact that I *know* they are self-exonerating does not, of course, exonerate me.)

1 June

Paul Desmond died yesterday; fifty-two, of lung cancer. The best continue to go first. I think the *LA Times* is right when it says he was the most original alto sax player since Charlie Parker;[1] his exquisite tone, threading its way through the difficult time-signature he delighted in, was always instantly recognisable, even on a transistor a hundred yards away on a beach. I knew him very well and saw him very seldom; jazz musicians travel too much to form close relationships except with other

1. Charlie Parker (1920–55). Legendary alto saxophonist and one of the great jazz improvisers.

jazz musicians. He carried himself with the same lanky elegance with which he played; he had real distinction of mind, gentleness, chivalry and the kind of wit that does not cancel out the ability to admire. Prematurely bald, melancholy eyes, imagine an ideal Jules Feiffer, with the neuroses ironed out and a handsomer face, and you have some idea of his looks. How can you miss someone you so rarely saw? But I shall. (I remember once, long ago, when we had scarcely met, he called to invite me to dinner at the French Shack in New York. Alone, with no purpose other than to tell me that he admired my writing.) According to the newspaper, he has requested that there be no services; simply that his ashes should be scattered from a plane over Big Sur. His composition, *Take Five*, now joins Viviani, the Beatles and Mozart in the programme for my own memorial service. Peace to you, Paul. Give my love to Alan and Dommie, and tell them from me what Cohan told the gang on 42nd Street.[1]

More about Paul: he was a genuine loner. There had been, I believe, an early divorce, after which he lived completely on his own – from choice, without loneliness. There would be the odd girl, sometimes picked up at one of the night spots which are the only places for jazzmen to go after concerts in strange cities; but mostly he was on his own, with his music and his books.

I am so glad that both Kathleen and Nicole knew him.

You can accept the world; fight to change it; or withdraw from it. Like so many good but non-combative men before him, Paul quietly withdrew. The paper says he died 'in bed'. I hope he wasn't alone, but fear that he probably was. If so, who found him? And had he taken pills to hasten his passage? (No matter: I don't really want to know.)

5 June

From *Journey of the Wolf* by Douglas Day: '*Hay que tomar la muerte como si fuera aspirina*'.[2]

---

1. 'Give my regards to Broadway/Remember me to Herald Square/Tell all the guys on Forty-Second Street/That I will soon be there. Whisper of how I'm yearning/To mingle with the old-time throng/Give my regards to old Broadway/And say that I'll be there, e'er long.'
2. 'You have to take death as if it were an aspirin.'

7 June

Rita Moreno[1] on the Merv Griffin show – bristling with energy at forty-five – my mind and prick go back to 1964, when she was the last woman to make me cry. (Much as we adored each other, there was too much spanking for her to take, and too many career chances in America.) Rita, whose anus I licked in Bristol, London and Newcastle (where we flew to see Larry's pre-London tour of *Othello*); whose firm, tawny bottom I joyfully smacked; who sucked me off by daylight in a train as it passed through Royal Oak station, a minute away from arrival at Paddington. Has she *gained* energy since then? Or is it merely that I have *lost* it? Because now I would shrink from the thought of bedding that ravenous, tireless-looking vixen, whom once I truly loved. She says on the show that constant fucking has kept her young. I believe it.

9 June

Bill Tennant of Columbia tells me over lunch that he wants me to continue with the script of *The Ripper* but that he proposes to ditch Donald C. as director, replacing him with either John Schlesinger or Nick Roeg. He then reveals totally haywire plan for solving problem of falling attendances at movies. He has been reading recent articles by Marshall McLuhan, the discredited sixties sage, on the interaction between the right hemisphere of the brain (which controls emotions) and the left hemisphere (which handles conceptual thought). (I may have got this wrong.) He has been so impressed that tomorrow he is paying McLuhan $2,000 to give the top brass at Columbia a seminar on how to select scripts and stars that will make both hemispheres react favourably. They will feed McLuhan with questions like 'How about Streisand and O.J. Simpson in a film about the French revolution?' And he will tell them what the hemispheric rating is going to be. I remark that it all sounds as if the situation at Columbia is like the last days of the Romanovs; suffering from haemophilia of the box-office (the bleeding away of audiences), they send for McLuhan as their Rasputin. (Next thing you know, all the executive vice-presidents will be shuffled off to

---

1. Rita Moreno (1931–). Actress and dancer; *The Guinness Book of Records* cites her as the only female performer to win an Academy, Grammy, Tony and Emmy Award.

a disused garage in Burbank. A volley of machine-gun fire will ring out . . .)

18 June

There's many a false word spoken in jest.

> When Lewis Carroll was a lad,
> He said to Edward Lear:
> 'First thing you do, you whip it out,
> And then you put it *here*.'
> So saying, Carroll shoved his prick
> Up Alice Liddell's[1] nose.
> 'The trouble is,' said Edward Lear,
> 'I've not got one of those.'
> 'I saw you blow it yesterday!'
> The irate Carroll cried.
> 'You didn't see me blow my *prick*,'
> Lear said, and, weeping, died.

I took the Buick to a carwash yesterday. There was a steady flow of cars entering it, and I noticed that almost all of them were perfectly clean. The institution of the carwash in California really has very little to do with the washing of cars. It's more of a ritual – a ceremony of self-purification. It is not your car but *you*, its owner, who feels cleaner and better as it emerges gleaming from the assembly line, to be polished by the *Chicano* staff. For an extra dollar (which I always spend) you can send the car through a device that subjects it to a boiling spray of Carnuba wax. This represents the annealing fire through which the soul must pass if it is to be purified. I always climb back into my cleansed car feeling, as I am sure Catholics must feel after Confession, a better man.

Another thing that the Californian carwash has to do with is simply passing the time.

---

1. Alice Liddell (1852–1934). The young Alice for whom Lewis Carroll wrote *Alice's Adventures in Wonderland*.

19 June

To a concert given by the pupils of Roxana's piano teacher at his Santa Monica home. Roxana erect, composed and breathtakingly pretty as ever, though the two Mozart pieces she played could have done with a little more practice. Moment of pure soap opera when the second performer, an eleven-year-old boy, attempts a trill in the opening bars and misses it. 'Damn!' he shouts. Tries again, misses again: 'Damn!' Failing for the third time, he rises in tears and shouts: 'I hate myself!' His father attempts to coax, then to drag him back to the piano, but of course he refuses. Later in the recital his mother plays a Bach Prelude and Fugue: a hard-faced lady in her late thirties whose blonde hair may be natural (but who would certainly dye it if it weren't). She stares at the harpsichord while playing with a murderous intensity, her eyes blazing.

Odd how diametrically contrasted Roxana and Matthew have turned out to be:

Roxana	*Matthew*
determined	vague
strides	drifts
imperious	submissive
jokerbutt	
assured	tentative

Yet both are gentle, open-minded, uncontaminated, and surpassingly beautiful.

20 June

The San Andreas Fault is a subterranean rift that traverses the state of California. Earthquakes happen when there is friction between the two sides of the rift. It is as if the earth were grinding its teeth. The San Andreas Fault runs through my mind.

Must remember on bad days (and this is one of the worst) that I am a performer who needs an audience, not a writer who likes writing for its own sake. K. said this today and it is true; in the *Observer* days Terry used to say: 'I say – you've performed rather well this week.' In LA I am cut off from audience reaction: hence – partially – my writing block.

Phone call from Cotton Caldwell in Mississippi.

K.T.: What are you doing in Mississippi?
Cotton: Tryin' to earn a livin . . . Tell me, when you were in Cuba, did your wife get an interview with the Bushy One? (i.e. Castro).

3 July

Lunch with Larry at the Bel-Air: he's here filming *The Betsy* and then going to Brazil to make another picture. His energy continues to daunt me. He tells me he learned his speech to the Queen at the opening of the Olivier Theatre by heart against the advice of Joan, who begged him to read it from notes and not run the risk of drying. 'But,' he says, 'I knew that smarmy bastard (i.e. P. Hall) wouldn't be using notes, and I was damned if I was going to let him outdo me. So I went to the theatre three times, the week before the opening, at eight in the morning and rehearsed the speech to the cleaners until I had it word perfect.'

On instructions from Andy Braunsberg I tell him about the script on Jack the Ripper and offer him $500,000 to play Sir William Gull. He says he likes the idea but the money is not what he's accustomed to. I say I think this could be adjusted (which Andy later confirms on the phone. 'Offer him *anything*!' he says, rather frantically). Yet Larry complains of financial straits, bewails the cost of educating his children, sees poverty on the doorstep. What nonsense.

4 July

Independence Day party at Pamela and Portland Mason's,[1] the house where I stayed on my first trip to Hollywood in 1954. It was built in the twenties by Buster Keaton, who called with his new wife while I was there and deferentially asked if he could show her over the place. I was shattered to see my idol so down-at-heel: his career was then in total

---

1. Pamela Mason (1916–96). Wife of the actor James Mason, mother of Portland.

eclipse, so much so that he was appearing in a sleazy saloon in Las Vegas doing a mime act three times nightly. Pamela is as noisy as ever: Portland has grown up svelte and bright and lovely; and the other guests include – an unlikely couple – Mort Sahl[1] and Nixon's legal adviser, John Dean, lately out of the slammer.

I finish at long last my profile of Tom Stoppard, four months later than I promised it. Length: over 28,000 words. On the same day I learn that Tom has just written 6,000 words about himself and his connection with the Czech dissidents for the *New York Review*, which will appear in two weeks, thus neatly pulling the carpet out from under my six months' ordeal.

14 July

Go to location in Pasadena watching Mel Brooks' last day of shooting *High Anxiety*, his new movie. A parody of a Hitchcock sequence involves 100 trained pigeons which pursue Mel across a park while men on motorised cranes squirt simulated bird-shit (actually mayonnaise) on him from a height of about 50 feet. As Mel does take after take, emerging from each one splattered with mayonnaise, Barry Levinson[2], one of the film's co-authors, says to me: 'We have enough equipment in this place right now to put a man on the moon and it's all being used to cover a Jew in bird-shit.' Mel's energy – in a smog-laden 85 degrees – is Napoleonic. He uses an instant playback videotape machine so that he can see each take without waiting for rushes: such an obviously good idea that one wonders why more directors don't adopt it. 'I stare at life through fields of mayonnaise,' he says later. He shows me his version of the shower-murder scene in *Psycho*,' in which he plays the Janet Leigh part. Camera shows his feet; bathrobe falling to floor; daintily stepping over it, he enters the shower, his back visible to just above buttock-level. 'I want people to see this and say: "He may be a small Jew, but I love him. He may be just a little Hebrew man, but I would go to the ends of the earth for him. I want every gay in LA to see this and say: "Will you look at that *back*?"'

1. Mort Sahl (1929–). Innovative, iconoclastic comedian who brought politics and social observation to American comedy in the early fifties.
2. Barry Levinson (1932–). Film director and screenwriter.

Evening: party at Lazar's to signal departure of Freddie de Cordova[1] and wife, who are going away for about ten days. (Any excuse will serve for a Lazar party.) Many guests arrive high on cocaine and many others get drunk; some are both coked and sodden. I meet and like Elizabeth Ashley[2] (coked) whose mother, if I understood her correctly, was a circus aerialist, while her father pushed dope. Noticing that she clenches her thumbs inside her fists as she talks, I tell her to take them out: 'If I do,' she says, 'I'll only suck them.' She is nutty, frenetic but very nice. Johnny Carson is there, without Joanna, about whose whereabouts he seems unclear. He is cool always. I decide that Carson is the visible tip of an iceberg named J. Carson. Tony Curtis, Tony Randall, Richard Brooks and the Gregory Pecks among guests.

Greg, rather drunk, is very defensive since he has just starred in an idolatrous film about General MacArthur and, as a one-time liberal turned conservative, is hyper-sensitive to accusations of being a reactionary. He plunges into unprovoked explanation of how MacArthur brought democracy and agrarian reform to Japan. I suggest that he is protesting too much. He complains that people treat him as if he had played Richard Nixon. 'That's different,' I say. 'Nixon only conspired to pervert the course of justice. MacArthur conspired to pervert the course of history.' 'I see I've fallen into a hot-bed of liberals,' says Greg.

He goes on to tell me the astonishing story of MacArthur's son and only child, who was encouraged by his parents (from infancy) to dress up in his mother's clothes. At dinner parties, when aged seven or eight, he would be told to put on Mom's things to entertain the guests. 'What a cute little fella!' they would cry. The result is that he became a full-time transverstite and now lives in Greenwich Village, a middle-aged drag queen. The bizarre thing is that MacArthur seems not to have objected, and would visit him in his apartment, imperially sipping a drink while a throng of transvestites cavorted around him. The tableau reminds one of a typical brunch with Tiberius at Capri.

Was MacArthur (a) too innocent to know about transvestism and homosexuality or (b) too tolerant and sophisticated to care? Fascinating question for some other film to answer: needless to say, Greg's movie avoids the whole subject.

---

1. Freddie de Cordova (1910–). Long-time producer of Johnny Carson's *The Tonight Show*.
2. Elizabeth Ashley (1939–) American actress and the author of a sensational memoir.

18 July

Mr Shawn calls to say he thinks my 28,000-word Stoppard profile is 'thrilling – absolutely marvellous'. I am overwhelmed.

21 July

A cheque for $22,000 – three times the amount specified in the contract for a single profile – arrives from *The New Yorker*. I am stunned. For a day I am surely the best-paid journalist in the world.

24 July

I have been reading *Iberia*, James Michener's book on Spain, with mounting respect. I thought I knew Spain but he shows me a face of it that I've ignored. Extremadura and Galicia, the tough, cast-hardened, indomitable Spanish core. Hardly a word about Andalucía, the easy and obvious Spain to which, via the bulls, I have enslaved myself. But to skirt the point: today Ivan Moffatt took us to lunch with a rich couple who own a ranch near the Mexican border. He tells a story about a Mexican he knew who referred to Christ as 'Jesse Christ', like Jesse James. Back in LA I return to Michener and the first section of his book, which deals with Santiago de Compostela, the burial place of St James, to which thousands of pilgrims have journeyed every year since the Moors left Spain. Michener reserves his highest praise and richest prose for the Portico de la Gloria in the cathedral of Santiago which (he says) is the greatest masterpiece of Romanesque art. (Sculptor Maestro Mateo, who finished it in 1188 after twenty-five years' work.) One of its central features is a column carved to represent 'the Tree of Jesse, from which Jesus sprang'. An interesting coincidence; but no more; except for the fact that as I read to Kathleen some of Michener's account of the annual festivities in St James' honour, she interrupts to ask when they take place. I find the answer in the text: 25 July. That is the Saint's Day and the culmination of the pilgrimage. The celebrations begin at dawn. I look at my watch. It is 9.45 p.m. on 24 July in Los Angeles; in Santiago de Compostela it is dawn on 25 July. We exchange looks that are only partly amused. I seriously consider kneeling. To anyone with the faintest trace of belief in the religions of the West, this must surely qualify as a sign; or, at the very least, a broad hint. I hereby swear to go to Santiago within the next twelve months. (The reason I have missed it so far is that its festival coincides with the Feria of San Jaime in Valencia. There are no bulls in Santiago.

Coughing again; also sleepless. Why? (I know the answer: cigarettes.) Excerpt from conversation *en route* to O'Neill ranch:

Ivan: . . . and he was a ship's chandler, whatever that is.
K.T.: A ship's chandler is the marine equivalent of a house dick.

25 July

Ivan M. tells us of a young Californian writer he has discovered. Her name is Victoria Looseleaf, and her first novel is called *Stalking the Wild Orgasm*. I congratulate him on this Firbankian invention. But he swears it is true.

30 July

Swifty takes me to lunch at USC in honour of Neil Simon. Hundreds of guests: we are seated next to Walter Matthau, husband of Carol Saroyan, the Dresden doll with whom I had a joyous but doomed affair in 1954–55. (She had twice married and twice divorced William Saroyan.) We met in Hollywood; fell merrily into bed; I loved her faux-naif wit and blonde beauty and awakened in her a lively taste for spanking. In 1955 she left the States, selling her home and possessions to meet me in Spain. It was the first extra-marital escapade of my life with Elaine and I was stricken with guilt. After a few nights at the Palace in Madrid we went to Valencia for the summer *feria*. Here we met a married couple of school teachers, strangers to Spain and the bulls, and both black: Tynan the lion-hearted liberal insisted on befriending them and took them out with us to supper on our first night in Valencia. They were very nice and very boring; but this was in the days when it was forbidden for white liberals to find blacks boring. When we finally got to our bedroom, Carol and I had our first row. 'I did not,' she cried, 'come 10,000 miles to have dinner with a couple of coons from Queens!' I yelled back; though with hindsight I see her rage was perfectly justified. By the end of the week we had made some unforgettable sexual explorations, shot through with fits of gloom whenever guilt struck me limp. I finally called Elaine and said I was coming back home. I then retired to one of the twin beds we were (by now) sharing chastely: I had booked a room of my own for the sake of appearances, and slept in Carol's that night only because she was miserable, feeling dumped and deserted, as she had every right to feel. Ironically, as soon as the lights were out, the door burst open and a private detective (who had, I learned later, been hired by Elaine to follow me from London) leaped in and took flash pictures of us in our twin beds. And so I went back to seven more years of the inferno with Elaine. I saw Carol several times afterwards in New York, but the bloom – to put it mildly – had gone, and in 1959 she married Walter[1]).

Anyway, Swifty introduced me to Walter, whom I'd never met. He leant across and shook hands, with the conversation-stopping remark: 'Good to meet ya. My wife is insanely in love with you.' I grinned feebly and shrugged stupidly, mumbling something about twenty years being a long time. (I gather he is a jealous man.) Two nights later Carol phoned me from her daughter Lucy's at 3.15 a.m. dragging me out of a drugged sleep. We talked for two hours. I said that I was husbanding my energies now that I was fifty. 'How strange,' she said, in that soft-edged child-like voice, 'when I'm only twenty-five.' I hope we can arrange to have a circumspect lunch – not for sexual reasons but to mend a link in my life that should never have been broken.

1 August

Feydeau was a realist and farce is the Theatre of Fact. Today, Kathleen being away in London for a fortnight, I called a girl who had advertised her availability for spanking purposes in the *LA Times* and made a date to see her at 2.30 p.m. at an apartment house in the tacky part of North Hollywood. Blinds drawn, rock music blaring, other girls flitting in and out of other rooms. I give her $60 and it's immediately clear that she is high on cocaine and is utterly uninterested in the spanking scene. However, I put her across my knee, where she lies wriggling in time to

---

1. Carol Saroyan quipped afterwards: 'The pain in Spain was mainly from Elaine.'

the music, and am about to experiment with a light tattoo on the rump when another girl dashes into the room and tells her to come at once.

I wait in my underwear for two minutes: then girl one (we'll call her Mandy) dashes back, her face white, and says: 'The cops are at the door. Get your clothes on and hide in the closet.' I do this at record speed and huddle in a clothes closet where I shake so much that the clothes hangers rattle. Suddenly I remember that my handbag, containing credit cards, chequebook and driver's licence, is on the bed. I am wondering whether to hurtle out and grab it when Mandy flies back and whispers: 'They're coming in to search the place. You'll have to jump off the balcony.' I seize the handbag. 'Hurry, for Christ's sake,' she hisses, dragging me through the window on to the balcony. I look over: it's a 12–15-foot drop into an alley, with garbage cans directly beneath. 'I can't make it,' I mutter. 'It's that or jail,' she says. (In LA, both the prostitute *and* her clients can be charged.) So I scramble over and drop. No injury; not even a tear.

My first reaction is that the whole thing has been a put-up job to get my $60 and that there were no cops. Later in the day, however, I call Mandy's number and another girl replies: she says Mandy and three other girls and four or five men are down at the court house, and: 'Who the hell are you anyway? Are you a cop?' So I hang up. Some kind of thanksgiving is in order. It would not have helped my relationship with K. or *The New Yorker* to have been picked up in a vice raid. I must have escaped literally by seconds.

7 August

To Tijuana with Tracy, Hercules, Theo Davis and Margarita Naish. Boring three-hour drive. The monumental bullring – an inverted bowl by the sea – is our destination: Antonio Lomelin, supposedly the best matador in Mexico, is on the *cartel*. Arriving at noon, we buy our tickets, select a seafood restaurant and order margaritas. Disgusted to find that it is an election day and no alcohol (not even beer or wine) can be sold. *Corrida* surprisingly good; bulls are small (around 400–420 kilos) but spirited, and Lomelin has real class – masses of *prudonor*, immense technical resource and great authority in the plaza, planted on the sand like a tree. He's about thirty and a classicist when he chooses; but this crowd, of course, wants *tremendisme*, so he supplies it with skill and tact.

(I've never seen a *corrida* in which more kneeling passes were executed.) He cuts four ears and a tail, killing very honourably: he'd have cut a couple of ears in Madrid.

Afterwards Theo asks whether he can drive us into Tijuana (the plaza is five miles out of town) for dinner. I agree, warning him not to leave the keys in the car before closing the doors – an error I've made once or twice, causing great inconvenience, since the doors are self-locking and the car is as impregnable as a tank. Having parked outside the restaurant, the imbecile disregards my instructions and we are locked out of the car, facing the prospect of (a) getting duplicate keys mailed from LA or (b) turning Mexican mechanics loose on the door with blow-torches. Theo insists on breaking in himself while we go off to eat. (By now, thank God, wine is legally available again.) Two hours later he arrives and announces success; he has probed through the rubber and chromium surrounding the window with steel wire and released the lock. The door, however, is nastily scratched and dented. Two good *faenas* are not, I conclude, enough recompense for six hours' driving and a repair job that will cost about $75.

11 *August*

Very swank party at the Lazars for bulky and beaming Australian authoress of best-selling novel called *The Thorn Birds*, which nobody present seems to have read. Swifty has skimmed the cream of his address book – guest list includes James Stewart, Gene Kelly, Jack Lemmon, Sue Mengers, Roger Vadim[1], Michael Caine, Johnny Carson, Ed McMahon[2], Natalie Wood, Robert Wagner, Richard Brooks – and Carol Saroyan Matthau, my *belle de jour* of twenty-two years ago, for whom I should have left Elaine. Her presence is still demure porcelain, a dainty rogue if ever George Meredith saw one, though bags have underlined her eyes and there has been some erosion of the once exquisite nose. We are placed side by side at dinner and gleefully reminisce. It seems that her husband (who is working early tomorrow) told her not to come, since he knew I would be present: after a flaming

1. Roger Vadim (1928–2000). French film director, famously married to Brigitte Bardot then Jane Fonda.
2. Ed McMahon (1923–). TV celebrity, long-time talk-show sidekick of Johnny Carson, who was the subject of one of Tynan's most celebrated profiles.

row, she defied him and walked out. (She says his first wife was 'satisfactorily hideous, like yours'.)

After a lot of white wine, she confesses that the most ecstatic moments of her life were spent with me here in Hollywood and later in Spain; and that she never makes love to Walter without a mental image of me. I am ravished by this flattery: I thought she would have looked back on Spain with contempt for my cowardice. She gives me two new kinds of pep pills, telling me that Dexamyl, my old standby, is long out of date. A wonderful reunion that gratifies us both: I hope we can manage the odd secret lunch. (Felicia Lemmon promises to act as go-between.)

Only jarring note at party is presence of a photographer from *Women's Wear Daily* gossip column. The Lemmons and I conspire to shock him: seeing him creeping up on us, we make a whispered plan, and as the flash bulb explodes, I press Felicia's face to my crotch with an expression of beatific delight while at the same time giving Jack a smacking kiss on the lips.

13 August

K.H. returns from two weeks in London. No matter what happens, we are the centre of each other's lives. In her absence, I am Saturn without its rings, a planet of leaden melancholy. (This is true despite the fact that at this moment more females are simultaneously and *avowedly* in love with me than ever before – four in all!)

21 August

Christopher Isherwood says on TV: 'In the eyes of eternity, of course, there are no such things as good and bad. It's too important for that.'

27 August

Astonishing news: Dustin Hoffman has agreed to play opposite Vanessa in K.'s film – although the part, as written, is of a young English aristocrat filling in as gossip columnist. (I suggest turning him into an American whose uncle is a British press lord, who has gone to Paris and joined the Lost Generation, discovered that, like George Dillon, he has 'all the symptoms of genius without the disease'[1], and settled for journalism instead.) Hoffman's name – one of the half-dozen which guarantee that a film will repay its investment – means that the picture is *actually going to happen* – and on schedule, too: Mike Apted intends to start shooting in October. (Feel, but do not mention, a pang of chagrin about my own film and all those years of still unforgotten frustration.) Hoffman gives a buffet dinner at his house to celebrate. He's forty, bearded, incredibly observant, quick and bright; feral might be the word, if he weren't so obviously nice. I naturally assume, from the speed of his reflexes and his restless energy, that he is on cocaine, as most people in this town seem to be; Bob Towne[2] says I'm right, others demur. He and I sniff around each other a little, somewhat warily; he of the critic and husband, I of the 'superstar' (hate that word) and charmer. Later that night I have an idea: he should play Mozart in a film based on the theory that the wee Salzburger was poisoned by his rival operatic composer Salieri.

18 November

Long pause in journal. Much – and nothing – happening. Shooting on K.'s film has started in England with Redgrave and Hoffman. I have spent two weeks in Madrid with Nicole researching piece for *New Yorker*. Amazed to discover that biggest theatrical hit in city is *Oh! Calcutta!*. Producer ropes me in for press receptions, luncheons and interviews, at once flattering and maddening, since all journalists assume the success of the show will make me a millionaire whereas in fact I get only 1 per cent of the gross. See three more films by Carlos Saura[3] and my admiration grows: his latest, *Elisa Vida Mia*, strikes me as his best – exquisite *intimiste* piece about elderly man who walks out of family life in early middle age and re-meets his daughter nearly twenty years later. Their late-blooming love for each other keeps reminding me of my present relationship in LA with Tracy. I tell Carlos: 'You've admitted that your films are semi-autobiographical. But the mystery is that you seem to be telling *my* autobiography.' (There's a scene in his *La*

---

1. John Osborne's 'Epitaph for George Dillon'.
2. Robert Towne (1934–). American screenwriter, renowned for *Chinatown* (1974).
3. Carlos Saura (1932–). Spanish film director and screenwriter.

Madriguera when Geraldine dresses as a schoolgirl and begs her husband – an older man – to punish her, which he does with a ruler on the seat of her knickers.)

But I return to the journal because K. telephoned today with the news that Clive Goodwin is dead. He was working in Hollywood with Trevor Griffiths and Warren Beatty, discussing the film Trevor is writing for Warren: in the lobby of the Beverly Wilshire he had a heart attack that produced vomiting. The management, thinking he was drunk, called the police, who took him off to the cells, where he died. This, at any rate, is the story so far. Garbled, since transmitted to her in London from LA: if true, it is horrific. (I gather Warren is already taking action against the police department.) But: so goes another of my few close friends, and as prematurely as the rest – Alan, Dommie, Steve Vinaver (with whom K. and I took Clive to Pamplona after Pauline's death in 1966, and about whose death I also learned by telephone while on holiday in an obscure south-eastern corner of Spain – I am now in Mojacar).

I go back a long way with Clive – to his editorship of *Encore*, certainly the best English theatre magazine of my time; through *Tempo*, on which he was my associate producer and frequent anchorman; through *The Black Dwarf*, his attempt to launch a really uncompromised English Leftist newspaper; in fact, through the battles so many of us fought in the fifties and sixties to forge links between the arts and politics. Whenever there was a good Leftist cause to be supported, demonstration to be organised or attended, letter of protest to be written or signed, Clive would always be the first on the phone. At the same time he never lost his balance, never sacrificed a certain detachment that enabled him to make a joke about the most serious political situation. Some of the fire went out of his life for good with the sudden death of Pauline (by a rare variety of cancer): he never formed another close attachment with a woman in the remaining eleven years of his life.

He became an extremely effective agent, gathering a list of clients that included many of the best socialist playwrights and directors in Britain; but he was aware that this was an essentially parasitic activity, and he took no special pride in it. (He appears, thinly disguised, in Trevor Griffiths' *The Party*, whose subject is the Parlour Pinks of London's intelligentsia.) He had superb taste in modern paintings, and the sale of his collection should see to it that his daughter does not want. So many of the most memorable occasions of my last twenty years have Clive in a central place – e.g. the great party he gave for Daniel Cohn-Bendit during the Paris student riots of 1968, that trip to Pamplona two years earlier, the time he made me and Richard Findlater pose for an *Encore* photo in full Victorian mourning clothes at the foundation stone of the National Theatre (some time in the early fifties) and hundreds of evenings when, with nothing particular to do, I've wondered who it would be most pleasant to dine with, called Clive and had a wonderful time. He cannot have been more than forty-one or forty-two. He lacked ambition (after Pauline's death) and application (but look who's talking): he did not lack commitment or friends. His death deprives me of one more strong reason for wanting to live.

20 November

Young bearded Madrid journalist interviews me at length with intense adulation and in the third person (e.g. 'What does Kenneth Tynan think of the new Spain?'). He asks me about politics, religion and philosophy as well as theatre and sex, and when I enquire why he should be interested in my views on these subjects, he says: 'Because to us Mr Kenneth Tynan represents might.' I protest that I am opposed to the exercise of might, which in any case I don't possess. 'No, no,' he says, 'to us, in our eyes, you are might.' Half an hour passes at cross purposes before he says: 'Let me explain it like this – in your own time of life, you are a *might* – M-Y-T-H – *might*!' I would never have guessed it. N.B. Spanish journalists all very much out of practice at being journalists. For forty years they have been employed mainly to carry official statements from ministries to printers, and they have grown rusty at the actual job of news gathering. One female reporter asks whether I see myself as the prophet of a heterosexual revolution in Spain. I casually point out that most of the night-clubs I've attended have featured transvestite (rather than heterosexual) shows. Headline next day: 'TYNAN SAYS SPANISH MEN ARE HOMOSEX-UALS'. Concierge at hotel (among others) gives me very beady eye when this appears. Some lady asks me whether *Oh! Calcutta!* isn't a little vulgar. I jocularly remind her that Voltaire called Shakespeare a vulgar barbarian. This appears in print as: 'TYNAN SAYS VOLTAIRE VULGAR'.

14 December

Less than $600 in the bank here, an overdraft of £5,100 at the bank in London, unpaid bills.

My 28,000-word piece on Stoppard appears in *The New Yorker*. It's not unimpressive, but I feel it's a bit overweight, and doesn't succeed in demonstrating why Tom deserves such extended treatment.

Dinner last night at Ma Maison with Howard (Austin), other guests including Michael and Pat York[1], Brooke Hayward[2] and Paul and Joanne Newman. Spend most of evening talking to Newmans, whom I haven't seen for ages. Paul's looks seem to improve with time: to call him a mature version of the Michelangelo *David* wouldn't be an exaggeration. He tells me that until a few years ago he could consume up to twenty-four cans of beer per day (on the set) plus a fifth of Scotch and a few bottles of wine. Now he drinks only beer, with the odd glass of wine after dinner. His face bears no signs of a hard-drinking past: I assume that cosmetic surgery has cleared up the pouches and broken veins. His politics have veered to the right since I first knew him, twenty years ago – e.g. 'I'd rather have illegal Mexican immigrants coming in to do the dirty jobs at low wages than legal ones living on welfare out of my pocket.' He expresses admiration for John Wayne.

Tells me of practical joke played on him by R. Redford after they finished *The Sting*. Redford bought a brand new Porsche (Paul loves fast cars), had the engine removed and rest of the car delivered to Paul, tied in pink ribbon. Paul, by way of riposte, had it taken to an automobile crushing yard, squeezed to a block of metal 5 feet square, and delivered to Redford's front door. The rich certainly pay for their laughs. Paul says he thinks it's about time he played Macbeth.

Forgot to mention that last weekend K.H. and I drove to border town of Mexicali (four–five hours on the road each way) to see *corrida* featuring Paco Camino, Manolo Martinez, and Miguel Espinosa 'Armillita' (son of the great Armillita). Paco is not more than decorous;

1. Michael York (1942–). British actor.
2. Brooke Hayward (1937–). Daughter of Leland Hayward, married to society bandleader Peter Duchin.

Martinez (one of the two best Mexican matadors, the other being Antonio Lomelin) cuts three ears with great craftsmanship, and a superb slow *estocada* in his first bull; but the revelation is young Armillita, who is only seventeen years old. He puts in brilliant sticks in the Arruza style, and in his second bull gives us some marvellous work with the left hand, extending the contrary leg and following all the classical rules. He can't yet kill well and for this reason cuts no ears: but if he can remedy this, Mexico will have an authentic *figura*.

On the way down we stop for lunch at the Rancho La Costa near San Diego, an absurdly expensive health farm where Gore V. has been paying $1000 a week to lose thirty pounds. The place has four restaurants, all with lengthy menus and wine lists for visitors. In five weeks there Gore has forged ahead with a new novel, working nine– ten hours a day, and his talk at lunch, on Perrier, is quite as vivacious as mine, on two vodka martinis and white wine.

1978

A sad and rainy Christmas. In the following week I finish my Carson piece – around 25,000 words – while bank account dwindles to under-zero and (due to an accounting error committed by my secretary) cheques begin to bounce. After a week of suspense, Mr Shawn calls. He thinks the piece 'stunning' and 'marvellous' and promises an immediate cheque to tide me over. It arrives ($15,000).

A recent TV showing of *Pandora's Box* brings back all my infatuation for Miss B. – she runs through my life like a magnetic threat, this shameless urchin tomboy, this unbroken, breakable porcelain colt, this prairie princess, equally at home in a slum pub or the royal suite at Neuschwaustein, creature of impulse, unpretentious temptress capable of dissolving into a fit of the giggles at a romantic climax, amoral but selfless, lesbian and hetero, with that sleek black cloche of hair that rings so many bells in my memory – Eton-cropped at the back with heavy fringe and kiss-curls bracketing the cheekbones – the only star actress I can imagine either being enslaved to or wanting to enslave.

Wake before dawn having dreamed all night of words. Why do all words that juxtapose the letters 'b' and 'l' (in that order) have connotations of clownish clumsiness? 'Bl' people dribble when they drink; their stomachs rumble after meals which they gobble. Rather than walk, they amble, stumble, hobble, shamble, or tumble; they are bloated and bleary-eyed; vocally they babble, bleat, burble, bluster, and mumble; physically, they are feeble. In the Pall Mall area they are Blimpish blighters; *en masse*, they are a rabble, always grumbling and in trouble. They fumble every task, and their lives are a jumble. If black, they have the blues. If women, they are blowsy, their minds are a blank, and rapidly crumble. At school they are blockheads who scatter their pages with blots. Their skin is blemished, covered in blotches and blackheads. They are blinkered against reality and unable to prevent their thoughts from rambling, they merely babble. Many of them are

Russian: Oblomov is the classic example (though some, like Leopold Bloom, are Irish and expert in blarney), terribly short of rubles. In a word, they are bumblers. Yet they are harmless blokes, for the most part humble, and although impossible to live with, they shall in good time be blessed. (In many ways I am their double.)

21 January

With children to the Norton Simon museum in Pasadena. Vast and fascinating collection, better than national gallery of most small European countries. Oriental sculpture especially fine; also strong right across the French spectrum up to Matisse; and a whole floor of Picassos. (Rather *too* strong on the Dutch, apart from the obligatory Rembrandt self-portrait.) Curator obviously addicted to Maillol: those majestic bums are everywhere, some to be fingered by me *en passant*. Collection is arranged however in total disorder, neither chronologically nor according to countries; and postcards of only about thirty exhibits are on sale. Matthew gets bored after a while but suddenly dashes up to me and says: 'Daddy, I've found a piece of sculpture that works!' It turns out to be a very well-designed drinking fountain. Feel this a remark of which Duchamp would have approved.

17 February

My Carson profile has appeared in *The New Yorker*. Fear the editing process has ironed out much that might have made it identifiably mine; also, when writing for the magazine, one automatically censors audacious phrases lest they should be demolished by the inquisitorial logicians on 43rd Street. Piece contains, moreover, far too many facts and figures and quotes and far too little analysis and interpretation – result of too much research.

Re-reading Boswell's Johnson, I find this, from the doctor's 'Meditations' in 1764, when he was fifty-five:

My indolence . . . has sunk into grosser sluggishness, and my dissipation spread into wilder negligence. My thoughts have been clouded with sensuality: and, except that from the beginning of this year I have, in some measure, forborne excess of strong drink, my appetites have predominated over my reason. A kind of strange oblivion has overspread me, so that I know not what has become of the last year; and perceive that incidents and intelligence pass over me without leaving any impression.

Exactly.

Conversation, a few days ago, with Mel Brooks, who had been saying that he would never think of making a picture that wasn't a comedy:

Mel: Let the people who can't make you laugh do that. It's all that's left to them. What if I became the next Jean Renoir? What the hell would be left for the other guys to do? I would take all their jobs away. No, with me, it's shoemaker, stick to your last.

21 February

K.H. complains that I spend too much time just chatting with my secretary Judy. Explain that without Judy's vivacity I would have great difficulty in overcoming my morning depression. 'She fills in the empty spaces,' I say, 'and prevents me from thinking of myself and the future.' Then I pick up Johnson and find this:

That man is never happy for the present is so true that all his relief from unhappiness is only forgetting himself for a little while. Life is a progress from want to want, not from enjoyment to enjoyment.

23 February

Note that people only use phrase 'by far' to introduce statement they know to be highly dubious – e.g. 'Angie Dickinson is *by far* the best actress the American cinema has produced.' '*Silk Stockings* is *by far* Fred Astaire's best film.'

4 March

Monroe Stahr in *Last Tycoon* refers to cinema as the 'furtive, privileged inspection of people under stress'.

8 March

Johnson, at seventy-five, baffles Boswell by his ability, though profess-ing himself miserable and transfixed by a horror of death, to remain so vivacious and animated in conversation. Johnson: 'Alas! it is all outside; I may be cracking my joke, and cursing the sun.' This is a poet speaking. A little later, in a letter: 'This is my history; like all other histories a narrative of misery.'

My sole claim to a link with the literary past is something my father once told me: that, as a child, he had known a man whose father lived in Lichfield and had met Samuel Johnson. This piece of information still unaccountably thrills me.

On Johnson's death-bed: Dr Warren hoped he was better. Johnson replied: 'No, sir; you cannot conceive with what acceleration I advance towards death.'

18 March

The Michelins are out, the lists are being made, the kilometres are being converted into miles, cables fly off to hotels in Spain and France as I embark on my favourite annual game: planning the summer holidays. (This year: the trip south from France to the villa I am taking in Mojacar, *and* the July trip *en famille* along the pilgrims' route to Santiago de Compostela. Joy!)

I invent a nice rumour: that Pauline Kael[1] nowadays refuses to review movies unless she has final cut. (With new directors she also insists on a solo credit: 'Reviewed by Pauline Kael'.)

23 March

Mock-Hammerstein lyric, to be sung in slow waltz-time by worldly European in Bora-Bora to native girl leaving to study in Europe:

---

1. Pauline Kael (1919–). Doyenne of American film critics; film critic of *The New Yorker*, 1968–91.

The more people you know –
That's fine, when you are young –
When there are so many jokes to be laughed at, and songs
To be sung:
But, when you *grow* old,
Clouds darken the sky,
And the more people you know,
   the more people you know . . .
Will die.

1 *April*

Someone asked me what the food was like at the Carson party. Found myself saying: 'The caviare was served out of a milk-churn with a soup-ladle – chuckwagon style. Then there was salmon in aspic with a TWA boarding pass in its mouth to show that it had just been flown in.'

6 *April*

Am reading C.S. Lewis's *Letters* (published to my amazement as long ago as 1966) having just finished Edmund Wilson's[1]. I knew both men, who were born – I think – in the same year, 1898. Startling to reflect that when I was Lewis's pupil, he was younger than I am now; startling because I feel still as I felt then, infinitely his junior. How good it would have been to bring Wilson and Lewis together – the resolute unbeliever and the great Christian persuader, the left-wing polemicist and the arch-traditionalist, the international traveller and the Oxford home-body, the guardian of contemporary letters and their amused scourge ('Why should one read authors one doesn't like because they happen to be alive at the same time as oneself,' C.S.L. writes to a friend. 'One might as well read everyone who had the same job or the same-coloured hair or the same income or the same chest measurement . . .'). But how much they would have had in common – the love of Tolstoy, of standards, of classic norms. The gap in Lewis is that he met too few people as unlike himself, yet as combatively well read, as Wilson. The

1. Edmund Wilson (1898–1972). Author and critic; *New Yorker éminence grise.*

gap in Wilson is that he never met a religious man as brilliant and provocative as Lewis.

May–September

I have not written about the events of this devastating summer – the most turbulent and shattering period of my life – and will do so now only in telegram form. I do not propose to relive it, even in words. In May I spent four happy days in Rochester, NY with Louise Brooks, who was a joy – bedridden but birdlike, hilariously indiscreet (she claims that when she masturbates, even at seventy-one – 'I sit on that couch and the spurt from my cunt goes Poww! clear across to that record player on the other side of the room. That's five and a quarter yards!'), together with detailed stories of her affairs with Chaplin, Hearst[1], Pabst[2] (!) etc.

I had planned to spend summer at a villa in Mojacar with Nicole, taking the month of July out to drive K.H. and children on tour across Spain to the celebrations of Saint James at Santiago de Compostela. Should have known fate disapproved when my plane from Rochester to New York was grounded by engine failure. Luggage transferred to second plane, which also develops engine trouble. Am finally shunted on to third plane and re-routed to Paris via Buffalo, Toronto and Amsterdam on four different airlines. Arrive to find all my baggage (eight pieces) has been lost. It turned up in Warsaw two days later. Meet Nicole (we stay at delicious little bandbox hotel near Etoile called La Residence du Bois) and go to public car-park to pick up the Jaguar, which my English secretary has driven from London. Discover that power-steering has broken down: car is undrivable (except by Superman) without it. Spend three days painfully guiding it round Paris in search of repair. Finally, in remote garage beyond Périphérique find mechanic who can cope. We set off south. Good couple of days, eating at Hotel de la Poste and chez Point. Then, just across Spanish border, a deafening bang: tyre has not deflated but exploded. We are doing 100 m.p.h. on motorway

---

1. William Randolph Hearst (1863–1951). Newspaper and Hollywood-film magnate.
2. George Pabst. Tynan wired Louise Brooks on her birthday, 13 November 1978: 'LIEBE LOUISE UPON MY KNEES WITH LOVE I HAVE COLLAPSED I WISH YOU HAPPY BIRTHDAY PLEASE YOURS TRULY GEORGIE PABST. K.T.'

and car bucks like bronco. Nicole blessedly changes tyre: old one is so battered and shredded that we throw entire wheel away. (Grave error: there are no Jaguar wheels in Spain and after months of seeking am forced to have replacement flown in from London at cost of nearly £200.)

Villa at Mojacar is superb, 100 yards from sea: coastline uncrowded, weather perfect. While fucking Nicole a little over-enthusiastically (having had no sex before this trip, since last November with Nicole in Spain), I twist and bend penis, experiencing stabbing pain. Thereafter penis is painful to the touch when more than half-erect, which severely restricts sexual activity. Months later, discover that I have burst blood vessel in penis: scar tissue has formed and hardened, causing prick to take on shape of hourglass and preventing flow of blood. This means I may never achieve full erection again: also, it becomes a long and exhausting business to reach the point of ejaculation.

I suffer from bouts of extreme lassitude, perhaps after-effect of 1,500-mile drive, so Nicole suggests I spend three days in bed. I agree. Around lunchtime on first day I am sleeping in bedroom; Nicole is at beach. I wake up at four when she returns, to find that my Nikkormat camera, gold pen, nearly a thousand dollars in pesetas, and handbag have been stolen, latter containing passport (with US visa), driver's licences (UK and California), credit cards, air tickets, and traveller's cheques worth about $14,000. All these were taken from my bedroom while I slept: handbag was on bedside table. Moreover, bedroom door was closed: suppose thief had entered to find me awake? Am assured by neighbours that I am lucky: woman in nearby house woke up while burglars were in her room some weeks ago, and had her kneecaps shot off.

Now begins horrendous routine of reports to police, to traveller-cheque companies, to banks, to embassies, to travel agencies, all complicated by fact that villa has no telephone, all Mojacar phones are out of order and nearest point of contact with outside world is public phone in village seven miles away. American Express refuse to refund a cent unless I travel 200 miles to their office in Granada to swear affidavit that report of theft is authentic; they also need signed verification from chief of police (three weeks passed before they made good the loss; will never use them again). Meanwhile a lorry, passing too close on a mountain road, nearly tore off left-hand side of Jaguar, which goes into garage looking like Al Capone's jowl. Finally (or so I thought) a prolonged paroxysm of coughing caused by a piece of meat stuck in my throat produces, next morning, my first hernia unpleasantly close to scrotum on left side. Local doctor advises immediate surgery and prescribes truss, which turns out to be medieval contraption as effectively anti-aphrodisiac as a chastity belt. Sexual activity now ceases completely.

Emotionally there is turmoil as date approaches for K.H. and children to take over from Nicole in villa. (How I ever thought I could get away with this I shall never know but I was surely punished for my hubris.) Nicole, unable to get seat on plane, remains in Mojacar, staying with friends after K.H. arrives. Atmosphere is electric. My reaction is a simple desire to go to sleep for ever.

I say a guilt-ridden *au revoir* to Nicole and embark on trip to north with family. K.H. takes wheel: I am no longer capable of driving. Remember magnificent hotels (Landa Palace outside Burgos, Reyes Catolicos in León, converted from a seventeenth-century monastery) and Romanesque churches of golden stone along the pilgrimage route to Santiago; also the astounding cathedral at León, which has a higher ratio of stained glass to brickwork than any other cathedral in the world: but I am virtually immobilised by lung problems and in León I collapse altogether and spend two days unable to move from my bed. According to K.H. I talk gibberish, making no sense: of this episode I remember nothing.

In Santiago (second only in beauty to Salamanca) I recover; the Plaza de Las Platerias seems to me the most exquisite Renaissance square I have ever seen. Then on to spend five wantonly luxurious days in the Grand Hotel, Isla de la Toja, just off the lovely Galician coast – a genuine 1906 Grand Hotel, populated exclusively by rich Spaniards, where dinner in the grand ballroom is accompanied by a pianist who plays a Bechstein grand in white gloves.

K.H. drives us back to Madrid, then flies off with children to South of France where they are to stay with the Anstruthers. Two friends from Mojacar, Roger and Hilary Bush, join me in Madrid. Hilary is to drive the Jaguar back to London while I fly to California. On their first night I take them to dinner at Valentin's. We leave restaurant at midnight; as I set foot on sidewalk a young Spaniard, sprinting at full speed, dashes up to me, snatches my (new) handbag and disappears down an alley. I give chase, but trip over a kerb, badly cutting both knees. Roger tries to pursue, but the thief soon loses him.

Inside the handbag, as I need hardly say, are my (replaced) traveller's cheques, (replaced) credit cards, passport (with US visa that expires in a week's time), driving licences, about $700 in pesetas – plus my diary, private financial documents (including the only record of Wilar's assets), and air tickets. The same bureaucratic rigmarole must start all over again, this time with the temperature at 102 degrees and with the disadvantage that many of the people to whom I now apply for refunds and replacements are frankly reluctant to believe that lightning could have struck twice within such a short time in the same place. Oh the agony of standing in line at embassies, police stations, travel agencies, banks, traveller-cheque companies, and filling in once again their interminable forms in triplicate – with one eye on the calendar, since if the US Embassy refuses to re-issue my visa by next Tuesday I shall be unable to re-enter the US and my job with *The New Yorker* will end. I recall what a Madrid friend told me just before Franco died: 'You will be able to tell when Spain has democracy because at the same time Spain will have crime.'

So much for my hard-luck story. I made the plane and got wheel-chair treatment to Los Angeles. Destiny gave me a final tap in the balls to remind me who was boss. Of my eight pieces of luggage, seven appeared on the carousel at LA Airport. The eighth, containing all my *New Yorker* research and the manuscript of the Mel Brooks profile (32,000 words) which I'd finished in Spain, was lost. It turned up next day in Rio de Janeiro.

22 September

On one page of the obituary section of this week's *Variety* I discover that four friends have died. Hy Kraft[1], who wrote *Top Banana* and whom I knew when he came to London as a refugee from McCarthyism in the fifties, is dead and has been since 1975: I learn this from an obit. of his wife Reata, which also mentions that their daughter recently died, like her mother, of cancer. Finally, the peerless Dwight Marfield is dead, aged seventy: the first great American eccentric comedian I ever met. He entertained, with his minute ukulele, at the first party I attended on my maiden trip to New York in 1951 – a

---

1. Hy Kraft (1900–75). Blacklisted New York playwright.

thin, rambling, grey-haired man with a high voice in which he delivered bizarre monologues (about trips round the world with Cole Porter, the Princess of Thurn und Taxis 'in one of her more bifurcated moments' and 'the Ranee of Rawalpindi, lately widowed and travelling in the company of her cook') interspersed with deservedly neglected songs of the twenties, which he sang in a haunting nasal whine.

Dwight was an acquired taste, like white truffles, and he had a cult following in which I was soon enrolled. I wrote a eulogy of him for an English magazine (he was my first American 'discovery'): moreover I recorded all his routines and recommended him to show-business friends as an after-dinner entertainer: he did not, however, flourish in the salons of the great where few were disposed to surrender their own right to the floor to this shy and wispy intruder, who resembled a cross between the White Knight and Don Quixote. He was also a painter. I bought one of his water-colours, showing two tiny heraldic animals escaping from a storm-threatened landscape: it was called *Les Echoués*. Whatever Shangri-La they were bound for, I hope he has joined them there. His flavour was too delicate for the coarse palate of show business. I last saw him, not inappropriately, as one of the gentle lunatics in the movie *One Flew Over the Cuckoo's Nest*. Though I saw little of him in the past fifteen years or so, I missed him and still do.

Merlin, by Robert Nye, who wrote the masterpiece *Falstaff*, reveals even more clearly its author's obsession with the world of spanking, e.g.:

Camelot the golden
Built upon a secret cesspool
A very perfect gentle knight,
Who likes to whip girls' bottoms.

1 October

Tested penis by masturbation. Can achieve moderate stiffness in lower part of trunk and upper inches next to tip: but in between is a soft waistline that causes organ to topple sideways like axed tree. Orgasm difficult to achieve and far from ecstatic. Deeply depressed. Can

imagine London gossip and press comments when this news gets out –
'MAN WHO SAID FUCK CAN'T FUCK' etc.

Reading Nancy Mitford[1] I come across an apt verse from a poem
Voltaire wrote to Madame du Châtelet announcing (at forty-six!) that
he was too old to make love:

> *On meurt deux fois, je le vois bien,*
> *Cesser d'aimer et d'être aimable*
> *C'est une mort insupportable:*
> *Cesser de vivre ce n'est rien.*

A good epitaph.

15 November

After a bad week – of exhaustion without explanation – I pick up
The New Yorker and find that Janet Flanner has died, aged eighty-six.
My Parisian *patronne*, who opened her eyes to my journalism and
welcomed me to her city nearly a quarter of a century ago, will not
be replaced, because the giants who peopled Paris during her lifetime
will not be replaced either. No other American was addressed on
equal terms by Cocteau, Gide, Matisse, Camus, Sartre, Valéry,
Malraux, Piaf, Josephine Baker – her memory was the most glittering
salon in the city. How she praised and reproached and enlightened
me, this blue-haired spinster with eyes that sparkled with sapphires!
There were few people whose approval I cherished more. Like
hundreds of other young writers, I can say that Janet discovered me.
(Which is not to say that I lived up to her.) I belonged to her inner
circle, and in Western Europe after the war there was no prouder
place to be.

When did I last take her out? Was it to Josephine Baker's comeback
at the Olympia, which Janet hailed by rising to her feet at the end and
clapping her hands high above her head? Enthusiasm, even at eighty,
never failed her for the promise of the day's doings. A queen bee if ever
I knew one; and how rich the honey! She always urged me to visit

---

1. Nancy Mitford (1892–1978). Novelist and biographer, best known for her witty *Love in a Cold Climate* (1949).

ageing celebrities and question them before they died: 'Tax their brains,' she would say. 'It's like lobsters. Go for the head – there's tasty chewing there.' As there was in Janet's, on which I contentedly fed whenever we met. One consolation, I suppose, is that here, at least, is a life-enhancer who outlived the shits – an American life with a perfectly resolved third act.

1979

3 January

Bad December, including week in hospital just before Christmas for exhaustion. The usual tests; no new discoveries. Am now on oxygen all night, with portable machine for daytime use. Spend New Year's Eve with K.H. and children at hotel in Death Valley, vast expanse of nothing that has *less* of anything than any tourist resort in the world – less water (indeed, no water at all), fewer flora and fauna (unless you count the coyote and the kangaroo rat), fewer hotels and buildings of interest (e.g. handful of very vestigial ghost towns and the unimpressive pseudo-Spanish mansion called Death Valley Scotty's Castle), less of everything attractive to the civilised mind except heat, of which there is far too much (the average summer temperature is around 120 degrees F). We drive back through ghastly company towns run by chemical firms and by the US navy's weapons research department. Death valley is minimal tourism, a gigantic natural monument to the theory that less is more. Query: Why is it that all man-made objects in the States – especially cars, trains, aircraft and modern buildings – look like outsize toys?

13 August

When we say that a man is a great classical actor, what we really mean is that he is good at playing antique soldiers who come to bad ends. In L.O.'s case: Antony, Caesar, Coriolanus, Titus, Hotspur, Macbeth, Oedipus. Edgar in *The Dance of Death* is a retired soldier; and Tyrone in *Long Day's Journey* has spent his life playing the Count of Monte Cristo.

November

Flashback to the sixties – I went to Rome to interview Richard Burton for BBC TV. He drank wine steadily all day as we filmed (around five bottles) and then invited me and the producer to dinner at the huge villa he and Elizabeth had rented outside Rome. (She was filming

Reflections in a Golden Eye. This took place the day after Brando presented them with the two memorial antique silver goblets, the first engraved 'Richard: Christ, I've pissed in my pants' and the second: 'Elizabeth: That's not piss, that's come.')

Large group of guests in entrance hall of villa. Richard, the producer and I are chatting when R. suddenly directs his wolfish grin at me and says: 'How do you think Elizabeth is looking, Ken?' 'Fine,' I say, inwardly meaning 'Fat'. Pause: still eyeing me, he says: 'How would you like to go to bed with her?' A no-win situation, as they say: to answer 'Very much' is to lech after the host's wife, to answer 'Not at all' is to stigmatise her as unattractive. I wiggle out by self-deprecation: 'To be quite candid, Richard, I doubt whether I'd be capable of making it with Elizabeth.' 'You mean you couldn't get it up?' I still refuse the provocation. 'Something like that.' 'Elizabeth!' Richard bellows at her across the room. She breaks away from a group by the fireplace, and teeters a little unsteadily across the hall to join us. 'Yes, Richard?' 'Do you know what our friend Ken just said about you?' 'No, dear.' 'He said he didn't think he'd be able to get it up for you in bed.' Elizabeth turned blazing eyes on me. '*That*,' she said noisily, 'is the most *insulting thing* that has ever been said to me. *Leave my house!*'

So here I am being ordered out of a house for *not* having made a pass at the hostess. I retire to avoid a drunken row in which goblets are likely to be thrown. Next day the phone in my hotel bedroom rings. It is Elizabeth, her voice honeyed with hungover apology – 'So terribly sorry. Don't know what got into me' (a crate of vodka?). 'Please forgive us both.' Flowers are delivered to my room. But the scene sticks in memory, not inspiring affection.

1980

11 January

Debts in excess of $75,000; no work achieved since last spring. Still in Puerta Vallarta: health failing rapidly, and, with it, energy and the desire to work. Hands now shake so much that I can barely write.

17 January

By bumpy boat from Puerto Vallarta to lunch at Las Caletas, the compound of huts – inaccessible by road – where John Huston and his entourage live. Kathleen and I make the trip with Tom and Toody Compatello. Tom is a professional backgammon player against whom John likes to match himself. They play twenty games at 100 pesos a point: John loses the first nine heavily but recovers, taking urbane and outrageous risks, so that he ends up only 600 pesos (about $27) in the red. Tom is an emotional player whose verbal exuberances slightly irritate John, provoking him to sleek one-line put-downs that pass quite unnoticed by Tom. E.g.:

Tom (*following an unsuspected move by John*): Aha! Coming in on the blind side, as they say in poker!
John (*an expert poker player*): They say that in poker, do they? (*Pause*) They have all kinds of quaint little sayings in poker. One of these days I think I'll make a collection of them. (*He wins the game.*)
Tom: Who was it who said, 'Nothing succeeds like success?'
John (*innocently*): Probably another of those quaint little sayings.

29 January

From Maugham's *The Summing Up* (apropos of Rousseau):

There is a sort of man who pays no attention to his good actions, but is tormented by his bad ones. This is the type that most often writes about himself. He leaves out his redeeming qualities and so appears only weak, unprincipled and vicious.

Shall I fall into this trap?

INDEX

1001 Nights 100
1789 73
2001: A Space Odyssey 221

Acapulco, Mexico 118
Ackerley, J.R. 369
Across the River and Into the Trees
 (Hemingway) 60–1
Acton, Harold 306
Adler, Larry 274
African Genesis 105
Agate, James 10–11, 312
Agatha 347
Aix-en-Provence, France 50
Akenfield 223
Akhnaten, Pharaoh 315–16, 321–2
Alan (KT's cousin) 299–300
Albee, Edward 74
Albery, Donald 55
Aldwych Theatre, London 161fn, 225
Alex and Sophie (KT's screenplay) 37, 102,
 224, 315, 393; finance 170, 175, 179–
 81, 183–4, 187, 191, 227; German
 interest 215; on location 184–5
Alexander of Yugoslavia 40
Algonquin Hotel, New York 61, 109fn,
 132, 274
Ali, Muhammad 33, 73, 130, 191, 200,
 209
Ali, Mukhta 85
Allen, Jim 273
Alsace 197
Altman, Robert 86fn, 273
Alvarez, Al 177
Ameche, Don 211
American Embassy, London 258, 269
Amis, Kingsley 228, 291, 317–18, 337,
 340, 374
Amis, Martin 278, 288
Amram, David 375, 377
Anderson, Lindsay 153
Anderson, Maxwell 173
Anderson, Sherwood 74

Anna (urban guerrilla) 196, 325–6
Annan, Noel 40
Anne, Princess Royal 139
Annis, Francesca 28
Another Bride, Another Groom 257
Anouilh, Jean 10
Antalya, Turkey 104
Anti-California (Lamott) 372
Antonioni, Michelangelo 107fn, 248–9,
 251, 255
Apted, Mike 393
Aquarius (LWT) 226, 279
Archibald, William 323
*Architect and the Emperor of
 Assyria* (Arrabal) 21fn, 25–6
Arena (BBC TV) 279, 288
Aristotle 342
Armallita, Miguel Espinosa 396
Arts Council 22, 45, 55fn
Arts Theatre Club 26, 311
As You Desire Me 327
As You Like It (Shakespeare) 141
Ashcroft, Peggy 197, 219
Ashley, Elizabeth 386
Askey, Arthur 260
Aspinall, John 288
Astaire, Fred 246
Astaire, Jarvis 330
Astor, Mary 211
Atkins, Eileen 141
Attenborough, Sir Richard 20, 89, 90
Attwell, Mabel Lucie 357
Auberge de Noves, Avignon 50, 155–6
Auden, Wystan Hugh 72, 76, 123, 208,
 306, 369
Austen, Jane 224
Austin, Howard 396
Avedon, Richard 182
Avignon, France 50, 63, 329
Axelrod, George 27, 44, 71, 87, 182
Axelrod, Joan 27, 44, 87, 182
Ayckbourn, Alan 272
Ayckbourn Trilogy 285

Ayer, Sir A.J. 'Freddie' 137, 138, 342
Aznavour, Charles 41

Baader-Meinhof group 325
Bacall, Lauren 105–6, 137, 182, 351
Bacchae (Euripides) 57, 117, 146
Bach, J.S. 29
Bacon, Francis 58
Bad News Bears 363
Baddeley, Hermione 110–11
Baden-Powell, Lord 327
Bailey, David 107, 231
Baker, Boty 239
Baker, Josephine 411
Baldwin, James 43–4, 230
Baldwin, Stanley 277
Ball of Fire 271–2
Bardot, Brigitte 41, 391fn
Barnum, Minnie 106
Barrault, Jean-Louis 245, 336
Barrie, J.M. 329
Barron, Keith 223
Barry, Gerald 76fn
Barry Lyndon 291, 293, 300–1
Barrymore, John 211
Bartok, Bela 37
Barton, John 139, 140, 225
Baryshnikov, Mikhail 284
Baxter, Beverly 144, 312
Bayesen, Hjalnar 110, 111
Baylis, Lilian 243, 279, 281
BBC 15, 53, 68, 97, 101, 218, 266, 279,
   339, 341, 415
BBC 3 86fn
Beardsley, Aubrey 357
Beat movement 286
Beatles 367, 380
Beaton, Cecil 39, 67, 96
Beatty, Warren 27, 229, 237, 341, 355,
   394
Beaumont, Hugh 'Binkie' 54, 129, 219,
   314, 337
Beckett, Samuel 25, 238
Beerbohm, Max 179, 258fn, 299
Beesley, Alan 31–2, 33–4, 207–8, 265,
   309, 320, 394
Behrman, S.N. 258
Belafonte, Harry 43–4, 169
Belfast, N. Ireland 31
Bennett, Alan 37, 79fn, 86
Bennett, Arnold 51
Bennett, J.A.W. 357
Bennett, Jill 34, 59, 60, 172, 201–2, 223

Benny, Jack 145, 171, 356
Benny, Mary 356
Beowulf 288
Berenson, Bernard 249
Berenson, Maria 354
Berger, John 83, 103, 113
Berghaus, Ruth 281
Bergner, Elizabeth 218
Berlin 280, 282, 315, 374
Berlin, Irving 246, 313, 376
Berliner Ensemble 34–5, 105fn, 129fn,
   280–1, 374
Bernstein, Burton 274, 281–2
Bernstein, Carl 327
Bernstein, Felicia 182
Bernstein, Leonard 44, 182
Bernstein, Sidney 70, 278
Bertolucci, Bernardo 341
Bessie, Mike 74
Best, George 148, 232
Betjeman, John 86
Betsy, The 384
Beuselinck, Oscar 201
Bevan, Aneurin 107
Bick, Jerry 364
Big Store, The 44
Billington, Michael 56, 176, 337
Bingham, Henrietta 210
Birkenhead, Earl of 277
Birkett, Michael 330
Birmingham 6, 194, 217; Rep 190
Birthday Party, The (Pinter) 57
Bishop, John 179, 181, 227
Black Dwarf, The 394
Black Panthers 113
Blackburn, Robin 138, 189, 196, 326
Blaine, Amory 178
Blake, Eubie 376fn
Blake, James 51, 157
Blake, William 29, 45, 48, 51
Blakemore, Michael 69, 98; and Dexter
   92; as director 35, 45, 54–5, 135, 149;
   on Finney 118; and Hall 88–90, 99,
   309; KH's lover 341; on Olivier 136;
   resigns from NT 330–1
Blithe Spirit (Coward) 173, 334
Blond, Peter 268
Blond, Virginia 117, 268
Bloom, Claire 101fn, 128, 172, 278
Bloomsbury set 209–10, 264, 323
Blow-Up 107fn, 248fn, 255
Blythe, Domini 187
Bocuse, Paul 154

Bogarde, Dirk 305, 311
Bogdanovich, Peter 355, 363, 366
Bond, Edward 13, 152
Booker McConnell 113
Books and Bookmen 324
Bormann, Martin 95
Boswell, James 402–4
Boty, Pauline 309, 338, 394
Boud, John 170
Bournemouth 171
Boxer, Mark 191, 269
Boycott, Rosie 129
Boylston, Saltonstall 109
Brackett, Charles 211, 271, 272
Braden, Bernard 138
Brancusi, Constantin 253
Brando, Marlon 19, 255, 324, 416
Brandt, Willy 52
Brassens, Georges 245
Braunsberg, Andy 37, 102, 179–81, 364, 384
Breathless 371
Brecht, Bertolt 13, 22, 46, 98, 103, 117, 240; and Berliner Ensemble 35, 105fn, 280–1; poems 318–19
Brenan, Gerald 210
Brenton, Howard 143, 336
Brideshead Revisited (Waugh) 51
Brien, Alan 187
Brighton, Sussex 70, 89, 227
British Museum, London 269
Britneva, Maria 110, 111
Brompton Hospital, London 230, 236, 263, 334–5
Brook, Dinah 357
Brook, Peter 83, 225, 297–9, 314, 325
Brooks, Lt.-Col. 205–6
Brooks, Louise 15, 97–8, 327, 401, 406; KT's study of 347
Brooks, Mel 235–6, 308, 385, 403; KT's study of 347, 409
Brooks, Richard 386, 391
Brooks, Victoria 193
Brown, George 47
Brown, Georgia 227
Brown, Pamela 270
Brown, Sophie 47
Bruce, Lenny 236, 259
Buchan, John 262
Buchanan, Jack 127fn
Buchwald, Art 71
Buckle, Richard 'Dickie' 284
Burgess, Guy 31, 306

Burney, Fanny 224
Burns, George 308, 356
Burton, Richard 12, 180, 415–16
Bush, Roger and Hilary 408
Butler, Samuel 23
Butt, Dame Clara 40
By Candlelight 105
Byron, Lord 24, 108, 187, 249, 327

Caesar's Palace, Las Vegas 353
Café Chauveron, New York 61
Caine, Michael 239, 391
Caldwell, Cotton 384
California 372, 373, 382, 383
Calley, Lt. William 32
Calthrop, Gladys 48
Cambridge University 199
Cameron, James 264
Camino, Paco 396
Cammell, Donald 364, 378, 381
Campiello, Il (Goldoni) 343
Capote, Truman 74, 107, 182, 231, 282, 373–4
Capron, Marion 305
Caretaker, The (Pinter) 53, 57
Carey, Joyce 48
Carrington, Dora 209–10
Carroll, Lewis 382
Carry On films 272
Carson, Frank 97, 373
Carson, Joanna 386
Carson, Johnny 308, 355, 366, 386, 391, 405; KT's study of 347, 401, 402
Carte Blanche 141fn, 242, 322; finance 302, 328; 'Triangle' 340–1, 372–3; opens 338, 341; rehearsals 340–1; reviews 118fn, 358; title chosen 336
Carter, Jimmy 352
Casement, Roger 327
Cassady, Neal 286
Castro, Fidel 215, 377–8, 384
Caute, David 75, 105
Cavett, Dick 47, 97
Chamberlain, Neville 6
Chandos, Lord 45, 128–9
Channel 5, New York 70
Chant d'Amour 79
Chapel, Alain 197
Chaplin, Charles 103, 287, 406
Château de Meyrargues, France 50–1
Château St Martin, Vence 61
Chayevsky, Paddy 365
Chekhov, Anton 59, 103, 149, 173, 253

Cherry Orchard, The (Chekhov) 35fn, 135, 149
Cheshire, David 288
Chester 231
Chesterton, G.K. 194, 204
Chevalier, Maurice 107–8
Chez la Mère Charles, Mionnay 155, 156, 197
Chicago 71
Chichester Festival Theatre 13, 105fn, 144fn
Children of the Sun (Green) 306
Chin, Tsai 73
Christ Church, Oxford 123
Christie, Agatha 338, 347
Christie, John 241
Christie, Julie 237
Christopher and His Kind (Isherwood) 369–70
Churchill, Winston 6
Churchill, Winston Jnr 94–5
CIA 31–2, 221, 366–7
Citizen Kane 42, 251, 358
Citkovitz, Caroline 42
Clark, Max Stafford 239
Clay, Cassius, *see* Ali, Muhammad
Clements, Sir John 105
Cleopatra (Shakespeare) 12, 369
Clore, Charles 199
Close, Brian 333
Clunes, Alec 26
Clurman, Harold 164, 252
Coburn, James 355
Cockburn, Claud 31
Cockburn, Emma 36
Cocteau, Jean 29–30, 359, 411
Coghill, Neville 144
Cohn-Bendit, Daniel 31, 73–4, 395
Colbert, Claudette 211
Coliseum, London 217
Columbia 378, 381
Comden, Betty 97fn, 120, 182
Comedians, The (Greene) 266
Comédie Française 129fn, 137
Common Market, *see* EEC
Commonwealth Day 249
Communism 23, 32, 43–4, 117, 135, 215, 234, 283
Compatello, Tom and Toody 419
Compton, Fay 26fn, 311
Concept of Mind, The (Ryle) 75
Confessions of Nat Turner (Styron) 230
Confucius 218

Conlon, 'Scooper' 62
Connery, Sean 239
Connolly, Cyril 16, 64, 67, 113, 159, 170, 306, 308, 357
Conquest, R. 265
Conrad, Joseph 227
Conservative Party 22, 49, 52, 70, 77, 86, 174, 193, 271, 320, 327
Cooch Behar, Maharajah of 110, 111
Cook, Peter 79–80, 86, 137
Cooper, Diana 278, 319
Cooper, Gary 271
Copenhagen, Denmark 322
Cordoba, Spain 62
Corelli, Marie 224
Coriolanus (Shakespeare) 34–5, 85–6
Corneille, Pierre 224
Cornwall 339
Costa Smeralda, Sardinia 62
Courtenay, Tom 12
Covent Garden 92, 143
Coward, Noël 48, 96, 145, 344; biography of 355; death 130; homosexuality 103, 312; KT's profile of 371; KT's review of 12; plays 164; songs 188–9; and Vidal 359
Cowdray Park 110, 111
Cowdrey, Colin 190
Crewe, Quentin 231
Croft, Michael 247–8
Cromwell (Storey) 152
Cromwell, Oliver 319–20
Crosby, John 61
Crumb, Robert 100fn
Cuba 215, 375, 376–8, 384
Cukor, George 180, 242, 366
Culloden (BBC TV) 339
Curran, Charles 144
Curry, John 308
Curtis, Tony 44, 386
Curtiss, Thomas Quinn 40, 184–5, 186
Cushman, Robert 337

Daily Express 63fn, 349
Daily Mail 320–1, 327
Daily Mirror 49
Daily Telegraph 20, 138fn, 174
Dale, Jim 278
Dance of Death 120, 190, 415
Dance to the Music of Time (Powell) 268
Dangerous Corner (Priestley) 173
Dangerous Edge, The (Lambert) 262
Dankworth, Johnny 49, 326

Dante Alighieri 177
Danton's Death 57–8
Darkness at Noon (Koestler) 337
Darrell, Peter 310
Daubeny, Peter 129
Davis, Bill 291
Davis, George 327
Davis, Miles 169
Davis, Sammy 373
Davis, Theo 390–1
Day, Douglas 380
Day by the Sea, A (Hunter) 59
Days of Hope (Garnett) 273, 277
De Cordova, Freddie 386
De Filippo, Eduardo 159
De La Falaise, Lulu 137
De Mille, Cecil B. 58, 293
De Niro, Robert 308
De Vries, Peter 257
Dean, John 385
Death in Venice 311
Death Valley 415
Deep Throat 204, 224
Deighton, Len 206
Delfont, Sir Bernard 128
DeLynn, Alan 61
Dench, Judi 321
Denmark 322
Denon, Dominique 85
Desmond, Paul 379–80
Devils, The 58
Dexter, John 48fn, 118, 119; and
    Blakemore 92; as director 35, 45, 54–5,
    126fn; on Goodman 93; and Hall 88–
    9, 92, 124; and Plowright 226
Dick Cavett Show 47
Dickens, Charles 83
Dickinson, Angie 355, 403
Didion, Joan 347
Dietrich, Marlene 12, 38–9, 96, 106, 132,
    242, 347
Diller, Barry 373
Disney, Walt 100–1
Docker, Lady 279
Dodd, Ken 319
Doll's House, A (Ibsen) 128
Donahue, Bernard 330
Donaldson, Willie 232, 342–3
Donne, John 178
Donnell, Patrick 89, 118, 119, 124
Dorchester Hotel, London 36
Douglas, Lord Alfred 108
Douglas, Kirk 20

Dourdou, Dr 263
Driberg, Tom 107
Drogheda, Lord 92
Duchin, Peter 396fn
Dud Avocado, The (Dundy) 41fn
Duffy, Maureen 117
Dumbville, Douglas 44
Dumont, Margaret 44
Dunbar, Paul 357
Dundy, Elaine 9, 83, 130, 274; affairs 374;
    as biographer 365fn; KT's happy times
    with 41, 110, 182, 186; KT's relations
    with 189, 261, 357, 389; and KT's
    sexual preferences 142, 254; and Leigh
    133; marriage 10; as novelist 41fn, 170;
    and Portman 241–2
Dunlop, Frank 88–9, 92
Dunne, John Gregory 347

Ealing Films 226, 359
Easterbrook, Tony 55
Eaton Hall 231
Eccles, Viscount 22, 40fn, 46
Eclipse, The 249
Eden End (Priestley) 173
Edinburgh Festival 88fn, 154
Edvard Munch 339
Edward My Son 234
Edwards, Charlie 261
EEC 49, 52, 70, 76, 234, 248
Egypt 84–5, 154, 175, 315
Einstein on the Beach 328–9
Eisenhower, Dwight D. 22–3
Eisenstein, Sergei 103, 131
Ekland, Britt 48, 49
Eliot, T.S. 10, 122, 208
Elisa Vida Mia 393
Elizabeth II, Queen 49, 78, 139, 231,
    250, 343, 344
Elizabeth, Queen Mother 49, 163–4, 231
Elizabethan Stage Society 299
Elle 172
Ellis, A.E. 96fn
Ellsberg, Daniel and Patricia 307
Elsom, John 128fn
Elstree 47, 226
Elwes, Dominic 65–6, 102, 113, 278–9,
    394; memorial service 288; suicide
    264–5, 266, 267–70, 309
Emmanuelle 200
Encore 394, 395
End Game (Beckett) 238

End of Me Old Cigar (Osborne) 223
Englewood, New Jersey 132
Enoch, Russell 207
'Epitaph for George Dillon' (Osborne) 393
Equus (P. Shaffer) 126–7, 147, 190
Ervine, St John 173
Esquire 247
Etting, Ruth 148
Evans, Dame Edith 123
Evans, Evans 42, 186
Evans, Laurie 90, 92
Evening News 118fn
Evening Standard 56, 88, 123, 144, 145, 162, 165

Falstaff (Nye) 410
Fanshen (Hare) 239–40, 298
Feiffer, Jules 63, 71, 360, 380
Ferreri, Marco 197fn
Festival Ballet 43
Festival of Light 68
Feydau, Georges 389
Fields, Gracie 188
Fields, W.C. 124
Financial Times 56
Finch, Peter 365
Findlater, Richard 243, 395
Finlay, Frank 32fn, 226, 336
Finlay, Neil 320
Finney, Albert 12, 118
Finney, Anouk 278
Firbank, Ronald 131
Fish, Michael 203
Fish in the Sun (McGrath) 228
Fitzgerald, F. Scott 25fn, 74, 83, 233
Flanders, Michael 236
Flanner, Janet 369, 411–12
Flea in his Ear 190
Flindt, Flemming 322
Flindt, Vivi 322
Flower Drum Song 11
Fonda, Jane 28, 391fn
Fonteyn, Margot 285
Foo Chow's, New York 182
Foot, Michael and Jill 95
Forbes, Bryan 123
Ford, Betty 194
Ford, Gerald 269, 307
Ford, John 74
Ford Foundation 31
Foreman, George 191, 200
Forster, E.M. 32, 359, 369

Forte, Charles 186
Fox, Edward 70
Frankenheimer, John 42
Franklin, Benjamin 269
Franklin, Sidney 299
Fraser, Lady Antonia 191, 242–3, 278, 316, 323; biographer 320
Frayn, Michael 155, 264
Frazier, Joe 33
Freud, Clement 187
Freud, Kitty 40
Freud, Lucian 40fn, 187fn
Freud, Sigmund 52, 103, 122, 153, 328
Frinys, Kurt 120
Fritz the Cat 100
From Here to Eternity 20
Front Page, The 35fn, 99, 112, 173, 190, 272fn
Frost, David 97, 191, 330
Fry, Christopher 10
Funny Girl 189
Funny Thing Happened on the Way to the Forum, A 171
Furstenberg, von 373

G (Berger) 83, 113
Gadsdon, Mrs 184
Galbraith, Kenneth 71
Gale, George 317
Garbo, Greta 327
Garcia, Victor 21–2, 25–6
Gardner, Ava 64fn, 144
Garland, Judy 12–13
Garland, Nick 160fn
Garland, Patrick 144, 231
Garnett, Tony 273
Gaskill, Bill 239, 281
Gaudí, Antonio 248
Gaulle, Charles de 74, 179, 371
Gaumont 179, 180
Gaumont Cinema, Kilburn 200
Genet, Jean 51, 79–80
Geneva, Switzerland 253
Genou de Claire, Le 53
Germany 196, 215, 326
Gershwin, George 313, 376
Gershwin, Ira 273fn
Getty, Paul 162–3
Getty, Paul Jr 183–4, 191, 193, 198
Getz, Stan 375, 377
Giaconda Smile, The 270
Gide, André 149, 153, 411
Gielgud, Sir John 105, 128, 352, 357;

eccentricity 157; homosexuality 103, 241, 312; impromptu of 83–4; at NT 238, 331
Gill, Brendan 50, 229, 252
Gillespie, Dizzy 370, 375–6, 377
Gilliatt, Penelope 34, 56fn, 132, 248
Ginsberg, Allen 286
Giorgi, Dr Elsie 373
Giori, Signor 253
Glenville, Peter 53
Glyndebourne 309
Go-Between, The 54, 57, 69–70
Godard, Jean-Luc 24, 371
Goddard, Paulette 40
Godfather, The 246
Goldoni, Carlo 343
Goldsmith, Sir James 323, 330
Goldsmith, Teddy 200
Goldwyn, Sam 134
Goodbody, Mary Ann 'Buzz' 141
Goodman, Benny 44
Goodman, Lord 55, 70fn, 90, 91, 92, 93, 125, 135, 191
Goodwin, Clive 31, 33, 69, 73, 129, 309fn, 394–5
Goosens, Eugene 130
Gordon, Emma 176
Gordon, Ruth 324
Gorme, Edie 313
Goya, Francisco de 249
Grade, Lew 266, 355
Graham, Billy 68
Grand Hotel, Las Vegas 353–4
Grande Bouffe, La 197
Grant, Cary 120
Granville-Barker, Harley 93
Graveney, Tom 190
Graves, Robert 86, 148, 318–19
Gray, Eddie 148
Great National Holiday, The (Caute) 105
Green, Adolph 97, 182, 305
Green, Benny 309
Green, Martin 306
Greene, Graham 266
Greenstreet, Sydney 72
Greenwich Theatre 172, 223
Greer, Germaine 55, 62, 118
Grew, Mary 101
Griffin, Merv 306–7, 381
Griffiths, Trevor 123, 141, 146, 181; and Carte Blanche 199; The Party 119, 160–1, 165
Grimond, Joseph 'Jo' 107

Grippo, Jimmy 353–4
Gross, John 75, 138, 166
Gross, Miriam 138–9, 166, 278
Grosvenor House, London 85
Guardian 26, 84, 88, 165, 176, 201, 337
Guess Who's Coming to Dinner? 326
Guinness, Alec 144, 234
Guthrie, Tyrone 25fn

Haden-Guest, Anthony 231, 329
Haigh, Kenneth 12
Hailsham, Lord (Quintin Hogg) 257
Half Moon Theatre, London 228
Halifax, Michael 55
Hall, Peter 136, 139, 291; Miller on 343; NT appointment 14, 88–92, 119, 124–5, 126, 152; and Olivier 14, 105, 190, 224–5, 384; personality 125, 190, 279, 309; plans for NT 98–9, 131, 135; at RSC 140, 225; regime at NT 160–1, 175–6, 219–20, 222, 224–6, 267, 288, 309; TV work 226, 279
Hall, Willis 195fn
Hamburg 27–8
Hamill, Pete 353
Hamlet (Shakespeare) 25, 144, 172–3, 176, 195–6, 285–6, 287
Hammerstein, Oscar II 11, 190
Hammond, Kay 105
Hands, Terry 137
Hanson, James 330
Hardwick, Elizabeth 42
Hardwicke, Cecil 61
Hardy, Thomas 227
Hare, David 239
Harewood, George 170
Harlech, Lord David and Lady Pamela 43, 44, 117, 137, 150, 159
Harper's and Queen 187
Harper's Bazaar 172
Harris, Richard 255, 319
Harrison, George 29
Harrison, Rex 26
Hart, Moss 129, 235–6
Hartley, L.P. 57
Hartwell, Lord 174
Harty, Russell 227
Harvey, Laurence 83, 110–12, 135
Hastings, Sussex 261
Havana, Cuba 376–7
Hawkins, Jack 47
Hawks, Howard 271
Haydon, Richard 272

Haynes, Jim 203
Hayton, Lennie 326
Hayward, Brooke 396
Hayward, Leland 258, 396fn
Hayward Gallery, London 190
He That Plays the King (KT) 6, 9, 11, 16, 19fn, 235
Healey, Lord Denis 320
Hearst, William Randolph 358, 406
Heath, Edward 22fn, 52, 144, 174, 206, 250
Hecht, Ben 272
Hefner, Hugh 71
Hegel, G.W.F. 342
Heighway, Steve 148
Heinz, Henry and Drue 138
Hellman, Lillian 230
Hemdale 191
Hemingway, Ernest 19, 60–1, 74, 83, 103, 232–3, 299, 374, 377
Henry IV (Shakespeare) 10, 12
Henry V (Shakespeare) 60, 243
Hepburn, Katharine 12, 40, 106, 180, 326
Herbert, Jocelyn 152
Herder, Addie 42, 186, 374
Hernani (Hugo) 337
Heseltine, Michael 303
Heston, Charlton 236
Hickey, William 349
High Anxiety 385
High Society 234
Hiller, Wendy 219
Hines, Earl 375, 376, 377
Histoire d'O, L' 192, 250
Hitchcock, Alfred 262, 385
Hitler, Adolf 49, 52, 91, 95fn
Hobsbawm, Eric 137, 302
Hobson, Harold 56, 127, 128–9, 337
Hockney, David 44
Hoffman, Dustin 347, 392–3
Hoffman, Jutta 280
Hogg, Min 166
Holly, Ellen 351–2
Hollywood 217, 272, 299, 347–50
Holroyd, Michael 191
Homolka, Oscar 272
Hope-Wallace, Philip 25
Hopkins, Anthony 21, 22, 35, 226
Hopkins, John 175
Horne, Lena 326
Hotel de la Paix, Geneva 50
Hotel de la Poste, Avallon 154, 155, 156

Hotel in Amsterdam, The (Pinter) 59
Houdini, Harry 298
Houston, University of 86
Howard, Alan 243
Howard, Anthony 191, 205
Howard, Brian 306
Howard, Elizabeth Jane 317, 337
Howard, Michael 91
Howard, Trevor 270
Howerd, Frankie 137
Huckleberry Finn (Twain) 74
Hughes, Howard 368–9
Hugo, Victor 49
Humes, Harold 'Doc' 366–7
Humphrey, Hubert 307
Humphries, Barry 160
Hunt, E. Howard 163
Hunter, N.C. 59–60
Hure, M. 156
Huston, Anjelica 355
Huston, John 233, 239, 278, 305, 419
Huxley, Aldous 58

Iberia (Michener) 387
Ibsen, Henrik 42, 219
ICA 239
Ifield, Frank 312
Ik, The 297–8
Impact Quadrant 183
Importance of Being Earnest (Wilde) 123fn, 129
In Cold Blood (Capote) 231
In Harm's Way 20
In My Own Way (Watts) 176
In Which We Serve 20
Industrial Relations Bill 22, 70
Inferno (Dante) 117, 177
Inge, William 258, 259
Ingrams, Richard 198
Injured Party, The (Dundy) 170
Innocents, The 323
Invasion of the Body Snatchers 22
Invocation, The 289
IRA 31
Irma la Douce 129
Isherwood, Christopher 306, 347, 359, 363, 366, 369–70, 392
Isis 31fn
Isla de la Toja, Spain 408
Israel 206–7

J'Accuse 226
Jack the Ripper 378, 381, 384

Jackson, Barry 190
Jackson, George 43
Jagger, Bianca 352, 366
Jagger, Mick 24
Jaipur, Maharajah of 111
James, Clive 232
James, Gerald 48, 56
James, Harry 299
Jaques, Elliott 177
Jay, Helen 65, 267
Jeanmaire, Zizi 301
Jefferson, Thomas 269
Jenkins, Roy 150, 248, 327
Jerez de la Frontera, Spain 65, 66
Jessel, George 357
Jewish War Veterans 38
Joffe, Roland 99, 117, 146
John Gabriel Borkman (Ibsen) 219–20, 222
Johnson, Lyndon B. 47
Johnson, Marigold 317
Johnson, Nunnally 368
Johnson, Paul 229, 317
Johnson, Dr Samuel 194, 402, 404
Joint, The (J. Blake) 51, 157
Jolson, Al 123
Jones, Gloria 374
Jones, James 366, 374–5
Journey of the Wolf (Day) 380
Jowett, Prof. Benjamin 246
Joyce, James 103, 122
Judson, Margaret Atwood 320
Judy (KT's secretary) 403
Jumpers (Stoppard) 99

Kael, Pauline 42, 404
Kafka, Franz 34, 103, 242
Kallman, Chester 208
Kanin, Garson 325
Karnak, Egypt 85, 315
Katz, Israel 180, 183
Kaufman, Bob 286, 308, 358
Kaufman, Eileen 286, 358
Kaufman, George S. 164, 272
Kay, Charles 57
Kaye, Danny 259
Kazan, Elia 'Gadge' 91
Keaton, Buster 103, 384–5
Keeler, Christine 24fn
Keller, Hans 36
Kelly, Barbara 138
Kelly, Gene 391
Kelly, Grace 234
Kempton, Murray 71

Kendall, Kay 172, 309
Kennedy, Edward 38, 71, 307
Kennedy, John F. 33, 38–9, 43fn, 163, 286
Kennedy, Joseph P. 6, 38, 39
Kennedy, Robert 38
Kern, Jerome 313, 376
Kernon, Pat 253–4
Kerouac, Jack 286
Kerr, Deborah 20
Kerr, Walter 287
Keynes, John Maynard 179
Kids-Aid 205
King, Martin Luther 43
King Edward's School Chronicle 9, 282fn
King Lear (Shakespeare) 131, 193, 287, 298
Kipling, Rudyard 239
Kirov Ballet 98, 161
Kiss Me Kate 281
Kitt, Eartha 357
Koltai, Ralph 141, 190
Kraft, Hy 409
Kraft, Reata 409
Kronhausen, Phyllis and Eberhard 332
Kubrick, Stanley 221, 291, 293, 300–1
Kurnitz, Harry 107–8
Kustow, Michael 176

LA Times 379, 389
Labour Party 22, 47fn, 49, 52, 70, 193, 273, 277, 284, 316
Lahr, Bert 272fn
Laine, Cleo 49, 326
Laing, R.D. 367
Lambert, Gavin 144, 262
Lamott, Kenneth 372
Lancaster, Burt 20
Landau, Martin 292, 297, 335, 336, 351
Landscape (Pinter) 57
Lang, Harold 264, 309
Langner, Lawrence 258
Laos 32
Lardner, Ring 74
Las Vegas 353
Lasdun, Denys 309
Last Tycoon, The (Fitzgerald) 25fn, 354, 403
Late Show, The 372
Lawrence, D.H. 147
Lawrence, Steve 313
Lawrence, T.E. 69, 262
Laye, Evelyn 145

Lazar, Irving 'Swifty' 308, 354–5, 366, 386, 388, 389, 391
Lear, Edward 159fn, 382
Leavis, F.R. 323
Lederer, Francis 211
Lee, Bruce 287
Lee, Jennie 70
Léger, Fernand 64
Lehmann, John 369
Leicester 311
Leigh, Janet 385
Leigh, Vivien 12, 36, 133–4, 164
Leisen, Michael 211
Lemmon, Felicia 392
Lemmon, Jack 363, 391
Lennon, John 117
León, Spain 408
Leonardo da Vinci 39
Lerner, Alan Jay 129
Lesley, Cole 355
Lessing, Doris 7, 137, 141, 264
Lester, Dick 330
Levin, Bernard 174
Levinson, Barry 385
Levy, Prof. Leonard W. 319
Lewis, C.S. 37, 208, 222–4, 357; on Akhnaten 321–2; KT's tutor 9, 194; Letters 405–6; The Problem of Pain 243–5
Lewis, Jerry 41
Liberal Party 327
Lichfield, Patrick 107, 231
Liddell, Alice 382
Life of Christ 266
Life of Kenneth Tynan, The (KH) 8, 102fn, 113fn
Likely Story, A (Morley) 164
Lilburne, John 319–20
Lilywhite Boys, The 153
Lindsay, Derek (Deacon) 96
Lindsay, Vera, see Russell, V.
Lipman, Maureen 141
Little Hut, The 234
Littlewood, Joan 137, 309
Littman, Marguerite 142, 278
Littman, Mark 142, 143, 199
Llanberis, Wales 150
Loach, Ken 273
Lockhart, Calvin 73
Loesser, Frank 190
Logan, Joshua 44, 134–5, 258
Logue, Christopher 69, 86–7
Lomelin, Antonio 390, 397
London: airport 186; theatre 103

London Life 78, 171
Long Day's Journey into Night (O'Neill) 35fn, 99, 120, 136, 190, 415
Longford, Lord 68, 233
Look Back in Anger (Osborne) 13, 58fn, 337
Loos, Anita 40
Looseleaf, Victoria 388
Lord of the Flies 298
Lord's cricket ground, London 340
Los Angeles 83, 135, 347–50
Losey, Joseph 54, 69–70, 351
Lovelace, Linda 301
Lowe, Frederick 129
Lowell, L. Cabot 109
Lowell, Robert 42, 122–3
LSD 71, 221–2
Lubitsch, Ernst 272
Lucan, Lord 202–3, 265, 269
Lukas, Paul 255
Lumet, Sidney and Gail 305, 326
Lutèce Hotel, Paris 41–2
Luther, Martin 222
Luxor, Egypt 84–5, 315
Lynch, Sean 156
Lyon, France 154
Lyons, Leonard 61
Lysistrata 55, 62

MacArthur, Charles 272
MacArthur, Gen. Douglas 386
Macbeth (Shakespeare) 27–9, 47, 79, 119
McCarthy, Joseph 242
McCarthyism 22–3, 274, 409
McCarthy, Mary 67, 103, 122, 132
McCowan, Alec 103, 226
McCullough, Colleen 391
McGee, Hetty 65
McGrath, John 228
MacGrath, Leueen 164
McKellen, Ian 103
McKenna, T.P. 187
MacLaine, Shirley 266, 301, 308, 353
MacLean, Donald 306
MacLeish, Archibald 134
McLuhan, Marshall 357, 381
McMahon, Ed 391
Madras House, The (Granville-Barker) 93
Madrid, Spain 247, 249, 367–8, 393, 395, 408
Madriguera, La 394
Maeterlinck, Maurice 170
Magic Christian, The (Southern) 325

Magnificence (Brenton) 143
Mailer, Norman 132–3, 313, 366
Maillol, Aristide 402
Makarova, Natalia 98
Malle, Louis 356, 375
Man Who Came to Dinner, The 234
Mankiewicz, Herman J. 42, 272
Manson, Charles 26fn
Marat/Sade 297fn, 298
Marfield, Dwight 409–10
Margaret, Princess 43, 49, 79–80, 112, 163, 231, 278, 324, 348
Markman Securities 170, 199
Markova, Alicia 285
Marlborough House, London 249
Marowitz, Charles 56
Marquand, Christian 341
Marquand, Johnny Jr 230
Mars, life on 333
Martin, Tony 44
Martinez, Manolo 396–7
Marx, Groucho 44, 97, 123, 171, 356
Marx, Karl 23, 179
Marx Brothers 44, 272fn, 273fn
Marxism, *see* Communism
Mary, Queen of Scots (ballet) 310, 311
Maschler, Thomas 113
Mason, Pamela and Portland 384–5
Mastersingers, The (Wagner) 217
Matthau, Walter 388, 389, 391–2
Maugham, Somerset 226, 419
Maxton, James 166
May, Elaine 182, 202
Meinhof, Ulrike 325
Melba, Dame Nellie 106
Melchett, Lord 94
Melly, George 32
Melnick, Danny 355
Mencken, H.L. 121fn
Mengers, Sue 348, 355, 356, 364, 366, 373, 391
Menotti, Gian-Carlo 354
Mentor 78
Merchant, Vivien 79
Meredith, George 391
Meriden 215
Merlin (Nye) 410
Merman, Ethel 188–90
Mexico 390–1, 396–7
Meyerhold, Vsevolod 25fn
Miami, Florida 305, 306, 307
Michener, James 387
Midgely, Robin 311

Midnight 211
Milbanke, Annabella 108
Millais, Hugh 86, 268
Miller, Arthur 74, 164
Miller, Henry 313
Miller, Jonathan 73, 79fn, 301, 316; as director 57, 172; on Hall 343; at NT 90, 92, 136, 176; social life 86, 252, 278
Miller, Karl 75, 191
Mills, John 20
Milton, John 215
Minnelli, Liza 137, 301, 355
Miracles (Lewis) 194
Miranda, Carmen 312, 377
Misanthrope, The (Molière) 190
Mitchell, Adrian 45, 46, 47–8, 54–5, 56fn, 137
Mitchell, James 206
Mitford, Nancy 411
Mnouchkine, Ariane 73
Moffatt, Ivan 'Boy' 356, 387, 388
Mojacar, Spain 394, 404, 406–8
Molnar, Ferenc 328
Monroe, Marilyn 27fn, 29
Montagu, Lord Edward 312
Montoire, France 87
Moore, Bobby 23–4, 148
Moore, Dudley 79fn, 138, 355
Moore, G.E. 218
Morales, Adele 133
Moravia, Alberto 71
More, Thomas 222
Morecambe, Eric 32, 135–6, 137, 172
Moreno, Rita 381
Morgan, Julia 358
Morley, Joan 232, 233
Morley, Robert 164–5, 232–4
Morocco 232–3
Mortimer, Sir John 88
Morton, Frederic 97
Morton, J.B. 63
Mostyn-Owen, Gaia 92, 122, 309
Mother Courage (Brecht) 105fn
Mountbatten, Lord 231
Mozart, Wolfgang Amadeus 36, 72, 288, 350, 367, 380, 393
Mrs Warren's Profession (Shaw) 280
Much Ado About Nothing (Shakespeare) 190, 321
Muir, Frank 97
Mullin, Frin 220, 260
Mullin, Mikayella 220, 297

Munich, Germany 215
Murderer (A. Shaffer) 227–8
Murdoch, Iris 191
Murrow, Edward R. 134, 242
Mutter, Die 281
My Fair Lady 129
My Lai, Vietnam 32

Nabokov, Vladimir 74
Naish, Margarita 390
Namier, Lewis 301
Nash, Ogden 272fn
Nashville 273
Nastase, Ilie 100
Nathan, George Jean 121
National Bottom 379
National Film Theatre (NFT) 124, 211, 287, 289
National Health, The 190
National Health Service 230
National Theatre 35fn, 36, 58, 234, 395; associate directors 330–1; Board 88–91, 92, 128fn, 226; collective leadership 35; financing 78, 288; gala opening 309, 343–4, 384; Hall's appointment 88–92, 124; Hall at 160–1, 175–6, 267, 288, 330–1; Hall's plans for 98–9, 131, 135; KT's position at 13–15, 98, 99; KT retires from 166, 177; new building 88, 125, 190; planning committee 225; productions 21fn, 29, 34, 45fn, 117, 146, 149, 159–60, 219–20, 222, 238, 331, 336; proposed merger with RSC 135, 136; success of 162
National Youth Theatre 60, 247fn
Neame, Christopher 185
Nefertiti, Queen 315–16
Neruda, Pablo 263
Network 365
Neville, Rupert 49
New Orleans 375
New Statesman 205, 229, 282
New Theatre, London 57
New Wave 12
New York 70, 72, 74, 97, 132, 270, 304, 351
New York 292
New York Herald Tribune 61
New York Post 61
New York Review of Books 40fn, 42, 132fn, 385
New York Times 280, 307fn
New Yorker 256–7, 274, 319, 393;

columnists 42, 252; Gill's book on 229; KT as drama critic 13; KT's earnings 387, 401; KT's profiles 15, 97fn, 292, 308, 332, 347, 351, 367, 371, 378, 385, 396, 402, 409; KT's Reich piece 96, 175; out-of-towners 74
Newman, Alfred 217
Newman, Joan 396
Newman, Paul 366, 396
Newman, Phyllis 97, 305
Next of Kin (Hopkins) 175
Nichols, Mike 34, 132, 182, 202
Nicholson, Jack 249, 347, 355, 372
Nicole 176, 199, 208, 256, 260, 322, 341; affairs 210, 273; KH and 138, 142, 177, 245; KT's guilt over 245; KT's trips with 171, 189–90, 220, 227, 261, 367, 393, 406–7; KT's row with 220–1; quoted 146, 160–3, 165, 174, 177, 185, 187, 195–6, 286; spanking sessions 121, 135, 198, 250–1, 260; and Waterhouse 195
Nietzsche, Friedrich 240
Nixon, Richard 33, 143, 163, 221, 237, 327, 386
No Man's Land (Pinter) 238, 285, 331, 351
Norman, Frank 61
Norton, Deborah 288
Norton, Elliot 259
Norton Simon museum, Pasadena 402
Nottley Abbey 133
Novello, Ivor 8, 312
Nunn, Trevor 136, 140
Nye, Robert 410

Oberon, Merle 355
O'Brien, Conor Cruise 31
O'Brien, Edna 137, 243, 252
O'Brien, Virginia 44
Observer 8, 14, 56fn, 87, 91, 129, 165, 205, 383
Odets, Clifford 173
Oedipus (Seneca) 84, 105, 287, 298
Oh! Calcutta! 15, 16, 26fn, 76, 141fn, 177, 231, 255, 325; cast 249; in Madrid 393, 395; in Paris 40–1; royalties 170, 228; title 255fn
Old-Fashioned Way, The 124
Old Times (Pinter) 53, 54, 57, 59
Old Vic Theatre, London 36, 48, 84, 175, 219, 225, 243fn, 270
Olivier 162
Olivier, Sir Laurence 26, 70, 160, 357; as

actor 119–20, 131, 160, 166, 324, 326, 384, 415; and Blakemore 136; as film producer 180; on filming 33; and Garcia 21–2; on Glenville 53; and Hall's appointment 88–92, 124–5; hatred of Hall 190, 224–5; ill health 225, 266–7; as imposer 19; interviewed by KT 266, 279; KH's biography of 166; language of 126; and Leigh 133; as NT director 13–14, 99, 105, 117–18; as NT President 225, 267; at opening of Olivier Theatre 343–4, 384; and Osborne 58, 60, 162; and Panovs 161; and Plummer 35; psychology of 91; quoted 69; resigns from NT 119; temperament of 57, 60, 98; and Theatre Exhibition 190; and *Tyger* 45–6, 47–8, 54–6

Olympia, Paris 41
On the Waterfront 324
One Flew Over the Cuckoo's Nest 410
One Plus One 24
O'Neal, Ryan 300, 355, 366, 373–4
O'Neal, Tatum 348, 355
Ordóñez, Antonio 190, 233
Orton, Joe 13, 103, 131fn, 153fn
Orwell, George 58
Osborne, John 34, 58–60, 153, 162, 201–2, 223
Osborne, Rafael 66–7
Osborne, Tomas 65–6
Osgood, Peter 148
Othello (Shakespeare) 190, 312fn, 324, 381
Otherwise Engaged 285
O'Toole, Peter 12, 184–5
Oxford 243, 270
Oxford University 5, 32, 69, 170, 194, 199, 228; Author-Critic Club 31fn; Balliol College 246; Magdalen College 9, 37fn; New College 342; Poetry Society 192
Oxford Book of Literary Anecdotes 246
Oxford Viewpoint 312fn

Pabst, George 97, 406
Page, Anthony 60
Palladium Theatre, London 188, 301, 312
Pamplona, Spain 394, 395
Pandora's Box 97, 401
Panovs (of Kirov) 161, 246
Pangborn, Franklin 139
Parade 287

Paramount 364
Parents Terribles, Les (Cocteau) 20, 26fn, 311
Paris 40, 113, 184, 186–7, 229, 374, 411; 1968 revolt 31, 73–4; De Gaulle airport 186; erotic theatre 331
Parker, Charlie 379
Parker, Dorothy 272
Parker, Sir Peter 194fn, 316
Parker, Stanley 200
Parkinson, Michael 202, 209, 341
Partridge, Ralph and Frances 209–10
Party, The (Griffiths) 119, 160–1, 165–6, 394
Pasadena, California 385, 402
Pasco, Richard 139
Passenger, The 248, 255
Pavlova, Anna 285
Payn, Graham 48, 359
Peacock, Sir Peter 7
Peck, Gregory 145, 386
Peer Gynt 332
Pelléas et Mélisande (Maeterlinck) 170
People 49, 205
Pepys, Samuel 52
Perelman, S.J. 272
Perkins, Maxwell 233
Perrine, Valerie 355
Peter Pan (Barrie) 329
Phelps, Diana 187–8
Philby, Kim 306
Philip, Prince, Duke of Edinburgh 49
Philips, Robin 103, 225
Phipps, Diana 316, 319
Picasso, Pablo 103, 402
Picnic (Inge) 258
Pilbrow, Richard 302, 328, 341
Pinewood Studios 180
Pinter, Harold 13, 79–80, 220, 278, 291, 308; appearance 323; cricket fan 340; as director 175; dislikes *The Party* 161fn; as imposer 19; at NT 175–6, 330; plays of 53, 59, 238, 240; relations with women 191fn, 197, 243, 316; and Roxana 323; as screenwriter 54, 57, 69–70; themes 57, 70, 285
Pirsig, Robert 366
Planchon, Roger 281
Playboy 71, 87, 180, 324
Plimpton, George 230
Plomley's 161
Plowright, Joan 12; on Hall 224–6; Olivier and 13, 55, 89, 90, 384; on

Osborne 60; repertory company plans 226
Plowright, Mr 166
Plummer, Christopher 34–5, 37, 57, 266
Plunder (Travers) 289fn, 309
Poel, William 299
Poitier, Sidney 169, 326
Poland 134
Polanski, Roman 14, 24, 26, 28–9, 60, 125; as imposer 19, 182–3; KT's piece on 37; *Macbeth* of 27, 28, 29; on politicians 77
Porter, Cole 74, 188, 189, 313
Portman, Eric 241–2
Post Office 24
Powell, Anthony 145–6, 268
Powell, Enoch 335
Preminger, Otto 184–5, 299
Present Laughter (Coward) 48fn, 173
Pretty Baby 375
Previn, André 203
Priestley, J.B. 173, 282
Princess Zoubaroff, The (Firbank) 131, 135
Principia Ethica (Moore) 218
Pritchett, V.S. 71
Private Eye 138fn, 160fn, 198, 254–5, 323, 329
Private Lives (Coward) 128
Privilege 340
Problem of Pain (Lewis) 243–5
Profumo scandal 24fn, 281
Prokofiev, Sergei 285
Proust, Marcel 30, 83, 103, 242
Pryce-Jones, David 247
Psycho 385
Puerto de Santa Maria, Spain 65–6
Punch 254
Punishment Park 340

Quarrier, Iain 24
Queensberry, Marquis of 108fn, 223
Quennell, Peter 138, 306, 319
Quesnet, Marie-Constance 371
Quinn, Anthony 53fn

Racine, Jean 224
Rack, The (Ellis) 96fn
Raffles, Gerry 309
Rahv, Philip 230
Ralph, George 166
Ramsey, Sir Alf 148
Randall, Tony 386
Random House 107

Rattigan, Terence 120, 241, 312, 340
Ravel, Maurice 30
Rayne, Sir Max 43, 88, 89, 90–1, 92fn, 225, 226
Reagan, Ronald 307
Real Inspector Hound (Stoppard) 364
Reckord, Barry 199
Redford, Robert 396
Redgrave, Vanessa 58, 347, 392–3
Reed, Oliver 58
Rees-Mogg, William 329
Reflections in a Golden Eye 416
Reflections on the Psalms (Lewis) 321–2
Reich, Wilhelm 91, 95, 98, 122, 204; KT's book on 15, 96, 135, 153, 175, 209
Revie, Don 148
Revolt of Islam (Shelley) 265
Richard II (Shakespeare) 139
Richard III (Shakespeare) 120, 137
Richards, Frank 47fn
Richards, Viv 340
Richardson, Ian 139
Richardson, Joely 58fn
Richardson, Maurice 20–1
Richardson, Natasha 58fn
Richardson, Sir Ralph 59, 119, 219–20, 238, 331; KT's study of 308, 332–3, 347, 351, 352
Richardson, Tony 58, 153, 156, 229, 347, 359, 366, 372
Rigg, Diana 226
Roberts, Rachel 223
Robin and Marion 330
Rockefeller, Nelson 269
Rodgers, Richard 11, 190, 313, 376
Roeg, Nick 381
Rollerball 273
Rolls Royce 34
Rome, Italy 415
Romeo and Juliet (Shakespeare) 225
Romney, Oliver Wendell 109
Ronda, Spain 65
Rosebud 184
Rosenberg, Harold 253
Rosewall, Ken 232
Rosmersholm (Ibsen) 42
Ross, Annie 156
Ross, Harold 281
Rossetti, Dante Gabriel 183
Roth, Philip 366
Rothermere, Lord and Lady 36
Rotherwick, Lord and Lady 36

Rothschild, Evelyn de 256
Rothschild family 165, 180
Rothschilds, The (Morton) 97
Roundhouse, London 73, 297
Rousseau, Jean-Jacques 419
Rowe-Dutton, Jill 194, 235, 316
Royal Ballet 98
Royal Court Theatre, London 60, 143, 152–3, 228, 239fn, 337
Royal Danish Ballet 322
Royal Hunt of the Sun, The (P. Shaffer) 126fn
Royal Opera House, Covent Garden 92, 284
Royal Shakespeare Company (RSC) 234, 321; Board 89; directors 140; proposed merger with NT 135, 136; style of 137, 139–40, 141, 144, 152, 225
Rozina (KT's secretary) 49, 87, 90, 92, 197
Runacre, Jenny 248
Runyon, Damon 74
Russell, Ken 58
Russell, Vera 76
Rutherford, Margaret 12
Ryle, Gilbert 75
Ryskind, Morrie 272

Sade, Marquis de 370, 371
Sahl, Mort 385
St Joan (Shaw) 134, 287
St Just, Maria 278
St Laurent, Yves 137fn
St Tropez, France 155, 263
Sakall, S.Z. 272
Salamanca, Spain 50
Salambo Erotic Theatre, Hamburg 27
Salieri, Antonio 393
Salinger, Pierre 87
Salisbury Cathedral 37
Sally (S-M devotee) 250–1, 260
Sampson, Anthony 75
Samson Agonistes (Milton) 215
San Andreas Fault 383
San Francisco 286, 358
San Simeon, California 358
Sandstone club, California 307
Santa Barbara, California 364
Santa Monica, California 347, 351
Santiago de Compostela, Spain 387–8, 404, 406, 408
Sardinia 62, 155
Saroyan, Carol 388–9, 391

Saroyan, William 388
Satie, Erik 30
Saturday, Sunday, Monday (de Filippo) 159–60, 161fn
Saunders, Peter 62
Saura, Carlos 393
Savage God, The (Alvarez) 177–8
Savile, Anne-Marie 157
Savo, Jimmy 41
Schlesinger, Arthur 71, 174, 176
Schlesinger, John 330, 381
Schneider, Maria 249
Schubert, Franz 26, 29, 40
Schulberg, Budd 209
Sciclounoff, Pierre 253–4, 336
Scofield, Paul 79, 90, 226
Scot, Reginald 43
Scott, Norman 327
Scott, Peter 235
Seagull, The (Chekhov) 173
Segal, George 366
Segovia, Spain 368
Sellers, Arlene 180
Sellers, Joy 256
Sellers, Peter 29, 137, 202, 256, 257, 308
Selway, Rose 187
Senft, Paul 303–4
Separate Tables (Rattigan) 241
Seven Year Itch, The 27fn
Shadow Play (Coward) 48
Shaffer, Antony 187, 227–8, 264
Shaffer, Peter 126–7, 128, 147, 187fn, 190
Shakespeare, William 43fn, 108, 227, 243, 249, 395
Shakin' Stevens at the Sunset 138
Shampoo 237
Shaw, G.B. 15, 103, 129, 287
Shaw, Irwin 229 30
Shaw, Sandie 121
Shaw, Susan 110, 111
Shaw Theatre, London 275
Shawn, Mr 257, 292, 304, 308, 387, 401
Shelley, Percy Bysshe 265
Sherek, Henry 145
Shevelove, Burt 138, 142–3
Shore, Dinah 259, 355
Shostakovich, Dmitri 203
Shulman, Milton 56, 144
Siegel, Don 22–3
Silent Clowns, The (Kerr) 287
Silvers, Phil 171–2
Silvers, Robert 132
Simon, Neil 272, 388

Simpson, O.J. 381
Sinatra, Tina 355
Sissle, Noble 376
Six Hits and a Miss 45
Skinner, B.F. 75
Slonimski, Antoni 134
Small World 134
Smith, Maggie 128, 226
Smith, Stan 100
Snow White 101
Snowdon, Earl of (A. Armstrong-Jones)
    49, 79, 86, 112
Soames, Emma 269
Soldiers 325
Soledad Brothers 43
Somerset, David 99
Sondheim, Stephen 137, 182
Sonnenberg, Ben 252
Sound of Music, The 35
Sound of Two Hands Clapping, The (KT)
    32fn
South Africa 36
South Sea Bubble (Coward) 164
Southern, Terry 230, 256, 325
Soyinka, Wole 117
Spain 63–7, 247, 367–8, 378, 387–8, 395,
    406–9
Spark, Dame Muriel 201
Spectorsky, Augie 71, 74
Spender, Natasha 123
Spender, Stephen 122–3, 369
Spiegel, Sam 316
Spielberg, Steven 355
Spinetti, Victor 264, 309
Spinoza, Benedict de 87
Stamp, Sally 165
Stanwyck, Barbara 271
Stark, Graham 202
Stark, Ray 355
Steiger, Rod 324
Stein, Jules 44
Steiner, Max 217
Stephens, Robert 172, 187, 227
Steppenwolf 333
Stern, Harold and Evelyn 96
Stevens, George 61
Stevens, Peter 330
Stewart, James 391
Stigwood, Robert 179, 239, 252
Stiles, Nobby 147
Sting, The 396
Stoker, Bram 364
Stoppard, Tom 291, 337, 342; as

cricketer 340; on KT 5; KT's profile
    of 308, 369, 378, 385, 387, 396; at
    NT 15, 117, 190; Santa Barbara
    festival 364
Storey, David 152, 153fn
Stout, Rex 96
Strachey, Lytton 199, 208, 209–10, 370
Stratford 243; see also Royal
    Shakespeare Company
Stravinsky, Igor 103, 208fn
Strehler, Giorgio 281
Streisand, Barbra 189, 301, 355, 381
Styne, Jule 137, 182
Styron, Rose 230
Styron, William 230
Suck 118
Sullivan, Frank 109
Summing Up, The (Maugham) 419
Sun 266
Sunday, Bloody Sunday 34fn, 53, 54
Sunday Times 56, 85–6, 91, 127fn, 162,
    265, 312fn, 330, 337, 376
Susskind, David 70
Suzman, Janet 197
Swain's Rats and Cats 356
Swan Lake 98
Swann, Donald 236fn
Switzerland 253
Sykes, C. 281
Sylvester, Victor 253, 309

Talese, Gay 341
Talloires 253
Tara hotel, London 257
Taroudant, Morocco 232
Tate, Sharon 27fn, 29
Tati, Jacques 287
Taylor, Elizabeth 415–16
Tempest, The (Shakespeare) 144–5, 190
Tempo 394
Temporary Kings (Powell) 145
Tenement Symphony (Martin) 44–5
Tennant, Bill 381
Tenschert, Joachim 34–5
Terkel, Studs 264
Terrail, Claude 184
Territorial Imperative 105
That Hideous Strength (Lewis) 37
That's Entertainment 201, 246
Thatcher, Dennis 138fn
Thatcher, Margaret 319
Théâtre des 2 Boules, Paris 332
Théâtre du Soleil 73

Theatre Exhibition, Hayward Gallery 190
Theatre Guild 258
They Shoot Horses, Don't They? 273
This Side of Paradise (Blaine) 178
Thomas, Dylan 192, 309
Thomas, J.H. 277
Thompson, J. Walter 86
Thomson of Fleet, Lord 86
Thorn Birds, The (McCullough) 391
Thorndike, Sybil 134
Thorpe, Jeremy 326
Three Sisters, The (Chekhov) 190
Thurber, Helen 274
Thurber, James 159, 274, 281–2
Tijuana, Mexico 390–1
Time Out 250
Times, The 36, 39, 56, 78, 91, 174, 192,
    301–2
Timon of Athens (Shakespeare) 298
Tiomkin, Dimitri 217
Titus Andronicus (Shakespeare) 298
Tom Jones 118, 300
Tomalin, Nick 128
Too True to Be Good 287
Topolski, Dan 308, 341
Tour d'Argent, Paris 42, 113, 156, 186,
    332
Towne, Bob 393
Toynbee, Philip 158
Tracy, Spencer 326
Travers, Ben 289, 344
Travers, Henry 272
Travesties (Stoppard) 364
Tree, Penelope 107, 183
Trevelyan, John 302
Troisgros restaurant, Roanne 156
Trollope, Anthony 106
Tropicana, Havana 377
Trouble Shooters, The 68
Trouille, Clovis 255
Trueman, Fred 333, 340
Tuckwell, Pat 170
Tunis 175, 232
Tunisia 108
Turkey 101, 104–5
Turn of the Screw (James) 323
Turnbull, Colin 297–8
Tushingham, Rita 12
TV Guide 180
Twelfth Night (Shakespeare) 144, 225
Twiggy 357
Two Gentlemen of Verona (Shakespeare)
    225

Two Sisters (Vidal) 141
Tyger (Mitchell) 29, 45–6, 47, 54–6, 58,
    165
Tynan, Kathleen Halton (KH) 87, 186,
    366, 371–2; affairs 102fn, 210, 308, 341,
    347; attitude towards Nicole 138, 142,
    177, 245; as biographer 2, 8, 166; and
    cars 30; and Churchill 94–5;
    conversations 62, 128, 207, 284; friends
    268; journalism 246, 376; knickers story
    49; and KT's diaries 1–2; and KT's
    illness 263; as KT's mistress 375; and
    KT's proposed film 102, 181; and KT's
    sexual tastes 121, 223, 347; and lease of
    house 23, 24; marriage 132; as mother
    48fn, 52, 338; moves to Beverly Hills
    227–9, 338, 341; nicknames 173; palm-
    reading 314; quarrels with KT 24, 63,
    102, 179, 317–18, 341, 350, 372–3;
    relations with KT 42, 97, 113fn, 121,
    138–9, 142, 145, 152, 154, 202, 308,
    392; as screenwriter 338, 347, 378
Tynan, Kenneth: affairs 42fn, 73fn, 194,
    341, 388–9; autobiography 43, 108,
    148, 347; as critic 5–6, 10–13, 15, 16,
    177; death 5; depression 26, 175, 228,
    232, 259, 261, 302, 303, 373, 403, 410;
    as director 10, 15, 26fn, 37, 102, 175,
    177, 234; fatherhood 37, 51, 343; film
    project, see Alex and Sophie; finances
    24, 178, 215, 216, 228, 254, 259, 292,
    310, 335–6, 348, 371, 379, 393, 396,
    401, 419; homes 23, 24, 178, 184, 252,
    323, 351; ill health 1, 16, 113, 194,
    229–30, 232, 245, 252, 254, 259, 261,
    263, 282, 284, 292, 305, 334, 339, 341,
    347–50, 356, 367, 379, 407–8, 415;
    journalism 10, 20, 177; life of 6–10,
    13–15, 347– 50; marriages 10, 41fn,
    132, 237; memorial service 2, 5, 350,
    367, 380; personality 5, 6, 8–9, 12, 29;
    as producer 15; sado-masochistic
    escapades 15, 102fn, 121–2, 198, 250–1,
    270, 347, 360, 374, 381, 388; screen-
    plays 28fn, 50, 381; sexual tastes 142,
    208, 328, 378, 379; spanking obsession
    69, 78, 103, 140, 147, 170, 205–6, 231–
    2, 281, 310, 341, 370–1, 410; stammer
    8, 41fn, 194; suicidal thoughts 95–6,
    177–8, 184, 187, 195, 252, 306, 395;
    will 1–2, 177; writer's block 130–1,
    378, 384
Tynan, Matthew Blake 23fn, 285, 402;

birth 51–2; and diaries 2; education 378; at memorial service 5; personality 383

Tynan, Rose 7, 217–18

Tynan, Roxana 23fn, 52, 150, 285, 321; acting offer 323; and diaries 2; education 378; on KT's illness 350; at memorial service 5; personality 383; piano lessons 383; quoted 119, 130, 163, 179, 241; theatre trips 243

Tynan, Tracy 41fn, 89, 102fn, 129, 343, 390; and KT's diaries 1–2; on KT's illness 349–50; KT's poem to 93–4; on KT's sado-masochism 347; on KT's social life 348; at memorial service 2, 5; relations with KT 299, 393; twenty-first birthday 137

Tynan Right and Left (KT) 6

Ulanova, Galina 285

Uncle Vanya (Chekhov) 190

Underground City, The (Humes) 366

United Nations Association 36

Up Against the Law 205

Up in Arms 259

Upper Slaughter, Cotswolds 285

US 298, 325

US Constitution 319–20

Ustinov, Peter 269

Vadim, Roger 391

Valencia, Spain 388

Valk, Frederick 220

Valley of the Kings, Egypt 85, 315

Van Doren, Mamie 83, 135

Variety 26, 409

Vaughan, Frankie 276

Vedado, Cuba 377

Vence, France 61

Versailles, France 358

Vidal, Gore 107, 226, 254, 255, 279, 347, 359, 363, 374, 397; battle for supremacy 141; as host 278, 366; KT's proposed profile of 308; on Nixon 143, 163

Viertel, Deborah and Peter 363

Vietnam 366

Vietnam War 44, 47, 325, 339

Vinaver, Steve 132, 309, 394

Vogue 246, 376

Volk, Frederick 312fn

Voltaire 395, 411

Wagner, Richard 63, 217, 342

Wagner, Robert 391

Waiting for Godot (Beckett) 275

Wajda, Andrzej 134

Wakefield, David and Divina 203–5, 221–2

Wales 150

Wall, Max 138, 275–6

Wallace, George 143, 163

Wallace, Liz 63

Wallace, Nellie 106

Walpole, Horace 32

War Game, The 339

Ward, Dorothy 53

Ward, Dr Stephen 24

Wardle, Irving 56

Warner, Philip 262

Wars of the Roses, The 176, 279

Warwick Castle 321

Washington Post 174, 327fn

Watergate 147, 163, 174, 221, 307, 327fn

Waterhouse, Keith 195

Watkins, Peter 339–40

Watts, Alan 71–2, 75, 176

Watts, Richard 61

Waugh, Auberon 281

Waugh, Evelyn 83, 253, 279–80, 281, 306, 337, 356

Way of the World (Congreve) 12

Way to the Stars, The 20

Way We Live Now, The (Trollope) 106

Wayne, John 20, 396

We Dive at Dawn 20

Weapons of Happiness (Brenton) 336–7

Weidenfeld, George 67, 137, 166, 199, 206, 291, 319, 330, 351, 371

Weidenfeld, Sandra 99

Weigel, Helene 105

Wekwerth, Manfred 34–5, 281

Weld, Tuesday 355

Welles, Orson 6, 19, 42, 96, 153, 239, 328, 348, 358

Wells, Dee 138

Wells, John 138

Wesker, Arnold 73

West, Anthony 72

West, Nathaniel 253

West, Rebecca 72fn, 282

West Indies 40; cricket side 333, 340

West of Suez (Osborne) 58–9

Westbrook, Mike 48, 55

Westminster, Duke of 231

Wheldon, Hugh 86

Whicker, Alan 86

White, Michael 26, 48, 207, 226; and
    Carte Blanche 302, 328, 336; and KT's
    film project 227, 232; sued by KT 341,
    372
Whitelaw, Alexander 'Sandy' 60
Whitman, Walt 6, 74
Wigram, Mr and Mrs 265, 269–70
Wilde, Oscar 108, 123fn, 129, 208, 223,
    249, 255, 327
Wildeblood, Peter 312
Wilder, Audrey 356
Wilder, Billy 27fn, 211, 229, 271, 272,
    356, 363, 366
Wilder, Thornton 324–5
William, David 90
Williams, Clifford 141, 199, 227– 8, 242,
    287, 302, 328, 331–2
Williams, Esther 64fn
Williams, John 339
Williams, Leonard 339
Williams, Marcia 174, 330
Williams, Tennessee 16, 74, 142, 143,
    164, 258; at Cowdray Park 110–12;
    Memoirs 307; on speed 278
Wilson, Edmund 371, 405–6
Wilson, Harold 70fn, 93, 174, 269, 329,
    330
Wilson, Robert 328–9, 372
Wilson, Sandy 358
Wilton, Robb 260–1
Wimbledon 100
Windsor, Duchess of 163–4

Wisdom of Father Brown, The (Chesterton)
    136
Wise, Ernie 32, 135–6
Witney, Oxfordshire 192
Wittgenstein, Ludwig 20
Wodehouse, P.G. 338, 340
Wolfe, Thomas 178
Wolfit, Donald 8
Women's Wear Daily 392
Wood, Natalie 28, 391
Woodward, Bob 327
Woolf, Virginia 122
Woollcott, Alexander 282
Woolly Monkey sanctuary, Cornwall 339
World Cup 182
World of Paul Slickey, The (Osborne) 223
World War II 20, 311
Worsthorne, Peregrine 228, 319
Worth, Irene 84
Wyler, William 363, 366

York, Michael and Pat 396
You're Telling Me 124
Young, B.A. 56
Young Frankenstein 235
Young Vic 120, 137

Zeffirelli, Franco 225, 266
Zen and the Art of Motorcycle
    Maintenance (Pirsig) 366
Zen Buddhism 71, 176, 218

Tracy Tynan thanks Roxana Tynan, Matthew
Tynan, Sharon Delano, Lyn Nesbit and
Jim McBride for their patience and support.